The Genius of the Place

The English Landscape Garden 1620–1820

Edited by
JOHN DIXON HUNT
and
PETER WILLIS

Paul Elek   London

Published in Great Britain by
ELEK BOOKS LTD
54–58 Caledonian Road
London NI 9RN

Printed in Great Britain by
Unwin Brothers Limited
The Gresham Press, Old Woking, Surrey
A member of the Staples Printing Group

ISBN 0 236 31033 X

Contents

Part Two

The Early Landscape Garden

Contents

Part Three

The Progress of Gardening

Contents

Part Four

Picturesque Taste and the Garden

Contents

Plates

Preface

This anthology and commentary on the English landscape garden is intended both for the general reader and for students in the visual arts. It has arisen partly out of our own needs as teachers of literature, architecture and painting to provide students with the documents upon which they can base their own thinking. But we also feel that the provision of many essential sources for the one art that England contributed to Europe since the Renaissance will enable those interested to support their studies of actual landscapes with primary literary and visual material. For this reason we have taken our texts from the original editions or manuscripts, and presented them with the minimum of editorial interference: unless otherwise indicated, extracts appear in their earliest form and are given the date of their earliest appearance.

Most of the debts we have incurred during the preparation of this book are listed in the Acknowledgements. To these we should like to add our particular gratitude to Mr Jack Baldwin, Dr William Brogden, Mr Tim Brownlow, Sir John Clerk of Penicuik, Bt, Mr Robert Holden, Mr George Howard, M. Denis Lambin, Professor Samuel Holt Monk, Professor Samuel A. Roberson, Mr Richard Robson, Dr James Sambrook and Professor Carl D. Sheppard. The Photographic Services of the University Libraries at Newcastle and York gave us invaluable assistance, whilst in the final stages of preparation we benefited from the diligent and enthusiastic editorial help of Miss Ann Douglas and Miss Jane Heller of Messrs Paul Elek Ltd.

J. D. H.
P. W.
Spring 1975

xix

Acknowledgements

Grateful thanks are due to the following for permission to reproduce paintings and drawings: Birmingham Museum and Art Gallery (Plates 1 and 14); Bristol City Museum (Plate 99); British Library, London (Plates 4, 10, 11, 19, 20, 21, 24, 25, 27, 29, 30, 32, 33, 41, 43, 53, 56, 58, 60, 62, 64, 65, 66, 67, 72, 77, 79, 80, 81, 83, 85, 88, 93 and 94); Duke of Buccleuch (Plate 76); Cambridge University Library (Plates 8, 31, 55, 69, 96); Trustees of the Chatsworth Settlement (Plates 23, 37 and 82); Christie, Manson and Woods Ltd. (Plate 48); Mr T. Cottrell-Dormer (Plate 22); Derby Museums and Art Gallery (Plate 17); Dr and Mrs John Dixon Hunt (Plate 95); Dumbarton Oaks, Washington, D.C. (Plates 7, 18, 28, 34, 68); Edinburgh University Library (Plates 54 and 90); Trustees of the Will of the Late J. H. C. Evelyn (Plates 44 and 46); Ferens Art Gallery, City of Kingston upon Hull (Plate 86); Folger Shakespeare Library, Washington, D.C. (Plate 2); Earl of Halifax (Plate 89); Mr George Howard (Plate 75); Huntington Library, San Marino, California (Plate 92); Kensington and Chelsea Public Libraries (Plate 6); Kunsthistorisches Institut, Florence (Plates 42 and 45); Duke of Marlborough (Plate 87); Mauritshuis, The Hague (Plate 49); Mr and Mrs Paul Mellon (Plate 39); Metropolitan Museum of Art, New York (Plates 40, 61, 73, 74); Warden, Moor Park College (Plate 52); National Gallery, London (Plate 38); National Library of Scotland (Plate 101); National Trust (Fairhaven Collection, Anglesey Abbey) (Plate 12); Nationalmuseum, Stockholm (Plate 84); Newcastle upon Tyne University Library (Plate 50); University of Newcastle upon Tyne (Shipley Bequest) (Plates 13 and 78); Castle Museum and Art Gallery, Nottingham (Plate 91); Royal Commission on Ancient Monuments, Scotland (Plate 71); Tate Gallery, London (Plate 38); Musée de Versailles (Plate 5); Victoria and Albert Museum (Plates 9, 15, 36, 47, 97); Mr G. H. H. Wheler (Plate 3); Whitworth Art Gallery, University of Manchester (Plates 26 and 98); Sir Marcus Worsley, Bt (Plate 57); York University Library (Plates 59, 63, 70, 95 and 100).

The Authors and Publishers would also like to thank the following copyright owners for quotations from their collections: Bodleian Library, Oxford, for *Castle Howard* (anonymous), *c.* 1733; Bristol City Museum for the 'Red Book' for Blaise Castle by Humphry Repton, 1795–6; British Library for letters by Lord Perceval, 1724, and Richard Pococke, 1756; Sir John Clerk of Penicuik, Bt, for 'The Country Seat' by Sir John Clerk, 1731; the James Marshall and Marie-Louise Osborn Collection, Yale University Library, for letter from Joseph Spence, 1765; Southampton City Council for letter by Samuel Molyneux, 1713; the Tucker-Coleman Collection, Earl Gregg Swem Library, the College of William and Mary in Virginia, for 'Memorandums' by Thomas Jefferson, 1786.

Bodley Head Ltd kindly gave permission to quote from *The Complete Works of Sir John Vanbrugh* ed. B. Dobrée and G. Webb; Faber and Faber Ltd from *The Works of Sir Thomas Browne* ed. Geoffrey Keynes; Oxford University Press from *The Diary of John Evelyn* ed. E. S. de Beer and *The Correspondence of Alexander Pope* ed. G. Sherburn; Yale University Press from *Horace Walpole's Correspondence* ed. W. S. Lewis. The quotation from Philip Yorke's 'Journal', 1744, owned by Lady A. R. Lucas and transcribed by Joyce Godber, was taken from the *Proceedings* of the Bedfordshire Historical Record Society.

Every effort has been made to trace copyright holders but, if any have not been acknowledged, the Publishers would be glad to hear in the event of a second edition.

Introduction

I

The typical English landscape garden as generally visualized would consist of undulating grass that leads somewhere down to an irregularly shaped piece of water over which a bridge arches, of trees grouped casually, with cattle or deer, about the slopes, and of houses and other buildings glimpsed in the middle or far distance. Such a scene is the one that Richard Wilson painted of Croome Court in Worcestershire (Plate 1). Yet the landscape that Wilson records in 1758 was created by Lancelot ('Capability') Brown at least half a century after the idea of such a scene was first mooted. If Brown realized and perfected what is thought of variously yet unanimously as 'the English landscape garden', '*le jardin anglais*' or '*der englische Garten*', his work is only the outcome of much exploration and experiment that had gradually transformed the stiff and geometric gardens of Tudor and Stuart England into an art that the rest of Europe imitated.

It is the history of that art which is the subject of this book. *The Genius*

1 Croome Court, Worcestershire. Painting by Richard Wilson, 1758.
Birmingham Museum and Art Gallery

of the Place brings together a selection of the most important literary and visual evidence, and chronicles the development of the English landscape garden from the early 1700s, when its distinctive features began to emerge, to its decline in the early nineteenth century. As the evidence reveals, it is not simply a history of design and stylistic change. The fortunes of the landscape garden involved the history of ideas, of taste, of the great English estates, of the other arts of poetry and painting that guided the course of landscape design — in short, of the complex manifestations of human intelligence and imagination which create and at the same time are mirrored in gardens. Garden art involves so many aspects of human endeavour that a special place might well be claimed for it in the inquiries of cultural history. 'As is the Gardener, so is the Garden', was how Thomas Fuller expressed it in 1732.[1]*

* Superior figures refer to Notes pp. 43–6.

II

The Tudor garden was a carefully organized realm. Thomas Hill's *The Gardener's Labyrinth* (1577) shows that the flowers are marshalled in geometrical shapes, the sections of the garden divided by rails, and the whole firmly separated from the world beyond the garden (Plate 2). Gervase Markham in *The English Husbandman* (1613) offered suggestions for embroidering the quarters with knots of flowers, emblems such as coats of arms,

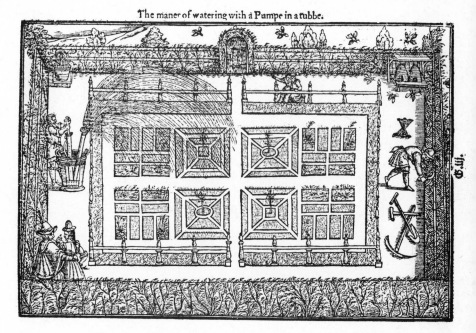

2 Plate from Thomas Hill, *The Gardener's Labyrinth*, 1577

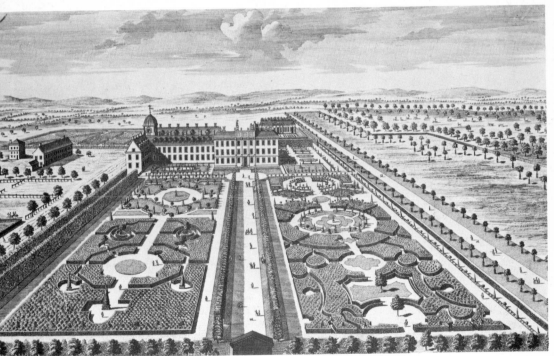

3 (*top*) Ledston Hall, Yorkshire. Painting by J. Settrington, 1728

4 (*bottom*) Kensington Gardens, London. Engraving, *c.* 1710

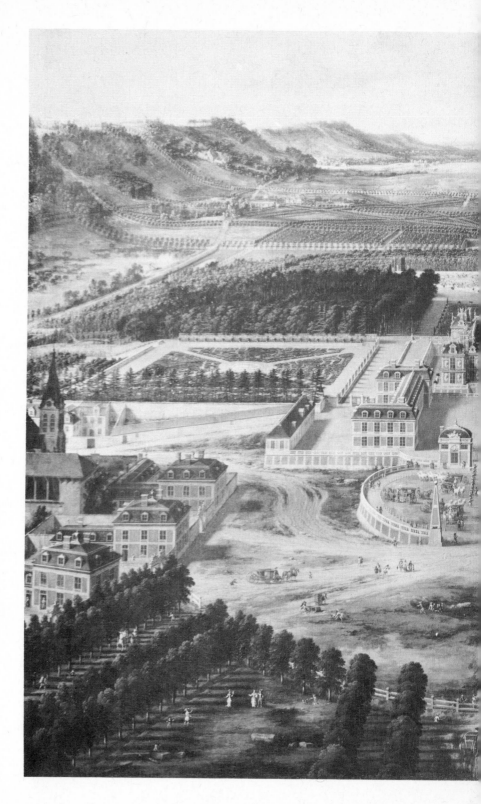

5 Versailles. Painting by Pierre Patel, 1666

6 Kensington Gardens, London. Drawing of the south-east corner by
Bernard Lens the Younger, 1736, showing mount and summerhouse

'a conduit of antic fashion . . . or else some dial or other pyramid'.[2] These
gardens were generally small, open-air extensions of the manor house or
hall which had barely been emancipated from the need for some form of
fortification. A few grandiose designs existed, as Daines Barrington notes
in his historical survey of gardening presented to the Society of Antiquaries
of London in 1782: at Nonsuch a garden was

cut out and divided into several allies, quarters and rounds, set about with thorn
hedges. On the north side was a *kitchen* garden very *commodious*, and surrounded
with a brick wall of fourteen feet high. On the west was a wilderness severed from
the little park by the hedge, the whole containing ten acres. In the privy garden
were pyramids, fountains, and basons of marble, one of which is set round with six
lelack trees, which trees bear no fruite, but only a very pleasaunte flower . . . Lastly,
before this palace was a *neate* and *haundsome* bowling-green, surrounded with a
balustrade of free stone.

   In this garden therefore at Nonsuch we find many such ornaments of old English
gardening, as prevailed till the modern taste was introduced by Kent.[3]

Barrington ignores the influence of Italian, French and Dutch gardens that
intervened before Kent, as well as contributions to the 'modern taste' prior
to Kent's, but he is still accurate in his sense of the persistence of Tudor

6

features. Ledston Hall in Yorkshire (Plate 3) still retained in 1728 its high walls and divided and embellished quarters; Kensington in *c.* 1710 (Plate 4) still displayed pyramids of evergreens (though this was as much a legacy from the Netherlands) and preserved as late as 1736 the old motif of a mount, from which views were achieved beyond the confines of a high-walled garden (Plate 6).

What the seventeenth century added to English garden design was a certain intricacy and a delight in waterworks, derived mainly from Italy, a sense of grandeur and vast scale from France, and more ideas of how to embroider flowerbeds and embellish shrubs and trees from the Netherlands. These legacies were, of course, not distinct in practice, and the dominant, mediating taste by the end of the century was French. And it was a rejection of the French formality, which dominated Europe throughout the seventeenth century, that initiated the English landscape garden.

The ideal of a French layout was Versailles ('*le miracle que fait M. Le Nôtre*', as Louis XIV termed it), with its dominant palace, axial and radial avenues and its vistas forming the skeleton of the plan (Plate 5). Within this framework were intricate parterres, canals, *bosquets*, statuary, domes, triumphal arches and *treillage*. The garden was an extension of the palace proper, providing a majestic setting for the firework displays, theatrical performances, and all the arts of the *fêtes galantes* which added savour and sophistication to courtly life. It also embodied concepts of Cartesian philosophy, the interpretation of the 'natural' in terms of the universal laws of geometry. Throughout Europe this resplendent and autocratic garden became a necessary adjunct to every great house or palace: today examples

7 St Cloud. Engraving of cascade by Jacques Rigaud, 1730

can be seen at Herrenhausen in West Germany, Fredensborg in Denmark, the Haus Petersberg in Holland, the Villa Crevelli Sormani-Verri at Castel-lozzo in Italy, and at Peterhof in Russia. In Northern Ireland there is Kilruddery, in England there are Melbourne and Hampton Court (Plate 66).

Dutch contributions, especially during the reign of William and Mary who brought their tastes with them from the Netherlands in 1688, super-imposed upon the French mode a greater use of clipped evergreens (the topiary Pope was to satirize), fussier and less grandiloquent ornament, and statues. But statuary was just as crucial an element of Italian Renaissance gardens (see Plate 45), on which the French and Dutch of course drew, and French water gardens, like that at St Cloud (Plate 7), were modelled upon Italian predecessors at Frascati or the Villa D'Este at Tivoli. The Italian example, much praised by Henry Wotton and John Evelyn among others, was transmitted mainly through France,[4] and it is difficult to disentangle what were its specific contributions to the ideas and practice of English 'gardenists' (to use Walpole's word).[5] What *is* certain is that Italian gardens were thought of as an art distinct from the French by many seventeenth-century travellers and garden theorists. The delightful variety and ingenious ways of involving the spectator in the enchantments of garden spaces (Plate 42) were a powerful if submerged continuity between early theorists of variety and the ideas of villa and garden held by the neo-Palladians around Lord Burlington.

The English reaction to French gardens in the early 1700s was vigorous. Earlier pleas for less contrived scenery, like Bacon's or Temple's, were remembered and called in aid of a new determination to reject French authority in the arts and in politics. It was an endorsement of liberty and tolerance against tyranny and oppression. Democracy against autocracy. And it was expressed in every facet of the creative arts, as Pope explained in *An Essay on Criticism* (1711):

> But *Critic Learning* flourish'd most in *France*.
> The *Rules*, a Nation born to serve, obeys,
> And *Boileau* still in Right of *Horace* sways.
> But *we*, brave *Britons*, *Foreign Laws* despis'd,
> And kept *unconquer'd*, and *uncivilised*,
> Fierce for the *Liberties of Wit* . . .
>
> (lines 712–17)

But the protests were largely in theoretical terms; gardening practice lagged behind. The idea of Wotton that '*Gardens* should be irregular', or the news Temple offered that the Chinese used 'extraordinary dispositions of Nature' in their landscapes, shaped actual designs very slowly. It was partly that revisions of key terms, like 'art', 'nature', or 'imitation', could still be linked to surviving gardens and even illustrated by a fresh consideration of old devices. Thus at Longleat the walks among woods and the wilderness with its summerhouse upon the hillside (Plate 8) could be read as a significant exercise in a 'natural' taste compared with the canal, basins, squared gardens and fountains round the house. Or at Ham House in 1730 (Plate 9) the pattern

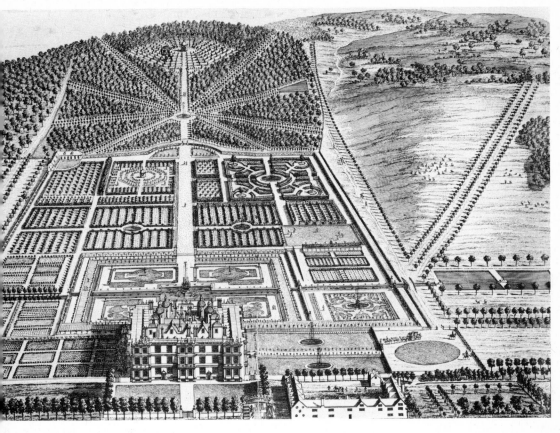

8 Longleat, Wiltshire. Engraving by Kip and Knyff, *c.* 1700

of tree-shaded walks may well have seemed to those who used them a pleasantly unartificial place. When the new ideas did get incorporated, they often seemed ridiculously contrived — at Hammels, for example (Plate 10) — and just as artful in their wavering lines and random trees as the geometry retained in the main garden below.

The same contradictions between language and visual evidence appear in the first professional gardener in England to write about the new style, Stephen Switzer. Others, like Timothy Nourse in *Campania Foelix* (1700), had recommended that a country seat be set 'not amongst Enclosures, but in a champaign, open Country'; Shaftesbury and Addison had celebrated the 'wide Fields of Nature'; but none of them had actually offered visual suggestions of how their ideas might be translated. But it was Switzer, the pupil of London and Wise and the collaborator with Vanbrugh and perhaps Bridgeman, who tried to give a practical turn to these theories. Soon after his first publication, *The Nobleman, Gentleman, and Gardener's Recreation*, appeared in 1715, Alexander Pope moved to Twickenham and began creating his remarkable and novel landscape (Plates 81 and 82).

9

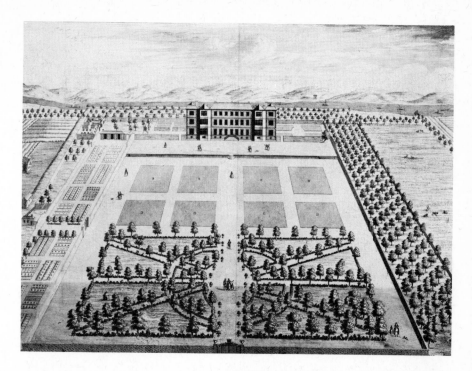

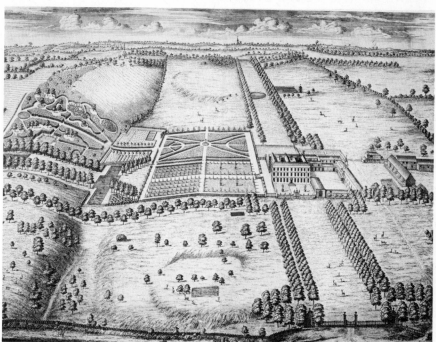

9 (*top*) Ham House, Surrey. Detail of engraving by Badeslade and
Rocque, *c.* 1730. Victoria and Albert Museum. Crown copyright

10 (*bottom*) Hammels, Hertfordshire. Engraving by Badeslade, 1722

III

The theories as well as the practical endeavours of men like Pope and Switzer
were sustained by the authority of literature and painting. It is no accident
that early landscapists, like Bridgeman and Kent, were members of literary
and artistic coteries that included Pope, Thornhill, Gibbs, Burlington and
Castell. For the contributions of literary and painterly connoisseurship to
landscape were enormously vital: as Walpole was to put it later — 'Poetry,
Painting & Gardening, or the science of Landscape, will forever by men of
Taste be deemed Three Sisters, or *the Three New Graces* who dress and
adorn Nature.'[6]

The most powerful literary influence was undoubtedly the celebration of
rural life by Virgil and Horace: the *topos* of '*beatus ille*',[7] the happy man,
whose contentment was attributed to his rural dwelling and his virtuous,
even pious, appreciation of the harmonious scheme of nature and its benevolent Creator. Matthew Prior, for whom Gibbs designed a villa at Down
Hall, set in a Bridgeman garden of the new mode, shaped one of the innumerable versions of this theme:

> GREAT MOTHER, let Me Once be able
> To have a Garden, House, and Stable;
> That I may Read, and Ride, and Plant,
> Superior to Desire, or Want;
> And as Health fails, and Years increase,
> Sit down, and think, and die in Peace.[8]

The magnificent illustrations in Dryden's translation of Virgil (1697) provide
a Restoration visual cast to this dedication to mother earth, with their
images of horticultural activity and of pastoral scenes where men in full-
bottomed wigs inhabit a Dutch Arcadian landscape. And however much the
early eighteenth century could only think of rural retirement in terms of
conventional country houses, it was yet evident that the Classical idea of
'*beatus ille*' could not be truly represented by 'Clipt Plants, Flowers, and
other trifling Decorations'. A happy country life presupposes that the house
will be placed in an open, rural setting. So Switzer divided his layouts into
what Walpole was to call 'the specific garden' near the house where 'a little
Regularity is allow'd', and the 'rural and extensive garden' beyond it where
the designer 'ought to pursue Nature'. Where possible, enclosing walls
should vanish, and by means of 'an easy, unaffected manner of Fencing' it
would 'look as if the adjacent Country were all a Garden'. The motif which
made this possible was the ha-ha: Walpole called it 'the capital stroke, the
leading step to all that has followed'.[9]

The first gardening book to describe the ha-ha was D'Argenville's *La
Théorie et la Pratique du Jardinage* (Paris 1709, trans. 1712), though there
is no reason to suppose that there were not earlier examples of its use both
in England and France. Moreover, the physical shape and situation of many
Italian gardens frequently contributed natural ha-ha's — from the Villa

D'Este one still looks out towards Rome across the plain, and Falda's engraving of the Duke of Parma's garden on the Palatine shows a southern aspect bounded by rocky descents (Plate 11).

Further support for what Pope termed 'calling-in the country' and for the traditions of Classical literature came from seventeenth-century painting. And since much of this was itself dedicated to Classical themes, the possibility of identifying them was greater. So Claude and Poussin, French artists working in Italy, could be taken as reliable illustrators of Virgil (see Plate 12), and their visual authority joined literature as precedent and endorsement of the new gardening. Their idealized visions of the countryside around Rome established an intricate relationship of water, distant hills, buildings (especially the effect of ruins or the formal contrasts of square and round temples), bridges and trees. When Pope writes of calling in the country, of catching opening glades and varying shades from shades, he is describing

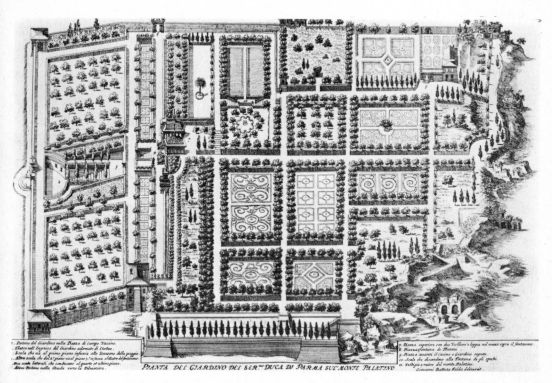

11 Palatine Hill, Rome. Engraving from Falda, *Li Giardini di Roma*, 1683

exactly the visual organization of a Claudean landscape and its application to Stowe. At the opposite extreme to the Arcadian scenes of Claude was the more turbulent vision of the Neapolitan artist, Salvator Rosa (Plate 13).

These paintings provided, above all, a sense of nature's *variety*, as one of their earliest French critics maintained:

car dans la grande variété dont-il est susceptible, le Peintre [du paysage] a plus d'occasions que dans tous les autres genres de cet Art de se contenter dans le choix des objets; la solitude des Rochers, la fraîcheur des Forêts, la limpidité des Eaux, & leur murmure apparent, l'étenduë des Plaines & des Lointains, le mélange des Arbres, la fermeté du Gazon . . .[10]

Variety became in its turn the central criterion of the landscape gardener.[11] So Nature's capabilities and potentialities were fully realized in accordance with the rules set by her artistic interpreters in Italy, and Pope's dictum, recorded by Spence in his *Anecdotes*, that 'all gardening is landscape-painting',[12] applied throughout the eighteenth century, though in varying ways. Addison recommended the man of taste to 'make a pretty Landskip of his own Possessions'.[13] And if the Duchess of Marlborough did not follow Vanbrugh's celebrated injunction to 'send for a landscape-painter'[14] who could advise on the retention of Old Woodstock Manor in the Blenheim

12 Claude Le Lorrain, 'Landscape with the Arrival of Aeneas at Pallanteum', 1675

13 Salvator Rosa, 'Soldier and Peasants in a Rocky Landscape', *c.* 1650

landscape (Plate 56), there were other patrons who virtually did. For they collected from Italy examples of the 'best of Landskip painters' — William Kent, for example, was sent abroad for that purpose. These pictures and engravings were destined for English walls and cabinets, while outside the grounds steadily assumed the forms the paintings had suggested.

It is difficult sometimes to see how designers transferred these landscape paintings to the three-dimensional world of English estates. At Castle Howard, Vanbrugh certainly invoked three of the most famous ingredients of such a Claude as the 'Pastoral Landscape with the Ponte Molle' (Plate 14), a square and a round building (the Temple of the Four Winds and the Mausoleum, built later by Hawksmoor and Daniel Garrett), and a Palladian bridge. At Stourhead its creator's Virgilian theme for the garden lends support to the suggestion that the layout and character are modelled upon Claude's 'Coast View of Delos with Aeneas'.[15] But with those exceptions and that of Painshill, where part of the lakeside is known to have been modelled on some Rosa sketches, it seems likely that the role of pictures as a pattern-book of designs has been exaggerated or misunderstood.[16]

What *is* beyond question is that landscape painting influenced men's thinking about natural scenery; it shaped their responses and gave them a vocabulary with which to articulate their experience of the new gardening. Thus Walpole reported to Richard Bentley in September 1753 that he had found a hermitage at Hagley, 'so exactly like those in Sadeler's prints' (Plate 15), and 'a pretty well under a wood, like the Samaritan woman's in

14 Claude Le Lorrain, 'Pastoral Landscape with the Ponte Molle', 1645.
Birmingham Museum and Art Gallery

a picture of Nicolò Poussin!' At Stowe likewise in 1770 he discovered a scene 'comprehending more beauties of light, shade and buildings, than any picture of Albano'.[17] The tone, colouring and light of English countryside is so different from its real Italian counterparts or their painted idealizations that such comparisons often seem absurd. John Constable saw the absurdity most strikingly in 'the landscapes of the English Woo[t]ton, who painted country gentlemen in their wigs and jockey caps, and top-boots, with packs of hounds, and placed them in Italian landscapes resembling those of Gaspar Poussin' (Plate 16).[18] Yet the vogue for such conversation pieces by Wootton, Hogarth or Devis, testifies to landowners' pride in their acquisition of the new landscape taste.[19]

Italian paintings cannot be separated from the English experience of actual Italian scenery. Addison travelled to Italy to 'compare the natural face of the country with the Landskips that the Poets have given us of it'.[20] Walpole on his way over the Alps in 1739 exclaimed, 'Precipices, mountains, torrents, wolves, rumblings, Salvator Rosa'.[21] This congruence of a taste for literature or painting with that for Italian scenery is an important element in William Mason's history of *The English Garden*, written in the 1770s:

> your eyes entranc'd
> Shall catch those glowing scenes, that taught a CLAUDE
> To grace his canvass with Hesperian hues:
> And scenes like these, on Memory's tablet drawn,
> Bring back to Britain; there give local form
> To each Idea; and, if Nature lend
> Materials fit of torrent, rock and shade,
> Produce new TIVOLIS.[22]

The country estate gave local form to various souvenirs of the Grand Tour. The proprietor of taste repeated the lessons of Europe as best he or his advisers could, prompted by the collections he had made abroad: paintings, engravings, sculpture, views of such famous places as Tivoli (Plate 78), folios on architecture, especially villas and gardens, books on Classical antiquity that might contain prints of the supposed sites of events first encountered in Roman literature, sketches by visiting Englishmen (Plate 17).[23]

The fortunes of the English landscape garden owed as much to practical matters as to aesthetic pursuits. A love of poetry and philosophy, painting and architecture, encountered problems of planting and transplanting, drainage and earthworks, in realizing visions of a garden. So the English milord also returned from his Grand Tour with trees, flowers and shrubs, and even hints on how to improve agricultural technique. His economic solvency depended upon taking agriculture and silviculture seriously.[24] Jethro Tull was one traveller who wrought a revolution in methods of cultivation as a result of observing the tillage operations of French wine-

15 (*opposite top*) Raphael Sadeler, after Paul Brill, 'Landscape with Two Figures on a Rock', c. 1600–20. Victoria and Albert Museum. Crown copyright

16 (*opposite bottom*) John Wootton, 'Hawking', c. 1740

17 Joseph Wright of Derby, 'Part of the Colosseum', *c.* 1774–5

growers. Farming methods were radically improved, and drainage, fertilization and crop rotation were introduced. The success, in fact, of the English garden owed much to the fact that in the early 1700s there were huge estates, mainly due to the development of the enclosure system, awaiting exploitation. Evelyn's *Sylva* (1664) had advised landowners to adorn their demesnes 'with trees of venerable shade and profitable timber'. So shrubs and trees were imported: oaks came from the Mediterranean countries and across the Atlantic; pines from Canada, Corsica, Georgia and New England; firs and spruces from Scandinavia and North America. Limes, sycamores, walnuts and plane trees were also imported, and nurseries sprang up specializing in such trees as horse chestnuts, laurels, mulberries, cedars of Lebanon or cypresses. If the landscape painter is the gardener's best designer, as Shenstone claimed, then the gardener's palette was becoming more colourful, richer and stronger.[25]

IV

Enormous expense was involved in these improvements. The French mode of gardening had been, certainly, more dependent upon a large budget, and John James, in his translation of D'Argenville's *La Théorie et la Pratique du Jardinage*, directed his book to 'Persons of greater and more elevated Minds' who were above all 'wealthy, and curious in the Art of Gardening'.[26] Though the English landscape garden was acknowledged to be less expensive than its French rival, cheaper to lay out and cheaper to maintain, many were still ruined by their undertakings. 'Every Man Now,' said the publication *Common Sense* in 1739, 'be his fortune what it will, is to be *doing something at his Place*, as the fashionable Phrase is; and you hardly meet with any Body, who, after the first Compliments, does not inform you, that he is *in Mortar* and *moving of Earth*; the modest terms for Building and Gardening.'

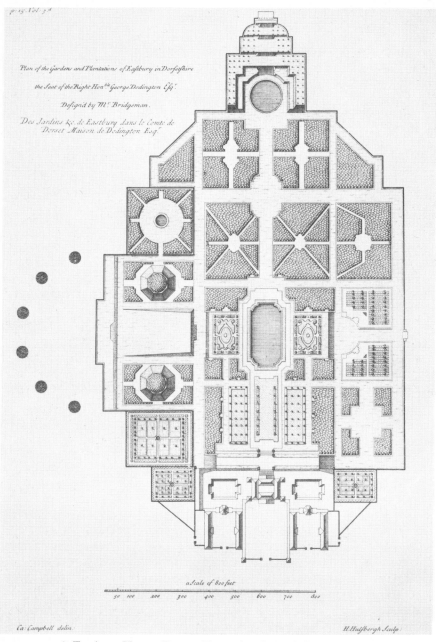

18 Eastbury House, Dorset. Engraving from Colin Campbell,
Vitruvius Britannicus, III, 1725

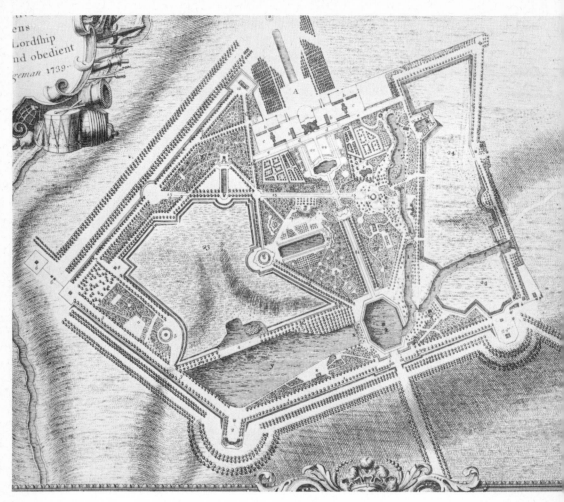

Within the image: "ens", "Lordſhip", "nd obedient", "geman 1739", "A"

19 Stowe House, Buckinghamshire. Detail of engraving by Rigaud and
Baron from *Views of Stowe*, published by Sarah Bridgeman, 1739

'The rapid progress of this happy enthusiasm', as it was called by a writer
in *The World* (No. 118), is evident from the writers, painters and engravers
who celebrated the beauties of the English scene.[27] To read in sequence the
published travel writings of those who undertook to explore the curiosities
of their own country during the eighteenth century is to register not only the
extraordinary amount of gardening carried out, but the steady spread of the
landscaping taste throughout the British Isles: first, there was Celia Fiennes,
who travelled between 1686 and 1705; then Defoe in the 1720s, Pococke in
the 1750s, Arthur Young in the next two decades, Gilpin's tours and
picturesque observations, and finally Cobbett's *Rural Rides* of 1821–32.
Foreigners, too, like Pehr Kalm, C. P. Moritz and Thomas Jefferson, found
English gardens and estates an essential part of their itinerary; visiting
artists, like the Swede, F. M. Piper, sketched them. Poems appeared on the
high points of the tour; guidebooks and many, often sumptuous, volumes of

engravings advertised the glories of the country house, beginning with Kip and Knyff's *Britannia Illustrata* (1707 *et seq.*) (Plate 8) and Colin Campbell's *Vitruvius Britannicus*[28] (1715 *et seq.*). These records, to which painters and watercolourists also contributed, all testify to what in 1755 *The World* (No. 118) called 'the peculiar happiness of this age . . . regularity banished, prospects opened, the country called in, nature rescued and improved, and art decently concealing herself under her own perfections'.

Throughout the first half of the century the divergences already noticed

20 Chiswick House, Middlesex. Engraving of bridge and canal by
Rysbrack, *c.* 1730

between early theory and practice continued to be visible: neither the interpretation of what *The World* saw as basic formulae nor the progress of their consolidation was always straightforward. Bridgeman, for example, worked at both Eastbury (Plate 18) and Stowe (Plate 19) at about the same time, yet the flexibility and irregularities of the latter are in striking contrast to the geometrical cadenzas of the former. Equally, the disposition of buildings beside water is conspicuously different at Chiswick and Claremont on the one hand (Plates 20 and 21), and in Kent's vision of the Vale of Venus at Rousham (Plate 22). The talent that Walpole identified in Kent was his ability to see 'that all nature was a garden'; but he could envisage a landscape (Plate 23) where the garden is all nature to an extent that his contemporaries could not achieve.

The responsibility for establishing the English landscape garden lay with a small group of professional architects and designers — mainly, Vanbrugh,

21 (*top*) Claremont House, Surrey. Engraving of lake, amphitheatre and island temple by Rocque, 1754

22 (*bottom*) Rousham, Oxfordshire. Sketch by Kent of Venus' Vale, *c.* 1737

23 Woodland landscape. Sketch by Kent, ?1730s

Bridgeman, Kent, and Gibbs — working for a limited number of patrons, who numbered among them several distinguished amateurs like Burlington and Pembroke. They produced landscapes for the Marlboroughs at Blenheim, for Cobham at Stowe, for Burlington at Chiswick, for Pelham at Esher (where Kent was 'Kentissime'), for Bathurst at Cirencester, for Aislabie at Studley Royal, and for the Dormers at Rousham. At each the 'Genius of the Place' is improved with the appropriate repertoire of sinuous walks and streams, Classical or Gothic temples and follies, all of which features join the ha-ha as the essence of this early English landscape. But it is perhaps the collaboration of architect with landscapist that was most crucial, and here Vanbrugh, with progressive ideas on landscape and the imagination to explore new relationships between buildings and garden, must have set a strong example. As Switzer advised, 'When you first begin to build, and make Gardens, the Gardener and Builder ought to go Hand in Hand, and to consult together'.[29] This consultation determined not only the relationship of house to grounds, but it ensured that a landscape was embellished with buildings.

The authority for much architectural design was antiquity, mediated by Italian Renaissance theory and practice. Even the title of *Vitruvius Britannicus* establishes the ambitions which Pope, for example, credited to Lord Burlington:

You show us, Rome was glorious, not profuse,
And pompous buildings once were things of Use,

24 (*top*) Marble Hill, Middlesex. View from Thames. Engraving by
Heckell and Mason, 1749

25 (*bottom*) Pope's villa, Twickenham. View from Thames.
Engraving by Heckell and Mason, 1749

as well as the unfortunate consequences of his example —

Yet shall (my Lord) your just, your noble rules
Fill half the land with Imitating Fools,
Who random drawings from your sheets shall take,
And of one beauty many blunders make.[30]

But at least half of the country could boast, as Ralph Allen did at Prior Park (Plate 83), a Palladian mansion of some distinction and villas like Marble Hill House and Pope's own place at Twickenham (Plates 24 and 25). While in more exclusively gardenist publications, like Castell's *Villas of the Ancients Illustrated* and Langley's *New Principles of Gardening*, both appearing in 1728, there was the same anxiety to base contemporary practice upon Classical example. Walpole's judgement on Rousham, in his *History* (p. 29), by invoking Roman parallels, confers upon the Dormers' estate the ultimate accolade: 'The whole is as elegant and antique as if the emperor Julian had selected the most pleasing solitude about Daphne to enjoy a philosophic retirement.' One of Rousham's architectural delights is the terrace with arcade below it that looks over the river and meadows, and it is significant that this was given an honoured Roman name — Praeneste.[31] Castell's

26 John Wootton, 'Classical Landscape', *c.* 1730

27 Fanciful landscape with Hampton Court and Esher Place.
Sketch by Kent, ?1730s

inquiry into Pliny's villas both confirmed and promoted the usage of temples
and other structures dotted around a landscape. And these scholarly,
archaeological tastes, together with memories of Roman remains in Italy,
must have encouraged the vogue for imaginary Classical landscapes:
Wootton's fantasies of scenery interspersed with temples and sculpture
(Plate 26), or the equivalent visions of garden designers — Kent, for example,
speculated in a mingled Gothic and Classical vein about improvements for
Hampton Court and Esher Place (Plate 27).

Gardening publications rapidly provided more practical plans and elevations of specimen structures. The ambitious but uncertain landowner would
have been faced with a baffling array of suggestions from Batty Langley's
exotic trelliswork (Plate 28), to the Halfpenny brothers' suggestions for
Gothic termination seats (Plate 29), or Queen Caroline's Classical ruin of a
hermitage (Plate 30). It was considered, as the century progressed, more
appropriate to Britain's cultural history to provide ruins in the Gothic taste:
Sanderson Miller became especially famous for his contributions in this
style (Plate 31).[32] More fortunate gardens could incorporate genuine ruins
on the site, as Shenstone did at The Leasowes, or as Aislabie did at Studley
Royal, where the Classical territory around the water gardens (Plate 77) was
extended to include the magnificent remains of Fountains Abbey (Plate 32).

Stowe had probably the richest array of temples, doubtless a determined
visual pun upon the family motto— *Templa quam dilecta* (How delightful
are thy temples!) — which was itself a verbal play with Cobham's family
name of Temple. But not only for its garden ornaments was Stowe the most
important garden of the period. Here Vanbrugh, Gibbs, Bridgeman and
Kent created the most magnificent and admired garden of early and mid-

28 Ornamental trelliswork. Engraving from Batty Langley,
New Principles of Gardening, 1728

eighteenth-century England. Bridgeman determined its basic structure; later, Vanbrugh, Gibbs and Kent added temples and other garden buildings. With its open and closed areas, its buildings, its use of various forms of water, and the integration of the park into the garden proper, Stowe provides us with a brilliant exercise in the co-operation of art with nature. Furthermore, Stowe is very well documented, providing an invaluable 'text' in which to study the scope and progress of English gardening.[33] When after Bridgeman's death in 1738 the Elysian Fields, with their satiric juxtaposition of buildings, were completed and the Grecian Valley was created further to the east, Stowe also anticipated the development of the landscape garden in the second half of the eighteenth century.

Stowe was essentially the creation of professional architects, painters and landscapists, though it would be unwise to neglect Cobham's enlightened patronage and the contributions of amateurs like Gilbert West or even perhaps Pope. Elsewhere, at Stourhead, the patron dominated, and its Virgilian landscape of arranged views, temples and meditation points along a determined circuit was a highly personal expression of Hoare's own imagination and learning. Other proprietors of taste were also engaged in small

29 (*opposite left*) Gothic summerhouse. Engraving from William Halfpenny,
Rural Architecture in the Gothic Taste, 1752

30 (*opposite right*) Hermitage in Richmond Gardens, Surrey.
Engraving by Gravelot and Du Bosc, 1735

31 (*top*) Gothic tower at Wimpole Hall, Cambridgeshire. Engraving *c.* 1777

32 (*bottom*) Studley Royal, Yorkshire. Fountains Abbey, mount and lake.
Engraving by Anthony Walker, 1758

33 Woburn Farm, Surrey. Engraving by Luke Sullivan, 1759

gardens of similarly personal scope. In Surrey, Philip Southcote created Woburn Park — Gray called it 'Southcote's Paradise' — which was much admired by contemporaries: it had prospects, a painterly disposition of temples, and its own special emphasis on providing a setting for a peaceful rural life (Plate 33). In Worcestershire, Staffordshire and Shropshire three gardens received unanimous praise from connoisseurs — Hagley, the property of George Lyttelton; Enville, that of Lord Stamford; and The Leasowes, belonging to the poet, William Shenstone, which Walpole called 'a perfect picture of his mind, simple, elegant and amiable' and, we might add, of his poetic fancy.

V

Three themes dominate the second half of the eighteenth century and the maturity of the English landscape gardening movement: one is the extensive and fresh work by 'Capability' Brown; a second is the rise of Orientalism; a third is the controversy about picturesque taste and its application to garden design, which involved Knight, Price and Repton. The three themes are closely related.

Brown's work was in one respect the most radical of all landscape designers'. He chose to emphasize the basic materials of a site — the lines and shapes and contours of its ground, waters and trees. He neglected buildings and statues, mottoes and inscriptions; he swept the lawn straight up to the walls of the house, eliminating terraces and other remains of the 'specific garden'. It is therefore to his work, above all, that the exact meaning of *formal* should be applied: for he rediscovered the forms of the landscape itself. Doubtless he developed what was already implicit in certain areas of early eighteenth-century gardens — the 'formal' qualities, for example, of Stowe's Elysian Fields and Grecian Valley, which he would have known when he was head gardener there in the decade after 1741.

Brown's influence on the face of the English countryside is unquestionable. His work inside parks consisted in treating them as *formally* as their natural materials allowed, which in its turn alerted his clients and their friends to the natural capabilities of the countryside that lay beyond their estates. But there were many contemporaries who found Brown's designs dull. Sir William Chambers, who advised some Chinese solutions, and Richard Payne Knight and Uvedale Price, who prescribed fidelity to the vision of Salvator Rosa, were at one in their dismay at Brown's work.[34] Even Humphry Repton, who rejected the picturesque notions of Knight and Price, discovered that his deliberate attempt to succeed Brown as the leader of British landscapists required some thorough re-assessments of Brownian principles.[35]

The trouble with Brown's designs proved to be, ironically, their studied elimination of designed elements. Joshua Reynolds is presumably glancing at Brown in his thirteenth *Discourse* (1786), when he writes: 'Gardening, as far as Gardening is an Art, or entitled to that appellation, is a deviation from nature; for if the true taste consists, as many hold, in banishing every appearance of Art, or any traces of the footsteps of man, it would then be no longer a Garden.' Chambers found Brown's gardens 'differ very little from common fields, so closely is common nature copied in most of them'.[36] Yet, as Repton was to point out, Brown's best designs do surreptitiously proclaim the art that recognizes and utilizes nature's forms; it was his 'illiterate followers', mimicking his work, who betrayed his high achievement.[37]

Repton's own contribution to landscape history was to reclaim gardens for social use and relate them again to the houses they served. He pushed back the park and reintroduced regular and architectural forms — terraces, raised flowerbeds, trelliswork, conservatories — which were a logical extension of the social spaces of the house and more convenient for his clients who could thus use them more readily: the shrubbery and gravel walks in *Mansfield Park* to which Fanny Price occasionally retreats would be typical of the Reptonian attention to the social function of his designs.[38] They were not calculated — Repton admits himself — to look well in a picturesque sketch, but they did answer to human requirements (Plates 101a and 101b). It is perhaps no accident that his career led him finally to design the gardens of London squares, in this anticipating the work both of his later editor, John Claudius Loudon, and of William Robinson.

Neither Chambers' views nor, in matters of garden design, even the picturesque attitudes prospered. Though Chambers thought his garden at Kew, with its pagoda and other Chinese trappings, made an 'Eden' of 'what was once a Desart', his critics found it neither appropriate to this country nor anything but spurious Orientalism anyway. Walpole considered Chambers' *Dissertation on Oriental Gardening* (1772) 'more extravagant than the worst Chinese paper, and is written in wild revenge against Brown; the only surprising consequence is, that it is laughed at, and it is not likely to be adopted'.[39] Mason's response, *An Heroic Epistle to Sir William Chambers*, was therefore greatly to the taste of Walpole, who wrote to the Countess of Upper Ossory that 'I laughed till I cried, and the oftener I read it, the better I like it'.[40] Kew represented the most exciting form of garden design only to the meretriciously fashion-conscious; but the effect of Kew and Chambers' writings together was in part to undermine the English authority for establishing the landscape garden. To the Frenchman, Le Rouge, for instance, '*tout le monde sait que les Jardins Anglais ne sont qu'une imitation de ceux de la Chine*',[41] and his proposals for a '*Superbe Jardin Anglais*' near Paris (Plate 34) is a risible concoction of Chinese pavilions and extravagant serpentine lines.

The picturesque taste among gardenists failed for different reasons. The debates that Repton conducted with Knight and Price were concerned with the minutiae of aesthetics and the *amour-propre* of the disputants. The main point to emerge was that, though Price and Knight created 'romantick', Salvator Rosa-like landscapes on their own estates, these were not transfer-

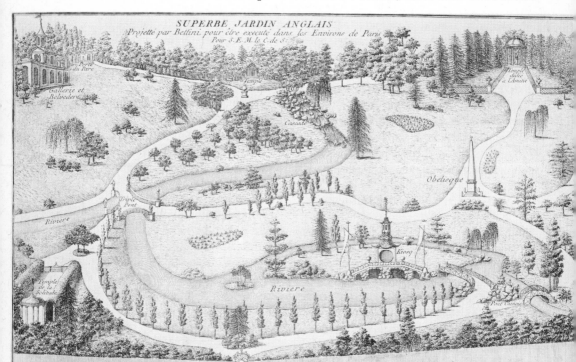

34 '*Superbe Jardin Anglais*'. Engraving from Le Rouge,
Détails des Nouveaux Jardins à la Mode, 1776–88

able to less sublime topography. Those who sought wilder scenery than the English country estate usually provided were following Gilpin's picturesque tours into Scotland and the Lake District, and had deserted the garden. Thomas Gray, in fact, advised precisely that in a letter to William Mason of 1765:

the Mountains are extatic, & ought to be visited in pilgrimage once a year. none but those monstrous creatures of God know how to join so much beauty with so much horror. a fig for your Poets, Painters, Gardiners, & Clergymen, that have not been among them: their imagination can be made up of nothing but bowling-greens, flowering shrubs, horse-ponds, Fleet-ditches, shell-grottoes, & Chinée-rails.[42]

VI

One further aspect of the controversies deserves separate treatment. When Brown chose to concentrate upon the natural forms of the landscape and eliminate temples, inscriptions and statues, he banished from the garden the objects which had provoked the minds and imaginations of their visitors. Both Chambers, with his 'Chinée-rails', and Knight and Price, with their variations upon Rosa, were attempting to bring back into the garden the opportunities for associationism which Brown seemed to have rejected and which had been endemic to the English landscape movement since its inception.

The English landscape garden was associated from the start with the idea of Liberty. Stowe actually incorporated a Gothic Temple of Liberty into its final scheme to recall visitors to an awareness of Britain's own cultural traditions, and it was once appropriately surrounded with busts of the Germanic deities who gave their names to the days of our week. But 'Liberty' was only one of a whole complex of ideas that a garden like Stowe was designed to promote; some were even of the rival, Classical traditions of culture. In the Elysian Fields the two encountered each other: a Temple of Ancient Virtue, with statues of the most famous Grecian lawgiver, general, poet and philosopher, faced a row of half-length busts placed in the niches of a Temple of British Worthies across the little valley, through which a stream flowed named the River Styx.

This particular confrontation illuminates some of the more intricate patterns of thought that gardens tried to instil in their visitors. Some were more simple and provided straightforward allusions to either Classical myth, like Rousham's Venus, with her attendant nymphs and peeping satyrs, or to Roman precedence. Castell's *Villas of the Ancients* offered encouragement for those by discussing the proper ornaments for a garden and by noting the deities who were aptly celebrated at a villa; hence the temples to Venus at Stowe, to Bacchus at Stowe, and to Flora at Stourhead. But the Elysian Fields present a much more ambitious scheme of associations; they require a visitor to compare ancient virtue with its modern counterpart (a ruined and Gothic Temple of Modern Virtue was established nearby), to register the political significance of the British Worthies, which in its turn involved noticing that a line was missing from a Virgilian quotation, and to appreciate that the Temple of Ancient Virtue called to mind the Roman Temple of Vesta (the so-called Sybil's Temple) at Tivoli, and the Temple of British Worthies some other modern Italian examples. And in these matters of English Augustanism, the assimilation of Classical ideas was not merely a question of 'imitation', but of 'translation', of making Homer (in Pope's phrase) 'speak good English', and of registering the difficulties as well as the opportunities for cultural obligations. When, for example, Pope came to translate Horace's lines about the gladiator's retirement deep into the countryside — '*Vejanius Armis Herculis ad postem fixit latet abditus agro*' — his version accommodates the Roman idea in its proper place in a contemporary nobleman's recreations:

> Our Gen'rals now, retir'd to their Estates,
> Hang their old Trophies o'er the Garden gates,
> In Life's cool evening satiate of applause,
> Nor fond of bleeding, ev'n in BRUNSWICK's cause.[43]
>
> (lines 7–10)

The English landscape garden acquired this apparatus of associative imagery in many ways. From Italian gardens, especially, which were often designed by poets and humanists to promote a series of reflections,[44] there must have come some experience in composing and in 'reading' a garden's ideas. Paintings, too, were visual events that had to be searched for meaning, and their symbols or emblems understood. But pictures provided experience of a different sort that was also transferred to gardens — their landscapes seem to exist as a means of expressing inward feeling and mood. A Claude painting that we know to have been in England in the 1720s defines both this expressive and the emblematic pictorial vocabulary: 'The Enchanted Castle' (more properly entitled 'Landscape with Psyche at the Palace of Cupid') affords a magically evocative scene, where the central figure, symbolizing the soul, finds its grief mirrored in the expressive landscape. Poussin's 'Landscape with a Man Killed by a Snake' (Plate 35) is also known to have been read as an account of the 'effects of terror'.[45] Salvator Rosa was valued for his exploration of the wilder emotions, for which his landscapes served as objective equivalents (Plate 13).

These habits of responding to the meaning and mood in landscape pictures were readily transferred to the experience of a landscape garden. At Castle Howard, for instance, the Mausoleum catches the eye across the fields, sombre and dark, a *memento mori* for the mind on the walk across from the Temple of the Four Winds; once inside, with a dramatic change, one is aware only of the serene lightness — the Christian point of which is fairly obvious, taking one from the gloom of death to its transcendence. Another example is that recorded in Pope's reactions to the scenes at Woburn Farm:

When I [i.e. Spence, Pope's 'biographer'] told Mr. Southcote that the sight of his ground near his house was always apt to lead me into a pleasing smile and into a delicious sort of feeling in the heart, of which I had nothing when I was in his much nobler views along the brow of the hill, he said that Mr. Pope had often spoke of the very same effect of it on him.[46]

One suspects that the eighteenth-century gardenists' invocation of pictures was a means of identifying moods which a landscape provoked in them. Gilpin's picturesque attention on his visit to Stowe is notably acute, but he also ends his *Dialogue* (1748) with a clear recognition of a garden's own emotional structures learnt from, but independent of, paintings: 'these Gardens are a very Epitome of the World: They are calculated for Minds of every Stamp, and give free Scope to Inclinations of every kind.'

Such emotions had always been a special province of the lyric or dramatic poet. And the garden's debt to poetry — Virgil's, Horace's, Milton's, Spenser's — was not only an obligation to ideas on design, but to verbal concentrations of associated ideas and meanings. So Milton provided an image of unrestricted natural scenery *and* ideas of edenic bliss in *Paradise Lost*; *Il Penseroso* suggested 'archèd walks of twilight groves' as the scenery for a 'peaceful hermitage', of which there were many in eighteenth-century gardens, but at the same time it identified the kinds of reflection and mood that a hermitage might instil. Spenser appears to have inspired Bridgeman and Kent with his landscape descriptions;[47] Kent especially chose to make the

35 Nicolas Poussin, 'Landscape with a Man Killed by a Snake', *c.* 1648.
National Gallery, London

35

36 James Thornhill. Sketch of set for *Arsinoë, Queen of Cyprus, c.* 1704.
Victoria and Albert Museum. Crown copyright

ideas of romance, strangeness and adventure that he discovered in *The Faerie Queene* part of a garden's scope (Plate 92).

The dramatic poets, too, explored psychological conditions, and though this anthology contains no examples of their work it is vital to remember that the garden and the theatre have been closely connected at various points in their history. The Italian Renaissance garden often contained a theatre, where plays or operas were performed, and this in its turn the English garden imitated with theatres or amphitheatres at Rousham, Claremont and Stowe: Pope's garden at Twickenham had its 'Bridgemannick Theatre'.[48] From placing theatres in gardens it was but a short step to thinking of the whole garden in theatrical terms. Thus Pope at Rousham, for example, admired 'the prettiest place for water-falls, jetts, ponds inclosed with beautiful scenes of green and hanging wood' — and his use of *scenes* surely implies a sense of places contrived like the theatre sets of Thornhill (Plate 36). But it is not simply that Thornhill (who was a friend of Bridgeman) could show in one of his stage designs a garden with urns, fountains, statues and a distant villa, but that such locations in opera or masque or drama were symbolic and expressive of the action displayed there. This identification of landscape and events that take place in them may be traced back at least to the Italian *intermezzi* and other court entertainments which were often held in gardens; it was partly from these that Inigo Jones derived his masque designs (Plate 37), which include landscapes symbolic of the ideas that the masques presented. It seems inconceivable that this aspect of Jones' work was not

37 Inigo Jones. Sketch of back shutter, probably for *The Shepherd's Paradise*, 1631

remarked by the eighteenth-century neo-Palladians.

But the English landscape garden was able to absorb and exploit this range of symbolic and expressive traditions in the other arts because its creation coincided with fresh theories of how the human mind operated. John Locke's *Essay Concerning Human Understanding* was published in 1690, and by 1706 had reached an enlarged fifth edition. Its influence throughout the eighteenth century was enormous, as its insights were elaborated and analysed by a succession of British philosophers.[49] Locke's basic arguments were the denial of 'innate ideas' and the insistence that we derive all our ideas from experience. The visible world is registered by the eyes which transfer to the mind simple ideas associated with the images seen; the mind is capable of forming complex patterns of ideas from this stock of simple ones. We begin to see the effect of Locke's theories in Addison's writings: in the *Spectator* papers on the 'Pleasures of the Imagination' he justifies our exploring the 'wide fields of Nature, where the sight wanders up and down without confinement, and is fed with an indefinite variety of Images'; these visual pictures promote our ideas, so 'any single Circumstance of what we have formerly seen often raises up a whole scene of Imagery and awakens numberless ideas that before slept in the Imagination'. And Addison continues in that issue of *The Spectator* (No. 417) with an account of the associative workings of the mind in the face of a garden prospect. One of his essays in *The Tatler* (No. 123) even seems to have provided the programme of images and their associated ideas for Stowe's Elysian Fields.[50]

The exciting relevance of these fresh mental perspectives for English landscapists lay in their ability to direct, if not control, the minds and imaginations of people who passed their temples, statues and mottoes, registering the images and inscribed words and releasing associated ideas. Such associationism was a central aspect of garden art from Pope (who objected to the statue of Dr Clarke in Queen Caroline's Hermitage)[51] to Price and the proponents of the picturesque. The various discussions of sublimity, beauty and the picturesque during this period all involved the mental adjudications of each idea and especially its visual character; aesthetics, accordingly, came to exercise considerable influence on gardenist matters.

As the eighteenth century progressed, some reservations came to be expressed about the kind of associationism appropriate to a garden, though nobody denied its fundamental role except perhaps, by implication, Brown. One reservation, undoubtedly a result of an established taste for the Brownian landscape, came from Thomas Whately:

Character is very reconcileable with beauty; and even when independent of it, has attracted so much regard, as to occasion several frivolous attempts to produce it; statues, inscriptions, and even paintings, history and mythology, and a variety of devices have been introduced for this purpose. The heathen deities and heroes have therefore had their several places assigned to them in the woods and the lawns of a garden; natural cascades have been disfigured with river gods; and columns erected only to receive quotations; the compartments of a summer-house have been filled with pictures of gambols and revels, as significant of gaiety; the cypress, because it was once used in funerals, has been thought peculiarly adapted to melancholy; and the decorations, the furniture, and the environs of a building have been crowded with puerilities, under pretence of propriety. All these devices are rather *emblematical* than expressive; they may be ingenious contrivances, and recall absent ideas to the recollection; but they make no immediate impression, for they must be examined, compared, perhaps explained, before the whole design of them is well understood; and though an allusion to a favourite or well-known subject of history, of poetry, or of tradition, may now and then animate or dignify a scene, yet as the subject does not naturally belong to a garden, the allusion should not be principle; it should seem to have been suggested by the scene: a transitory image, which irresistibly occurred; not sought for, not laboured; and have the force of a metaphor, free from the detail of an allegory.[52]

When landscape gardens are no longer, as Stowe had been, filled with emblematic devices that initiate meditations upon Liberty, British Worthies or Ancient Virtue, the mind is necessarily freer, its associations more flexible, more vague even, certainly more private. One difference, then, between Stowe and a Brownian park (or alternatively Knight's own landscape at Downton Vale) is that the garden scenes of the former instilled the same pattern of thought and reflection in visitors, who would have shared the same tastes and education; as Rigaud's 'Views of Stowe' reveal (Plates 61, 73 and 74) there does not appear to be any solitary meditation. Whereas in later gardens the scope for personal reverie was as great as the absence of directives allowed. Chambers, Knight and Price, trying to compensate for

38 Joseph Wright of Derby, Brooke Boothby, 1780–1

what they took to be an associationist poverty in Brown's designs, perhaps erred on the side of over-direction of a visitor's responses, which might explain their lack of a substantial following.

By the second half of the eighteenth century the English landscape garden had, as we have seen, ceased to hold many men of taste. Walpole announced this tendency when he exclaimed 'how picturesque the face of the country' was and how 'every journey is made though a succession of pictures'.[53] Like Gray and Gilpin, connoisseurs of scenery ventured into the world beyond the ha-ha in a fashion that leaves even Walpole's praise of Kent far behind. We see this search for rural scenery and for the private introspection it allows through an increasing number of paintings, from Wright of Derby's superb portrait of Brooke Boothby in the forest with his copy of Rousseau (Plate 38) to Francis Danby's views of private excursions in Leigh Woods or other Bristol landscapes (Plate 39). A compelling reason for the flight from the garden had been, in fact, announced as early as Addison:

The Beauties of the most stately Garden or Palace lie in a narrow compass, the Imagination runs them over, and requires something else to gratify her; but, in the wide Fields of Nature, the sight wanders up and down without confinement . . .[54]

Yet if the imagination was rewarded with more stimulation in the 'wide Fields of Nature', we think that the habits of mind and patterns of meditation that were relied upon there were precisely those learnt among landscape gardens. Wordsworth, himself something of a gardener in the eighteenth-

39 Francis Danby, 'Landscape Near Clifton', *c.* 1822–3

century mould,[55] called the countryside into his gardens at Dove Cottage and Rydal Mount, which were so contrived that psychological effects were stimulated by the prospects over lake and mountain. These expressive images of landscape become the central mode of his imagination in poetry:

> How exquisitely the individual mind
> . . . to the external world
> Is fitted.

This congruence of inward and outward, creative transactions between mind and nature, become central to the romantic imagination.[56] Their provenance, it is not too extreme to argue, is in the landscape gardening movement of the eighteenth century.

VII

Although the landscape garden was an English creation, it became an international style, copied (not to say parodied) extensively.[57] It had its counterparts in Scotland and Ireland, and it dominated Europe in much the same way that the French garden of Le Nôtre had done earlier. Foreign tourists visited the English parks to learn and admire, and theoretical books on the

40 Parc Monceau, near Paris. Engraving from Carmontelle, *Jardin de Monceau,* 1779

new style came out rapidly. Often these took their cue from English writers: Watelet's *Essai sur les Jardins* of 1774, for instance, is dependent upon Addison and Whately and was the outcome of experience at the Maison-Joli, near Paris; Louis Carmontelle's celebrated views of the Parc Monceau of 1779 (Plate 40) were accompanied by a text derived in part from Whately. Other examples of the new style on the Continent were not hard to find: at Wörlitz in Austria there was a Gothic house and grotto, as well as a pedimented Temple of Flora; in 1771 Mme du Barry built two temples at Louveciennes

41 Ermenonville, near Paris. Engraving of Rousseau's tomb on an island of poplars, and Temple of Philosophy, from Laborde, *Description des Nouveaux Jardins de la France et des Anciens Châteaux*, 1808

copied from Stowe and Kew; at Versailles itself there was Le Petit Hameau; in Russia there was Tsarskoye Selo, with fanciful garden buildings designed by Charles Cameron. In the United States both Mount Vernon and Jefferson's Monticello benefited from English examples, while in Italy, where the most celebrated example was the Villa Torlonia in Rome, *il giardino inglese* settled like a blight throughout a country as little apt for its particular effects as perhaps England had been for Palladian villas where owners, as Pope wrote, were proud to catch cold at a Venetian door.

But probably nowhere more than in France was the enthusiasm for the English style more pronounced. Walpole was in Paris in 1771 (the year his *History of the Modern Taste in Gardening* was printed at his press at Strawberry Hill) and he reported exultantly that 'English gardening gains ground here prodigiously . . . This new *anglomanie* will literally be *mad English*.'[58] But the English garden was something more than just another manifestation of Anglomania. Itself a result and expression of a new relationship between man and nature, it became a symbol of those fresh treaties: Rousseau in *La Nouvelle Héloïse* set his beloved Julie in an Elysium free of all man-made structures (and compared such an Elysium unfavourably with Stowe); Goethe made a landscape garden the setting for *Die Wahlverwandtschaften* (1808); Flaubert used it in *Bouvard et Pécuchet* (1881) to express the aspirations of his two central figures.[59]

Rousseau died at Ermenonville, the estate of the Marquis de Girardin, who had published in 1777 the most authoritative French book on the English landscape style, *De la Composition des Paysages, ou des Moyens d'Embellir la Nature*. With its grotto, temples and monuments, Ermenonville (Plate 41) is France's answer to Stowe.[60] But whereas Stowe is an affirmation of public and private life, Ermenonville is dominated by death. It is Rousseau's tomb, erected in 1778, that casts its spell over the garden: set on an island of poplars, it can be glimpsed from the shore as if it were a fragment of antique marble in some landscape by Hubert Robert. Like those shrines to Augustan poets in English gardens — Thomson's seat at Hagley, Congreve's monument at Stowe, Pope's seat at Cirencester — its inscription is a testimony to the varying fortunes of basic words in our vocabulary: '*Ici repose l'homme de la nature et de la vérité.*'

1   *Gnomologia: Adagies and Proverbs, Wise Sentences and Witty Sayings, Ancient and Modern, Foreign and British* (London 1732), no. 701.

2   See Ellen C. Tyler, *Early English Gardens and Garden Books*, Folger Booklets on Tudor and Stuart Civilization (Washington, D.C. 1963); the Markham quotation is taken from the caption to Plate 6.

3   'On the progress of gardening', *Archaeologia*, VII (1785), pp. 119–20. Barrington cites various Elizabethan sources for his remarks and quotes phrases from them.

4   See especially Claude Mollet, *Théâtre des Plans et Jardinages* (Paris 1652).

5   See Isabel W. U. Chase, *Horace Walpole: Gardenist* (Princeton, N.J. 1943), p. 184. All further references, unless otherwise stated, are to this critical edition of Walpole's *History of the Modern Taste in Gardening*.

6   MS annotation to William Mason's *Satirical Poems*, published in an edition of the poems by Paget Toynbee (Oxford 1926), p. 43. On the literary and artistic coteries see Peter Willis, *Charles Bridgeman and the English Landscape Garden* (London 1976), ch. 3; for essays on Walpole's 'sister arts' see John Dixon Hunt, *The Figure in the Landscape: Poetry, Painting and Gardening during the Eighteenth Century* (Baltimore and London 1976).

7   On this theme see Maren-Sofie Røstvig, *The Happy Man: Studies in the Metamorphoses of a Classical Ideal*, 2 vols. (2nd ed., Oslo and New York 1962–71); John Chalker, *The English Georgic* (London 1969); A. J. Sambrook, 'The English Lord and the Happy Husbandman', *Studies on Voltaire and the Eighteenth Century*, LVII (Geneva 1967), pp. 1357–75.

8   'Written at Paris, 1700. In the Beginning of Robe's *Geography*', lines 8–13, in *The Literary Works of Matthew Prior*, ed. H. Bunker Wright and Monroe K. Spears, 2 vols. (2nd ed., Oxford 1971), I, p. 189.

9   Walpole's remarks are in *Horace Walpole: Gardenist*, p. 25, and Switzer's are taken from his *Ichnographia Rustica* (London 1718), III, pp. 5–6 and *The Nobleman, Gentleman, and Gardener's Recreation* (London 1715), pp. xiii and xxviii. For Switzer's style see William A. Brogden, 'Stephen Switzer: "La Grand Manier" ', in *Furor Hortensis: Essays on the History of the English Landscape Garden in Memory of H. F. Clark*, ed. Peter Willis (Edinburgh 1974), pp. 21–30.

10 Roger de Piles, *Cours de Peinture par Principes* (Paris 1708; reprinted Geneva 1969), p. 200.

11 See Pope's remarks recorded by Joseph Spence, *Observations, Anecdotes, and Characters of Books and Men*, ed. James M. Osborn, 2 vols. (Oxford 1966), I, p. 254 (item 612). For other remarks on 'variety' see the following extracts *passim*.

12 ibid., I, p. 252 (item 606).

13 'Landskip' is, of course, a painterly term signifying a painted landscape.

14 Cited by Uvedale Price, *Essays on the Picturesque* (London 1810), II, p. 116. The basis for this presumably apocryphal remark is Vanbrugh's letter printed below, pp. 120–1.

15 Kenneth Woodbridge, *Landscape and Antiquity: Aspects of English Culture at Stourhead 1718 to 1838* (Oxford 1970), especially part I.

16 Similar scepticisms have been expressed by Derek Clifford, *A History of Garden Design* (2nd ed., London 1966), pp. 136 and 140, and by S. Lang, 'The genesis of the English landscape garden', *The Picturesque Garden and its Influence Outside the British Isles*, ed. N. Pevsner (Washington, D.C. 1974), pp. 3–8. However, Dr Lang's argument is based apparently upon the fact that Claude's name is not mentioned by any gardenist before Walpole, and she ignores (even though she quotes) references to painted 'landskips'.

17 *Yale Edition of Horace Walpole's Correspondence*, ed. W. S. Lewis *et al.* (London and New Haven 1937 *et seq.*), XXXV, p. 149 and X, p. 315.

18 C. R. Leslie, *Memoirs of the Life of John Constable* (London 1951; first published 1843), p. 320.

19 See Sacheverell Sitwell, *Conversation Pieces* (London 1936) and Mario Praz, *Conversation Pieces* (London 1971).

20 *The Works* (London 1721), II, A₄ verso. Joseph Spence similarly remarks (*Anecdotes*, I, p. 250, item 603), 'whence did Mr. Southcote take his idea of a Ferme Ornée — Fields, going from Rome to Venice'.

21 *Yale Walpole*, XIII, p. 181: Walpole writing to Richard West, 28 September 1739.

22 Book I, lines 64–71 in the York edition of 1783, provided with commentary by W. Burgh.

23 The enormous number of guidebooks and 'souvenir' volumes available to the Italian visitor is a subject yet to be explored thoroughly; but some hints may be taken from the invaluable editorial commentary in *The Diary of John Evelyn*, ed. E. S. de Beer, 6 vols. (Oxford 1955), and from A. Lytton Sells, *The Paradise of Travellers: The Italian Influence on Englishmen in the Seventeenth Century* (London 1964).

24 Many writers, including John Evelyn, had urged massive rehabilitation of the countryside after the ravages and disruptions of the Civil War.

25 For a history and bibliography of the 'gardener's palette' see (most recently) Blanche Henrey, *British Botanical and Horticultural Literature Before 1800*, 3 vols. (London 1975).

26 (London 1712; reprinted 1969), p. 4.

27 See Esther Moir, *The Discovery of Britain: The English Tourists: 1540 to 1840* (London 1964).

28 For details of these see Hugh Prince, *Parks in England* (Pinhorns, Isle of Wight 1967) and John Harris, *A Country House Index* (also Pinhorns, Isle of Wight 1971).

29   *Ichnographia Rustica* (2nd ed., London 1742), II, p. 154.

30   *Epistles to Several Persons* (*Moral Essays*), ed. F. W. Bateson (London and New Haven 1961, vol. III, pt. 2 of the 'Twickenham Edition' of Pope's poetry), pp. 139–40.

31   The modern Palestrina, near Rome: it has been argued that the Renaissance garden in Italy was derived from the Temple of Fortune at Praeneste — see Georgina Masson, *Italian Gardens* (London 1966; first published 1961), pp. 123–5.

32   See Anthony C. Wood and William Hawkes, *Sanderson Miller of Radway* (forthcoming).

33   Gilbert West's poem of 1732 and Gilpin's *Dialogue* of 1748 are both represented in this volume; there were also Seeley's guides and various sets of engravings, starting with those issued in 1739 by Sarah Bridgeman. For modern accounts, see Christopher Hussey, *English Gardens and Landscapes 1700–1750* (London 1967); *Apollo*, XCVII (June 1973), an issue devoted to Stowe; and the series of articles appearing each term in *The Stoic*.

34   On Knight and Price see the first volume of essays by N. Pevsner, *Studies in Art, Architecture and Design*, 2 vols. (New York and London 1968); on Price, see Marcia Allentuck, 'Sir Uvedale Price and the picturesque garden: the evidence of the Coleorton Papers', *The Picturesque Garden*, ed. Pevsner, pp. 59–76.

35   See *The Landscape Gardening and Landscape Architecture of the Late Humphry Repton, Esq. Being His Entire Works on These Subjects*, ed. J. C. Loudon (London 1840; reprinted 1969), *passim*. There is an article on Repton by Pevsner in his collection cited in the previous note.

36   William Chambers, *A Dissertation on Oriental Gardening* (London 1772; reprinted 1972), p. v.

37   Loudon, op. cit., pp. 327–8.

38   See John Dixon Hunt, 'Sense and sensibility in the landscape designs of Humphry Repton: with a Postscript on *Mansfield Park*', *Art Quarterly* (forthcoming).

39   *Yale Walpole*, XXVIII, p. 34: Walpole writing to William Mason, 25 May 1772.

40   ibid., XXXII, p. 101: Walpole's letter is dated 11 March 1773.

41   *Détails des Nouveaux Jardins à la Mode* (Paris 1776–87), *cahier* 15, inscription on Plate 1.

42   *The Correspondence*, ed. Paget Toynbee and Leonard Whibley, 3 vols. (Oxford 1935), II, p. 899.

43   *Imitations of Horace*, ed. John Butt (London and New Haven, 1961, vol. IV of the 'Twickenham' Pope), p. 279. It is interesting to note that Poussin also is thought to have painted a version of these lines from Horace: see Anthony Blunt, *Nicolas Poussin* (London and New York, 1968), p. 292n and plate 185 ('Landscape with a Man Washing His Feet at a Fountain').

44   The garden of the Villa D'Este is discussed in David Coffin, *The Villa D'Este at Tivoli* (Princeton, N.J. 1960), especially ch. 5. An earlier garden at Castello, near Florence, is the subject of L. Châtelet-Lange's essay, 'The grotto of the unicorn and the garden of the Villa di Castello', *Art Bulletin*, L (March 1968), pp. 51–8.

45   Blunt, op. cit., pp. 286–91. See also Dean Tolle Mace, '*Ut pictura poesis*: Dryden, Poussin and the parallel of poetry and painting in the seventeenth century', *Encounters: Essays on Literature and the Visual Arts*, ed. John Dixon Hunt (London 1971), p. 81.

46 Spence, op. cit., I, p. 255 (item 615).

47 See Willis, *Charles Bridgeman*, chs. 2 and 3.

48 The term 'Bridgemannick Theatre' occurs in *The Correspondence of Alexander Pope*, ed. George W. Sherburn (Oxford 1956), II, p. 372; the later remarks on Rousham are from ibid., II, p. 513. Little has yet been done on the whole theatrical theme in garden design, but see S. Lang, 'The genesis of the English landscape garden', op. cit., pp. 22–9.

49 See, among other works, the excellent discussion of Locke's contribution to romanticism in Ernest Tuveson's *The Imagination as the Means of Grace: Locke and the Aesthetics of Romanticism* (Berkeley and Los Angeles 1960).

50 G. B. Clarke, 'The History of Stowe — X: Moral Gardening', *The Stoic*, XXIV (July 1970), pp. 115–16.

51 'Ev'n in an ornament its place remark,/Nor in an Hermitage set Dr Clarke': *Epistles to Several Persons*, ed. Bateson, p. 144.

52 *Observations on Modern Gardening* (Dublin 1770), pp. 119–20.

53 Chase, op. cit., p. 36. On the picturesque habit see Christopher Hussey, *The Picturesque* (New York and London 1927; reprinted 1967) and E. W. Manwaring, *Italian Landscape in Eighteenth Century England* (New York 1925; reprinted 1965).

54 *The Spectator*, No. 412. For Pope's similar excursions outside the garden see 'A new Pope letter', *Philological Quarterly*, XLV (1966), pp. 409–18, with its account of his visit to Netley Abbey.

55 See Russell Noyes, *Wordsworth and the Art of Landscape* (Bloomington and London 1968).

56 The literature on this is enormous, but see especially M. H. Abrams, *The Mirror and the Lamp: Romantic Theory and the Critical Tradition* (New York and Oxford 1953) and *Natural Supernaturalism: Tradition and Revolution in Romantic Literature* (London 1971).

57 See the essays by Anna Zádor, 'The English garden in Hungary', and by Brian Knox, 'The arrival of the English landscape garden in Poland and Bohemia', in *The Picturesque Garden*, ed Pevsner, pp. 79–98, 101–16.

58 *Yale Walpole*, XXXV, pp. 125–6: Walpole writing to Chute, 5 August 1771.

59 See Eva Maria Neumeyer, 'The landscape garden as a symbol in Rousseau, Goethe and Flaubert', *Journal of the History of Ideas*, VIII (1947), pp. 187–217.

60 See Peter Willis, 'Rousseau, Stowe and *le jardin anglais*. Speculations on visual sources for *La Nouvelle Héloïse*', *Studies on Voltaire and the Eighteenth Century*, XC (1972), pp. 1791–8.

Part One

Prelude:
The Seventeenth Century
and the Reign of
Queen Anne

Henry Wotton (1568–1639)

Wotton is one of the earliest English writers to celebrate a garden's irregularity. He writes of gardens that involve and exercise the mind in the exploration of their spaces; in this he anticipates the emphasis on surprise and variety by eighteenth-century exponents of the landscape garden, with whom his work, *The Elements of Architecture*, was popular. Otherwise he reveals himself more firmly of his age, especially with his delight in the conceits that artifice could engineer in a garden. He is certainly influenced here by the example of Italian gardens, experienced while Ambassador to Venice (1604–12 and 1621–4). Italian garden art could be almost as symmetrical in design as the French gardening it influenced; yet it promoted a sense of variety (see Plate 42), flexibility and irregularity both by the steepness of its sites and by its attention to the psychological dimensions of a garden (such items as the arcade of water Wotton discusses intrigue the mind by a deliberate confusion of elements).

from *The Elements of Architecture* (1624)

Now there are *Ornaments* also without, as *Gardens*, *Fountaines*, *Groves*, *Conservatories* of rare *Beasts*, *Birds*, and *Fishes*. Of which ignobler kind of Creatures, *Wee ought not* (saith our greatest Master among the sonnes of Nature) *childishly to despise the Contemplation; for in all things that are naturall, there is ever something, that is admirable.* Of these externall delights, a word or two.

First, I must note a certaine contrarietie betweene *building* and *gardening*: For as Fabriques should bee *regular*, so Gardens should bee *irregular*, or at least cast into a very wilde *Regularitie*. To exemplifie my conceit; I have seene a *Garden* (for the maner perchance incomparable) into which the first Accesse was a high walke like a *Tarrace*, from whence might bee taken a generall view of the whole *Plott* below but rather in a delightfull confusion, then with any plaine distinction of the pieces. From this the *Beholder* descending many steps, was afterwards conveyed againe, by severall *mountings* and *valings*, to various entertainements of his *sent*, and *sight*: which I shall not neede to describe (for that were poeticall) let me onely note this, that every one of these diversities, was as if hee had beene *Magically* transported into a new Garden.

But though other *Countreys* have more benefite of Sunne then wee, and thereby more properly tyed to contemplate this delight; yet have I seene in

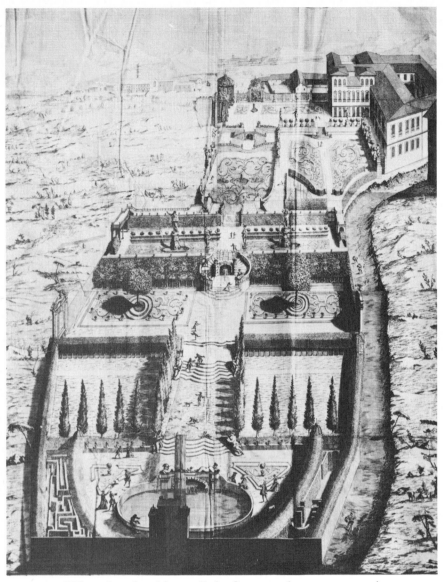

42 Villa and garden, Merate, Italy. Seventeenth-century engraving,
artist unknown

our *owne*, a delicate and diligent *curiositie*, surely without *parallel* among
foreigne *Nations*: Namely, in the Garden of Sir *Henry Fanshaw*, at his seat
in *Ware-Parke*, where I wel remember, hee did so precisely examine the
tinctures, and *seasons* of his *flowres*, that in their *setting*, the *inwardest* of
those which were to come up at the same time, should be alwayes a little
darker then the *outmost*, and to serve them for a kinde of gentle *shadow*, like
a piece not of *Nature*, but of *Arte*: which mention (incident to this place)
I have willingly made of his *Name*, for the deare *friendship* that was long

49

betweene us: though I must confesse, with much wrong to his other *vertues*; which deserve a more solide *memoriall*, then among these vacant observations. So much of *Gardens*.

Fountaines are *figured*, or only plaine *Water'd-workes*: Of either of which, I will describe a matchlesse patterne.

The first, done by the famous hand of *Michael Angelo da Buonaroti*, in the figure of a sturdie *woman*, *washing* and *winding* of linnen clothes; in which Acte, shee *wrings* out the water that made the *Fountaine*; which was a gracefull and naturall conceit in the Artificer, implying this rule; That all *designes* of this kind, should be *proper*.

The other doth merite some larger expressio[n]; There went a long, straight, mossie walke of competent breadth, greene, and soft under foot, lifted on both sides with an *Aquaeduct* of white stone, breast-high, which had a hollow *channell* on the top, where ranne a pretty trickling streame; on the *edge* whereof, were couched very thicke all along, certaine small *pipes* of lead, in little holes; so neatly, that they could not be well perceived, till by the turning of a cocke, they did sprout over interchangeably from side to side, above mans height, in forme of *Arches*, without any intersection or meeting aloft, because the pipes were not exactly opposite, so as the *Beholder*, besides that, which was fluent in the *Aquaeducts* on both hands in his view, did walke as it were, under a continuall *bowre* or *Hemisphere* of water, without any drop falling on him. An *invention* for refreshment, surely farre excelling all the *Alexandrian* delicacies, and *Pneumatiques* of *Hero*.

Groves, and artificiall devices under ground, are of great expence, and little dignitie; which for my part I could wish converted here into those *Crypteria*, whereof mention is made among the curious provisions of *Ticho Braghe* the *Danish Ptolemie*, as I may well call him: which were deepe *concaves* in gardens, where the *starres* might be observed even at *noone*. For (by the way) to thinke that the brightnesse of the Sunnes body above, doth drowne our discerning of the lesser lights, is a popular errour; the sole impediment being that lustre, which by *reflection*, doth spread about us, from the face of the Earth; so as the *caves* before touched, may well conduce, not to a delicious, but to a learned pleasure.

In *Aviaries* of wire, to keepe Birdes of all sorts, the *Italians* (though no wastfull Nation) doe in some places bestow vast expence; including great scope of *ground*, varietie of *bushes*, *trees* of good height, running *waters*, and sometimes a *Stove* annexed, to contemper the *Aire* in Winter. So as those *Chanteresses*, unlesse they be such as perhaps delight as much in their wing, as in their voice, may live long, among so good provisions and roome, before they know that they are prisoners, reducing often to my memory, that conceit of the *Romane Stoicke*, who in comparison of his owne free *contemplations*, did thinke divers great and splendent fortunes of his time, little more then *commodious captivities*.

Francis Bacon (1561–1626)

Bacon, like Wotton, inclines towards a more natural garden. His essay, 'Of Gardens', urges 'diversity' and 'variety' in certain parts of a garden's design and above all in its horticultural profusion. To this he brings his considerable scientific and experimental intelligence, anticipating the more substantial contribution that gardenist members of the Royal Society like John Evelyn would make to the art, and contriving to realize the paradisal myth of perpetual spring (*Ver Perpetuum*) in terms of horticultural skills and knowledge. His vision of a garden is otherwise compounded of old-fashioned items (the mediaeval mount), Tudor features (the knot garden by the house) and some suggestions of more up-to-date Italianate features (the fountains). Some contemporary equivalent of Bacon's taste in gardens might be Wilton House (Plate 43), laid out in the 1630s. In his rejection of topiary and in his plea for some eminence from which 'to look abroad into the fields' Bacon is a hundred years ahead of Pope's satire on trees cut into statues, and his reminder to garden designers to 'call in the country'.

'Of Gardens' (1625)

GOD *Almightie* first Planted a *Garden*. And indeed, it is the Purest of Humane pleasures. It is the Greatest Refreshment to the Spirits of Man; Without which, *Buildings* and *Pallaces* are but Grosse Handy-works: And a Man shall ever see, that when Ages grow to Civility and Elegancie, Men come to *Build Stately*, sooner then to *Garden Finely*: As if *Gardening* were the Greater Perfection. I doe hold it, in the Royall Ordering of *Gardens*, there ought to be *Gardens*, for all the *Moneths* in the Yeare: In which, severally, Things of Beautie, may be then in Season. For *December*, and *January*, and the Latter Part of *November*, you must take such Things, as are Greene all Winter: Holly; Ivy; Bayes; Juniper; Cipresse Trees; Eugh; Pine-Apple-Trees; Firre-Trees; Rose-Mary; Lavander; Periwinckle, the White, the Purple, and the Blewe; Germander; Flagges; Orenge-Trees; Limon-Trees; And Mirtles, if they be stooved; & Sweet Marjoram warme set. There followeth, for the latter Part of *January*, and *February*, the Mezerion Tree, which then blossomes; Crocus Vernus, both the Yellow, and the Gray; Prime-Roses; Anemones; The Early Tulippa; Hiacynthus Orientalis; Chamairis; Frettellaria. For *March*, There come Violets, specially the Single Blew, which are the Earliest; The Yellow Daffadill; The Dazie; The Almond-Tree in

Blossome; The Peach-Tree in Blossome; The Cornelian-Tree in Blossome; Sweet-Briar. In *Aprill* follow, The Double white Violet; The Wall-flower; The Stock-Gilly-Flower; The Couslip; Flower-De-lices, & Lillies of all Natures; Rose-mary Flowers; The Tulippa; The Double Piony; the Pale Daffadill; The French Honny-Suckle; The Cherry-Tree in Blossome; The Dammasin, and Plum-Trees in Blossome; The White-Thorne in Leafe; The Lelacke Tree. In *May*, and *June*, come Pincks of all sorts, Specially the Blush Pincke; Roses of all kinds, except the Muske, which comes later; Hony-Suckles; Strawberries; Buglosse; Columbine; The French Mary-gold; Flos Africanus; Cherry-Tree in Fruit; Ribos; Figges in Fruit; Raspes; Vine Flowers; Lavender in Flowers; The Sweet Satyrian, with the White Flower; Herba Muscaria; Lilium Convallium; The Apple-tree in Blossome. In *July*, come Gilly-Flowers of all Varieties; Muske Roses; The Lime-Tree in blossome, Early Peares, and Plummes in Fruit; Ginnitings, Quadlins. In *August*, come Plummes of all sorts in Fruit; Peares; Apricockes; Berberies; Filberds; Muske-Melons; Monks Hoods, of all colours. In *September*, come Grapes; Apples; Poppies of all colours; Peaches; Melo-Cotones; Nectarines; Cornelians; Wardens; Quinces. In *October*, and the beginning of *November*, come Services; Medlars; Bullises, Roses Cut or Removed to come late; Hollyokes; and such like. These Particulars are for the *Climate* of *London*, But my meaning is Perceived, that you may have *Ver Perpetuum*, as the Place affords.

And because, the *Breath* of Flowers, is farre Sweeter in the Aire, (where it comes and Goes, like the Warbling of Musick) then in the hand, therfore nothing is more fit for that delight, then to know, what be the *Flowers*, and *Plants*, that doe best perfume the Aire. Roses Damask & Red, are fast Flowers of their Smels; So that; you may walke by a whole Row of them, and finde Nothing of their Sweetnesse; Yea though it be, in a Mornings Dew. Bayes likewise yeeld no Smell, as they grow, Rosemary little; Nor Sweet-Marjoram[.] That, which above all Others, yeelds the *Sweetest Smell* in the *Aire*, is the Violet; Specially the White-double-Violet, which comes twice a Yeare, About the middle of *Aprill*, and about *Bartholomew tide*. Next to that is, the Muske-Rose. Then the Strawberry Leaves dying, which a most Excellent Cordiall Smell. Then the Flower of the Vines; It is a little dust, like the dust of a Bent, which growes upon the Cluster, in the First comming forth. Then Sweet Briar. Then Wall-Flowers, which are very Delightfull, to be set under a Parler, or Lower Chamber Window. Then Pincks, and Gilly-Flowers, specially the Matted Pinck, & Clove Gilly-flower. Then the Flowers of the Limetree. Then the Hony-Suckles, so they be somewhat a farre off. Of Beane Flowers I speake not, because they are Field Flowers. But those which *Perfume* the Aire most delightfully, not *passed by* as the rest, but being *Trodon upon* and *Crushed*, are Three: That is Burnet, Wilde-Time, and Water-Mints. Therefore, you are to set whole Allies of them, to have the Pleasure, when you walke or tread.

For *Gardens*, (Speaking of those, which are indeed *Prince-like*, as we have done of *Buildings*) the Contents, ought not well to be, under *Thirty Acres of Ground*; And to be divided into three Parts: A *Greene* in the Entrance;

43 Wilton House, Wiltshire. Engraving from Isaac de Caus, *Wilton Garden*, ?1645

A *Heath* or *Desart* in the Going forth; And the *Maine Garden* in the midst; Besides *Alleys*, on both Sides. And I like well, that Foure Acres of Ground, be assigned to the *Greene*; Six to the *Heath*; Foure and Foure to either *Side*; And Twelve to the *Maine Garden*. The Greene hath two pleasures; The one, because nothing is more Pleasant to the Eye, then Greene Grasse kept finely shorne; The other, because it will give you a faire Alley in the midst, by which you may go in front upon a *Stately Hedge*, which is to inclose the *Garden*. But, because the Alley will be long, and in great Heat of the Yeare, or Day, you ought not to buy the shade in the *Garden*, by Going in the Sunne thorow the *Greene*, therefore you are, of either *Side* the *Greene*, to Plant a *Covert Alley*, upon Carpenters Worke, about Twelve Foot in Height, by which you may goe in Shade, into the *Garden*. As for the Making of *Knots*, or *Figures*, with *Divers Coloured Earths*, that they may lie under the Windowes of the House, on that Side, which the *Garden* stands, they be but Toyes: You may see as good Sights, many times, in Tarts. The *Garden* is best to be Square; Incompassed, on all the Foure Sides, with a *Stately Arched Hedge*. The *Arches* to be upon *Pillars*, of Carpenters Worke, of some Ten Foot high, and Six Foot broad: And the *Spaces* between, of the same Dimension, with the *Breadth* of the *Arch*. Over the *Arches*, let there bee an *Entire Hedge*, of some Foure Foot High, framed also upon Carpenters Worke: And upon the *Upper Hedge*, over every *Arch*, a little *Turret*, with a *Belly*, enough to receive a *Cage* of *Birds*: And over every *Space*, betweene the *Arches*, some other little *Figure*, with Broad Plates of *Round Coloured Glasse*, gilt, for the *Sunne*, to Play upon. But this *Hedge* I entend to be, raised upon a *Bancke*, not Steepe, but gently Slope, of some Six Foot, set all with *Flowers*. Also I understand, that this *Square* of the *Garden*, should not be the whole Breadth of the Ground, but to leave, on either Side, Ground enough, for diversity of *Side Alleys:* Unto which, the Two *Covert Alleys* of the *Greene*, may deliver you. But there must be, no *Alleys* with *Hedges*, at either *End*, of this great *Inclosure*: Not at the *Hither End*, for letting your Prospect upon this Faire Hedge from the *Greene*; Nor at the *Further End*, for letting your Prospect from the Hedge, through the Arches, upon the *Heath*.

For the Ordering of the Ground, within the *Great Hedge*, I leave it to Variety of Device; Advising neverthelesse, that whatsoever forme you cast it into, first it be not too Busie, or full of Worke. Wherein I, for my part, doe not like *Images Cut out* in *Juniper*, or other *Garden stuffe*: They be for Children. *Little low Hedges*, Round, like Welts, with some Pretty *Pyramides*, I like well: And in some Places, *Faire Columnes* upon Frames of Carpenters Worke. I would also, have the *Alleys*, Spacious and Faire. You may have *Closer Alleys* upon the *Side Grounds*, but none in the *Maine Garden*. I wish also, in the very Middle, a *Faire Mount*, with three Ascents, and Alleys, enough for foure to walke a breast, Which I would have to be Perfect Circles, without any Bulwarkes, or Imbosments; And the *Whole Mount*, to be Thirty Foot high; And some fine *Banquetting House*, with some *Chimneys* neatly cast, and without too much *Glasse*.

For *Fountaines*, they are a great Beauty, and *Refreshment*; But *Pooles* marre all, and make the *Garden* unwholsome, and full of Flies, and Frogs. *Fountaines* I intend to be of two Natures: The One, that *Sprinckleth* or *Spouteth Water*; The Other a *Faire Receipt* of *Water*, of some Thirty or Forty Foot Square, but without Fish, or Slime, or Mud. For the first, the *Ornaments* of *Images Gilt*, or of *Marble*, which are in use, doe well: But the maine Matter is, so to Convey the Water, as it never Stay, either in the Bowles, or in the Cesterne; That the Water be never by Rest *Discoloured*, *Greene*, or *Red*, or the like; Or gather any *Mossinesse* or *Putrefaction*. Besides that, it is to be cleansed every day by the Hand. Also some *Steps* up to it, and some *Fine Pavement* about it, doth well. As for the other Kinde of *Fountaine*, which we may call a *Bathing Poole*, it may admit much Curiosity, and Beauty; wherewith we will not trouble our selves: As, that the Bottome be finely Paved, And with Images: The sides likewise; And withall Embellished with Coloured Glasse, and such Things of Lustre; Encompassed also, with fine Railes of Low Statua's. But the Maine Point is the same, which we mentioned, in the former Kinde of *Fountaine*; which is, that the *Water* be in *Perpetuall Motion*, Fed by a Water higher then the *Poole*, and Delivered into it by faire Spouts, and then discharged away under Ground, by some Equalitie of Bores, that it stay little. And for fine Devices, of Arching Water without Spilling, and Making it rise in severall Formes, (of Feathers, Drinking Glasses, Canopies, and the like,) they be pretty things to looke on, but Nothing to Health and Sweetnesse.

For the *Heath*, which was the Third Part of our Plot, I wish it to be framed, as much as may be, to a *Natural wildernesse*. *Trees* I would have none in it; But some *Thickets*, made onely of *Sweet-Briar*, and honny-suckle, and some *Wilde Vine* amongst; And the Ground set with *Violets, Strawberries*, and *Prime-Roses*. For these are Sweet, and prosper in the Shade. And these to be in the *Heath*, here and there, not in any Order. I like also little *Heaps*, in the Nature of *Mole-hils*, (such as are in *Wilde Heaths*) to be set, some with Wilde Thyme; Some with Pincks; Some with Germander, that gives a good Flower to the Eye; Some with Periwinckle; Some with Violets; Some with Strawberries; Some with Couslips; Some with Daisies; Some with Red-Roses; Some with Lilium Convallium; Some with Sweet-Williams Red; Some with Beares-Foot; And the like Low Flowers, being withal Sweet, and Sightly. Part of which *Heapes*, to be with *Standards*, of little *Bushes*, prickt upon their Top, and Part without. The *Standards* to be Roses; Juniper; Holly; Beare-berries (but here and there, because of the Smell of their Blossome;) Red Currans; Goose-berries; Rose-Mary; Bayes; Sweet-Briar; and such like. But these *Standards*, to be kept with Cutting, that they grow not out of Course.

For the *Side Grounds*, you are to fill them with *Varietie* of *Alleys*, Private, to give a full Shade; Some of them, wheresoever the Sun be. You are to frame some of them likewise for Shelter, that when the Wind blows Sharpe, you may walke, as in a Gallery. And those Alleys must be likewise hedged, at both Ends, to keepe out the Wind; And these *Closer Alleys*, must bee ever finely Gravelled, and no Grasse, because of Going wet. In many of these *Alleys* likewise, you are to set *Fruit-Trees* of all Sorts; As well upon the Walles, as in Ranges. And this would be generally observed, that the *Borders*, wherin you plant your *Fruit-Trees*, be Faire and Large, and Low, and not Steepe; And Set with *Fine Flowers*, but thin and sparingly, lest they Deceive the Trees. At the End of both the *Side Grounds*, I would have a *Mount* of some Pretty Height, leaving the Wall of the Enclosure Brest high, to looke abroad into the Fields.

For the *Maine Garden*, I doe not Deny, but there should be some Faire *Alleys*, ranged on both Sides, with *Fruit Trees*; And some Pretty *Tufts* of *Fruit Trees*, And *Arbours* with *Seats*, set in some Decent Order; But these to be, by no Meanes, set too thicke; But to leave the *Maine Garden*, so as it be not close, but the Aire Open and Free. For as for *Shade*, I would have you rest, upon the *Alleys* of the *Side Grounds*, thereto walke, if you be Disposed, in the Heat of the Yeare, or day; But to make Account, that the *Maine Garden*, is for the more Temperate Parts of the yeare, And in the Heat of Summer, for the Morning, and the Evening, or Over-cast Dayes.

For *Aviaries*, I like them not, except they be of that Largenesse, as they may be *Turffed*, and have *Living Plants*, and *Bushes*, set in them; That the *Birds* may have more Scope, and Naturall Neastling, and that no *Foulenesse* appeare, in the *Floare* of the *Aviary*. So I have made a Platforme of a *Princely*

Garden, Partly by Precept, Partly by Drawing, not a Modell, but some generall Lines of it; And in this I have spared for no Cost. But it is Nothing, for *Great Princes,* that for the most Part, taking Advice with Workmen, with no Lesse Cost, set their Things together; And sometimes adde *Statua's,* and such Things, for State, and Magnificence, but nothing to the true Pleasure of a *Garden.*

John Evelyn (1620–1706)

Evelyn is certainly the central figure in Restoration gardening. His travels took him to the most famous of French and Italian gardens (Plate 45) in the mid-seventeenth century, while his first-hand experience was matched with a wide historical knowledge — he added an essay, for example, on 'the Sacrednesse, and Use of standing Groves' to the 1670 edition of his *Sylva, or a Discourse of Forest-Trees* (1664). But he was also an eager practitioner, first at the family home at Wotton in Surrey (Plate 44), where he made a 'fishpond, an island, and some other solitudes and retirements', and later at Sayes Court, Deptford (Plate 46), where he created a garden from a field of one hundred acres. Here he exercised his experimental interests in arboriculture and horticulture, like another contemporary, John Rose (Plate 47); he had his nursery gardens, an 'elaboratorie' where he practised chemistry, a transparent beehive and a walled private garden of choice flowers and simples. And he was in addition a dedicated and prolific author. From this vast repertoire we have selected, first, his letter to Sir Thomas Browne, another future member of the Royal Society (founded in 1660): it concerns Evelyn's projected work, 'Elysium Britannicum' (see our third extract), and explains Evelyn's dedication to gardenist activities; it ends with a long list (not given here) of all the most notable gardens in mythology, literature and the various parts of the world, including China and South America. Some sense of Evelyn's alert and close attention to gardens he knew himself is conveyed by the second extract, comprised of entries in his Diary: though what he sees is generally of a carefully ordered, even geometrical, design, he is yet particularly quick to notice variety and whether layouts 'agreed with the nature of the place' (his remark about Sayes Court). The third passage by which he is represented is the outline of his never completed project, an encyclopaedic survey of all matters that pertain to both the philosophy and practice of the garden art: this formed an appendix to his *Acetaria, a Discourse of Sallets* (1699).

from a Letter to Sir Thomas Browne (1657)

The truth is, that which imported me to discourse on this subject after this sorte, was the many defects which I encounter'd in Bookes and in Gardens, wherein neither words nor cost had bin wanting, but judgement very much; and though I cannot boast of my science in this kind, as both unbecoming my yeares and my small experience, yet I esteem'd it pardonable at least, if in doing my endeavour to rectifie some mistakes, and advancing so usefull and innocent a divertisement, I made some essay, and cast in my Symbole with the rest. To this designe, if forraine observation may conduce, I might likewise hope to refine upon some particulars, especially concerning the ornaments of Gardens, which I shall endeavor so to handle, as that they may become usefull and practicable, as well as magnificent, and that persons of all conditions and faculties, which delight in Gardens, may therein encounter something for their owne advantage. The modell, which I perceive you have seene, will aboundantly testifie my abhorrency of those painted and formal projections of our Cockney Gardens and plotts, which appeare like Gardens of past board and March pane, and smell more of paynt then of flowers and verdure: our drift is a noble, princely, and universall Elysium, capable of all the amoenities that can naturally be introduced into Gardens of pleasure, and such as may stand in competition with all the august designes and stories of this nature, either of antient or moderne times; yet so as to become usefull and significant to the least pretences and faculties. We will endeavour to shew how the aire and genious of Gardens operat upon humane spirits towards virtue and sanctitie, I meane in a remote, preparatory and instrumentall working. How Caves, Grotts, Mounts, and irregular ornaments of Gardens do contribute to contemplative and philosophicall Enthusiasms; how *Elysium, Antrum, Nemus, Paradysus, Hortus, Lucus*, &c., signifie all of them *rem sacram et divinam*; for these expedients do influence the soule and spirits of man, and prepare them for converse with good Angells; besides which, they contribute to the lesse abstracted pleasures, phylosophy naturall and longevitie: and I would have not onely the elogies and effigie of the antient and famous Garden Heroes, but a society of the *Paradisi Cultores*, persons of antient simplicity, paradisean and hortulan saints, to be a society of learned and ingenuous men, such as Dr Browne, by whome we might hope to redeeme the tyme that has bin lost, in pursuing vulgar errours, and still propagating them, as so many bold men do yet presume to do. Were it to be hoped, *inter hos armorum strepitus*, and in so generall a Catalysis of integrity, interruption of peace and propriety, the hortulane pleasures, these innocent, pure, and usefull diversions might enjoy the least encouragement, whilst brutish and ambitious persons seeke themselves in the ruines of our miserable yet dearest country, *quis talia fando* . . .

Extracts from Evelyn's Diary (late 1630s–1706)

The Place of my birth was Wotton, in the Parish of Wotton or Black-Heath in the County of Surrey, the then Mansion house of my Father, left him as above by my Grand-father, and now afterwards my Eldest Brothers. (In the red-Chamber having 2 windows directly towards the N and South respecting the Gardens.) It is situated in the most Sothern part of the Shire, and though in a Vally; yet realy upon a very greate rising, being on part of one of the most eminent hills in England for the prodigious prospect to be seen from its summit, though by few observed . . . in a serene day. The house is large and antient, suitable to those hospitable times, and so sweetely environ'd with those delicious streames and venerable Woods, as in the judgment of strangers,

44 Wotton, Surrey. View of the garden by John Evelyn, 1653

as well as English-men, it may be compared to one of the most tempting and pleasant seates in the Nation for a great person & a wanton purse to render it Conspicuous: for it has risings, meadows, Woods & Water in aboundance; not destitute of the most noble and advantagious accommodations; being but within little more than 20 miles from Lond: and yet so securely placed, as if it were an hundred . . . I will say nothing of the ayre because the praeeminence is universaly given to Surrey; the soile being dry and sandy; but I should speake much of the Gardens, Fountaines and Groves that adorne it were they not as generaly knowne to be amongst the most natural & most magnificent that England afforded til this later & universal luxury of the whole nation since abounding in such expenses, and which indeede gave one of the first examples to that elegancy since so much in vogue and followd, for the managing of their Waters and other elegancies of that Nature . . .

Accompanyd with some English Gent: we tooke horse [on 27 February 1644] to see St. Germains en Lay, which is a stately Country-house of the Kings, some 5 leagues from Paris: By the way we alighted at St. Cloes, where upon an Eminence neere the River, the Arch-Bishop of Paris, has a Garden (for the house is not very considerable) so rarely waterd, & furnish'd with fountaines, statues, & groves: as I had never seene an[y]thing exceeding it: The Walkes are very faire; above all that fountaine of the Laocoon in a very ample square poole or Piscina, casting waters neere 40 foote in height, and having about it a multitude of Statues and basines, is a most glorious & surprizing object: Those three at descent of the hill, and dispos'd in a round Walke are very remarkable; but nothing is more esteem'd than the Cascada falling from the greate stepps into the lowest & longest Walke from the Mons Parnassus, which consists of a Grotto or shell house erected on the summit of the hill; & herein are divers water-workes, and unlucky contrivances to wet the Spectators: This is coverd with a fayre Cupola, the Walls paynted with the Muses, statues placed thick about it, whereof some antique and good: In the upper Walkes are two Perspectives very pretty ones, seeming to enlarge the allys; and in this Garden there are a world of other incomparable diversions . . .

I went [on 1st April 1644] more exactly to see the roomes of that incomparable Palace of Luxemburge in the Fauxbourgs St. Germains, built by Mary de Medices and I thinke one of the most noble, entire and finish'd Pile[s] that is standing in any Citty of the World, taking it with the Garden and all its accomplishments . . . The Gardens containe neere an English mile in Compasse, enclos'd with a stately wall, & in good ayre, which renders it certainly one of the sweetest places imaginable; The Parterr is indeede of box; but so rarely designd, and accurately kept cut; that the [e]mbrodery makes a stupendious effect, to the Lodgings which front it; 'tis divided into 4 Squares, & as many circular knots; having in the Center a noble Basin of Marble neere 30 foot diameter (as I remember) in which a Triton of brasse holds a Dolphin that casts a girandola of water neere 30 foote high which plays perpetualy, & the water is excellent, being convey'd from Arceuil, whence it is derived by an Aquaeduct of stone built after the old Roman magnificence. About this ample Parter, the spacious Walkes & all included, runs a bordure of free-stone adorn'd with Pedistalls for Potts & Statues; and part of it neere the Stepps of the Terrace, with a raile & baluster of pure white marble: The Walkes are exactly faire, long & variously descending, & so justly planted with limes, Elmes & other Trees, that nothing can be more delicious & surprizing, especially that of the hornebeame hedge, which being high & stately, butts full upon the fountaine: Towards the farther end is an excavation intended for a Vast Piscina, but never finish'd; & neere it is an enclosure for a Garden of simples, rarely entertaind, & here the Duke keepes Tortoises in greate number who use the pole of Water at one side of the Garden: here is also a Conservatory for Snow: At the upper part (towards the Palace) is a grove of tall Elmes cutt into a Starr, every ray being a Walke whose center is a large fountaine: The rest of the Ground is made into severall enclosures (all hedge Worke or rowes of Trees) of whole fields, meadowes, boscages, some of them containing divers ackers: Next the streete side, & more contiguous to the house are knolls in trayle or grasse Worke, where likewise runs a fountaine; Towards the Grotto, & Stables, inclos'd within a Wall is a Garden of choyce flowers, in which the Duke spends many thousand pistoles: In summ, nothing is wanting to render this Palace, & Gardens perfectly beautyfull & magnificent; nor is it one of the least diversions, to behold the infinite numbers of Persons of quality, & Citizens, & strangers who frequent it, and to whom all accesse is freely permitted . . .

This Palas of Negros [at Genoa on 17 October 1644] is richly furnish'd with the rarest Pictures, & other collections & moveables: but nothing which more delighted me than the terrac, or hilly Garden, where there stands a grove of

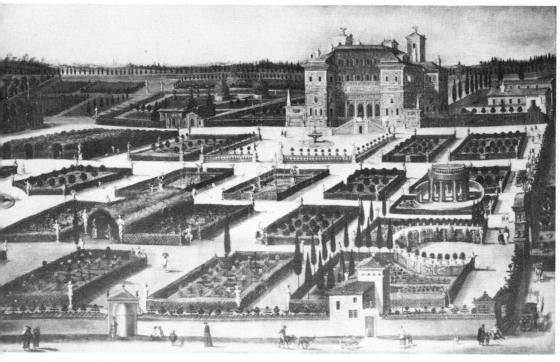

45 Gardens of Villa Borghese, Rome. Seventeenth-century painting,
artist unknown

stately trees, furnish'd with artificial Sheepe, Shepheards, & Wild beasts,
so naturaly cut in a grey-stone, fountaines, rocks, & Piscina's, that casting
your eyes one way, you would imagine your selfe in a Wildernesse & silent
Country, side-ways in the heart of a great Citty, & backwarde in the middst
of the Sea; and that which is most admirable, all this within one Aker of
ground, and I thinke the most stupendious & delightfull in the whole
World . . .

Returning home [to Rome on 8 November 1644], we had time to view the
Palazzo de Medici, which was an house of the Duke of Florence neere our
Lodging upon the brow of Mons Pincius: having an incomparable Prospect
towards the Campo Marzo. This is a very magnificent strong building, having
a substruction very remarkable, and a Portico supported with Columns
towards the Gardens with two huge Lions of marble at the end of the
Balustrads: The whole out side of this facciata is [incrusted] with antique
& rare Basse-relievis & statues: Descending into the Garden is a noble
fountaine govern'd by a Mercury of brasse, and a little distance on the Left
hand, a Lodge full of incomparable Statues, amongst which the Sabines,
antique & singularly rare: In the Arcado neere this stand 24 statues of
infinite price; and hard by a Mount planted with Cypresses, representing a
fortresse, with a goodly fountaine in the middle: Here is also a row balustr'd
with white marble, on which are erected divers statues and heads, covered

over with the natural shrubbs, Ivys & other perennial Greenes, as in nices: At a little distance Those fam'd statues of the Niobe & her family, in all 15 as big as the life, of which we have ample mention in Pliny, being certainly to be esteemed amongst the best pieces of worke in the world, for the passions they expresse, & all other perfections of that stupendious art. There is likewise in this Garden a faire Obelisque full of Hieroglypics: At our going out, I tooke notice of the fountaine before the front, which cast water neere 50 foote in height, receiving it into a most ample basin of marble . . .

I walked [on 17 November 1644] to Villa Burghesi, which is an house and ample Gardens on Mons Pincius, yet somewhat without the Citty-Wales; circumscrib'd by another wall full of small turrets and banqueting houses, which makes it appeare at a distance like a little Towne, within it tis an Elysium of delight; having in the center of it a very noble Palace (but the enterance of the Garden, presents us with a very glorios fabrick, or rather dore-Case adorned with divers excellent marble statues): This Garden abounded with all sorts of the most delicious fruit, and Exotique simples: Fountaines of sundry inventions, Groves, & small Rivulets of Water: There is also adjoyning to it a Vivarium for Estriges, Peacocks, Swanns, Cranes, &c: and divers strange Beasts, Deare & hares: The Grotto is very rare, and represents among other devices artificial raines, & sundry shapes of Vessells, Flowers &c: which is effected by [changing] the heads of the Fountaines: The Groves are of Cypresse and Lawrell, Pine, Myrtil, Olive &c: The 4 Sphinxes are very Antique and worthy observation: To this is a Volary full of curious birds . . .

On the 28 [November] I went to se[e] the Garden and house of the Aldobrandini, but now Cardinal Burghezes: . . . about a Mile without the Cittie, being rather a Park or Paradise contrivd & planted with Walkes & shades of *Myrtils, Cypresse* & other trees & groves, adornd with aboundance of Fountains, statues & Bassrelievos: Here they had hung large Netts to Catch Wood-Cocks: there were fine glades, & several pretty murmuring rivulets trickling downe the declining Walkes: There was also a Vivarie where among other exotic soules there was an Ostridge, besids a most capacious Aviarie & in another inclosed part, an heard of Deere: Before the Palace (which might become the Court of a greate Prince) stands a noble Fountaine of white Marble, inrich'd with statues: The walles of the house without are incrusted with excellent Basse relievos antique of the same marble, incornish'd with Festoones, & Niches set with statues from the very roofe to the foundation: A stately Portico joynes the Palace full of Statues, Columns, Urnes & other Curiosities of Sculpture . . .

We descended [on 18 January 1645] into the Vatican Gardens, cald Belvedere, where entring first into a kind of Court, we were shew'd those incomparable statues (so fam'd by Pliny & Others) of Laocoan with his three sonns embrac'd by an huge serpent, all of one entire parrian stone, very

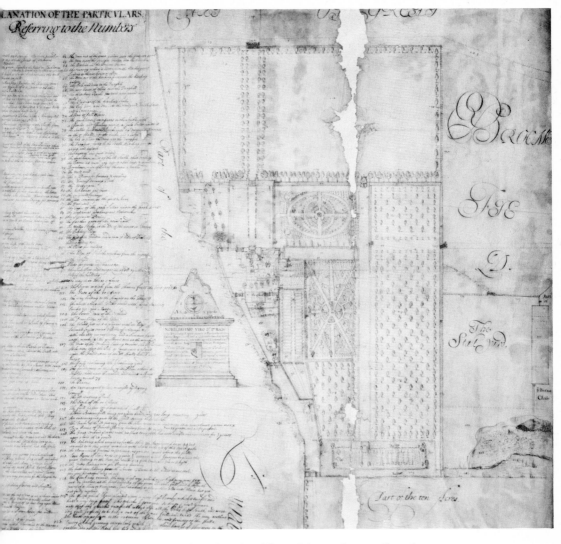

46 Sayes Court, Deptford, London. Plan of the garden, attributed to
John Evelyn, 1653

white & perfect, somewhat bigger then the life, & the Worke of those three
celebrated Sculptors, Agesandrus, Polidorus, and Artimadorus Rhodians, as
it was found amongst the ruines of Titus's Baths, and placed here: Plynie
says this Statue is to be esteem'd before all pictures & statues in the World,
and I am altogether of his opinion, for in my life I never beheld anything
of Art approch it: Here is also Those two famous Images of Nylus with the
children playing about him, and that of Tyber. Romulus & Rhemus about
the Wolfe, that incomparable figure of the dying Cleopatra; The Venus and
Cupid, rare pieces; The Mercury, Cybel; Hercules, Apollo, Antinous; most
of which, are for defence against the Weather shut up in their Neeches with

dores of Wainscot; We were likewise shew'd those Reliques of the Hadrian Moles; viz. the Pine, a vast piece of Mettall which stood on the summit of that Mausoleum; also a Peacock of Coper, supposed to have been part of Scipios Monument.

In the Garden without this (which containes a very Vast circuit of ground) are many stately Fountaines, especialy two, casting water into Antique lavors brought from Titus's Bathes: some faire Grotts & Water-works, with that noble Cascade where the ship daunces with divers other pleasant inventions, Walkes, Terraces, Meanders, Fruite-trees, and a most goodly Prospect over the greatest part of the Citty: One Fountaine under the Gate I must not omitt, consisting of three jettos of Water gushing out of the mouthes or proboscis of Bees (the Armes of the Late Pope) because of the Inscription

Quid miraris Apem, quae mel de floribus haurit?
Si tibi mellitam gutture fundit aquam . . .

The 5 [May 1645] we tooke Coach and went 15 miles out of the Cittie to *Frascati* formerly *Tusculanum*, a villa of Card: *Aldobrandini*, built for a Country house but for its elegance, situation & accommodation of plentifull water, Groves, Ascents & prospect, surpassing in my opinion the most delicious places that my eyes ever beheld: Just behind the Palace (which is of excellent Architecture) and is in the center of the Inclosure, rises an high hill or mountaine all over clad with tall wood, and so form'd by nature, as if it had ben cut out by Art, from the summit whereof falls a horrid Cascade seeming rather a greate River than a streame, precipitating into a large Theater of Water representing a[n] exact & perfect Raine-bow when the sun shines out: Under this is made an artific[i]all Grott, where in are curious rocks, hydraulic Organs & all sorts of singing birds moving, & chirping by force of the water, with severall other pageants and surprizing inventions: In the center of one of these roomes rises a coper ball that continualy daunces about 3 foote above the pavement, by virtue of a Wind conveyed seacretly to a hole beneath it, with many other devices to wett the unwary spectators, so as one can hardly [step] without wetting to the skin: In one of these Theaters of Water, is an *Atlas* spouting up the streame to an incredible height, & another monster which makes a terrible roaring with an horn; but above all the representation of a storme is most naturall, with such fury of raine, wind and Thunder as one would imagine ones selfe in some extreame Tempest: To this is a Garden of incomparable walkes & shady groves, aboundance of rare Fruit, Orangs, Lemons, &c: and the goodly prospect of Rome above all description, so as I do not wonder that *Cicero* & others have celebrated this place with such encomiums . . .

Ariv'd at *Tivoli* [on 7 May] we went first to see the Palace *d'Estè* erected on a plaine, but where was formerly an hill: The Palace is very ample & stately: In the Garden at the right hand are plac'd 16 vast Conchas of marble jetting out Waters: in the midst of these stands a *Janus* quadrifrons that cast forth 4

47 After Hendrick Danckerts, 'Rose, the Royal Gardener, Presenting Charles II
with the First Pineapple Grown in England, 1787.
Victoria and Albert Museum. Crown copyright

girandolas, calld from the resemblance the *fontana di Speccho*; neere this a
Place for Tilting: before the Ascent of the Palace is that incomparable
fountain of *Leda*, & not far from that 4 sweete & delicious Gardens; descending thence two pyramids of Water, & in a Grove of trees neere it, the
Fountaines of *Tethys, Esculapius, Arethusa, Pandora, Pomona* & *Flora*, then
the pransing *Pegasus, Bacchus*, The Grott of *Venus*, The two Colosses of
Melicerta & *Sybilla Tibertina*, all of exquisite Marble, Coper & other suitable
adornments, The *Cupids* especialy are most rare, pouring out Water, & the
Urnes on which are plac'd the 10 Nymphs: The Grotts are richly pav'd with

pietra Commessa, Shells, Corall &c: Towards *Roma Triumphans,* leades a long & spacious Walk, full of Fountaines, under which is historiz'd the who[le] *Ovidian* Metamorphosis in *mezzo Relievo* rarely sculptur'd, at the end of this, next the wall the Cittie of *Rome,* as it was in its beauty, all built of small models, representing that Citie with its Amphitheaters, Naumachia, Thermae, Temples, Arches, Aquaeducts, streetes & other magnificences, with a little streame running through it for the River Tybur, gushing out of the Urne next the statue of that River: In another Garden a noble Aviarie, the birds artificial, & singing, til the presence of an Owle appeares, on which the[y] suddainly chang their notes, to the admiration of the Spectators: Neere this is the Fountaine of Dragons belching large streames of water, with horrid noises: In another Grotto calld the *Grotta di Natura* is an hydraulic Organ, below this divers stews and fish-ponds, in one of which is the Statue of *Neptune* in his Chariot, on a sea-horse, in another a *Triton,* & lastly a Garden of simples . . .

We tooke horses for *Bologna,* & by the way alighted at a Villa of the *Grand Dukes* call'd *Pratoline,* The House is a Square of 4 Pavilions, with a faire platform about it, balustr'd with stone, 'tis situate in a large meadow like an amphitheater, ascending, having at the bottom a huge rock, with Water running in a small Chanell like a Cascade, on the other side the Gardens, the whole place seemes Consecrated to pleasure, & retirement in Summer: The Inside of the Palace may well compare with any in Italy for furniture of Tapissry, beds &c: The Gardens delicious & full of fountaines: In the Grove sits Pan feeding his stock, the Water making a melodius sound through his pipe, & an Hercules whose Club yeilds a Showre of Water, which falling into a huge *Concha* has a Naked Woman riding on the backs of Dolphins: In another Grotto is *Vulcan* & his family, the walls richly composd of Coralls, Shells, Coper & Marble figures; with the huntings of Severall beasts, moving by the force of Water: Here having ben well wash'd for our Curiosity, we went down a large Walk, at the sides whereof gushes out of imperceptible pipes, couched under neath, slender pissings of water, that interchangeably fall into each others Chanells, making a lofty & perfect arch, so as a man on horseback may ride under it and not be wet with one drop, nay so high, as one may walk with a speare in ones hand under each spout, this Canopi or arch of Water, was mi thought one of the surprizings[t] magnificences I had ever seene, & exceedingly fresh during the heate of summer, at the End of this very long Walk stands a Woman in white marble in posture of a Laundresse wringing Water out of a piece of linnen very naturaly, into a vast Lavor, the work & invention of the famous *Michael Angelo Buonaroti*: Hence we ascended *Monte Parnasso,* where the Muses plaid to us on Hydraulic Organs; neere this a greate Aviarie: The Sourse of all these Waters are from the Rock in the Garden, on which the statue of a Gyant representing the *Appennines* at the foote of which stands this *Villa*: Last of all we came to the Labyrinth in which a huge Colosse of *Jupiter,* that throws out a streame over the Garden; This Moles is 50 foote in height, having in his body a pretty Square chamber, his Eyes and mouth serving for the Windos & dore:

Having view'd these rarities we tooke horse & supped that night at *il Ponte*, passing a dreadfull ridge of the *Appennines*, in many places cap'd with Snow, which covers them the whole summer long.

Outline of 'Elysium Britannicum' (1699)

THE
PLAN
OF A
ROYAL GARDEN:

Describing, and Shewing the *Amplitude*, and *Extent* of that Part of *Georgicks*, which belongs to *Horticulture*;

In Three Books.

BOOK I.

Chap. I. OF *Principles* and *Elements* in general.
Ch. II. Of the Four (vulgarly reputed) Elements; *Fire, Air, Water, Earth.*
Ch. III. Of the Celestial *Influences*, and particularly of the *Sun, Moon,* and of the *Climates.*
Ch. IV. Of the Four *Annual Seasons.*
Ch. V. Of the Natural *Mould* and *Soil* of a Garden.
Ch. VI. Of *Composts*, and *Stercoration, Repastination, Dressing* and *Stirring* the *Earth* and *Mould* of a Garden.

BOOK II.

Chap. I. A Garden *Deriv'd* and *Defin'd*; its *Dignity, Distinction,* and *Sorts.*
Ch. II. Of a *Gardiner*, how to be *qualify'd, regarded* and *rewarded*; his *Habitation, Cloathing, Diet,* Under-*Workmen* and *Assistants.*
Ch. III. Of the *Instruments* belonging to a Gardiner; their various *Uses*, and *Machanical* Powers.
Ch. IV. Of the *Terms* us'd, and affected by Gardiners.
Ch. V. Of *Enclosing, Fencing, Platting*, and disposing of the Ground; and of *Terraces, Walks, Allies, Malls, Bowling-Greens,* &c.
Ch. VI. Of a *Seminary, Nurseries*; and of Propagating *Trees, Plants* and *Flowers, Planting* and *Transplanting,* &c.
Ch. VII. Of *Knots, Parterres, Compartiments, Borders, Banks* and *Embossments.*
Ch. VIII. Of *Groves, Labyrinths, Dedals, Cabinets, Cradles, Close-Walks, Galleries, Pavilions, Portico's, Lanterns,* and other *Relievo's*; of *Topiary* and *Hortulan Architecture.*
Ch. IX. Of *Fountains, Jetto's, Cascades, Rivulets, Piscina's, Canals, Baths,* and other Natural, and Artificial *Water-works.*

48 Cornelius Holsteyn, 'Reynier Pauw with His Wife Adriana, and Four of Their Children, in the Gardens of Westwijk House', *c.* 1650

Ch. X. Of *Rocks, Grotts, Cryptae, Mounts, Precipices, Ventiducts, Conservatories,* of *Ice* and *Snow,* and other Hortulan Refreshments.

Ch. XI. Of *Statues, Busts, Obelisks, Columns, Inscriptions, Dials, Vasa's, Perspectives, Paintings,* and other Ornaments.

Ch. XII. Of *Gazon-Theatres, Amphitheatres,* Artificial *Echo's, Automata* and *Hydraulic Musick.*

Ch. XIII. Of *Aviaries, Apiaries, Vivaries, Insects,* &c.

Ch. XIV. Of *Verdures, Perennial Greens,* and *Perpetual Springs.*

Ch. XV. Of *Orangeries, Oporotheca's, Hybernacula, Stoves,* and Conservatories of Tender *Plants* and *Fruits,* and how to order them.

Ch. XVI. Of the *Coronary* Garden: *Flowers* and *Rare Plants,* how they are to be *Raised, Governed* and *Improved;* and how the Gardiner is to keep his *Register.*

Ch. XVII. Of the *Philosophical Medical* Garden.

Ch. XVIII. Of *Stupendous* and *Wonderful Plants.*

Ch. XIX. Of the *Hort-Yard* and *Potagere;* and what *Fruit-Trees, Olitory* and *Esculent Plants,* may be admitted into a Garden of Pleasure.

Ch. XX. Of *Sallets.*

Laudato ingentia rura,
Exiguum colito.

Andrew Marvell (1621–78)

Marvell wrote his long and intricate poem, 'Upon Appleton House', 'to my Lord Fairfax', while tutor to his daughter Maria at their estate in Yorkshire; it was published in 1681. Like many country house poems (Ben Jonson's 'To Penshurst' is an earlier English example, though the genre has Classical origins), Marvell's uses the topographical facts as the occasion, and in part the topic, of his meditations. The poem invokes and plays with so many other traditional forms and ideas — ideas of paradise, of retreat, of gardens, of the relative claims upon men of art and nature — that it is difficult to isolate what is of particular interest to this anthology. (But Marvell's stanza numbers have been retained so that the selections can easily be rediscovered in a text of the complete poem.) Marvell is of prime interest on two counts: he reveals, if indirectly, something of English garden design in mid-century before the French and Dutch tastes triumphed (see Plate 48), and he displays a rich array of attitudes to gardens and of the mental habits they elicited. Fairfax's flower garden, formed like a fort to recall its owner's military career, was adjacent to the new house and the ruined nunnery (an early example, perhaps, of Gothic setpiece in a landscape). The ordered area by the house was adjoined by the 'abyss' of groves and meadows. Here Marvell seems to imagine various features that are familiar in Italian gardens, which he might have seen while abroad in 1642. He compares himself to some river god (stanza LXXXI), Maria Fairfax to some goddess of the woods or *genius loci* (stanza LXXXVII), and the changing scenery of these groves (stanza XLIX), compared to theatrical masques, recalls Henry Wotton's delight in the sequence of scenes in the 'incomparable' garden he saw in Italy. Marvell's attitudes towards these varied landscapes are partly those of the old *hortus conclusus* — reading a garden as a series of symbols or emblems of larger ideas, a mode wittily conspicuous in his own poem 'The Garden' and more woodenly deployed by Henry Hawkins in *Parthenia Sacra*. But besides its adroit manoeuvres in what a contemporary called the 'holy garden of Speculation', Marvell's mind also seems to delight in real 'landskips'; these natural prospects, invoked with characteristically agile intelligence, occupy a prominent part in the second half of 'Upon Appleton House'. Remnants of the Fairfax landscape still survive today.

from 'Upon Appleton House' (early 1650s)

IX.

A Stately *Frontispice of Poor*
Adorns without the open Door:
Nor less the Rooms within commends,

Daily new *Furniture of Friends*.
The House was built upon the Place
Only as for *a Mark of Grace*;
And for an *Inn* to entertain
Its *Lord* a while, but not remain.

X.

Him *Bishops-Hill,* or *Denton* may,
Or *Bilbrough,* better hold then they:
But Nature here hath been so free
As if she said leave this to me.
Art would more neatly have defac'd
What she had laid so sweetly wast;
In fragrant Gardens, shaddy Woods,
Deep Meadows, and transparent Floods . . .

XXXVI.

From that blest Bed the *Heroe* came,
Whom *France* and *Poland* yet does fame:
Who, when retired here to Peace,
His warlike Studies could not cease;
But laid these Gardens out in sport
In the just Figure of a Fort;
And with five Bastions it did fence,
As aiming one for ev'ry Sense.

XXXVII.

When in the *East* the Morning Ray
Hangs out the Colours of the Day,
The Bee through these known Allies hums,
Beating the *Dian* with its *Drumms*.
Then Flow'rs their drowsie Eylids raise,
Their Silken Ensigns each displayes,
And dries its Pan yet dank with Dew,
And fills its Flask with Odours new.

XXXVIII.

These, as their *Governour* goes by,
In fragrant Vollyes they let fly;
And to salute their *Governess*
Again as great a charge they press:
None for the *Virgin Nymph*; for She
Seems with the Flow'rs a Flow'r to be.
And think so still! though not compare
With Breath so sweet, or Cheek so faire.

XXXIX.

Well shot ye Firemen! Oh how sweet,
And round your equal Fires do meet;
Whose shrill report no Ear can tell,
But Ecchoes to the Eye and smell.
See how the Flow'rs, as at *Parade*,
Under their *Colours* stand displaid:
Each *Regiment* in order grows,
That of the Tulip Pinke and Rose.

XL.

But when the vigilant *Patroul*
Of Stars walks round about the *Pole*,
Their Leaves, that to the stalks are curl'd,
Seem to their Staves the *Ensigns* furl'd.
Then in some Flow'rs beloved Hut
Each Bee as Sentinel is shut;
And sleeps so too: but, if once stir'd,
She runs you through, or askes *the Word.*

XLI.

Oh Thou, that dear and happy Isle
The Garden of the World ere while,
Thou P[a]radise of four Seas,
Which *Heaven* planted us to please,
But, to exclude the World, did guard
With watry if not flaming Sword;
What luckless Apple did we tast,
To make us Mortal, and The Wast.

XLII.

Unhappy! shall we never more
That sweet *Militia* restore,
When Gardens only had their Towrs,
And all the Garrisons were Flowrs,
When Roses only Arms might bear,
And Men did rosie Garlands wear?
Tulips, in several Colours barr'd,
Were then the *Switzers* of our *Guard*.

XLIII.

The *Gardiner* had the *Souldiers* place,
And his more gentle Forts did trace.
The Nursery of all things green
Was then the only *Magazeen*.

The *Winter Quarters* were the Stoves,
Where he the tender Plants removes.
But War all this doth overgrow:
We Ord'nance Plant and Powder sow.

XLIV.

And yet their walks one on the Sod
Who, had it pleased him and *God*,
Might once have made our Gardens spring
Fresh as his own and flourishing.
But he preferr'd to the *Cinque Ports*
These five imaginary Forts:
And, in those half-dry Trenches, spann'd
Pow'r which the Ocean might command.

XLV.

For he did, with his utmost Skill,
Ambition weed, but *Conscience* till.
Conscience, that Heaven-nursed Plant,
Which most our Earthly Gardens want.
A prickling leaf it bears, and such
As that which shrinks at ev'ry touch;
But Flowrs eternal, and divine,
That in the Crowns of Saints do shine.

XLVI.

The sight does from these *Bastions* ply,
Th' invisible *Artilery*;
And at proud *Cawood Castle* seems
To point the *Battery* of its Beams.
As if it quarrell'd in the Seat
Th' Ambition of its *Prelate* great.
But ore the Meads below it plays,
Or innocently seems to gaze.

XLVII.

And now to the Abbyss I pass
Of that unfathomable Grass,
Where Men like Grashoppers appear,
But Grashoppers are Gyants there:
They, in there squeking Laugh, contemn
Us as we walk more low then them:
And, from the Precipices tall
Of the green spir's, to us do call.

XLVIII.

To see Men through this Meadow Dive,
We wonder how they rise alive.
As, under Water, none does know
Whether he fall through it or go.
But, as the Marriners that sound,
And show upon their Lead the Ground,
They bring up Flow'rs so to be seen,
And prove they've at the Bottom been.

XLIX.

No Scene that turns with Engines strange
Does oftner then these Meadows change.
For when the Sun the Grass hath vext,
The tawny Mowers enter next;
Who seem like *Israaliies* to be,
Walking on foot through a green Sea.
To them the Grassy Deeps divide,
And crowd a Lane to either Side . . .

LV.

When after this 'tis pil'd in Cocks,
Like a calm Sea it shews the Rocks:
We wondring in the River near
How Boats among them safely steer.
Or, like the *Desert Memphis Sand*,
Short *Pyramids* of Hay do stand.
And such the *Roman Camps* do rise
In Hills for Soldiers Obsequies.

LVI.

This *Scene* again withdrawing brings
A new and empty Face of things;
A levell'd space, as smooth and plain,
As Clothes for *Lilly* stretcht to stain.
The World when first created sure
Was such a Table rase and pure.
Or rather such is the *Toril*
Ere the Bulls enter at Madril.

LVII.

For to this naked equal Flat,
Which *Levellers* take Pattern at,
The Villagers in common chase
Their Cattle, which it closer rase;

And what below the Sith increast
Is pincht yet nearer by the Breast [*sic*].
Such, in the painted World, appear'd
Davenant with th' Universal Heard.

LVIII.

They seem within the polisht Grass
A Landskip drawen in Looking-Glass.
And shrunk in the huge Pasture show
As Spots, so shap'd, on Faces do.
Such Fleas, ere they approach the Eye,
In Multiplying Glasses lye.
They feed so wide, so slowly move,
As *Constellations* do above.

LIX.

Then, to conclude these pleasant Acts,
Denton sets ope its *Cataracts*;
And makes the Meadow truly be
(What it but seem'd before) a Sea.
For, jealous of its *Lords* long stay,
It try's t'invite him thus away.
The River in it self is drown'd,
And Isl's th' astonish[t] Cattle round . . .

LXXVII.

Bind me ye *Woodbines* in your 'twines,
Curle me about ye gadding *Vines*,
And Oh so close your Circles lace,
That I may never leave this Place:
But, lest your Fetters prove too weak,
Ere I your Silken Bondage break,
Do you, *O Brambles*, chain me too,
And courteous *Briars* nail me through.

LXXVIII.

Here in the Morning tye my Chain,
Where the two Woods have made a Lane;
While, like a *Guard* on either side,
The Trees before their *Lord* divide;
This, like a long and equal Thread,
Betwixt two *Labyrinths* does lead.
But, where the Floods did lately drown,
There at the Ev'ning stake me down.

LXXIX.

For now the Waves are fal'n and dry'd,
And now the Meadows fresher dy'd;
Whose Grass, with moister colour dasht,
Seems as green Silks but newly washt.
No *Serpent* new nor *Crocodile*
Remains behind our Little Nile;
Unless it self you will mistake,
Among these Meads the only Snake.

LXXX.

See in what wanton harmless folds
It ev'ry where the Meadow holds;
And its yet muddy back doth lick,
Till as a *Chrystal Mirrour* slick;
Where all things gaze themselves, and doubt
If they be in it or without.
And for his shade which therein shines,
Narcissus like, the *Sun* too pines.

LXXXI.

Oh what a Pleasure 'tis to hedge
My Temples here with heavy sedge;
Abandoning my lazy Side,
Stretcht as a Bank unto the Tide;
Or to suspend my sliding Foot
On the Osiers undermined Root,
And in its Branches tough to hang,
While at my Lines the Fishes twang!

LXXXII.

But now away my Hooks, my Quills,
And Angles, idle Utensils.
The *young Maria* walks to night:
Hide trifling Youth thy Pleasures slight.
'Twere shame that such judicious Eyes
Should with such Toyes a Man surprize;
She that already is the *Law*
Of all her *Sex*, her *Ages Aw.*

LXXXIII.

See how loose Nature, in respect
To her, it self doth recollect;
And every thing so whisht and fine,
Starts forth with to its *Bonne Mine.*

The *Sun* himself, of *Her* aware,
Seems to descend with greater Care;
And lest *She* see him go to Bed,
In blushing Clouds conceales his Head . . .

LXXXVII.

'Tis *She* that to these Gardens gave
That wondrous Beauty which they have;
She streightness on the Woods bestows;
To *Her* the Meadow sweetness owes;
Nothing could make the River be
So Chrystal-pure but only *She*;
She yet more Pure, Sweet, Streight, and Fair
Then Gardens, Woods, Meads, Rivers are.

LXXXVIII.

Therefore what first *She* on them spent,
They gratefully again present.
The Meadow Carpets where to tread;
The Garden Flow'rs to Crown *Her* Head;
And for a Glass the limpid Brook,
Where *She* may all *her* Beautyes look;
But, since *She* would not have them seen,
The Wood about *her* draws a Skreen . . .

LXXXXIV.

Mean time ye Fields, Springs, Bushes, Flow'rs,
Where yet She leads her studious Hours,
(Till Fate her worthily translates,
And find a *Fairfax* for our *Thwaites*)
Employ the means you have by Her,
And in your kind your selves preferr;
That, as all *Virgins* She preceds,
So you all *Woods, Streams, Gardens, Meads.*

LXXXXV.

For you *Thessalian Tempe's Seat*
Shall now be scorn'd as obsolete;
Aranjeuz, as less, disdain'd;
The *Bel-Retiro* as constrain'd;
But name not the *Idalian Grove*,
For 'twas the Seat of wanton Love;
Much less the Dead's *Elysian Fields*,
Yet nor to them your Beauty yields.

LXXXXVI.

'Tis not, what once it was, the *World*;
But a rude heap together hurl'd;
All negligently overthrown,
Gulfes, Deserts, Precipices, Stone.
Your lesser *World* contains the same.
But in more decent Order tame;
You Heaven's Center, Nature's Lap.
And Paradice's only Map.

John Milton (1608–74)

'How noble and Majestic,' wrote Stephen Switzer, 'that Inimitable Description of Paradise by Mr Milton.' The passage in *Paradise Lost* which he (among many others) praises became almost a sacred text for later gardenists: Horace Walpole compared Stourhead with lines 223–7, and Hagley Park with the following three — 'What colouring, what freedom of pencil, what landscape . . .' From Milton was derived authority for serpentine lines, natural treatment of water, rural mounds, wooded theatres, and for the rejection of 'nice Art/In Beds and curious knots' in favour of 'Nature boon/Poured forth profuse on Hill and Dale and Plaine'. Admirers of Milton's prototype landscape garden were content to ignore the ambiguities of the passage: its invocation of the art term, 'Lantskip', for what is supposed to be a scene free of art; Milton's linking of his Eden with 'Hesperian Fables', as if to suggest the ultimate unreality of such a scene. Nevertheless, upon Milton's picture of the garden inhabited by our first parents were to be based many rural seats of various view during the century that followed *Paradise Lost*. Milton's choice of such a landscape to imagine his prelapsarian world probably owes less to any specific visual sources than to the idea that only after the Fall did man have to invoke art to shore a damaged nature; Walpole was to agree that topiary was unworthy of God's first garden. (A rival theory, looking to the geometrical-planned French gardens, argued that man began in a bestial state, from which his technical and intellectual supremacy gradually removed him.) Milton may possibly be recalling certain features of gardens seen on his Italian journey, which are invoked explicitly in *Paradise Regained* IV, or such literary ones as that of Alcina in Ariosto's *Orlando Furioso*, or any number of Italian and Flemish paintings with landscape backgrounds (see Plate 49).

from *Paradise Lost*, Book IV (1667)

So on he fares, and to the border comes
Of *Eden*, where delicious Paradise,
Now nearer, Crowns with her enclosure green,
As with a rural mound the champain head
Of a steep wilderness, whose hairie sides
With thicket overgrown, grottesque and wilde,
Access deni'd; and over head up grew
Insuperable highth of loftiest shade,
Cedar, and Pine, and Firr, and branching Palm,
A Silvan Scene, and as the ranks ascend

49 Peter Paul Rubens and Jan Breughel, 'Adam and Eve in Paradise', *c.* 1620

Shade above shade, a woodie Theatre
Of stateliest view. Yet higher then thir tops
The verdurous wall of Paradise up sprung:
Which to our general Sire gave prospect large
Into his neather Empire neighbouring round.
And higher then that Wall a circling row
Of goodliest Trees loaden with fairest Fruit,
Blossoms and Fruits at once of golden hue
Appeerd, with gay enameld colours mixt:
On which the Sun more glad impress'd his beams
Then in fair Evening Cloud, or humid Bow,
When God hath showrd the earth; so lovely seemd
That Lantskip: And of pure now purer aire
Meets his approach, and to the heart inspires
Vernal delight and joy, able to drive
All sadness but despair: now gentle gales
Fanning thir odoriferous wings dispense
Native perfumes, and whisper whence they stole
Those balmie spoiles . . .   [lines 131–59]

Southward through *Eden* went a River large,
Nor chang'd his course, but through the shaggie hill
Pass'd underneath ingulft, for God had thrown
That Mountain as his Garden mould high rais'd
Upon the rapid current, which through veins
Of porous Earth with kindly thirst up drawn,
Rose a fresh Fountain, and with many a rill
Waterd the Garden; thence united fell
Down the steep glade, and met the neather Flood,
Which from his darksom passage now appeers,
And now divided into four main Streams,
Runs divers, wandring many a famous Realme
And Country whereof here needs no account,
But rather to tell how, if Art could tell,
How from that Saphire Fount the crisped Brooks,
Rowling on Orient Pearl and sands of Gold,
With mazie error under pendant shades
Ran Nectar, visiting each plant, and fed
Flours worthy of Paradise which not nice Art
In Beds and curious Knots, but Nature boon
Powrd forth profuse on Hill and Dale and Plaine,
Both where the morning Sun first warmly smote
The open field, and where the unpierc't shade
Imbround the noontide Bowrs: Thus was this place,
A happy rural seat of various view;
Groves whose rich Trees wept odorous Gumms and Balme,
Others whose fruit burnisht with Golden Rinde
Hung amiable, *Hesperian* Fables true,
If true, here onely, and of delicious taste:
Betwixt them Lawns, or level Downs, and Flocks
Grasing the tender herb, were interpos'd,
Or palmie hilloc, or the flourie lap
Of som irriguous Valley spread her store,
Flours of all hue, and without Thorn the Rose:
Another side, umbrageous Grots and Caves
Of coole recess, o're which the mantling Vine
Layes forth her purple Grape, and gentle creeps
Luxuriant; mean while murmuring waters fall
Down the slope hills, disperst, or in a Lake,
That to the fringed Bank with Myrtle crownd,
Her chrystall mirror holds, unite thir streams.

[lines 223–63]

René Rapin (1621–87)

This famous example of French garden criticism from *Of Gardens* (originally published in 1666) is offered in the English version of John Evelyn. It was a widely read document (another translation by Gardiner appeared in 1706) and provided instruction upon all kinds of garden matters, while also celebrating French examples (Plate 7). The first extract treats of rural retirement: its opening phrase, echoing the '*beatus ille . . .*' of both *Georgics* II, lines 485 ff., and Horace's *Epodes* II, exemplifies the habit of offering late Renaissance ideas and themes through the mediating vision and language of the Classics. Rapin not only wrote his poem in Latin, but in his Preface claimed to be providing for the garden what Virgil had done for agriculture. If the descriptions of the first extract seem to fit the later English garden as much as the French, the account of waterworks clearly defines the Continental mode of geometrical designs. Yet even here there are some surprises among the injunctions for 'square Ponds and long Canals' and further devices that will proclaim *grandeur* and *gloire*: there is the plea for variety, and the taste for seemingly natural conditions of water, notably the sublime cascade falling from a precipice.

from *Of Gardens*, translated by John Evelyn (1673)

And blest is he, who tir'd with his affairs,
Far from all noise, all vain applause, prepares
To go, and underneath some silent shade,
Which neither cares nor anxious thoughts invade,
Do's, for a while, himself alone possess;
Changing the Town for Rural happiness.
He, when the Suns hot steeds to th' Ocean hast,
E're sable night the world ha's over-cast,
May from the hills the fields below descry,
At once diverting both his mind and eye.
Or if he please, into the woods may stray,
Listen to th' Birds, which sing at break of day:
Or, when the Cattle come from pasture, hear
The bellowing Oxe, the hollow Valleys tear
With his hoarse voice: Sometimes his flow'rs invite:
The Fountains too are worthy of his sight.
To ev'ry part he may his care extend,
And these delights all others so transcend,

That we the City now no more respect,
Or the vain honours of the Court affect.
But to cool Streams, to aged Groves retire,
And th' unmix'd pleasures of the fields desire.
Making our beds upon the grassie bank,
For which no art, but nature we must thank.
No Marble Pillars, no proud Pavements there,
No Galleries, or fretted Roofs appear,
The modest rooms to *India* nothing owe;
Nor Gold, nor Ivory, nor Arras know:
Thus liv'd our Ancestors, when *Saturn* reign'd,
While the first Oracles in Okes remain'd.
A harmless course of life they did pursue;
And nought beyond their hills their Rivers knew.
Rome had not yet the Universe ingrost,
Her Seven Hills few Triumphs then could boast.
Small herds then graz'd in the *Laurentine* Mead;
Nor many more th' *Arician* Valleys feed.
    Of Rural Ornaments, of Woods much more
I could relate, then what I have before:
But what's unfinish'd my next care requires,
And my tir'd Bark the neighb'ring Port desires . . .

    When in your gardens entrance you provide,
The waters, there united, to divide:
First, in the middle a large Fountain make;
Which from a narrow pipe its rise may take,
And to the air those waves, by which 'tis fed,
Remit agen: About it raise a bed
Of moss, or grass, or if you think this base,
With well-wrought Marble circle in the place.
Statues of various shapes may be dispos'd
About the Tube; sometimes it is inclos'd
By dubious *Scylla*; or with Sea-calves grac'd;
Or by a brazen *Triton* 'tis embrac'd.
A *Triton* thus at *Luxembourg* presides,
And from the *Dolphin*, which he proudly rides,
Spouts out the streams: This place, though beautified
With Marble round, though from *Arcueill* supply'd;
Yet to Saint *Cloud* must yield in this out-shin'd,
That there the *Hostel d'Orleans* we find.
The little Town, the Groves before scarce known,
Enabled thus, will now give place to none.
So great an owner any seat improves;
One whom the King, one whom the people loves.

This Garden, as a Pattern, may be shown
To those who would adde beauty to their own.
All other Fountains this so far transcends,
That none in *France* besides with it contends.
None so much plenty yields; none flows so high,
A Gulf, i' th' middle of the Pond do's lye,
In which a swollen tunnel opens wide;
Through hissing chinks the waters freely slide;
And in their passage like a whirlwind move,
With rapid force into the air above;
As if a watry dart were upward thrown,
But when these haughty waves do once fall down,
Resounding loud, they on each other beat,
And with a dewy show'r the *Basin* wet . . .

Hence spouting streams in verdant Groves we see,
And noble Gardens to a luxury,
By Art diversify'd: for pow'rful Art
To the ambitious water can impart
Such diff'rent shapes, as great *Ruel* can boast,
Where glorious *Richlieu* with excessive cost,
And pains, the waves into subjection brings,
And still survives in Monumental Springs.
All this he did, while he, not *Lewis* raign'd,
And *Atlas*-like the tott'ring State sustain'd.
Here variously dispos'd the Fountains run,
First head-long fall, then rise where they begun.
Receive all forms, and move on ev'ry side;
With horrid noise, *Chimara* gaping wide,
Out of her open mouth the water throws.
For from her mouth a rapid torrent flows,
From her wide throat, as waves in circles spout,
A Serpent turning sprinkles all the rout.
A brazen Hunter watchfully attends;
And threatning death the crooked tunnel bends.
Instead of shot, thence pearly drops proceed;
Drops not so fatal as if made of Lead.
This soon the laughter of the vulgar moves,
Whose acclamation the deceit approves.

But why should I repeat how many ways
In the deep Caves Art with the water plays?
The place grows moist with artificial Rain,
And hissing Springs, which here burst out amain.
Rebounding high, streams ev'ry where sweat through,
And with great drops the hanging stones bedew.
They who the Grotts, and Fountains over-see,

May as they please the streams diversifie.
Though the kind *Naiades* comply with those,
Who when they Grotts of Pebble do compose,
And Springs bring in, still beautifie the Cells,
With Eastern stones, or *Erythraean* shells.
Others of hollow Pumice may be made,
And well-plac'd shells may on the top be laid.
But all these arts, which modern ages own,
Were to our happy ancestors unknown,
These sights must be expos'd to th' peoples view,
Whose greedy eyes such novelties pursue . . .

 Rivers diffus'd a thousand ways may pass,
With hast'ning waves through the divided grass.
Like sudden torrents, which the rain gives head,
Through *precipices* some may swiftly spread;
And in the pebbles a soft noise excite.
Some on the surface with a tim'rous flight,
May steal; if any thing its speed retard,
Then its shrill murmurs through the fields are heard.
Inrag'd it leaps up high, and with weak strokes
The pebbles, which it overflows, provokes.
Threatning the bank it beats against the shore,
And roots of trees which froth all sprinkles o're.
That slender brook, from whence hoarse noises came,
Which as it had no substance, had no name;
When other riv'lets from the Vales come in,
Th' ignoble current then will soon begin
To gather strength; for bridges may be fit,
And by degrees great Vessels will admit,
Sometimes by grassie banks the River goes;
Sometimes with joy it skips upon green moss;
Sometimes it murmurs in exalted Groves,
And with its threats the narrow path reproves.
When 'tis dispers'd, then let the Meads be drown'd,
Let slimy mud inrich the barren ground.
If it runs deep, with dams its force restrain;
And from the Meadows noxious water drain.
Where from their fountains rivers do break loose,
And the moist Spring the Valleys overflows;
When on the Meads black showers do descend,
With mounds of earth the Groves from clouds defend.

 As diff'rent figures best with streams agree,
So on the sides let there some diff'rence be.
Still with variety the borders grace,
There either grass, or fragrant flowers place;

Or with a wharf of stone the bank secure;
But troubled Fens let their own reeds obscure:
Or Weeds, where croaking Frogs and Moorhens lye;
Nothing but grass your banks must beautifie,
Where silver Springs afford transparent waves,
And glist'ring sand the even bottom paves,
On which green Elms their leaves in *Autumn* sheed.
Thus Rivers both our care and culture need.
While in their channels they run headlong down,
We must take heed, that, as they hast, no stone
Fall'n from the hanging brink, may keep them back,
And through the Vales their course uneasie make.

    Ye Springs and Fountains in the Woods resound,
And with your noise the silent Groves confound.
Frequent their windings, all their avenues,
And into the dry roots new life infuse.

    While pleasant streams invite your thoughts and eyes,
And with resistless charms your sense surprize;
Of humane life you then may meditate,
Obnoxious to the violence of fate,
Life unperceiv'd, like Rivers, steals away.
And though we court it, yet it will not stay.
Then may you think of *its incertainty,*
Constant in nothing but inconstancy.
See *what rude waves disturb the things below,*
And *through what stormy voyages we go.*
So Hypanis, you'l say, *and* Peneus *so,*
Simois, *and* Volsoian Amasenus *flow;*
Naupactian Achelous, Inachus,
With slow Melanthus, *swift* Parthenius,
Thus ran along, and so Dyraspes *went,*
Whose current Borysthenian *streams augment.*

    Besides the Fountains, which to art we owe,
That falls of water also can bestow
Such, as on rugged *Jura* we descry,
On Rocks; and on the *Alps* which touch the Sky.
Where from steep *precipices* it descends,
And where *America* it self extends
To the rude North; expos'd to *Eurus* blast:
On *Canadas* bold shore the Ocean past.
There among Groves of Fir-trees ever green,
Streams falling headlong from the Cliffs are seen:
The cataracts resound along the shore;
Struck with the noise, the Woods and Valleys rore.

These wonders which by nature here are shown,
Ruellian Naiads have by Art out-done,
Into the air a Rock with lofty head
Aspires, the hasty waters thence proceed.
Dash'd against rugged places they descend,
And broken thus themselves in foam they spend.
They sound, as when some torrent uncontroll'd,
With mighty force is from a Mountain roll'd.
The earth with horrid noise affrighted grones,
Flints which lye underneath, and moistned stones,
Are beat with waves; th' untrodden paths resound,
And groves and woods do loudly eccho round.

John Woolridge (fl. 1669–98)

Woolridge (or Worlidge) provides prescriptions for modest gardens of schematic and geometrical forms that mirror as much a Dutch as a French taste. His motives, explained in the Preface to *Systema Horti-Culturae*, were 'not only to excite or animate such that have fair Estates, and Pleasant Seats in the Country, to adorn and beautify them; but to encourage the honest and plain countryman in the improvement of his Ville, by enlarging the bounds and limits of his Gardens'. As the first extract shows, he was aware of the need for variety, eager to promote gardens that influence 'the Passions of the Mind', and apparently concerned with visitors' *experiences* of a garden. His instinct for 'our florid and purely ornamental Garlands, delightful unto Sight and Smell; not framed according to mystical and symbolical Considerations' reveals a characteristic Enlightenment bias and a post-Restoration mistrust of any religious argument. As one of the foremost advocates of Italian gardening in this period, he is represented in the following extracts by an anthology of items on waterworks, in which Italy was acknowledged to excel, on grottoes and on statues. His attention at one point to Roman precedents recalls his more lengthy essay on Latin gardenist writings in the 'Prooemium' to *Systema Agriculturae* (3rd edition 1681) (Plate 50).

from *Systema Horti-Culturae: or The Art of Gardening* (1677)

THE Excellency of a *Garden* is better manifested by Experience, which is the best Mistress, than indicated by an imperfect Pen, which can never sufficiently convince the Reader of those transcendent pleasures, that the Owner of a Complete *Garden* with its Magnificent *Ornaments*, its Stately *Groves*, and infinite variety of never dying *Objects of Delight* every day enjoys: Nor how all his Senses are satiated with the great variety of Objects it yields to every of them: Nor what an influence they have upon the passions of the mind, reducing a discomposed fancy to a more sedate temper by contemplating on those miracles of Nature *Gardens* afford; deemed Miracles, because their admired and strange forms and effects proceed from occult causes . . .

Of Rivers.

ALthough small Crystalline Springs brought in Pipes may be sufficient to irrigate your Groves and Plants, and supply your Grotts and Fountains and add very much to the splendor of your Garden; yet, a Fair stream or Current flowing through or neer your Garden adds much to the Glory, and pleasure of it, On the banks of it may you plant several aquatick Exoticks, & have your seats or places of repose under their Umbrage, and there satiate your self with the view of the Curling Streams and its nimble Inhabitants. These Gliding Streams refrigerate the Air in a Summer evening, and render their banks so pleasant, that they become resistless Charms to your Senses, by the murmuring Noise, the Undulation of the Water, the verdant Banks and Shades over them, the sporting Fish confin'd within your own limits, the beautiful Swans, and by the pleasant notes of singing Birds, that delight in Groves on the Banks of such Rivulets.

Where such a Stream or Rivulet cannot naturally glide through your Garden but near unto it, it's probable that part of it may be raised by some Machine, at some distance from your Garden, and by an Aquaeduct conveyed through it, which will be more commodious (the charge only excepted in the bringing it thither) than the natural Current. 1. Because natural Currents are usually in the lowest grounds, which are not so proper for a Garden, as a declining or ground above the level of the adjacent Lands. 2. For that an Artificial Current is not subject to those extravagancies, that the natural usually are, by over-flowing after hasty Rains. 3. Those waters that are brought by Art are easily carried off again, and may be conducted to several parts of your Garden on the edges of your declining Walks whether they decline little or much, if but little then may Canals be made in the natural Earth, without any danger of decay or wearing.

Of Fountains.

FOuntains are Principal Ornaments in a Garden, scarce a famous Garden in *Europe* [is] without its *Fountains* which where primarily intended for Bathing and are in the more southern Countries used for that purpose to this day. The *Italians* bestow very great cost in Beautifying them for that use: the French are very prodigal in their Expences about Fountains: and several Curious Gardens in *England* have them; but here only for Ornament, they are generally made of Stone, some square others round or Oval, and of divers other forms, some flat in the bottom, others round like a Bason.

Into some the Water is cast by Pipes from the sides out of the Mouths of several figures representing Animals or out of the Pipes of *Eurs* of Stone standing on the Brim of the Fountain, or the Water is cast from some *Figure* or *Statue* erected in the middle of the *Fountain*, or from *Pipes* standing upright in the midst of it.

There must also be wast Pipes or Cavities to convey away the Water from such Fountains, which must be so made that at your pleasure you may drain your Fountain and cleanse it, and must be of capacity to carry off all the Water as it comes, lest it annoy your Garden, for the greater quantity of Water you have, the more pleasant will it appear.

Plenty in Fountains always graceful shows,
And greatest Beauty from abundance flows . . .

50 John Woolridge, *Systema Agriculturae*, 3rd ed., 1681, frontispiece

Of Grotto's.

IT oftentimes happens that in these *Northern Climes*, the *AEstival* heats are more troublesome than they are nearer the *Zodiack*, the Sun continuing here longer above the *Horizon* in the Summer season, than in those parts, which occasions that intemperancy that many times we are sensible of, for as we have less of the presence of the Sun in the Winter, so have we that defect supplied in the Summer.

But those that inhabit more southerly, and have the Sun more perpendicularly over them, are more sensible of the acute heat of that bright Orb about the middle of the day, generally than we are, and therefore about the heat of the day, they usually sequester themselves from their ordinary occupations, and betake themselves to their shades and cool places of Recess for some few hours.

Such that have convenient places in their Villes, make themselves Grotto's or Caves in the Earth for that only purpose, on which some have bestowed so much cost and labour that those Grotts have been the object of admiration of, and part of the Subject of several Histories written by several Travellers and Strangers, as are their Baths and Fountains.

For the same reason may our Grotts be as necessary for us, to repose our selves in the time of our Summer faint heats, although they are not here so constant every year as in those parts, yet are they less tolerable, for want of these nocturnal breezes they usually enjoy.

Therefore either in the side of some declive of a Hill, or under some Mount or Terrace artificially raised, may you make a place of repose, cool and fresh in the greatest heats. It may be Arched over with stone or brick, and you may give it what light or entrance you please. You may make secret rooms and passages within it, and in the outer Room may you have all those before mentioned water-works, for your own or your friends divertisements.

It is a place that is capable of giving you so much pleasure and delight, that you may bestow not undeservedly what cost you please on it, by paving it with Marble or immuring it with Stone or Rock-work, either Natural or Artificially resembling the excellencies of nature. The Roof may be made of the same supported with pillars of Marble, and the partitions made of Tables of the same.

The most famous of this kind that this Kingdom affords, is that *Wiltonian Grotto* near unto *Salisbury*, on which no cost was spared to make it compleat, and wherein you may view or might have lately so done the best of waterworks ...

Of Statues, Obelisks, Dyals, and other invegetative Ornaments.

IN all places where there is a Summer and a Winter, and where your Gardens of pleasure are sometimes clothed with their verdant garments, and bespangled with variety of Flowers, and at other times wholly dismantled of all these; here to recompence the loss of past pleasures, and to buoy up their hopes of another Spring, many have placed in their Gardens, Statues, and Figures of several Animals, and great variety of other curious pieces of

Workmanship, that their walks might be pleasant at any time in those places of never dying pleasures.

Herein the ancient *Romans* were excessively prodigal, sparing of no cost, to adorn their avenues with curious figures for their Winter diversions, as well as with rare plants for their Summer delights. Which vanity (although one of the most excusable) is descended on the *Italians*, whose Gardens are the mirrors of the world, as well for those ornaments as for their excellency of the Plants that are propagated in them.

This mode of adorning Gardens with curious workmanship is now become *English*, how many Statues made by excellent Art, are there to be seen in his Majesties Gardens, and in the Gardens of divers of the nobility of *England*? But what great pity is it that in many places remote from Cities and great Towns, these Statues should drive out of their view, those natural Beauties that so far exceed them?

Much more ornamental are Statues placed in Groves and Shades, and in or near your borders of the choicest Plants than on the naked surface of the Earth, which beget not that surprise in the Spectators as the other.

Statues are commendable in the midst of Fountains, and Green Squares, in Groves and at the ends of obscure walks.

In the room of Statues in the midst of your Green Squares, Obelisks or single Columns may not be improper, so that the Workmanship be accordingly. Neither can there be a more proper use for an obelisk, than to support a Globe with its Axis duely placed respecting both Poles, and its circumference on the Equinoctial Line, exactly divided into twenty four parts, and marked with twice twelve hours, that on it at a distance by the shadow only of the Globe on its self, you may discern the hour of the day, and observe how the Day and Night, and Summer and Winter happen throughout the Universe.

Charles Cotton (1630–87)

The house and gardens at Chatsworth are the seventh wonder of the Peak District in Cotton's poem, *The Wonders of the Peake*, extracted here from the second edition of 1683. The gardens, which he says rival Italy's, are a paradise preserved from the wild country outside (Plate 51); he celebrates their splendours with the hyperbole that claims for their '*Landskips*' a superiority far above painters' art. Yet Cotton's indifferent poem is also interesting for the insights it gives into the growing contemporary fascination with more savage natural scenes. Though Cotton vilifies the deformed countryside in Derbyshire, terming it the warts and boils, the *Pudenda*, of nature, he is also obviously intrigued and delighted by torrents, precipices, chasms, mouldering ruins and caves — the apparatus we find in the paintings of Salvator Rosa (Plate 13) and which become standard ingredients of the later Gothic and picturesque tastes.

from *The Wonders of the Peake* (1681)

This *Palace*, with wild prospects girded round,
Stands in the middle of a falling ground,
At a black *Mountains* foot, whose craggy brow
Secures from *Eastern-Tempests* all below,
Under whose shelter *Trees* and *Flowers* grow,
With early *Blossom*, maugre native snow;
Which elsewhere round a *Tyranny* maintains,
And binds crampt *Nature* long in *Crystal-Chains*.
The *Fabrick's* noble Front faces the *Pest*,
Turning her fair broad shoulders to the *East*,
On the *South*-side the stately *Gardens* lye,
Where the scorn'd *Peak* rivals proud *Italy*.
And on the *North* sev'ral inferior *plots*,
For servile use do scatter'd lye in spots.

The outward *Gate* stands neat enough, to look
Her *Oval* Front in the objected *Brook*;
But that she has better reflexion
From a large *Mirror* nearer of her own.
For a fair *Lake*, from wash of *Floods* unmixt,
Before it lies, an *Area* spread betwixt.

51 Chatsworth, Derbyshire. Detail of painting by Sieberechts, *c.* 1710

Over this *Pond*, opposite to the Gate,
A *Bridge*, of a queint structure, strength, and state,
Invites you to pass over it, where dry
You trample may on shoals of wanton *Fry*,
With which those breeding waters do abound,
And better *Carps* are no where to be found.
A Tower of *Antick model* the *Bridge* foot
From the *Peak-rabble* does securely shut,
Which by stone stairs, delivers you below
Into the sweetest *Walks* the world can s[h]ow.
There *Wood* and *Water*, *Sun* and *Shade* contend,
Which shall the most delight, and most befriend;

There *Grass*, and *Gravel* in one path you meet,
For *Ladies* tend'rer, and mens harder feet.
Here into open *Lakes* the *Sun* may pry,
A priviledge the closer *Groves* deny,
Or if confed'rate Winds do make them yield
He then but chequers what he cannot guild.
The *Ponds*, which here in double order shine,
Are some of them so large, and all so fine,
That *Neptune* in his *progress* once did please
To frolick in these *artificial Seas*;
Of which a noble *Monument* we find,
His Royal *Chariot* left, it seems, behind;
Whose *wheels* and *body moor'd* up with a Chain,
Like *Drake's* old *Hulk* at *Deptford*, still remain.
No place on Earth was ere discover'd yet,
For *contemplation*, or *delight* so fit.
The *Groves*, whose curled brows shade every *Lake*,
Do every where such waving *Landskips* make,
As *Painters* baffl'd *Art* is far above,
Who waves, and leaves could never yet make move.
Hither the warbling *People* of the Air
From their remoter *Colonies* repair,
And in these shades, now setting up their rests,
Like *Caesars Swiss*, burn their old native nests.
The *Muses* too pearch on the bending spraies
And in these thickets chant their charming *Laies*;
No wonder then if the *Heroick Song*
That here took birth, and voice do flourish long.

To view from hence the glittering *Pile* above
(Which must at once wonder create, and love)
Environ'd round with *Natures* Shames, and Ills,
Black Heaths, wild Rocks, bleak Craggs, and naked Hills,
And the whole *Prospect* so informe, and rude?
Who is it, but must presently conclude
That this is *Paradice*, which seated stands
In midst of *Desarts*, and of barren *Sands*?
So a bright *Diamond* would look, if set
In a vile *socket* of ignoble *jet*,
And such a face the new-born *Nature* took,
When out of *Chaos* by the *Fiat* strook.
Doubtless, if any where, there never yet
So brave a *Structure* on such ground was set,
Which sure the *Foundress* built, to reconcile
This to the other members of the *Isle*,
And would therein, first her own *Grandeur* show,
And then what *Art* could, spite of *Nature*, do.

William Temple (1628–99)

In his long meditation, *Upon the Gardens of Epicurus* (first published in 1692 in Part II of his *Miscellanea*), Sir William Temple contributes an important historical perspective to the idea of the English landscape garden, locating its natural inclinations in those of Adam and Eve before the Fall (on this see also p. 79) and in various Classical texts; some sense of these may be gathered from the first part of the extract. In the second part, Temple's historical sense and nostalgia invoke earlier English as well as Chinese gardens. The glimpse of Moor Park in Hertfordshire reveals a gardenist style prior to the French vogue at the Restoration, a change in taste that Temple, with his own preference for following Nature, seems to find uncongenial. Moor Park, both in its site and its treatment, recalls Italian models. But perhaps Temple is most remarkable for being the first to urge the Chinese example of planting ('*Sharawadgi*'), which has been seen to have played such an important role in the English landscape movement.

from *Upon the Gardens of Epicurus: or, Of Gardening, in the Year 1685* (1692)

If we believe the Scripture, we must allow that God Almighty esteemed the Life of a Man in a Garden the happiest he could give him, or else he would not have placed *Adam* in that of *Eden*; that it was the State of Innocence and Pleasure; and that the Life of Husbandry and Cities came after the Fall, with Guilt and with Labour.

Where Paradise was has been much debated, and little agreed; but what Sort of Place is meant by it may perhaps easier be conjectured. It seems to have been a *Persian* Word, since Xenophon and other Greek Authors mention it, as what was much in Use and Delight among the Kings of those *Eastern* Countries. *Strabo*, describing Jericho, says, *Ibi est palmetum, cui immixtae sunt etiam aliae stirpes hortenses, locus ferax, palmis abundans, spatio stadiorum centum, totus irriguus, ibi est Regi & Balsami Paradisus.* He mentions another Place to be *prope Libanum & Paradisum.* And *Alexander* is written to have seen Cyrus's Tomb in a Paradise, being a Tower not very great, and covered with a Shade of Trees about it. So that a Paradise among them seems to have been a large Space of Ground, adorned and beautified with all Sorts of Trees, both of Fruits and of Forest, either found there before it was inclosed, or planted after; either cultivated like Gardens, for Shades and for Walks, with Fountains or Streams, and all Sorts of Plants usual in the Climate,

52 Moor Park, Surrey. Drawing of Sir William Temple's garden, *c.* 1690, artist unknown

and pleasant to the Eye, the Smell, or the Taste; or else employed, like our Parks, for Inclosure and Harbour of all Sorts of Wild Beasts, as well as for the Pleasure of Riding and Walking: And so they were of more or less Extent, and of differing Entertainment, according to the several Humours of the Princes that ordered and inclosed them . . .

The perfectest Figure of a Garden I ever saw, either at Home or Abroad, was that of *Moor-Park* in *Hertfordshire*, when I knew it about thirty Years ago. It was made by the Countess of Bedford, esteemed among the greatest Wits of her Time, and celebrated by Doctor *Donne*; and with very great Care, excellent Contrivance, and much Cost; but greater Sums may be thrown away without Effect or Honour, if there want Sense in Proportion to Money, or if Nature be not followed; which I take to be the great Rule in this, and perhaps in every Thing else, as far as the Conduct not only of our Lives, but our Governments. And whether the greatest of Mortal Men should attempt the forcing of Nature may best be judged, by observing how seldom God Almighty does it Himself, by so few, true, and undisputed Miracles, as we see or hear of in the World. For my own part, I know not three wiser Precepts for the Conduct either of Princes or Private Men, than

Servare Modum, Finemque tueri,
Naturamque sequi.

Because I take the Garden I have named to have been in all Kinds the most beautiful and perfect, at least in the Figure and Disposition, that I have ever seen, I will describe it for a Model to those that meet with such a Situation, and are above the Regards of common Expence. It lies on the Side of a Hill, (upon which the House stands) but not very steep. The Length of the House, where the best Rooms and of most Use or Pleasure are, lies upon the Breadth of the Garden, the Great Parlour opens into the Middle of a Terras Gravel-Walk that lies even with it, and which may be, as I remember, about three hundred Paces long, and broad in Proportion; the Border set with Standard Laurels, and at large Distances, which have the Beauty of Orange-Trees out of Flower and Fruit: From this Walk are Three Descents by many Stone Steps, in the Middle and at each End, into a very large Parterre. This is divided into Quarters by Gravel-Walks, and adorned with Two Fountains and Eight Statues in the several Quarters; at the End of the Terras-Walk are Two Summer-Houses, and the Sides of the Parterre are ranged with two large Cloisters, open to the Garden, upon Arches of Stone, and ending with two other Summer-Houses even with the Cloisters, which are paved with Stone, and designed for Walks of Shade, there being none other in the whole Parterre. Over these two Cloisters are two Terrasses covered with Lead, and fenced with Balusters; and the Passage into these Airy Walks is out of the two Summer-Houses, at the End of the first Terras-Walk. The Cloister facing the *South* is covered with Vines, and would have been proper for an Orange-House, and the other for Myrtles, or other more common Greens; and had, I doubt not, been cast for that Purpose, if this Piece of Gardening had been then in as much Vogue as it is now.

From the Middle of the Parterre is a Descent by many Steps flying on each Side of a Grotto that lies between them (covered with Lead, and Flat) into the lower Garden, which is all Fruit-Trees ranged about the several Quarters of a Wilderness which is very Shady; the Walks here are all Green, the Grotto embellish'd with Figures of Shell-Rock-work, Fountains, and Water-works. If the Hill had not ended with the lower Garden, and the Wall were not bounded by a common Way that goes through the Park, they might have added a Third Quarter of all Greens; but this Want is supplied by a Garden on the other Side the House, which is all of that Sort, very Wild, Shady, and adorned with rough Rock-work and Fountains.

This was *Moor-Park*, when I was acquainted with it, and the sweetest Place, I think, that I have seen in my Life, either before or since, at Home or Abroad; what it is now I can give little Account, having passed through several Hands that have made great Changes in Gardens as well as Houses; but the Remembrance of what it was is too pleasant ever to forget, and therefore I do not believe to have mistaken the Figure of it, which may serve for a Pattern to the best Gardens of our Manner, and that are most proper for our Country and Climate.

What I have said, of the best Forms of Gardens, is meant only of such as are in some Sort regular; for there may be other Forms wholly irregular, that may, for aught I know, have more Beauty than any of the others; but they must owe it to some extraordinary Dispositions of Nature in the Seat, or some great Race of Fancy or Judgment in the Contrivance, which may reduce many disagreeing Parts into some Figure, which shall yet upon the whole, be very agreeable. Something of this I have seen in some Places, but heard more of it from others, who have lived much among the *Chineses*; a People, whose Way of Thinking seems to lie as wide of ours in *Europe*, as their Country does. Among us, the Beauty of Building and Planting is placed chiefly in some certain Proportions, Symmetries, or Uniformities; our Walks and our Trees ranged so, as to answer one another, and at exact Distances. The *Chineses* scorn this Way of Planting, and say a Boy, that can tell an Hundred, may plant Walks of Trees in straight Lines, and over-against one another, and to what Length and Extent he pleases. But their greatest Reach of Imagination is employed in contriving Figures, where the Beauty shall be great, and strike the Eye, but without any Order or Disposition of Parts, that shall be commonly or easily observ'd. And though we have hardly any Notion of this Sort of Beauty, yet they have a particular Word to express it; and, where they find it hit their Eye at first Sight, they say the *Sharawadgi* is fine or is admirable, or any such Expression of Esteem. And whoever observes the Work upon the best *Indian* Gowns, or the Painting upon their best Skreens or Purcellans, will find their Beauty is all of this Kind (that is) without Order. But I should hardly advise any of these Attempts in the Figure of Gardens among us; they are Adventures of too hard Achievement for any common Hands; and though there may be more Honour if they succeed well, yet there is more Dishonour if they fail, and 'tis Twenty to One they will; whereas, in regular Figures, 'tis hard to make any great and remarkable Faults.

Timothy Nourse (d. 1699)

Nourse added his essay, 'Of a Country House', to the end of *Campania Foelix*, a work that brings to its traditional Virgilian theme the fresh scientific interests in horticulture, arboriculture and husbandry which characterized the Restoration and in which Evelyn's role has already been noticed (see p. 57). Nourse's essay, extracted here, is interesting because it comes from a man who elsewhere objects to the 'dead plains' and little variety of Versailles and yet still offers a recipe for a mostly controlled and organized, if varied, garden. In contrast to Lawrence's project (see pp. 132 f.), Nourse's proposals concern a fairly grand country seat, though his frontispiece (Plate 53) offers little clue to this emphasis in the essay. There is some Italian influence in the courtyard that mediates between the interior of a house and the exterior world of the garden beyond, in the fountains, grotto and aviary (Nourse has already commended Italian waterworks), and in the triple-terraced site, which affords views into the countryside beyond. If the wood before the house and the two lower gardens behind it answer the forms and spaces of the architecture to which they are adjacent, the third garden is much more 'Natural-Artificial'. It again recalls the groves that adjoin many Italian gardens and is characterized by more private alleys and the 'negligent order' that can be seen also in the 'Landskip' beyond. Nourse's use of this painterly term recalls the large role played by landscape painting in the development of a taste for the English garden of the eighteenth century. We have already been told that a gallery inside the house should be hung with 'all sorts of landskip'.

from *Campania Foelix: or A Discourse of the
Benefits and Improvements of Husbandry* (1700)

All the Ground betwixt the Entrance of this Inclosure or Park, and the second Region alotted for the Dwelling-House, I would have planted with Trees, and above all with Beech, if the Soil will admit; or if the Place be already planted, and in the form of a Wood, I would have a large Walk or Road, of Thirty Paces breadth, leading directly from the Entrance of the Park to the Dwelling-House, which I would have to stand in full front or view; which Walk or Road I would have regularly pitch'd for a considerable breadth, to prevent the Dirt which a constant Intercourse of Horses and Carriages might make. On each side of which Ground-walk I would have private Foot-walks within the Wood, well gravell'd, or clean kept, in breadth of about Sixteen Foot each, which, like a dark Arbour-walk, should butt directly upon the corners of the front in the Dwelling-House; so that the

Trees meeting at the top, would make it wonderful cool and delightful in the Summer, the long Shade-alleys or Glades being terminated in the building. But in case it may be thought that such Walks or Glades through Woods might hinder the View and Prospect of the House, the Avenue or Approach may be cast into a Figure something resembling a Theatre; in which case we may allow what wideness we please, provided still that the principal Mansion, with all its Courts, Gardens, Out-buildings, and Offices, stand full in front to the Entrance, the shady Groves regularly contracting themselves the nearer Approach we make unto it. By this means the Palace will be seen at a vast distance, without Reserve or Mask upon its Face, resembling the same stately Canopy at the head of the inbearing Woods. But whatsoever Fancy may be pitch'd upon, this must carefully be taken heed to, that the tops of the Trees do not rise higher than the Rooms upon the first Floor, to the hinderance of Air and Prospect; and it may easily be allow'd that they will not, considering that the House is to be built upon a Rising-Ground, and at some distance from the tending Woods . . .

As for the Inward-Court of this Building, I would have it neatly Pav'd or Pitch'd, and not to be of Earth, with Gravell'd Walks and Grass-Plats; for these in the Winter-time will loosen after a Frost, and stick to the Feet; besides, the Washings of Rain will fill the lower Draughts with Filth: Nor is there any Danger of too much Heat to be reflected from the Stones, as my Lord *Verulan* [Bacon] does object; for the sides of the House will guard the Courts sufficiently from such Annoyance: But this, as many other things, must be left to the Fancy of the Builder. However, I should like two Fountains, or *Jetteauz*, with their Basons, in the midst of the Court, on each side one; and the further end of the Court, or fourth Side, answering the double-Building, to be all of Grate-work, with Freestone-Pillars, and Statues on the tops, giving a View or Prospect into the Grand Garden, the Doors or Gates being of Azure and Gilded, opening in the middle, and giving Entrance thereinto . . .

The next thing to be consider'd of is the Gardens, *viz.* that of the Kitchen, and that of Pleasure.

I shall begin with the Pleasure-Garden, into which, as I said before, we are to make our Entrance through the side of Grate-Work, which makes up the Quadrangle of the inner Court: The Par-terries or Plan of the Ground to be allow'd for the Garden, ought at least to be Six-Score Paces or Yards in breadth, and Nine Score in length; which I divide into three equal Parteries or Gardens, allowing to each Garden one hundred and twenty Paces, and sixty for depth, the Garden equally extending it self on both sides the House. As to the Pattern of the First Garden, let it be subdivided into Two Plats or Plans by a grand Alley in the middle, of thirty Foot in breadth; the side or round about Alleys to be fifteen in breadth, the borders on the sides of the Alleys six foot breadth, as also three foot along the Walls or Sides of the Garden where Fruit-Trees may be planted. Within which Borders on the sides, let there be other lesser Gravell'd Alleys of about six foot breadth with paths through the middle of the Borders, of a just breadth, to pass from Alley to Alley. When this is done there will remain a Quadrangular Plat in

53 Timothy Nourse, *Campania Foelix*, 1700, frontispiece

the middle, which may serve for a Grass-Plat, and in the midst thereof let there be a fair Fountain with a Bason of thirty foot Diameter, well pav'd and flankd with Free-Stone, and in the Centre of this let there be some Statue delivering the Water into the Fountain, such as *Neptune* riding upon a *Tritan*, out of whose Shell let the Water spout, or a Sea-Monster thrusting up his Head, and spouting out the Water into the Air, or a *Diana* with her Nymphs bathing themselves, and the Water trickling down the Linnen wherewith she drys her self; Or some other naked Female Figure, with water letting out at her Nipples, with a thousand such Inventions. The like Curiosities of Walks, Fountains, Statues, &c. to be in the other Partern or Partition of this First Garden.

The Borders which may be made, more or fewer, wider or narrower, according to the Genius of the Gardner, I would have replenished with Flowers, for every Month or Season of the Year: For to see a Flower-Garden without its decorations, is all one as to sit down to a Table furnisht with Cloth, Plates and Napkin, and nothing serv'd in. To enumerate the particular Flowers would be too tedious, the Curious may find Varieties to entertain themselves in Mr. *Wooldrige's Collection*, and especially Mr. *Evelyn's Kalendar*, a Gentleman who has oblig'd all lovers of planting, by his Excellent Books upon that Subject.

All throughout the Borders at an equal distance, let there be little Bushes of Ever-Greens, as Dwarft, Cypresses, Philyreas, Rosemary, Lavender, Bays, Lawns, Limes, Savine and Rue; for these also are Green in Winter and Sticky. Also some kinds of Holly would be Ornamental, as likewise little Firr-Trees, but these must be remov'd every three Years, because they cannot be drest without spoiling their Figure; let there be planted likewise up and down some little Tufts or Matts of Peaks for these look prettily in the Winter, as also some Mizerean Trees and the like.

Along the Grand Alley, as also from the ends of the long Upper-Walks, we may have three Ascents to Mount by, into the Second Garden, each Ascent to consist of sixteen or seventeen Steps, which second Garden I would have to stand nine foot above the first, which may easily be brought about, the whole Design both of the House and Garden being on a Rising Ground, as I said at the beginning; so that the Second Garden will be as a Terras to the first; and in the sides of the Bank which parts the two Gardens, and looking full to the Sun, we have a place for our Green-Houses . . .

The Furniture of the Green-Houses ought to be this, *viz.* Orange and Lemon-Trees, Myrtles, of which the small leav'd Myrtle is more difficult to be preserv'd: *Tuberosus's*, which will hold their Flowers in Winter, *Jessamins* of all sorts, as the Spanish, or *Jessamine* of *Catalonia*, the *double-blossom'd Jessamine*, with a Flower like to a Double Cherry, the *Persian Jessamine*, and the like; as likewise *Mavyn*, *Syriacum*, which tho a little Shrub, or a sort of *Mastick Thyme*, is much to be valued for its rich Balsamick Smell: the Olive-Tree, the Pomegranate-Tree, the Oleander or Rose-Lawrel. Likewise in the same Bank let there be Variety of Seats, and in the midst a *Grotto* made of Shell-work, with some little Imagery, delivering the Water through little Pipes, with some wetting-Places, as also a Bathing-Place or

Bason in the midst; likewise some artificial Birds murmuring or chirping, a Serpent hissing, with some contiguous Furies, would very much contribute to the pleasure of such *Grotto's*. All which Water-works, whether of *Grotto's* or *Fountains* are to be fram'd with proportionable Pipes for the clearer Conveyance of the Water to some of the lower Fountains, and from them to the Offices of the House. On the Tops of the Degrees or Stairs by which we ascend to the Second Garden, let there be erected little Pyramids with gilded Balls, or little Angels on the tops of them.

The Second Garden being of the same Dimensions with the first, I would have distributed into the same Order of Walks, Alleys, Borders, Grass-Plots and Fountains; only for Variety let the Grass-Plots and Alleys about them be of an Oval Figure: Also let the Borders be planted with Flowers of different kinds from those of the lower Garden, yet serving the several Months or Seasons, which may easily be done, if we except the Winter-Quarter, which admits but of little Variety: And as the first were adorn'd with Ever-Greens, so let the Borders of this be adorn'd with dwarft Fruit-Trees, as Cherries, Apples, some choice Pears, &c. cut and shap'd into little round hollow Bushes: likewise to have little Lath-Walkes for Climbers or Honey-suckles, *Indian Ciestes*, and the like. On the sides of this Garden I would have Two Terras-Walks, overlooking the Country on either side, each Walk being sixty Paces long. From this Second Garden let there be three Ascents (as from the former) landing into the third and last Garden: Also about the Walls of the Terras of this second or Middle-Garden, let there be planted some sorts of Fruit-Trees, and here and there some Common Jessamines, the White and the Yellow. Trial likewise may be made of the *Spanish* Jessamine, and of the broad-leav'd Myrrh, as we see in the *Tuilleries* at *Paris*, but I fear they will not resist the Injuries of our Climate, tho they be fenc'd with Mattings.

The Third or last Region of our Pleasure-Garden I would have wholly to be design'd for Boscage: Only Three long Alleys running to the farther end by way of continuance of those which traverse to the lower Gardens. Let there be likewise up and down little private Alleys or Walks of Beech, for this is a delicate Green: Here likewise let there be Tufts of Cypress-Trees, planted in the Form of a Theater, with a Fountain at the bottom, and Statues round about; likewise Fir-Trees in some negligent Order, as also Lawrels, Philyrea's, Bays, Tumarist, the Silac Tree, *Althea* Fruits, Pyracanthe, Yew, Juniper, Holly, Cork Tree, and in a word, with all sorts of Winter Greens which may be made to grow, together with wild Vines, Bean-Trefoile, *Spanish Ash*, Horse-Chesnut, Sweet-Brier, Honey-Suckles, Roses, Almond-Trees, Mulberries, &c. Also up and down let there be little Banks or Hillocks, planted with wild Thyme, Violets, Primroses, Cowslips Daffadille, Lillies of the Valley, Blew-Bottles, Daisies, with all kinds of Flowers which grow wild in the Fields and Woods; as also amongst the Shades Strawberries, and up and down the Green-Walks let there be good store of Camomile, Water-Mint, Organy, and the like; for these being trod upon, yield a pleasant Smell; and let the Walls be planted with Hedera, Canadensis, and Philyrea's, &c. So that this Third Garden, Grove or Wilderness, should be made to represent a perpetual Spring; To which end and purpose let there be large Aviaries in convenient places, which should have Ever-Green Trees growing in them, especially such as bear Berries, together with little Receptacles for Fresh Water. Likewise for Variety's sake, let there be here and there a Fruit-Tree, as Plumbs and Cherries, Haw-Thorn, which such like as will not run to Timber; for these Trees also have their Beauties in their several Seasons. In a word, let this Third Region or Wilderness be Natural-Artificial; that is, let all things be dispos'd with that cunning, as to deceive us into a belief of a real Wilderness or Thicket, and yet to be furnished with all the Varieties of Nature: And at the upper end of this Wilderness, let there be a Grate-Gate, answering the Entrance to the Garden; beyond which, and without the Territory of our Garden, let there be planted Walks of Trees to adorn the Landskip; Likewise a Bowling-Green and Poddock would be suitable to this higher Ground; and thus at length the Prospect may terminate on Mountains, Woods, or such Views as the Scituation will admit of.

George London (d. 1714)
and Henry Wise (1653–1738)

The Retir'd Gard'ner is a translation and adaptation (to 'render it proper for our English Culture') of two further French treatises by the famous Restoration partners in nursery gardening and landscape design. London started his nurseries at Brompton Park in 1681 and was joined six years later by Wise. The senior partner travelled round the country on horseback, advising clients on planting and securing orders which were dispatched from London to all parts of the kingdom: this professional concern for planting and growing is at the centre of *The Retir'd Gard'ner*, as of their earlier book, published in 1699, an abridgement of Evelyn's 1693 translation of De La Quintinie's *The Compleat Gard'ner* (Plate 54). Wise, who was appointed Master Gardener to Queen Anne, concerned himself also with matters of design and layout. Undoubtedly influenced by his partner's experience of French gardens (London had even been conducted around some of them by Le Nôtre himself and had returned from France with various plans, which Wise inherited in 1714), Wise was responsible for establishing the French taste and adapting it to the royal grounds at Kensington, St James's, Windsor and Hampton and to Chatsworth (see Plate 51). Melbourne in Derbyshire was designed by Wise after the manner of Versailles and Vaux-le-Vicomte, and following the Battle of Blenheim (1704) Wise moved to Woodstock to help Vanbrugh in the design of Marlborough's palace, and his partner prepared for the defeated Marshal Tallard at Nottingham a miniature French garden with *broderies* that recalled the sunflowers of Louis XIV (Plate 55). The extracts illustrate their professional concerns (their Preface advises 'the buying of Trees only of Persons of an establish'd reputation' — like themselves) and their ideas on the parterre, a typical French importation.

from *The Retir'd Gard'ner* (1706)

GARD'NER.

And that you may not be deceiv'd in the Kinds of 'em, you ought to buy 'em of some Nursery-Man you can depend upon, who observe the best Order in their Nurseries, and who, you are sure, will give you the Sorts for which you ask: For it would be very inconvenient, if at any time, you should happen to buy one sort for another, seeing you would thereby lose Three or Four Years in Prospect of Fruit, that fails at last to answer your Expectation. I advise you likewise to take the trouble of buying your Trees your self; and not trust your Servants to do it for you: For I have known several Gentlemen, who have been cheated by so doing; their Servants going to Places, where they bought

54 Engraving from De La Quintinie, trans. John Evelyn,
The Compleat Gard'ner, 1693

ill Plants at low Rates, and reckoning to their Masters the Prices of good. This is what I advise all my Friends to do; and they that follow my Advice, find no Reason to repent of it . . .

GENTLEMAN.

Is there nothing else I am to be inform'd of, in Relation of the Trees of my Plantation?

GARD'NER.

Yes, there is one thing more, no less Important than any of the rest; you ought never to buy your Trees before you are well acquainted with the Nature of the Ground, in which they are to be Set; for instance, if it be properest for Pears grafted upon a Quince, or Free-stock: For in some sort of Grounds the former will never thrive with all your Care, whilst the later flourish to a Miracle; whereas on the other side, in some Soils, a Pear-tree grafted on a Quince-stock, has by much the advantage over one grafted on a Free, which shoots out only Branches for Wood, and bears Fruit but seldom.

'Tis the same thing, *say the* French *Gard'ners*, with the Peach grafted upon a wild Almond, or a Plum: For Example, in a warm light Soil, as likewise in a hearty Soil, inclinable to be Hot, rather than Cold, the Almond-stock does perfectly well, whilst a Peach on a Plum-stock never comes to any thing; the Reason they give, is because the Sap of the Plum is not sufficient in light Soils for the Nourishment of the Graft of the Peach, which shoots forth many Wood-branches; but in a moist heavy Ground, the Peach grafted upon a Plum will thrive beyond Expectation; but if grafted upon an Almond, it will only languish and die away in a little time. *Now we cannot but wonder very much, that a Peach inoculated on a Plum, and planted in a warm light Soil, or in a hearty Soil, inclinable to be rather Hot than Cold, should never come to any thing in* France; *since in* England, *where the Climate is not so warm, we often find the contrary, as many Gentlemen can Witness in their own Plantations: For generally speaking, we find Peaches or Plum-stocks succeed very well in most Places; tho' we own, that in some particular dry, light, barren Soils, Peaches on Almond-stocks are preferable to 'em.*

GENTLEMAN.

After all these Precautions, which I'm resolv'd to observe, I desire your Instructions in the following Case: Suppose I have some Trees sent me in Cases from abroad, and they having been long a coming, I find, when I receive 'em, my Ground lock'd up by a Frost, which makes me unable to plant 'em, what must I do with 'em in the mean time 'till a Thaw comes?

GARD'NER.

There are Two Things to be observ'd; the First is, That upon Receipt of your Trees, which I suppose sent in Cases with Moss laid round the Roots, as they ought always to be, you must keep 'em in a Cellar 'till your Ground is capable of receiving 'em.

In the next Place, *says the Author of* Le Jardinier Solitaire, as soon as the Frost is over, you are to take your Trees out of their Cases, and trim the Roots in the manner I shall explain to you hereafter. After that, you must steep the Roots in Water for a Day, and then set 'em after the manner I shall prescribe to you by and by. I can assure you, that if you observe this Rule you won't lose one of your Trees, tho' they have been out of Ground for Three or Four Months together. *But we have had an Instance to the contrary of this in our Plantation at* Brumpton, *in some Trees which were brought us from* France *in the Year* 1698, *particularly in a Hundred Peach Trees, grafted on Almond Stocks, which were not Three Months out of the Ground; and notwithstanding all requisite Care was taken of 'em, by watering them duly, and skreening them with Mats from the Sun and piercing Winds, yet we could not save Ten Trees out of the whole Hundred. We are therefore surpriz'd at the Story that Author tells us* of a Present he receiv'd, above Twenty Years since, of some *Spanish* Jessamines from *Genoa*, every one as large as his Finger, and which by that time he receiv'd 'em were grown so dry, that they seem'd properer for the Fire than the Garden: However he steep'd 'em in Water for Seven or Eight Days, and after that ventur'd to set 'em in Pots; and assures us that to the best of his Remembrance he did not lose above Two out of a Dozen, and that the rest did shoot up as well as if they never had been dry.

He presumes that the same Care observ'd in Orange Trees would succeed, but says, that having never made any Experiment that way, he can't affirm it for a Truth. *Now to confirm his Opinion about Orange Trees, we have found, by Experience, that they have succeeded very well after they had been Nine Months out of the Ground; but all this depends upon a right and good Management, with a great deal of Attendance and Care . . .*

The PLAN of
M.r Tallard's Garden
att Nottingham

55 Plan of Marshal Tallard's garden from London and Wise,
The Retir'd Gard'ner, 1706

Of the different Situations proper for Parterres.

SEEING all the Designs we form to our selves are nothing but the pure Effects of our Fancy, we should be very often deceiv'd, if by Study and Reflection we did not endeavour to find out Means to render the Execution of them easie, which can no way be better effected, than by having Recourse to the most solid and obvious Rules of Art. For this Reason, I thought, that since my Design was to present the Publick with a general Treatise of the Culture of Flowers, I could not better begin my Book, than with a Discourse on the different Situations requir'd in Parterres, and thereby show, that to have a good Flower-Garden, it is not only necessary to have it well made, but also to pitch upon a proper Place for it.

I pretend not, as several Authors have done, to confine the Lovers of a Garden of this kind to any particular Situation, as being the best and most advantagious; that would be to restrain them too much, in case they had not the good Fortune to light upon just such a Piece of Ground as I should prescribe, without which, according to that Rule, all their Endeavours would be but imperfect.

In Matters of Art, the Mind ought by no means to be check'd; but after a Way is open'd for the entire Knowledge of a Thing, the Execution of it ought to be made as easie as possible.

'Tis true, a Piece of Ground that lyes sloping, and looks towards the rising Sun, is most esteem'd, because the Water runs easier from it, and the Sun at his Rising coming to dart on the Flowers in a Parterre thus situated, so enlivens them, that by means of his Heat on the Morning Dew still remaining upon them, they become much more vigorous in their Growth, than if the Parterre were in another Situation.

This Sloping nevertheless, which is so much esteem'd, is not always necessary, especially in very dry Soils, where the stopping of the Water does rather good than harm; so that in light, sandy, lean Soils, and the like, no Regard is to be had to such a Declivity.

As for Soils that are extreamly wet, this sloping Situation must be had if possible, because the Flowers we commonly cultivate in our Gardens by no means love to have their Roots always in Water. However, if it should be a Man's Lot to have a House situated upon a Flat, I would not have him, for that Reason only, abandon his Design of making a Flower-Garden, since where the Nature of a Place will not allow us all we could wish, Art comes to our Relief, supplying our Wants to that degree, that we may easily have wherewithal to content our Desires, as I hope I shall make appear in the Chapter of Soils.

This sloping Situation is not likewise to be consider'd in relation to stony Soils, which being easily warm'd, not only by the Heat of the Sun, but by means of the Stones retaining that Heat, they can hardly ever have Moisture enough.

Those happy Soils which naturally afford good Productions, how little soever they are cultivated, do very well either with or without this Sloping; for let the Parterre, or Ground-Plot of such a Flower-Garden, be situate where it will, all may succeed in it, providing nothing be omitted to make the Plants grow, but all the Instructions observ'd that I shall prescribe hereafter, for the Improvement of bad Earths.

Some pretend the Vapours which arise from marshy Grounds are pernicious to Flowers, and consequently that a Flower-Garden ought, by no means, to be planted near Marshes: But I am of Opinion this is a needless Scruple, since in many of these Places Flowers may thrive as well as elsewhere, provided no Pains or Care be spar'd to make them do so, and that the Parterre be not plac'd too near a Wood, whose Shade would be apt to hinder it from enjoying the free Air and Sun. Flowers have naturally no Antipathy to Moisture, in case it be not immoderate; on the contrary, it makes them more lively, and last the longer.

As to the Aspects that agree best with Parterres, there are some who would impose Laws upon us concerning them, affirming that a Garden design'd for Flowers will come to little unless it be expos'd to the East, and be shelter'd from the North Winds by a Wall: But Experience teaches us every Day, there are Flower-Gardens in all Aspects which produce excellent Flowers. Thus without troubling his Head any further about preferring one Aspect before another, a Florist may succeed well enough with his Flowers, whatever Exposition his Garden lyes in, provided it be not too much in the Shade; for where the Sun comes but little, or not at all, whatever we plant never thrives well.

'Tis agreed by all, that the South Aspect is not so kindly to Flowers, which are Plants of a tender Constitution, as that of the East, and when a Man is at liberty to chuse his Parterre where he pleases, the latter is preferable to the former; but when one is oblig'd to make use of a Piece of Ground as one finds it, every Situation, as I have said before, may do well enough for cultivating Flowers, especially if what I have order'd in the following Chapter be observ'd.

Roger de Piles (1635–1709)

De Piles was one of the most influential writers of his time on art history and theory. His *Cours de Peinture*, published in Paris, would have been widely known in England among connoisseurs, collectors, and gardenists before the first translation appeared as *The Principles of Painting*. Though the extract here is taken from that translation, which was issued towards the end of the first phase in English landscape gardening, its earlier currency dictates its proper place in the chronology. A serious appraisal of landscape painting as a genre by itself was somewhat unusual in French art criticism then, and further marks de Piles's appeal to the landscape garden movement. His recipes for the painter were readily transferred to the gardenist, as the language and emphases of the English translator in 1743 imply. When de Piles urges the imitation of the masters of landscape painting and when he argues that 'nature should be studied at all times, because she is to be represented in all seasons', he proposes what early gardenists also advocated. His insistence upon variety and upon the imagination of a painter and viewer alike, together with his discussion of temples and altars in landscapes, is in line with early landscaping theories. There is also an intriguing parallel between his division of landscapes into heroic and pastoral and the kinds of gardens that were being created in the mid-eighteenth century: Stowe or Chiswick, comparable with the heroic; Woburn Farm or The Leasowes, with the pastoral.

from *Cours de Peinture par Principes* (1708)
'First Translated into English by a Painter' (1743)

Of Landskip

LANDSKIP is a kind of painting that represents the fields, and all the objects that belong to them. Among all the pleasures which the different talents of painting afford to those who employ them, that of drawing landskips seems to me the most affecting, and most convenient; for, by the great variety, of which it is susceptible, the painter has more opportunities, than in any of the other parts, to please himself by the choice of his objects. The solitude of rocks, freshness of forests, clearness of waters, and their seeming murmurs, extensiveness of plains and offskips [i.e. distant views], mixtures of trees, firmness of verdure, and a fine general scene or opening, make the painter imagine himself either a hunting, or taking the air, or walking, or sitting, and giving himself up to agreeable musings . . .

AMONG the many different styles of landskip, I shall confine my self to two; *the heroick*, and *the pastoral* or *rural*; for all other styles are but mixtures of these.

THE heroick style is a composition of objects, which, in their kinds, draw, both from art and nature, every thing that is great and extraordinary in either. The situations are perfectly agreeable and surprising. The only buildings, are temples, pyramids, antient places of burial, altars consecrated to the divinities, pleasure-houses of regular architecture: And if nature appear not there, as we every day casually see her, she is at least represented as we think she ought to be. This style is an agreeable illusion, and a sort of inchantment, when handled by a man of fine genius, and good understanding, as *Poussin* was, who has so happily expressed it. But if, in the course of this style, the painter has not talent enough to maintain the sublime, he is often in danger of falling into the childish manner.

THE *rural style* is a representation of countries, rather abandoned to the caprice of nature than cultivated: We there see nature simple, without ornament, and without artifice; but with all those graces with which she adorns herself much more, when left to herself, than when constrained by art.

IN this style, situations bear all sorts of varieties: Sometimes they are very extensive and open, to contain the flocks of the shepherds; at others, very wild, for the retreat of solitary persons, and a cover for wild beasts . . .

Of Openings or Situations.

THE word *site*, or situation, signifies the view, prospect or opening of a country: It is derived from the *Italian* word *sito*; and our painters have brought it into use, either because they were used to it in *Italy*, or because, as I think, they found it to be very expressive.

SITUATIONS ought to be well put together, and so disengaged in their make, that the conjunction of grounds may not seem to be obstructed, tho' we should see but a part of them.

SITUATIONS are various, and represented according to the country the painter is thinking of: As, either open or close, mountainous or watery, tilled and inhabited, or wild and lonely; or, in fine, variegated by a prudent mixture of some of these. But if the painter be obliged to imitate nature in a flat and regular country, he must make it agreeable by a good disposition of the *claro-obscuro*, and such pleasing colouring as may make one soil unite with another.

'TIS certain, that extraordinary situations are very pleasing, and chear the imagination by the novelty and beauty of their makes, even when the local colouring is but moderately performed; because, at worst, such pictures are only look'd on as unfinish'd, and wanting to be completed by some skilful hand in colouring: Whereas common situations and objects require good colouring, and absolute finishing, in order to please. It was only by these properties, that *Claud Lorrain* has made amends for his insipid choice in most of his situations. But in whatever manner that part be executed, one of the best ways to make it valuable, and even to multiply and vary it without altering its form, is properly to imagine some ingenious accident in it.

Of Accidents.

AN accident in painting is an obstruction of the sun's light by the interposition of clouds, in such manner, that some parts of the earth shall be in light, and others in shade, which, according to the motion of the clouds, succeed each other, and produce such wonderful effects and changes of the *claro-obscuro*, as seem to create so many new situations. This is daily observed in nature. And as this newness of situations is grounded only on the shapes of the clouds, and their motions, which are very inconstant and unequal, it follows, that these accidents are arbitrary; and a painter of genius may dispose them to his own advantage, when he thinks fit to use them; for he is not absolutely obliged to do it. And there have been some able landskip-painters, who have never practised it, either thro fear or custom; as *Claude Lorrain*, and some others.

Of the Sky and Clouds.

THE sky, in painters terms, is the ethereal part over our heads; but more particularly the air in which we breathe, and that where clouds and storms are ingendered. Its colour is blue, growing clearer as it approaches the earth, because of the interposition of vapours arising between the eye and the horizon; which, being penetrated by the light, communicates it to objects in a greater or less degree, as they are more or less remote.

BUT we must observe, that this light being either yellow or reddish in the evening, at sun-set, these same objects partake not only of the light, but of the colour: Thus the yellow light, mixing with the blue, which is the natural colour of the sky, alters it, and gives it a tint more or less greenish, as the yellowness of the light is more or less deep . . .

IN short, the character of the sky is to be luminous; and, as it is even the source of light, every thing that is upon the earth must yield to it in brightness: If however there is any thing that comes near it in light, it must be waters, and polish'd bodies, which are susceptible of luminous reflexions.

BUT, whilst the painter makes the sky luminous, he must not represent it always shining throughout.

ON the contrary, he must contrive his light so, that the greatest part of it may fall only upon one place; and, to make it more apparent, he must take as much care as possible to put it in opposition to some terrestrial object, that may render it more lively, by its dark colour; as a tree, tower, or some other building, that is a little high.

THIS principal *light* might also be heightened by a certain disposition of clouds having a supposed light, or a light ingeniously inclosed between clouds, whose sweet obscurity spreads itself by little and little, on all hands. We have a great many examples of this in the *Flemish* School, which best understood landskip; as *Paul Bril, Brugel, Saveri*: And the *Sadelers* and

Merian's prints give a clear idea of it, and wonderfully awaken the genius of those who have the principles of the *claro-obscuro*.

Of Off-skips and Mountains.

OFF-SKIPS have a near affinity with the sky; it is the sky which determines either the force or faintness of them: They are darkest when the sky is most loaded, and brightest when it is most clear. They sometimes intermix their shapes and lights; and there are times, and countries, where the clouds pass between the mountains, whose tops rise and appear above them. Mountains that are high, and covered with snow, are very proper to produce extraordinary effects in the off-skip, which are advantageous to the painter, and pleasing to the spectator.

THE disposition of off-skips is arbitrary; let them only agree with the *whole together* of the picture, and the nature of the country we would represent. They are usually blue, because of the interposition of air between them and the eye: But they lose this colour by degrees, as they come nearer the eye, and so take that which is natural to the objects.

IN distancing mountains, we must observe to join them insensibly by the *roundings off*, which the reflections make probable; and must, among other things, avoid a certain edginess in their extremities, which makes them appear in slices, as if cut with scissors, and stuck upon the cloth.

WE must further observe, that the air, at the feet of mountains, being charged with vapours, is more susceptible of light than at their tops. In this case, I suppose the main light to be set reasonably high, and to enlighten the mountains equally, or that the clouds deprive them of the light of the sun. But if we suppose the main light to be very low, and to strike the mountains; then their tops will be strongly enlighten'd, as well as every thing else in the same degree of light.

THO' the forms of things diminish in bigness, and colours lose their strength, in proportion as they recede from the first plan of the picture, to the most remote off-skip; as we observe in nature and common practice; yet this does not exclude the use of the accidents. These contribute greatly to the wonderful in landskip, when they are properly introduced, and when the artist has a just idea of their good effects.

Of Verdure, or Turfing.

I CALL turfing, the greenness with which the herbs colour the ground: This is done several ways; and the diversity proceeds not only from the nature of plants, which, for the most part, have their particular verdures, but also from the change of seasons, and the colour of the earth, when the herbs are but thin sown. By this variety, a painter may chuse or unite, in the same tract of land, several sorts of greens intermixed and blended together, which are often of great service to those who know how to use them; because this diversity of greens, as it is often found in nature, gives a character of truth to those parts, where it is properly used. There is a wonderful example of this part of landskip, in the view of *Mechlin*, by *Rubens*.

Of Rocks.

THOUGH rocks have all sorts of shapes, and participate of all colours, yet there are, in their diversity, certain characters which cannot be well expressed without having recourse to nature. Some are in banks, and set off with beds of shrubs; others in huge blocks, either projecting or falling back; others consist of large broken parts, contiguous to each other; and others, in short, of an enormous size, all in one stone, either naturally, as free-stone, or else through the injuries of time, which in the course of many ages has worn away their marks of separation. But, whatever their form be, they are usually set out with clefts, breaks, hollows, bushes, moss, and the stains of time; and these particulars, well managed, create a certain idea of truth.

ROCKS are of themselves gloomy, and only proper for solitudes; but, where accompanied with bushes, they inspire a fresh air; and, when they have waters, either proceeding from, or washing them, they give an infinite pleasure, and seem to have a soul which animates them, and makes them sociable.

Of Grounds or Lands.

A GROUND or land, in painters terms, is a certain distinct piece of land, which is neither too woody nor hilly. Grounds contribute, more than any thing, to the gradation and distancing of landskip; because they follow one another, either in shape, or in the *claro-obscuro*, or in their variety of colouring, or by some insensible conjunction of one to another.

MULTIPLICITY of grounds, though it be often contrary to grand manner, does not quite destroy it; for, besides the extent of country which it exhibits, 'tis susceptible of the accidents we have mentioned, and which, with good management, have a fine effect.

THERE is one nicety to be observed in grounds, which is, that in order to characterize them well, care must be taken, that the trees in them have a different verdure and different colours from those grounds; though this difference, withal, must not be too apparent.

Of Terraces.

A TERRACE, in painting, is a piece of ground, either quite naked, or having very little herbage, like great roads and places often frequented. They are of use chiefly in the foregrounds of a picture, where they ought to be very spacious and open, and accompanied, if we think fit, with some accidental verdure, and also with some stones, which, if placed with judgment, give a terrace a greater air of probability.

Of Buildings.

PAINTERS mean by buildings any structures they generally represent, but chiefly such as are of a regular architecture, or at least are most conspicuous. Thus building is not so proper a name for the houses of country-people, or the cottages of shepherds, which are introduced into the rural taste, as for regular and showy edifices, which are always brought into the heroick.

BUILDINGS in general are a great ornament in landskip, even when they are *Gothick*, or appear partly inhabited, and partly ruinous: they raise the imagination by the use they are thought to be designed for; as appears from antient towers, which seem to have been the habitations of fairies, and are now retreats for shepherds and owls.

POUSSIN has very elegantly handled the *Roman* manner of architecture in his works, as *Bourdon* has done the *Gothick*; which, however *Gothick*, fails not to give a sublime air to his landskips. *Little Bernard* has introduced into his sacred story, what I may call a *Babylonian* manner; which, extraordinary as it is, has its grandeur and magnificence. I would not quite reject such pieces of architecture; they raise the imagination, and I am persuaded, they would succeed in the heroick style, if they were placed among half-distant objects, and if we knew how to use them properly.

Of Waters.

MUCH of the spirit of landskip is owing to the waters which are introduced in it. They appear in divers manners; sometimes impetuous, as when a storm makes them overflow their banks; at other times rebounding, as by the fall of a rock; at other times through unusual pressure, gushing out and dividing into an infinity of silver streams, whose motion and murmuring agreeably deceive both the eye and ear; at other times calm and purling in a sandy bed; at other times so still and standing, as to become a faithful looking-glass, which doubles all the objects that are opposite to it; and, in this state, they have more life than in the most violent agitation . . .

WATERS are not proper for every situation: But, to express them well, the artist ought to be perfect master of the exactness of watry reflexions; because they only make painted water appear as real: For practice alone, without exactness, destroys the effect, and abates of the pleasure of the eye. The rule for these reflexions is very easy, and therefore the painter is the less pardonable for neglecting it.

BUT it must be observed, that tho' water be as a looking-glass, yet it does not faithfully represent objects, but when 'tis still; for if it be in any motion, either in a natural course, or by the driving of the wind, its surface, becoming uneven, receives, on its surges, such lights and shades, as, mixing with the appearance of the objects, confound both their shapes and colours.

Of the Foreground of a Picture.

AS it is the part of the foreground to usher the eye into the piece, great care must be taken, that the eye meet with good reception; sometimes by the opening of a fine terrace, whose design and workmanship may be equally curious; at other times, by variety of well distinguished plants, and those sometimes flowered; at other times, by figures in a lively taste, or other objects, either admirable for their novelty, or introduced, as by chance.

IN a word, the artist cannot too much study his foreground objects, since they attract the eye, impress the first character of truth, and greatly contribute to make the artifice of a picture successful, and to anticipate our esteem for the whole work.

I AM sensible, that there are very fine landskips, with foregrounds, appearing to be well chosen, and carrying a great idea, but which are, nevertheless, very slightly finished: I own, indeed, that this slightness ought to be pardoned, when it is ingenious, when it suits with the nature of the ground, and bears the character of truth: But it must be owned likewise, that this effect is very rare, and that it is to be feared, lest this slight working should give some idea of poverty, or of too great negligence: So that in whatever manner the foregrounds of a picture be disposed, I would have the artist prescribe it as a law to himself, to finish them with skill, and accurate workmanship . . .

Of Figures.

IN composing landskip, the artist may have intended to give it a character agreeable to the subject he has chosen, and which his figures ought to represent. He may also, and it commonly happens, have only thought of his figures, after finishing his landskip: The truth is, the figures, in most landskips, are made rather to accompany than to suit them.

I KNOW there are landskips so disposed and situated, as to require only passing figures; which several good masters, each in his style, have introduced, as *Poussin* in the heroick, and *Fouquier* in the rural, with all possible probability and grace: I know also, that resting figures have been made to appear inwardly active. And these two different ways of treating figures are not to be blamed, because they act equally, though in a different manner. It is rather inaction that ought to be blamed in figures; for in this condition, which robs them of all connexion with the landskip, they appear to be pasted on. But, without obstructing the painter's liberty in this respect, I am persuaded, that the best way to make figures valuable is, to make them so to agree with the character of the landskip, that it may seem to have been made purely for the figures. I would not have them either insipid or indifferent, but to represent some little subject to awaken the spectator's attention, or else to give the picture a name of distinction among the curious.

John Vanbrugh (1664–1726)

This dramatist and architect was an important agent in the development of the landscape garden, and the idea floated in his letter on the old manor at Blenheim, a crucial item in his contribution. Vanbrugh's work in such early gardens as Castle Howard, Stowe, Claremont in Surrey, or Eastbury in Dorset was largely to design buildings in the landscape: but their very positioning — the Temple of the Four Winds at Castle Howard, the 'singularly romantick' and pseudo-mediaeval belvedere at Claremont — suggests a distinctly imaginative conception of setting. And this is supported by his plea for the retention of the old ruined manor house at Blenheim (Plate 56). His letter contains three major points of interest: his concern for associationism, for shaping and controlling the ideas of visitors to a garden; the emphasis upon assisting nature in order to augment its variety; the argument from painting to support his proposals for the inclusion of Woodstock Manor in the design of the park. Not only does he enclose a sketch of his proposal (sadly lost), but he claims that the proposed design would resemble what the 'best of Landskip Painters can invent'. Unfortunately, his recommendation was turned down and the letter survives with a dictated note by the Duchess of Marlborough: 'This paper has something ridiculous in it to preserve the house for himself, ordered to be pulled down; but I think there is something material in it concerning the occasion of building Blenheim.' Our text is taken from the Nonesuch Press edition of Vanbrugh's letters, published in 1928.

56 Woodstock Manor, Blenheim, Oxfordshire. Drawing of 1714,
artist unknown

'Reasons Offer'd for Preserving some Part of the Old Manor' at Blenheim (11 June 1709)

There is perhaps no one thing, which the most Polite part of Mankind have more universally agreed in; than the Vallue they have ever set upon the Remains of distant Times Nor amongst the Severall kinds of those Antiquitys, are there any so much regarded, as those of Buildings; Some for their Magnificence, or Curious Workmanship; And others; as they move more lively and pleasing Reflections (than History without their Aid can do) On the Persons who have Inhabited them; On the Remarkable things which have been transacted in them, Or the extraordinary Occasions of Erecting them. *As I believe it cannot be doubted, but if Travellers many Ages hence, shall be shewn The Very House in which so great a Man Dwelt, as they will then read the Duke of Marlborough in Story; And that they Shall be told, it was not only his Favourite Habitation, but was Erected for him by the Bounty of the Queen And with the Approbation of the People, As a Monument of the Greatest Services and Honours, that any Subject had ever done his Country: I believe, tho' they may not find Art enough in the* Builder, to make them *Admire the Beauty of the Fabrick* they will find Wonder enough in the Story, to make 'em pleas'd with the Sight of it.

I hope I may be forgiven, if I make some faint Application of what I say of Blenheim, to the Small Remains of ancient Woodstock Manour.

It can't indeed be said, it was Erected on so Noble nor on So justifiable an Occasion, But it was rais'd by One of the Bravest and most Warlike of the English Kings; And tho' it has not been Fam'd, as a Monument of his Arms, *it has been tenderly regarded* as the Scene of his Affections. Nor amongst the *Multitude of People who come daily to View what is raising to the Memory of the Great Battle of Blenheim; Are there any that do not run eagerly to See* what Ancient Remains are to be found. of Rosamonds Bower. *It may perhaps be worth some Little Reflection Upon what may be said, if the Very footsteps of it Are no more to be found.*

But if the Historicall Argument Stands in need of Assistance; there is Still much to be said on Other Considerations.

That Part of the Park which is Seen from the North Front of the New Building, has Little Variety of Objects Nor dos the Country beyond it Afford any of Vallue, It therefore Stands in Need of all the helps that can be given, which are only Five; Buildings, And Plantations[.] These rightly dispos'd will indeed Supply all the wants of Nature in that Place. And the Most Agreable Disposition is to Mix them: in which this Old Manour *gives so happy an Occasion* for; that were the inclosure filld with Trees (principally Fine Yews and Hollys) Promiscuously Set to grow up in a Wild Thicket. So that all the Building left, (which is only the Habitable Part and the Chappel) might Appear in Two Risings amongst 'em, it wou'd make One of the Most Agreable Objects that the best of Landskip Painters can invent. And if on the Contrary this Building is taken away; there then remains nothing but an Irregular, Ragged Ungovernable Hill, the deformitys of which are not to be cured *but by a Vast Expence; And that at last will only remove an Ill Object* but not produce a good One, whereas to finish the present Wall for the Inclosures, to forme the Sloops and make the Plantation (which is all that is now wanting to Compleat the Whole Designe) wou'd not Cost Two Hundred pounds.

I take the Liberty to offer this Paper with a Picture to Explain what I endeavour to Describe, That if the Present Direction for destroying the Building, shou'd happen hereafter to be Repented of, I may not be blam'd for Neglecting to set in the truest Light I cou'd, a Thing that Seem'd at least to me so very Matteriall.

Anthony Ashley Cooper, 3rd Earl of Shaftesbury (1671–1713)

Shaftesbury was one of the most influential writers of the Enlightenment, and his ideas and habits of thought may be tracked through the works of most English writers of the eighteenth century. At the centre of his doctrines was what he himself called *enthusiasm*, a state of enhanced spirituality, fullness of being and intense sympathy for all that is true, good and beautiful. The following are extracts from his life-work, *Characteristicks of Men, Manners, Opinions, Times*, in its first edition in three volumes of 1711. The first, from *The Moralists* (first issued in 1709 and later gathered into *Characteristicks*), features Theocles, the spokesman of Shaftesbury's enthusiasm, glorifying the world of nature unmediated by artificial controls (see Plate 57), and the response to this of the sceptical Philocles, who is nevertheless much moved. (On the encounter between an enthusiast's genius and the *genius loci* or spirit of place, a crucial item in landscapist philosophy, see the essay by Geoffrey Hartman in the list of further critical reading.) The second extract, from a long footnote in *Miscellaneous Reflections*, contained in the third volume of *Characteristicks*, offers a complementary passage of ironical attack on the pursuit of beauty and order, as Shaftesbury says, in 'outward things' only; significantly it chooses the French style of gardening to illustrate its point.

from *The Moralists* (1709)

"YE Fields and Woods, my Refuge from the toilsom World of Business, "receive me in your quiet Sanctuarys, and favour my Retreat and thoughtful "Solitude. — Ye verdant Plains, how gladly I salute ye! — Hail all ye "blissful Mansions! Known Seats! Delightful Prospects! Majestick Beautys "of this Earth, and all ye Rural Powers and Graces! — Bless'd be ye chast "Abodes of happiest Mortals, who here in peaceful Innocence enjoy a Life "unenvy'd, tho Divine; whilst with its bless'd Tranquillity it affords a "happy Leisure and Retreat for Man; who, made for Contemplation, and to "search his own and other Natures, may here best meditate the Cause of "Things; and plac'd amidst the various Scenes of Nature, may nearer view "her Works.

"O GLORIOUS *Nature!* supremely Fair, and sovereignly Good! All-"loving and All-lovely, All-divine! Whose Looks are so becoming, and of "such infinite Grace; whose Study brings such Wisdom, and whose Contem-"plation such Delight; whose every single Work affords an ampler Scene, and "is a nobler Spectacle than all that ever Art presented! — O mighty *Nature!*

"Wise Substitute of *Providence!* impower'd *Creatress!* Or Thou impowering
"DEITY, Supreme Creator! Thee I invoke, and Thee alone adore. To thee
"this Solitude, this Place, these Rural Meditations are sacred; whilst thus
"inspir'd with Harmony of Thought, tho unconfin'd by Words, and in loose
"Numbers, I sing of Nature's Order in created Beings, and celebrate the
"Beautys which resolve in Thee, the Source and Principle of all Beauty and
"Perfection . . .

"The Wildness pleases. We seem to live alone with Nature. We view her
"in her inmost Recesses, and contemplate her with more Delight in these
"original Wilds, than in the artificial Labyrinths and feign'd Wildernesses of
"the Palace . . .

" — See! with what trembling Steps poor Mankind tread the narrow
"Brink of the deep Precipices! From whence with giddy Horrour they look
"down, mistrusting even the Ground which bears 'em; whilst they hear the
"hollow Sound of Torrents underneath, and see the Ruin of the impending
"Rock; with falling Trees which hang with their Roots upwards, and seem to
"draw more Ruin after 'em. Here thoughtless Men, seiz'd with the Newness
"of such Objects, become thoughtful, and willingly contemplate the incessant
"Changes of this Earth's Surface. They see, as in one instant, the Revolutions
"of past Ages, the fleeting Forms of Things, and the Decay even of this our
"*Globe*; whose Youth and first Formation they consider, whilst the apparent
"Spoil and irreparable Breaches of the wasted Mountain shew them the
"World it-self only as a noble Ruin, and make them think of its approaching
"Period. — But here mid-way the *Mountain*, a spacious Border of thick
"Wood harbours our weary'd Travellers: who now are come among the
"ever-green and lofty Pines, the Firs, and noble Cedars, whose towring
"Heads seem endless in the Sky; the rest of Trees appearing only as Shrubs
"beside them. And here a different Horrour seizes our shelter'd Travellers,

57 Hercules Seghers, landscape, *c.* 1620

"when they see the Day diminish'd by the deep Shades of the vast Wood;
"which closing thick above, spreads Darkness and eternal Night below. The
"faint and gloomy Light looks horrid as the Shade it-self: and the profound
"Stillness of these Places imposes Silence upon Men, struck with the hoarse
"Ecchoings of every Sound within the spacious Caverns of the Wood. Here
"*Space* astonishes. *Silence* it-self seems pregnant; whilst an unknown
"Force works on the Mind, and dubious Objects move the wakeful Sense.
"Mysterious *Voices* are either heard or fancy'd: and various Forms of
"*Deity* seem to present themselves, and appear more manifest in these
"sacred Sylvan Scenes; such as of old gave rise to Temples, and favour'd the
"Religion of the antient World . . ."

"... Your *Genius*, the *Genius* of the Place, and the GREAT GENIUS have
"at last prevail'd. I shall no longer resist the Passion growing in me for
"Things of a *natural* kind; where neither *Art*, nor the *Conceit* or *Caprice*
"of Man has spoil'd their *genuine Order*, by breaking in upon that
"*primitive State*. Even the rude *Rocks*, the mossy *Caverns*, the irregular
"unwrought *Grotto's*, and broken *Falls* of Waters, with all the horrid Graces
"of the *Wilderness* it-self, as representing NATURE more, will be the more
"engaging, and appear with a Magnificence beyond the formal Mockery of
"Princely Gardens. — But tell me, I intreat you, how comes it That, except-
"ing a few *Philosophers* of your sort, the only People who are enamour'd in
"this way, and seek the *Woods*, the *Rivers*, or *Sea-shores*, are your poor
"vulgar LOVERS?"

from *Miscellaneous Reflections* (1711)

How fares it with our *Princely Genius*, our *Grandee* who assembles all these
Beautys, and within the Bounds of his sumptuous Palace incloses all these
Graces of a thousand kinds? — What Pains! What Study! Science! —
Behold the Disposition and Order of these finer sorts of Apartments, Gar-
dens, *Villa's!* — The kind of Harmony to the Eye, from the various Shapes
and Colours agreeably mixt, and rang'd in Lines, intercrossing without
confusion, and fortunately co-incident. — A *Parterre*, Cypress's, Groves,
Wildernesses. — Statues, here and there, of *Virtue, Fortitude, Temperance*. —
Hero's-Busts, *Philosophers*-Heads; with sutable Motto's and Inscriptions. —
Solemn Representations of things deeply natural. — *Caves, Grotto's, Rocks*.
— *Urns* and *Obelisks* in retir'd places, and dispos'd at proper distances and
points of Sight: with all those Symmetrys which silently express a reigning
Order, Peace, Harmony, and *Beauty!* — But what is there answerable to this,
in the MINDS of *the Possessors*? — What *Possession* or *Propriety* is theirs?
What *Constancy* or *Security* of Enjoyment? What *Peace*, what *Harmony*
WITHIN?

A. J. Dézallier D'Argenville (1680–1765)

D'Argenville's *La Théorie et la Pratique du Jardinage*, published anonymously in Paris in 1709, provides the most comprehensive statement of French formal gardening as it existed in the years immediately following the death of Le Nôtre in 1700. There had been earlier books on the Cartesian garden, or *le jardin de l'intelligence*, notably Jacques Boyceau de la Barauderie's *Le Traité du Jardinage* (1638), André Mollet's *Le Jardin de Plaisir* (1651), and Claude Mollet the Elder's *Théâtre des Plans et Jardinages* (1652). D'Argenville's treatise was enormously popular and the English translation by John James of Greenwich testifies to the high regard that the French style of gardening continued to enjoy in England. It provides a sure and lucid exposition of the basis of that style; debts to Italian garden design are obvious, but the resolutely geometrical temper of D'Argenville's proposals is characteristically French, as is his insistence on redressing the imperfections of the ground. Yet it should be noticed that variety and respect for 'the Situation of the Place' appear as important here as to Pope and the later English landscapists. Above all, we have here the first advocacy in garden literature of the use of the ha-ha, the motif which made the English landscape garden possible. Only the first of the plates referred to in the text is reproduced (Plate 58): the others are cadenzas or variations upon the theme.

from *The Theory and Practice of Gardening*,
translated by John James (1712)

TO make a complete Disposition and Distribution of a general Plan, Respect must be had to the Situation of the Ground: For the greatest Skill in the right ordering of a Garden is, throughly to understand, and consider the natural Advantages and Defects of the Place; to make use of the one, and to redress the other: Situations differing in every Garden.

THE Variety and Diversity of the Composition contributes no less to complete a Garden, than the most discreet and well-contriv'd Distribution; since, in the Opinion of every one, the Gardens that afford the greatest Variety, are the most valuable and magnificent.

'TIS, therefore, the great Business of an Architect, or Designer of Gardens, when he contrives a handsome Plan, with his utmost Art and good OEconomy to improve the natural Advantages, and to redress the Imperfections, Shelvings, and Inequalities of the Ground. With these Precautions he should guide and restrain the Impetuosity of his Genius, never swerving from

58 Plate from A. J. Dézallier D'Argenville, trans. James, *The Theory and Practice of Gardening*, 1712

Reason, but constantly submitting, and conforming himself to that which suits best with the natural Situation of the Place.

THIS is no such easy Task, as some imagine, a fine Garden being no less difficult to contrive and order well, than a good Building; and that which makes a great many Architects, and such as take upon them to give Designs of Gardening, often miscarry, is, that most of them form Designs in the Air, no way proper for the Situation of the Place, and at best but stoln, and pick'd here and there from others . . .

THE first Plate presents you with one of the noblest and most magnificent Designs that can be: It is made for a flat Ground, of about 50 or 60 Acres Extent. A great Avenue is supposed to lead to the Grill, or Gate of the Outer-Court, separated by the Walls of the two Bass-Courts, upon the Wings, which are environed with very regular Buildings, serving on one Side for

Stables, *Menagery*, Stalls for Cattle; Granarys, Barns, and other Convenien-
cies required in a Bass-Court; and on the other Side, for Lodging-Rooms for
Servants, and a long Green-house fronting the Orangery. This Fore-Court
leads you into the Castle-Court, which is parted from the other only by a wet
Mote. The Building consists of a large double Pavilion in the Middle, with
Sides stretching each way to two Pavilions at the Ends; in Front of which are
two small Terrasses, from which you discover on the Left a Parterre of
Compartment, and above it a Grass-work, encompassed with Cases and
Yews, with Water-works in the Middle. Beyond is a large Kitchen-Garden
walled in, which contains two Squares, each having four Quarters, with
Basons. It is terminated by a long Arbour, with three Cabinets facing the
Walks and Pavilions. On the Right are Green-Plots cut, to answer the Walks,
having Water-works, as on the other Side. These are bounded by a double
Line of Cases and Yews, and behind, by green Niches for Seats and Figures.
On the Side is a Parterre of Orange-Trees walled in, having Iron Grills
against the Walks; and at the End is a Bason, with Cabinets and green
Niches for Seats.

THE Entrance of the great Garden is by the Descent of Steps from the
Building, where you have a large Cross-walk, terminated by Grills of Iron;
and another great double Walk, which runs from one End of the Garden to
the other, as do those two also by the Walls which inclose the Ground.
Immediately under your Eye, are four Pieces of Parterre, two of Embroidery,
and two of Compartment, with Basons in the midst. These are accompanied
by two open Groves, adorned with Bowling-greens; and beyond them is
another large Cross-walk of Yews, in the Middle of which is the great Bason.
The Head of this Parterre is composed of four small Grass-Plots, with
Edgings of Box and Yews; and above is a Half-Moon of Palisades, whose
circular Walks run through that which divides the four great Quarters of the
Parterre before the House. This Half-Moon is parted into a Goose-foot, and
its Alleys are very fine, leading you to other Basons and Cabinets quite
different. Between each Alley, it is set out with Niches for Figures, which
makes a beautiful Ornament every way. The Groves are accompanied with
two Quincunces, set off with Cabinets, and a Hall in the Middle, with Figures.
There is also a Cross-walk made by the Palisades and Trees of the Groves,
where there are two Basons, whose Spouts are in a Line with the great ones of
the Middle Walk. Beyond are four Groves, cut like St. *Andrew's* Cross, all
different. The two upon the Right of the great Walk, contain a Hall adorned
with Seats and Figures, with a Bowling-green, and another Hall with Benches
of Earth, which may serve for an Amphitheater, or Theater for playing
Comedies. In the two on the Left, there is an Oval Hall, with a Bowling-
green, different from the other, and a little Hall of Fountains, contrived in the
four Middles, without interrupting the Line. All these Works appear very
magnificent when executed, being divided by Alleys, that range with those of
the upper and lower Parts of the Garden, either in their Square Lines or
Diagonals, which makes the Views and Glades of a very great Length.

BEYOND these Groves is a large Canal, reaching the whole Breadth of the
Garden; in the midst of which is a Group of Figures, as *Neptune* with *Tritons*

throwing one great Spout, and many lesser every way. At each End of this Canal, the Walls are opened, with wet Ditches, to preserve the Prospect. Farther on are two large Woods of high Trees cut into a Star, the Alleys of which are double, and planted with Trees that stand detached. In the middle of these Woods are two different Isles with Figures and Yews. At the End of the great Walk, and beyond these Woods, you meet with a low Terrass-Wall, from whence you have a View of the Country round about; a wet Ditch runs the whole Length of this Wall; and in the Front of the Half-Moon, at the End of the great Walk, is made a Cascade, which has three Mask-heads, and a Sheet of Water, that falls again into a Water-work of two Jets, the Water of which comes from the Canal, and supplies all the Ditch without the Garden. A Termination of this Kind is certainly the most magnificent that can be; and, without enlarging farther upon the fine Lines and Views from one End of the Garden to the other, and the Convenience of the Parts, together with what is to be found in the several Alleys, Figures, Fountains, Openings, Grills, and the like, it must be acknowledged this Design is sufficient to satisfy any one in its Disposition, Variety, Ornaments, and Distribution of the Water.

THE second Plate gives the Idea of a Garden, in its Kind not much inferior to the other, but nothing near so large, containing no more than 25 Acres: It is seated in a Ground divided into Terrasses that face the Building, which is here supposed to be planted in the midst of a Park, or Country, where the Lines of the Walks are continued quite through the Woods and Fields. You enter into a handsome Fore-Court with Grass-Plots, and a Fence of Wood, which on the Left leads to a large Kitchen-Garden, parted into six Squares, with a Bason; and on the Right into a Bass-Court, surrounded with Buildings; from whence you pass into another Court, where is a Wat'ring-Place, and a Dove-House, with other Conveniencies; you enter this Court likewise from the Fields, and it serves as a Store-Yard to the Bass-Court. Above is a Parterre of Orange-Trees with a Bason, terminated by an Arbor of Lattice-Work in a circular Form, adorn'd with three Cabinets, behind which is contrived a very curious small Grove. At the End of the Fore-Court you find a great Court, bounded by Galleries, Pavilions, and a long Range of Building at the Bottom, which renders the whole very regular.

YOU go down Steps to the Gardens, which present you first of all with a great Terrass, laid quite open for the Sake of the Prospect, and filled with two Pieces of Parterre of Embroider'd-Work, with Counter-Borders, accompanied with Bowling-greens, the Bottoms of which are enriched with Cut-work in Grass. On the other Side are two Heads of Water, which are Conservatories for the Fountains at the lower End of the Garden. You descend from this Terrass at each End, and in the Front of the middle Walk, by great Stairs made Horse-shoo-Fashion, ornamented with three small Jets, which are level with the first Terrass, and throw a Sheet of Water into the Bason below. On the second Terrass you find four Groves, two of which are open in Compartments, and the other two are planted in Quincunce, or Squares, which do not interrupt the Prospect. The Designs of them are very curious, and they are set off with Basons and Figures. The great Walk in the Middle, and the others, are continued, and planted with Yews, and Trees that stand detached. There is a great Bason with Water-works facing the Middle-Walk, and a Cross-Walk, planted with Horse-Chestnuts beyond the Groves. The Alley round this Bason makes the Terrass advance in a circular Form, where are two Flights of Stairs with Steps, Rests and Landings against the Goose-Foot, which is cut in the Wood of Forest-Trees below, and forms a Half-Moon of Horn-beam, adorn'd with Figures in Niches. You go down likewise by Steps, which lie at each End of this Terrass.

THE two Flights of great Stairs in the Middle inclose a Bason with Water-Spouts, which fall into another, where there are four Jets that throw a Sheet of Water into a Bason below, which makes the Head of a Cascade that runs into the great Canal at the Bottom. All this Water runs along little Channels, and falls foaming into Basons, where there are Water-Spouts: On the Side of these Channels are small Stands of Water, which are continu'd to the very lower End, as well as the Basons and Spouts of this Cascade; all which discharge their Water into the Canal, out of the Middle whereof rises a very large Jet d'eau. There may be small Boats to go upon this Canal, and it serves likewise for an Inclosure, and to separate the Park and Garden. The Forest-Wood that accompanies this Cascade is cut with diagonal Walks, and a large circular one, where you find Cross-Paths and Green-Plots. The Diagonals lead you by Alleys that return Square into four Cabinets all different. In the two upon the Right you have a great Circle, environ'd with a Palisade cut into Arcades, with an octangular Bowling-green in the Middle, and a long Hall, with Niches cut for Figures, and two Sinkings for Shells and Buffets of Water: In the Middle is a Grass-work after the *English* Manner, encompassed with a Flower-Border. The two Groves on the Left consist of a green Hall, with a Row of Trees that stand detached, and a close Walk in Cants, formed by plashing the Trees into a natural Arbor; the Middle is filled with a Bowling-green set out with Yews. 'Tis to be observ'd, that the Level of the Walks of these Groves ought to be kept to that of the great Walk in the middle, and of those on the Sides, which is supposed to be a gentle Sloping, by reason of the Cascade.

THE general Disposition of the third Plate describes a Garden situated on the Rising of a Hill, whose Terrasses are upon the Side, to distinguish it from the foregoing Design, where they are in Front. The Building here is very plain, and has no Out-Courts, which makes this Design less expensive to execute than the others. The Court has two Pavilions, with a large Grill between them, and a Bass-Court surrounded with Buildings, where there is a Dove-House and Watering-Place: Behind the Bass-Court are four Squares of Kitchen-Garden, with a Bason in the Middle. On the other Side of the Court is a small Terrass, which ranges with the Left Pavilion at the Entrance and the Corner of the House, and leads you along by the Court into the Garden. In Front of the House, you find upon a long Terrass six Quarters of Parterre, with a large Alley in the Middle, and one on each Side, with Cross Alleys to divide the Quarters; two of which are of Embroidery, two of Compartment, with a great Bason in the Middle; and the two others after the *English* Manner, surrounded with a Border cut, and garnished with Flowers, Yews, and Shrubs. The End of this Terrass is terminated by an Opening, which the

French call a *Claire-voïe*, or an Ah, Ah, with a dry Ditch at the Foot of it. From this Terrass you go up Steps at each End, and against the Bason, to a higher Terrass, where you have a large Wood-work cut into a Star, with a circular Alley, and eight Cross-ways; in the Middle is a Water-work, with a Jet d'eau, which serves for a Reservoir, or Conservatory, for the other Bason below; on the Side is a green Gallery, compassed about with Standards and Grass-Plots with Figures. This Gallery is accompanied with a large double Walk, and a Green-Plot in the Middle, which leads to the House.

As to the Gardens below, you go down from the Terrass before the House by two Descents of Steps, which bring you on another Terrass, that has two Bowling-greens with Oval Basons, an open Grove in Compartment, and a Quincunce; all of them set out with Figures and Green-Plots, and divided by Alleys, answering those of the upper Terrasses. This Terrass is supported by a Slope of Grass, in which are three several Descents to another Terrass, half of which is taken up by a Canal, or large Square of Water, with a Jet in the Middle of it. The rest is a Wood-work, planted in a very handsome Compartiment: This Terrass is sustained, as the other, by a Slope of Grass, with a Ditch at the Foot of it, which lies without the Garden. These four Terrasses are bordered with Yews, Cases, and Flowering-Shrubs; and are set off with many other Ornaments, as may be easily conceived, without farther Explication . . .

THE Ends and Extremities of a Park are beautified with Pavilions of Masonry, which the *French* call *Belvederes*, or Pavilions of *Aurora*, which are as pleasant to rest ones self in, after a long Walk, as they are to the Eye, for the handsome Prospect they yield; they serve also to retire into for Shelter when it rains. The Word *Belvedere* is *Italian*, and signifies a beauteous Prospect, which is properly given to these Pavilions; for that being always built upon some Eminence, they open and command the Country round about.

PERSPECTIVE Works and Grottos are now but little in use; especially Grottos, which are very subject to Ruin. They are commonly made at the End of Walks, and under Terrasses. As to Perspectives, they are of use to cover the Walls of Gable-ends, and such Walls as terminate Alleys that can be pierced no farther. They make a handsome Decoration enough, and their fallacious Openings are very surprizing. They are painted either in Oil, or in Fresco; and are secured above by a small Roof, which throws off the Rain-Water that would otherwise run along the Wall, and entirely spoil the Painting.

GRILLS of Iron are very necessary Ornaments in the Lines of Walks, to extend the View, and to shew the Country to Advantage. At present we frequently make Thorough-Views, call'd *Ah, Ah*, which are Openings in the Walls, without Grills, to the very Level of the Walks, with a large and deep Ditch at the Foot of them, lined on both Sides to sustain the Earth, and prevent the getting over, which surprizes the Eye upon coming near it, and makes one cry, *Ah! Ah!* from whence it take its Name. This Sort of Opening is, on some Occasions, to be preferred, for that it does not shut up the Prospect, as the Bars of a Grill do . . .

SEATS, or Benches, besides the Conveniency they constantly afford in great Gardens, where you can scarce ever have too many, there is such need of them in walking, look very well also in a Garden, when set in certain Places they are destin'd to, as in the Niches or Sinkings that face principal Walks and Vistas, and in the Halls and Galleries of Groves: They are made either of Marble, Free-stone, or Wood, which last are most common; and of these there are two Kinds, the Seats with Backs to them, which are the handsomest, and are usually removed in Winter; and the plain Benches, which are fixed to their Place in the Ground.

John Lawrence (d. 1732)

The following passage comes from the third chapter of Lawrence's *The Clergy-Man's Recreation*, 'Concerning the most agreeable Disposition of a GARDEN'. His preference for geometrical planning ('figures') does not prevent his advocacy of 'an irregular piece of Ground'. This open-mindedness, together with his emphasis on the surprises to be found while exploring gardens and their impact on the imagination ('Fancy'), makes him typical of writers in whose work we may see the beginnings of a taste for less ordered sites. He inclines towards the landscapists in recommending that an owner respect the ground as he finds it and not force patterns upon it. This is further supported by his suggestion that a man's land be arranged to his own taste and fancy rather than submit to *a priori* schemes, often of a more grandiloquent (and expensive) scope than would be apt for modest estates. Yet his description of 'a little wilderness' is reminiscent of that contrived by London and Wise in an old gravel pit in Kensington Gardens (Plate 59), which became famous for its ingenious and orderly conversion of 'a common pit' into 'several little Plantations' (as even Addison praises it in *The Spectator*, No. 477).

from *The Clergy-Recreation* (1714)

My purpose is not to give you all the varieties of Platforms, not to lay out great Designs. Every one may easily please himself in a Form that strikes most his own Fancy in so small a piece of Ground as I suppose a Garden need contain: Only, it may be, I may happen to give some useful Hints to those who are desirous to hear what others can say to direct their own Fancies.

I would say then, that if I were to chuse a Figure, that could be as cheap and as easily had as another, it should be a Square, or rather an Oblong-square, leading from the middle of my House; a Gravel-Walk in the middle, with narrow Borders of Grass on each side for Winter-use, and on each side of them Rows of all the Varieties of Winter-greens set at due Distances, which will appear with an agreeable Beauty from the House all the Year. But then I say too, that I should be under no sort of Uneasiness to be confined to an irregular piece of Ground, which may be made to have its Beauties as well as the most regular. Strait Lines bring any thing into Order, and I see not but a Triangle in a Garden has its Beauty as well as a Square, and yet an irregular piece of Ground may be made to have both by vertue of straight Lines, *viz.* Borders and Walks.

I confess indeed an Irregularity is not so easily hid in a little Ground as it is in a Garden of larger extent, where long Walks, and tall Hedges interrupt a distant and thorough View, and where, though the Walks and Hedges terminate in obtuse or acute Angles, no ways disagreeable to the Eye; yet you are insensibly led into new and unexpected Beauties still as you advance. Three or four Walks and double Rows of Hedges may be there contrived to open themselves at once to view, all terminating in the place where you stand, and the Triangular Spaces by an ingenious Fancy may be there agreeably disposed and filled up either with Borders of Flowers, or with Dwarff-Trees, or with Flowring Shrubs, or with Ever-Greens; or lastly with a little Wilderness of Trees rising one above another, till you come to the point of a tall one in the middle; this last may be made to look very beautiful with Charge and Care to clip them; for I am now got into a large Garden that requires a good Purse; and therefore before I part with it, I will only add, that methinks Gentlemen should not be over sollicitous, at great Charges, so to level or square their Gardens as to throw them open to one single view from the House; (which doubtless may be made a very beautiful one) because it may be worth while to consider, whether matters may not be so contrived, as to afford you many uncommon Prettinesses wholly owing to the Irregularity or Unevenness of the Ground. Insomuch that every little advance you make, you shall be presented with something new to strike the Fancy.

But altho' (as you see) Irregularities are best disguised and set off in a large Plot of Ground, yet even in a lesser Garden, an irregular Form, if it be not very aukward indeed, may be educed to a Regularity sufficiently agreeable as well as useful . . .

59 Gravel pit in Kensington Gardens. Engraving from Thomas Tickell, *Kensington Gardens*, 1722, title-page

Charles Evelyn (pseud.) (dates unknown)

Evelyn's charming and unpretentious book, *The Lady's Recreation: or The Art of Gardening Improv'd*, allows us a sight of the kind of modest garden (Plate 60) that London and Wise might have supplied and even designed. Though the extract envisages a plan of symmetry and mathematically contrived spaces — the wilderness, too, must be 'well form'd' — Charles Evelyn (conceivably the pseudonym of John Lawrence) allows both solitudes with seats for single people and some 'Enlargement of Prospect' beyond the garden into 'Parks and Meadows', which (as he writes elsewhere in the book) 'are too often neglected or forgotten'.

from *The Lady's Recreation: or
The Art of Gardening Improv'd* (1717)

The great Variety of Forms and Plans of Gardens, that might be drawn and represented, and the working Part of them, I leave to the practical *Gardener*, whose immediate Business it is; and since it would be no small Difficulty to prescribe Rules in a Case where Fancy entirely governs, and every Builder is most capable of pleasing himself, I shall therefore be contented with the small Scheme I have given in the Front of this Treatise, and the following short Explanation of it, *viz*. You are no sooner out of the House, but you are in a Walk of *Orange-Trees*, whose fragrant Smell, especially in the Blooming Season, excels that of all other Plants and Flowers; from thence you proceed to Grass-Plots and Squares, fill'd with the most beauteous Greens, and Borders set off with the most delightful Flowers. From those Entertainments you advance to a Fountain of the best Architecture: From thence you come to other Grass-Plots of various Forms, fine Greens, and beautiful Flower-Hedges; with the Addition of an excellent contriv'd Statue representing *Flora*; from whence you enter a well-form'd flourishing Wilderness; and being no longer pleas'd with a solitary Amusement, you come out into a large Road, where you have the Diversion of seeing Travellers pass by, to compleat your Variety.

   This is the Design of my Print prefix'd in the Front, to which I shall add my Intentions, in Respect to Seats and Out-door Edifices; at each End of the *Orange*-Walk, I would have an arch'd Seat equal in Wideness to the Walk, *to wit*, about eight or ten Foot; these Seats would not be a little pleasurable, as an immediate Resort from the House. The next Thing I would do, should be

60 Charles Evelyn (pseud.), *The Lady's Recreation*, 1717, frontispiece

to erect small Seats of a Size fit to receive two or three Persons, to be plac'd on each Side the Garden, at the Termination of the Cross-Walks; then, for cool Recesses, there's no Part of the Wilderness, but might with Facility, and for a trifling Expence, be converted into a most commodious Arbour; and that I might be perfectly retir'd, in the Middle of each Square of the Wilderness, or of two of them at least, there should be a large Elm or Fir, with a small Seat enclosing the Body thereof, and the Ground open in a Grass-Walk, for about the Space of six, seven, or eight Foot, &c. round, according to your Room, having a very narrow and almost conceal'd Entrance from the Walks; and for more publick Use, there might be large Trees planted in the Center of the Wilderness, with small Seats erected round them likewise; these Seats, with one or two small moveable ones, of a Size to contain one Person only, and a small Pleasure-House erected at one Corner of the Wilderness, under the Wall, opening to the Walk of the Side of the Garden, to resort to in wet and unpleasant Weather, or upon any other Occasion; with a small Edifice on the other Side the Garden, at the other Corner, of the same Extent and Form of the Pleasure-House, and answering to the same, as a Conservatory for your fine Greens in the Winter, and for the keeping of the *Gardener's* Utensils; with the Addition of some high Mount, or exalted Terras-Walk, near, for the Enlargement of Prospect, would compleat a Garden, to the Satisfaction of the most Curious.

In Respect to the laying out, and proportioning of Gardens in general, I shall advance very few Rules; the Reverend Mr. *Laurence* having very handsomely descanted on this Subject. The Extent of your Garden always determines the Extent of your Walks, Parterres, Grass-Plots, &c. if your Garden be large, of Course they must be large too; and if small, of Consequence they must be small likewise: But to give one Example, a Garden, or rather a Parterre, of seventy Foot every way, will require the Squares, or Grass-Plots, to be about twenty five Foot square, calculating four Squares for the Disposition of the Ground; the middle Walk may be about six or seven Foot wide; and the side Walks about four Foot each; which, with the Borders under the Walls, will employ the whole Ground: Each of these Squares may very well receive nine fashionable Greens regularly dispos'd, such as Pyramid *Eughs*, round-headed *Laurels* and *Bays*, silver Pyramid *Hollies, Junipers, &c.* the Borders being fill'd up between with the most odorous and beautiful Flowers: And by this Proportion may a larger or smaller Plot of Ground be laid out.

Having given you the Dimensions of a small Garden of Pleasure, I have only to observe, that it is most uniform to make the Entrance into your Garden out of one of the most magnificent Rooms in your House, or very near the same; and to preserve that Entrance from common Use, you may have some other Door into your Garden for Gardeners, Labourers, &c. and let your principal Walk extend it self as far as you can, directly from your House, adorn'd with the choicest Plants for Beauty and Scent, wherein, the longer the Walk is, the larger are the Plants to be, and the wider in Extent the Gravel-Walk.

Part Two

The Early Landscape Garden

Joseph Addison (1672–1719)

Addison must be counted among the foremost promoters of the landscape garden. His *Tatler* paper, which forms the first extract, establishes what is to become an essential part of the ideology of the English landscape garden, its freedom from unnecessary constraints. Just as England itself is happily spared the absolutism of French politics, its gardens should also be cleared of the ordered and fiercely prescriptive designs that mirror it. The theme is later rehearsed by Thomson in *Liberty* (1735–6). But by casting his paper in the form of a dream, Addison suggests the as yet only fanciful vision of this ideal garden, though the Goddess of Liberty and her attendant train of Arts and Sciences are presented like statues in an Italianate garden, or as Gilbert West was to see them around Stowe's parterre in 1732 (Plate 61). The second extract equally insists upon the romantic fantasy behind Leonora's garden, where its freedom from geometrical contrivance promotes a sense of some enchanted ground. These imaginative dimensions of a garden are discussed more philosophically in Addison's celebrated essays on 'the Pleasures of the Imagination' (from which the third and fourth extracts are taken). Here his concerns are with the appeal of natural rather than artificial effects to the spectator's mind, and with those arranged landscapes that still contrive to resemble nature. It is therefore perhaps odd that he champions French and Italian gardens: the reasons are probably their freedom from the niceties of Dutch design, which dominated England, and their scale, which admitted more variety and 'artificial Rudeness'.

61 Stowe, Buckinghamshire. Drawing by Jacques Rigaud, *c.* 1733, of the 'View of the *Perterre* [*sic*] from the *Portico* of the *House*'

This versatility, as *The Spectator*, No. 417, goes on to establish, better answers the workings of the human mind. Addison adapts Locke's theories of mental activity, illustrating them (significantly) with his visions of how a landscape garden works upon its visitors. The sublime or Homeric, and the magical or Ovidian garden are obviously Addison's preferred styles, because they mirror as well as elicit a more various imagination. The final extract, perhaps the most personal, is couched in the form of an unsolicited letter to *The Spectator*. In it Addison celebrates a 'Pindarick' manner of garden design, that prefers the 'beautiful Wildness of Nature' to the 'nicer Elegancies of Art'; it also involves its creator's mind at all points and in all seasons, the first of such personalized landscapes in the eighteenth century where, as Addison wrote in *The Spectator*, No. 583, 'you may trace [a Man] . . . in the Place where he has lived'. Yet the letter-writer is catholic and flexible in his tastes, admiring one of London and Wise's notable designs (Plate 59): this should remind us at least of how Addison's ideas were generally in advance of the practice of garden design at this time.

Papers from *The Tatler* and *The Spectator* (1710–12)

I Was walking Two or Three Days ago in a very pleasing Retirement, and amusing my self with the Reading of that ancient and beautiful Allegory, call'd, *The Table of Cebes*. I was at last so tired with my Walk, that I sat down to rest my self upon a Bench that stood in the midst of an agreeable Shade. The Musick of the Birds, that filled all the Trees about me, lull'd me asleep before I was aware of it, which was followed by a Dream, that I impute in some Measure to the foregoing Author, who had made an Impression upon my Imagination, and put me into his own Way of Thinking.

I fancied my self among the *Alpes*, and, as it is natural in a Dream, seemed every Moment to bound from one Summit to another, till at last, after having made this airy Progress over the Tops of several Mountains, I arrived at the very Center of those broken Rocks and Precipices. I here methought saw a prodigious Circuit of Hills, that reached above the Clouds, and encompassed a large Space of Ground, which I had a great Curiosity to look into. I thereupon continued my former Way of travelling through a great Variety of Winter Scenes, till I had gained the Top of these white Mountains, which seemed another *Alpes* of Snow. I looked down from hence into a spacious Plain, which was surrounded on all Sides by this Mound of Hills, and which presented me with the most agreeable Prospect I had ever seen. There was a greater Variety of Colours in the Embroidery of the Meadows, a more lively Green in the Leaves and Grass, a brighter Chrystal in the Streams, than what I ever met with in any other Region. The Light it self had something more shining and glorious in it than that of which the Day is made in other Places. I was wonderfully astonished at the Discovery of such a Paradise amidst the

Wildness of those cold, hoary Landskips which lay about it; but found at length, that this happy Region was inhabited by the Goddess of *Liberty*; whose Presence softened the Rigours of the Climate, enriched the Barrenness of the Soil, and more than supplied the Absence of the Sun. The Place was covered with a wonderful Profusion of Flowers, that, without being disposed into regular Borders and Parterres, grew promiscuously, and had a greater Beauty in their natural Luxuriancy and Disorder, than they could have received from the Checks and Restraints of Art. There was a River that arose out of the South Side of the Mountain, that by an infinite Number of Turns and Windings, seemed to visit every Plant, and cherish the several Beauties of the Spring, with which the Fields abounded. After having run to and fro in a wonderful Variety of Meanders, as unwilling to leave so charming a Place, it at last throws it self into the Hollow of a Mountain, from whence it passes under a long Range of Rocks, and at length rises in that Part of the *Alpes* where the Inhabitants think it the First Source of the *Rhone*. This River, after having made its Progress through those Free Nations, stagnates in a huge Lake at the leaving of them and no sooner enters into the Regions of Slavery, but runs thro' them with an incredible Rapidity, and takes its shortest Way to the Sea . . .

In the Train of the Goddess of *Liberty* were the several Arts and Sciences, who all of them flourished underneath her Eye. One of them in particular made a greater Figure than any of the rest, who held a Thunderbolt in her Hand, which had the Power of melting, piercing, or breaking every Thing that stood in its Way. The Name of this Goddess was *Eloquence*.

There were Two other dependent Goddesses, who made a very conspicuous Figure in this blissful Region: The First of them was seated upon an Hill, that had every Plant growing out of it which the Soil was in its own Nature capable of producing. The other was seated in a little island, that was covered with Groves of Spices, Olives, and Orange-Trees; and in a Word, with the Products of every Foreign Clime. The Name of the First was *Plenty*; of the Second, *Commerce*. The First learned her Right-Arm upon a Plough, and under her Left held a huge Horn, out of which she poured a whole Autumn of Fruits. The Other wore a rostral Crown upon her Head, and kept her Eyes fixed upon a Compass.

I was wonderfully pleased in ranging through this delightful Place; and the more so, because it was not incumbered with Fences and Enclosures . . .

The Tatler, No. 161, 18–20 April 1710

LEONORA was formerly a celebrated Beauty, and is still a very lovely Woman. She has been a Widow for two or three Years, and being unfortunate in her first Marriage, has taken a Resolution never to venture upon a second . . . But as the Mind naturally sinks into a kind of Lethargy, and falls asleep, that is not agitated by some Favourite Pleasures and Pursuits, *Leonora* has turned all the Passions of her Sex, into a Love of Books and Retirement

... As her Reading has lain very much among Romances, it has given her a very particular Turn of Thinking, and discovers it self even in her House, her Gardens, and her Furniture. Sir ROGER has entertained me an Hour together with a Description of her Country-Seat, which is situated in a kind of Wilderness, about an hundred Miles distant from *London*, and looks like a little enchanted Palace. The Rocks about her are shaped into Artificial Grottoes, covered with Woodbines and Jessamines. The Woods are cut into shady Walks, twisted into Bowers, and filled with Cages of Turtles. The Springs are made to run among Pebbles, and by that means taught to murmur very agreeably. They are likewise collected into a beautiful Lake, that is inhabited by a Couple of Swans, and empties it self by a little Rivulet which runs through a green Meadow, and is known in the Family by the Name of *The Purling Stream.*

The Spectator, No. 37, 12 April 1711

IF we consider the Works of *Nature* and *Art*, as they are qualified to entertain the Imagination, we shall find the last very defective, in Comparison of the former; for though they may sometimes appear as Beautiful or Strange, they can have nothing in them of that Vastness and Immensity, which afford so great an Entertainment to the Mind of the Beholder. The one may be as Polite and Delicate as the other, but can never shew her self so August and Magnificent in the Design. There is something more bold and masterly in the rough careless Strokes of Nature, than in the nice Touches and Embellishments of Art. The Beauties of the most stately Garden or Palace lie in a narrow Compass, the Imagination immediately runs them over, and requires something else to gratifie her; but, in the wide Fields of Nature, the Sight wanders up and down without Confinement, and is fed with an infinite variety of Images, without any certain Stint or Number. For this Reason we always find the Poet in love with a Country-Life, where Nature appears in the greatest Perfection, and furnishes out all those Scenes that are most apt to delight the Imagination ...

BUT tho' there are several of these wild Scenes, that are more delightful than any artificial Shows; yet we find the Works of Nature still more pleasant, the more they resemble those of Art: For in this case our Pleasure rises from a double Principle; from the Agreeableness of the Objects to the Eye, and from their Similitude to other Objects: We are pleased as well with comparing their Beauties, as with surveying them, and can represent them to our Minds, either as Copies or Originals. Hence it is that we take Delight in a Prospect which is well laid out, and diversified with Fields and Meadows; Woods and Rivers; in those accidental Landskips of Trees, Clouds and Cities, that are sometimes found in the Veins of Marble; in the curious Fret-work of Rocks, and Grottos; and, in a Word, in any thing that hath such a Variety or Regularity as may seem the Effect of Design, in what we call the Works of Chance.

IF the Products of Nature rise in Value, according as they more or less resemble those of Art, we may be sure that artificial Works receive a greater Advantage from their Resemblance of such as are natural; because here the Similitude is not only pleasant, but the Pattern more perfect. The prettiest Landskip I ever saw, was one drawn on the Walls of a dark Room, which stood opposite on one side to a navigable River, and on the other to a Park. The Experiment is very common in Opticks. Here you might discover the Waves and Fluctuations of the Water in strong and proper Colours, with the Picture of a Ship entering at one end, and sailing by Degrees through the whole Piece. On another there appeared the Green Shadows of Trees, waving to and fro with the Wind, and Herds of Deer among them in Miniature, leaping about upon the Wall. I must confess, the Novelty of such a Sight may be one occasion of its Pleasantness to the Imagination, but certainly the chief Reason is its near Resemblance to Nature, as it does not only, like other Pictures, give the Colour and Figure, but the Motion of the Things it represents.

WE have before observed, that there is generally in Nature something more Grand and August, than what we meet with in the Curiosities of Art. When, therefore, we see this imitated in any measure, it gives us a nobler and more exalted kind of Pleasure than what we receive from the nicer and more accurate Productions of Art. On this Account our *English* Gardens are not so entertaining to the Fancy as those in *France* and *Italy*, where we see a large Extent of Ground covered over with an agreeable mixture of Garden and Forest, which represent every where an artificial Rudeness, much more charming than that Neatness and Elegancy which we meet with in those of our own Country. It might, indeed, be of ill Consequence to the Publick, as well as unprofitable to private Persons, to alienate so much Ground from Pasturage, and the Plow, in many Parts of a Country that is so well peopled, and cultivated to a far greater Advantage. But why may not a whole Estate be thrown into a kind of Garden by frequent Plantations, that may turn as much to the Profit, as the Pleasure of the Owner? A Marsh overgrown with Willows, or a Mountain shaded with Oaks, are not only more beautiful, but more beneficial, than when they lie bare and unadorned. Fields of Corn make a pleasant Prospect, and if the Walks were a little taken care of that lie between them, if the natural Embroidery of the Meadows were helpt and improved by some small Additions of Art, and the several Rows of Hedges set off by Trees and Flowers, that the Soil was capable of receiving, a Man might make a pretty Landskip of his own Possessions.

WRITERS, who have given us an Account of *China*, tell us, the Inhabitants of that Country laugh at the Plantations of our *Europeans*, which are laid out by the Rule and Line; because, they say, any one may place Trees in equal Rows and uniform Figures. They chuse rather to shew a Genius in Works of this Nature, and therefore always conceal the Art by which they direct themselves. They have a Word, it seems, in their Language, by which they express the particular Beauty of a Plantation that thus strikes the Imagination at first Sight, without discovering what it is that has so agreeable an Effect. Our *British* Gardeners, on the contrary, instead of humouring Nature, love to deviate from it as much as possible. Our Trees rise in Cones,

Globes, and Pyramids. We see the Marks of the Scissars upon every Plant and Bush. I do not know whether I am singular in my Opinion, but, for my own part, I would rather look upon a Tree in all its Luxuriancy and Diffusion of Boughs and Branches, than when it is thus cut and trimmed into a Mathematical Figure; and cannot but fancy that an Orchard in Flower looks infinitely more delightful, than all the little Labyrinths of the most finished Parterre. But as our great Modellers of Gardens have their Magazines of Plants to dispose of, it is very natural for them to tear up all the Beautiful Plantations of Fruit Trees, and contrive a Plan that may most turn to their own Profit, in taking off their Evergreens, and the like Moveable Plants, with which their Shops are plentifully stocked.

The Spectator, No. 414, 25 June 1712

WE may observe, that any single Circumstance of what we have formerly seen often raises up a whole Scene of Imagery, and awakens numberless Ideas that before slept in the Imagination; such a particular Smell or Colour is able to fill the Mind, on a sudden, with the Picture of the Fields or Gardens where we first met with it, and to bring up into View all the Variety of Images that once attended it. Our Imagination takes the Hint, and leads us unexpectedly into Cities or Theatres, Plains or Meadows. We may further observe, when the Fancy thus reflects on the Scenes that have past in it formerly, those, which were at first pleasant to behold, appear more so upon Reflection, and that the Memory heightens the Delightfulness of the Original. A *Cartesian* would account for both these Instances in the following Manner.

THE Sett of Ideas, which we received from such a Prospect or Garden, having entered the Mind at the same time, have a Sett of Traces belonging to them in the Brain, bordering very near upon one another; when, therefore, any one of these Ideas arises in the Imagination, and consequently dispatches a flow of Animal Spirits to its proper Trace, these Spirits, in the Violence of their Motion, run not only into the Trace, to which they were more particularly directed, but into several of those that lye about it: By this means they awaken other Ideas of the same Sett, which immediately determine a new Dispatch of Spirits, that in the same manner open other Neighbouring Traces, till at last the whole Sett of them is blown up, and the whole Prospect or Garden flourishes in the Imagination. But because the Pleasure we received from these Places far surmounted, and overcame the little Disagreeableness we found in them, for this Reason there was at first a wider Passage worn in the Pleasure Traces, and, on the contrary, so narrow a one in those which belonged to the disagreeable Ideas, that they were quickly stopt up, and rendered incapable of receiving any Animal Spirits, and consequently of exciting any unpleasant Ideas in the Memory.

IT would be in vain to enquire, whether the Power of imagining Things strongly proceeds from any greater Perfection in the Soul, or from any nicer Texture in the Brain of one Man than of another. But this is certain, that a noble Writer should be born with this Faculty in its full Strength and Vigour, so as to be able to receive lively Ideas from outward Objects, to retain them long, and to range them together, upon occasion, in such Figures and Representations as are most likely to hit the Fancy of the Reader. A Poet should take as much Pains in forming his Imagination, as a Philosopher in cultivating his Understanding. He must gain a due Relish of the Works of Nature, and be throughly conversant in the various Scenary of a Country Life.

WHEN he is stored with Country Images, if he would go beyond Pastoral, and the lower kinds of Poetry, he ought to acquaint himself with the Pomp and Magnificence of Courts. He should be very well versed in every thing that is noble and stately in the Productions of Art, whether it appear in Painting or Statuary, in the great Works of Architecture which are in their present Glory, or in the Ruins of those which flourished in former Ages.

SUCH Advantages as these help to open a Man's Thoughts, and to enlarge his Imagination, and will therefore have their Influence on all Kinds of Writing, if the Author knows how to make right use of them. And among those of the learned Languages who excell in this Talent, the most perfect in their several kinds, are perhaps *Homer, Virgil,* and *Ovid*. The first strikes the Imagination wonderfully with what is Great, the second with what is Beautiful, and the last with what is Strange. Reading the *Iliad* is like travelling through a Country uninhabited, where the Fancy is entertained with a thousand Savage Prospects of vast Desarts, wide uncultivated Marshes, huge Forests, mis-shapen Rocks and Precipices. On the contrary, the *AEneid* is like a well ordered Garden, where it is impossible to find out any Part unadorned, or to cast our Eyes upon a single Spot, that does not produce some beautiful Plant or Flower. But when we are in the *Metamorphosis*, we are walking on enchanted Ground, and see nothing but Scenes of Magick lying round us.

HOMER is in his Province, when he is describing a Battel or a Multitude, a Heroe or a God. *Virgil* is never better pleas'd, than when he is in his *Elysium*, or copying out an entertaining Picture. Homer's Epithets generally mark out what is Great, *Virgil's* what is Agreeable. Nothing can be more Magnificent than the Figure *Jupiter* makes in the first *Iliad*, nor more Charming than that of *Venus* in the first *AEneid* . . . Homer's Persons are most of them God-like and Terrible: *Virgil* has scarce admitted any into his Poem, who are not beautiful, and has taken particular Care to make his Heroe so . . . In a Word, *Homer* fills his Readers with Sublime Ideas, and, I believe, has raised the Imagination of all the good Poets that have come after him. I shall only instance *Horace*, who immediately takes Fire at the first Hint of any Passage in the *Iliad* or *Odyssee*, and always rises above himself, when he has *Homer* in his View. *Virgil* has drawn together, into his *AEneid*, all the pleasing Scenes [that] his Subject is capable of admitting, and in his *Georgics* has given us a Collection of the most delightful Landskips that can be made out of Fields and Woods, Herds of Cattle, and Swarms of Bees.

OVID, in his *Metamorphosis*, has shewn us how the Imagination may be affected by what is Strange. He describes a Miracle in every Story, and always gives us the Sight of some new Creature at the end of it. His Art consists chiefly in well-timing his Description, before the first Shape is quite worn off, and the new one perfectly finish'd, so that he every where entertains us with something we never saw before, and shews Monster after Monster, to the end of the *Metamorphosis* . . .

The Spectator, No. 417, 28 June 1712

HAVING lately read your Essay on the Pleasures of the Imagination, I was so taken with your Thoughts upon some of our *English* Gardens, that I cannot forbear troubling you with a Letter upon that Subject. I am one, you must know, who am looked upon as an Humorist in Gardening. I have several Acres about my House, which I call my Garden, and which a skillful Gardener would not know what to call. It is a Confusion of Kitchin and Parterre, Orchard and Flower Garden, which lie so mixt and interwoven with one another, that if a Foreigner who had seen nothing of our Country should be conveyed into my Garden at his first landing, he would look upon it as a natural Wilderness, and one of the uncultivated Parts of our Country. My Flowers grow up in several Parts of the Garden in the greatest Luxuriancy and Profusion. I am so far from being fond of any particular one, by reason of its Rarity, that if I meet with any one in a Field which pleases me, I give it a Place in my Garden. By this Means, when a Stranger walks with me, he is surprized to see several large Spots of Ground covered with ten thousand different Colours, and has often singled out Flowers that he might have met with under a common Hedge, in a Field, or in a Meadow, as some of the greatest Beauties of the Place. The only Method I observe in this Particular, is to range in the same Quarter the Products of the same Season, that they may make their Appearance together, and compose a Picture of the greatest Variety. There is the same Irregularity in my Plantations, which run into as great a Wildness as their Natures will permit. I take in none that do not naturally rejoyce in the Soil, and am pleased when I am walking in a Labyrinth of my own raising, not to know whether the next Tree I shall meet with is an Apple or an Oak, an Elm or a Pear-tree. My Kitchin has likewise its particular Quarters assigned it; for besides the wholsome Luxury which that Place abounds with, I have always thought a Kitchin-garden a more pleasant Sight, than the finest Orangerie, or artificial Green-house. I love to see every Thing in its Perfection, and am more pleased to survey my Rows of Colworts and Cabbages, with a thousand nameless Pot-herbs, springing up in their full Fragrancy and Verdure, than to see the tender Plants of foreign Countries kept alive by artificial Heats, or withering in an Air and Soil that are not adapted to them. I must not omit, that there is a Fountain rising in the upper Part of my Garden, which forms a little wandring Rill, and administers to the Pleasure as well as the Plenty of the Place: I have so conducted it, that it visits most of my Plantations, and have taken particular Care to let it run in the same Manner as it would do in an open Field, so that it generally passes through Banks of Violets and Primroses, Plats of Willow, or other Plants, that seem to be of its own producing. There is another Circumstance in which I am very particular, or, as my Neighbours call me, very whimsical: As my Garden invites into it all the Birds of the Country, by offering them the Conveniency of Springs and Shades, Solitude and Shelter, I do not suffer any one to destroy their Nests in the Spring, or drive them from their usual Haunts in Fruit-time. I value my Garden more for being full of Blackbirds than Cherries, and very frankly give them Fruit for their Songs. By this Means I have always the Musick of the Season in its Perfection, and am highly delighted to see the Jay or the Thrush hopping about my Walks, and shooting before my Eye across the several little Glades and Alleys that I pass through. I think there are as many Kinds of Gardening as of Poetry: Your Makers of Parterres and Flower Gardens, are Epigrammatists and Sonneteers in this Art, Contrivers of Bowers and Grotto's, Treillages and Cascades, are Romance Writers. *Wise* and *London* are our heroick Poets; and if, as a Critick, I may single out any Passage of their Works to commend, I shall take Notice of that Part in the upper Garden at *Kensington*, which was at first nothing but a Gravel-Pit. It must have been a fine Genius for Gardening, that could have thought of forming such an unsightly Hollow into so beautiful an *Area*, and to have hit the Eye with so uncommon and agreeable a Scene as that which it is now wrought into. To give this particular Spot of Ground the greater Effect, they have made a very pleasing Contrast; for as on one Side of the Walk you see this hollow Basin, with its several little Plantations lying so conveniently under the Eye of the Beholder; on the other Side of it there appears a seeming Mount, made up of Trees rising one higher than another in Proportion as they approach the Center. A Spectator, who has not heard this Account of it, would think this Circular Mount was not only a real one, but that it had been actually scooped out of that hollow Space which I have before mentioned. I never yet met with any one who had walked in this Garden, who was not struck with that Part of it which I have here mentioned. As for my self, you will find, by the Account which I have already given you, that my Compositions in Gardening are altogether after the *Pindarick* Manner, and run into the beautiful Wildness of Nature, without affecting the nicer Elegancies of Art. What I am now going to mention will, perhaps, deserve your Attention more than any Thing I have yet said. I find that in the Discourse which I spoke of at the Beginning of my Letter, you are against filling an *English* Garden with Ever-Greens; and indeed I am so far of your Opinion, that I can by no Means think the Verdure of an Ever-Green comparable to that which shoots out annually, and cloaths our Trees in the Summer Season. But I have often wondered that those who are like my self, and love to live in Gardens, have never thought of contriving a *Winter Garden*, which should consist of such Trees only as never cast their Leaves. We have very often little Snatches of Sun-shine and fair Weather in the most uncomfortable Parts of the Year, and have frequently several Days in *November* and *January* that are as agreeable as any in the finest Months. At such Times, therefore, I think there could not be a greater Pleasure, than to walk in such a *Winter Garden* as I have proposed. In the Summer Season the whole Country blooms, and is a Kind of Garden, for which Reason we are not so sensible of those Beauties that at this Time may be every where met with; but when Nature is in her Desolation, and presents us with nothing but bleak and barren Prospects, there is something unspeakably chearful in a Spot of Ground which is covered with Trees that smile amidst all the Rigours of Winter, and give us a View of the most gay Season in the Midst of that which is the most dead and melancholy. I have so far indulged my self in this Thought, that I have set apart a whole Acre of Ground for the executing of it. The Walls are covered with Ivy instead of Vines. The Laurel, the Hornbeam, and the Holly, with many other Trees and Plants of the same Nature, grow so thick in it, that you cannot imagine a more lively Scene. The glowing Redness of the Berries, with which they are hung at this Time, vies with the Verdure of their Leaves, and are apt to inspire the Heart of the Beholder with that vernal Delight which you have somewhere taken Notice of in your former Papers. It is very pleasant, at the same Time, to see the several Kinds of Birds retiring into this little green Spot, and enjoying themselves among the Branches and Foliage, when my great Garden, which I have before-mentioned to you, does not afford a single Leaf for their Shelter.

YOU must know, Sir, that I look upon the Pleasure which we take in a Garden, as one of the most innocent Delights in humane Life. A Garden was the Habitation of our first Parents before the Fall. It is naturally apt to fill the Mind with Calmness and Tranquillity, and to lay all its turbulent Passions at Rest. It gives us a great Insight into the Contrivance and Wisdom of Providence, and suggests innumerable Subjects for Meditation. I cannot but think the very Complacency and Satisfaction which a Man takes in these Works of Nature, to be a laudable, if not a virtuous Habit of Mind. For all which Reasons I hope you will pardon the Length of my present Letter.

The Spectator, No. 477, 6 September 1712

Samuel Molyneux (1689–1727)

The following recently discovered description in a manuscript letter-book is possibly the earliest account of an actual English landscape garden, as opposed to merely theoretical formulations of the idea. Molyneux, an Irishman who was later to become famous as Secretary to Frederick, Prince of Wales, records his visits to several gardens and shows himself obviously well-versed in such writers as Shaftesbury or Addison's recently published essays. Petersham Lodge, just across the river from Twickenham (see Plate 62) appears as an astonishing approximation to Addison's ideal and anticipates the work of Alexander Pope, who from at least 1717 was friendly with the Earl of Rochester and his wife, the lessees of Petersham. That Molyneux appreciated the radical nature of the gardens there is clear from the contrasts he makes with other local examples in the French taste of 'regular manner of greens and gravel gardening'. In 1721 Petersham Lodge was destroyed by fire, but rebuilt soon afterwards to designs by Lord Burlington. Our text is taken from the manuscript in the Civic Records Office, Southampton.

from a Letter on Petersham Lodge (14 February 1713)

The Scituation of Hampton Court is on a dead Flatt and for such a one, I think the Gardens, the great Canall, the Park and the Bowling green are beautifully dispos'd enough, The Thames which runs at the Foot of one of the Gardens and along the great Terras going to the Bowling Green makes one of it's greatest beautys, and has given an Agreeable Scituation to a very handsome banquetting house, which is built close on the bank of the River; As I have not Botanicks enough to tell you all the Exotick Plants they shew'd us here in two or three different green houses and as I believe the Comon prints of Hampton Court will give you a better notion of it's Walks, Labyrinths & Scituation than I can if you have not seen this Palace yourself, I shall confine my Self to say no more of it than this, that I did by no means think it adequate in the whole to the notion I had of the Palace of a great Prince; From Hampton Court we went to see a lodgeing Park call'd Bushy Park belonging to the Palace which is now in the hands of my Lord Hallifax as Ranger I beleive of that Park, there was here little or nothing remarkeable but the Cascade which was not very high, but little and yet very beautifully dispos'd so as to fall between two fine pieces of Grotto Work where are places left for Paintings representing two Caves in which the little walks round the Basin of the Cascade end the Paintings are moveable so as to be taken away in Winter, From hence we went down the River by Boat, and saw a Beautiful Country all along a great many Villages and several pretty Seats along the Banks, and in about an hour I think we came to Richmond which is indeed a very pretty village as I have seen from thence we went to see new Park which is a Seat just by belonging to my Lord Rochester; if Hampton Court did not fill my Expectation the Gardens here I assure you did pay the Pains of my Journey and gave me perfect Satisfaction. I think I have never yet seen any peice of Gardening that has so much as this the true taste of Beauty. There is a certain sort of Presumption appears in the comon restrain'd formal & Regular Parteres & Gardens that one meets with But here art has nothing Sawcy and seems to endeavour rather to follow than alter nature, and to aim at no beautys but such as she before had seem'd to dictate: The Partere behind the house and the Hornbeam walks beyond it are well enough but a very high hill to the left of the Gardens part of which is beautifully and wildly dispos'd into Slopes, the rest and upper part cover'd with a fine wood so interspers'd with Vistos & little innumerable private

62 View of Twickenham. Engraving by Green after Muntz, 1756

dark walks thro every part of it lin'd on both sides with low hedges with the unconfin'd Prospects you meet every now and then of the Garden below the Country and the River beyond you is what in my opinion makes the Particular & distinguish'd preferable beauty of this place beyond any thing that I have ever seen. I should not forget to tell you that in every walk you meet here and there a little opening in the wood with Seats, a Statue, a grass plott, a Basin of water or the like, for you must know that here is a Fountain playing on the side of the hill (the Spring being at the Top) which is much higher, the Basin of which lyes higher than the house Roof as well as I remember they shew'd us here a huge Cedar of Libanus, in the house I think I observ'd nothing remarkeable at all. From hence persueing our Journey to London you meet Fulham the residence of the Bishop of London whose Garden of Exotick Plants is worth seeing and opposite on the other side Putney a pretty Village, Soon after we landed at the Colledge of Physicians garden at Chelsea where we saw several Exotick Plants more, Particularly four very fine Cedars of Libanus and a Cork tree . . . the gardens of [Kensington] it seems are counted a Master peice of Art in the new regular manner of greens and gravel-gardening, for my part I must confess I have no opinion of this way at all, and tho I own that the gravel pit at Kensington is happily enough dispos'd, the antique Busts and Statues very well plac'd at the end of the little walks, tho the mount made in Appearance on Level ground by trees of Different heights, and the small circular compartment of high greens I observ'd with a Statue in the middle of it of about 40 or 50 yards Diameter with 8 walks centering there and as many Seats let into the hedge between them tho I say all this be in it's way very agreable yet in my opinion all this falls so low and short of the sublime unconfinedness of nature, and there is something so infinitely more exalting in the beautiful Scaravagie of noble grown Trees in a wild Wood that I cannot conceive how the world is so entirely fall'n into this way of Gardening[.] The pleasure a great man takes in being able to force nature, and to make and finish a Garden in a season is what has certainly introduc'd this, whereas I think a well chosen exalted Scituation with natural Wood and Water & a distant prospect in spight of all these little vain Efforts of mankind does still display greater beautys, and is in it's wild variety more inviteing to the noble Seat than this in all it's finish'd Regularity is pleaseing after all; Variety is confess'd to be the Beauty of a Garden, now there can be no variety in that that one sees all the parts of so plainly at once, and this seems to be a natural Reason against this kind of gardening, a Friend of mine that walk'd with me there and happen'd to be of my opinion methought sayd a pleasant thing enough on this head, that he for his part did not like these Epigrams in gardening and was much more pleas'd with the Epick Style or the Pindarick.

Stephen Switzer (?1682–1745)

Although also a nurseryman, seedsman and garden designer, it is as a writer that Switzer is best known. He brought to his publications an attentive reading of Addison and various poetic appreciations of natural scenery, and this in its turn was mediated by a firm commitment to the practical exigencies of gardening. By 1742 he considered that he had promoted a larger and better understanding of the 'Operations of Nature'. His frequent insistence that gardening combined the useful and profitable with the pleasurable is, like Pope's praise of Burlington, a familiar Classical idea. *The Nobleman, Gentleman, and Gardener's Recreation*, the pioneering volume of 1715, outlined Switzer's proposals for what he called 'Rural and Extensive Gardening': allowing the 'Beauties of Nature' to remain 'uncorrupted by

63 Stephen Switzer, *The Nobleman, Gentleman, and Gardener's Recreation*, 1715, frontispiece

Art' — not straightening serpentine lines of path or river — and directing that 'all the adjacent Country be laid open to View, and that the Eye should not be bounded with High Walls, Woods misplac'd, and several Obstructions, that one sees in too many places, by which the eye is as it were imprisoned'. The frontispiece to *Recreation* (Plate 63) gives little hint of Switzer's fresh vision; its vaguely French manner reminds us that he actually invoked the 'extensive Way of Gard'ning . . . the French call *La Grand Manier*' (*sic*) to attack 'those crimping, Diminutive and wretched Performances we every where meet with'. Yet if he used the French to argue against the Dutch garden, his text already announces the sensitivity to scale and proportion and the feeling for nature that distinguish the English landscape garden. The first volume was obviously popular and in 1718 was expanded into the three-volume *Ichnographia Rustica*, of which an augmented version appeared in 1742. As Switzer himself recognized, the years since the publication of *Recreation* in 1715 had seen a prodigious advance in landscape taste and design, not a little due to his own writings; accordingly, the 1742 edition is more confident and radical in its prescriptions (a 'Design must submit to Nature, and not Nature to his Design': see Plate 64), as well as more loosely organized and repetitive. The first extracts demonstrate his animadversions upon scale and his promotion of statuary in imitation of mainly Italian models; passages follow on the management of woods, with the famous account of how Wray Wood at Castle Howard was preserved in its natural state; and we conclude with two descriptions of gardens that earned Switzer's approval — a lengthy one of Dyrham Park and a brief notice of Riskins (i.e. Richings in Buckinghamshire), probably one of the earliest discussions of the *ferme ornée* in England.

from *Ichnographia Rustica* (1718 and 1742)

from Volume III, 1718 and 1742

The Chief of our Design in this Book, being the Decoration and Embellishment of a whole Estate, or at least, that Part of it that lies most contiguous to the Mansion House, instead of such vast and expensive Gardens, that the Folly of this and the past Ages hath run into, whereby that most innocent and harmless Employ, is become a Burthen too great for the biggest Estate, and the Gardens themselves not at all answerable to the needless Expence that is laid out upon them.

For, supposing a Person should be possess'd of a Garden, thirty, forty, fifty, nay, as it is sometimes seen, of a hundred Acres of Ground; the Beauty is soon discover'd, and at the same time that that is, the Love of it too often vanishes, and when we come to add the Expence thereto, we soon find it a lothsome Burden, or the Owner whilst perhaps at the same time his Estate that lies contiguous to him, is as much neglected, when by spread-in Money more lightly at home, it might in a great measure be dress'd and improv'd, and be made altogether as beautiful as the most elaborate Garden; besides, the affording him a continual Profit and Employ.

To confirm this Supposition; if his Grounds were handsomly divided by Avenues and Hedges; and if the little Walks and Paths that ought to run through and betwixt them, were made either of Gravel or Sand; and if there were Trees for Shades with little Walks and purling Streams, mix'd and incorporated one with another, what cou'd be more diverting? And why, is not a level easy Walk of Gravel or Sand shaded over with Trees, and running thro' a Corn Field or Pasture Ground, as pleasing as the largest Walk in the most magnificent Garden one can think of? And why, are not little Gardens and Basons of Water as useful and surprizing (and indeed why not more so) at some considerable Distance from the Mansion House, as they are near it? Besides as these Hedge Rows, little natural Coppices, large Woods, Corn Fields, &c. mix'd one amongst another, are as delightful as the finest Garden; so they are much cheaper made, and still cheaper kept. And more than all, the careless and loose Tresses of Nature, that are easily mov'd by the least Breath of Wind, offer more to the Imagination than the most delicate Pyramid, or any of the longest and most elaborately clip'd Espalier, that it is possible to make; for, altho' we don't by this absolutely reject, in some few proper Places something of that kind, yet why should that be thought such a Beauty, as to exclude things more Natural? And why should not a judicious Mixture and Incorporation, of one with the other quite thro' a large Estate, be of more value, (*viz.*) as at or near the House, a little more exactitude is required; so after that view is over one would sometimes be passing thro' little Padducks and Corn Fields, sometimes thro' wild Coppices, and Gardens, and sometimes by purling Brooks and Streams, Places that are set off not by nice Art, but by luxury of Nature, a little guided in her Extravagancies by the Artists Hand, while sometimes it may not be improper unexpectedly to fall into a little correct, and elaborate Garden; but, as those should not be too often so, they ought not to be too large.

Again, why should we be at that great Expence of levelling of Hills, or filling up of Dales, when they are the Beauty of Nature? Why should we esteem nothing but large regular Walks, the only Characteristicks of a noble Seat? But, for diversity, should not rather mix therewith Serpentine Meanders; and instead of levelling Hills or filling up Dales, should think it more entertaining to be sometimes on the Precipice of a Hill viewing all round and under us, and at other times in a Bottom, viewing those goodly Hills and Theatres of Wood and Corn that are above us, and present themselves every where to our View? And, if we have not such by Nature, to create them by Art, by digging a Hole in one place, to make a Hill in another; and so to make the most level Country (which of all others is the least beautiful) as delightful as any thing that Nature throws in our way or Art can create . . .

from 'A Prooemial Essay' to Volume I, 1742

IN Parterres and open Lawns indeed, something of Regularity ought to be observed. 'Tis proper to make all level open Spaces equal as near as can be on every side; but even that may be insisted on to a Fault: for if the Boundaries of any Lawn be of Wood and Lawn well intermixt together, and which succeed one another, there is no great occasion for its being exactly level; Slopings down, and from such Lawns, adding to the Variety of the Place, the open Lawn or Parterre before the House being brought to a proper level as before set down.

BUT in all cases the Lawn or Parterre should not be too large, since 'tis a very wrong way of thinking, to imagine that true Greatness consists in Size and Dimension; whereas let the Works be ever so large, unless the Parts cohere in Harmony, there will be but a great many Littlenesses put together.

THIS aiming at an incomprehensible Vastness, and attempting at Things beyond the reach of Nature, is in a great measure owing to a late eminent Designer* in Gardening, whose Fancy could not be bounded; and this Notion has been in many Places carried so far, that no Parterre or Lawn that was not less than 50 or 60 Acres, some of them 80, 90, or 100, were by him esteemed capacious enough, though it sometimes took up the whole Area of Ground, and made the Building or Mansion-house in the middle look very small, and by no means proportionable to it.

THE same extravagant way of thinking prevailed also to a great degree, in that otherwise ingenious Designer, in his Plan of Lakes and Pieces of Water, without any regard to the Goodness of the Land, which was to be overflowed: But which he generally designed so large, as to make a whole Country look like an Ocean.

FROM all which it is justly infer'd, that the whole Art of Designing consists in a just Agreement of the several Parts one with another; and the adapting the whole to the Nature and Uses of the Place, for which your Design is formed.

THUS far of the Imperfections, Faults and Extravagancies of some late Designers of Gardens; to which might be added, that of the setting up of too many; and sometimes the misplacing of Buildings, Statues, and other Ornaments, with which some of the best of our modern Designs have been crouded.

I HAVE one thing more to add, as to Design, which has been generally omitted by all that have wrote, and by many that have practised Rural and Extensive Gardening; and that is the Ambit, Circuit, or Tour of a Design, such as in all large Designs can be only done on Horseback, or in a Chaise or Coach: And is by the *French* called *Anfilade*, probably from *Unum Filum*, a Clue or Continuation of Thread, of which this *Anfilade* or Circuit is composed.

THIS *Anfilade* or Circuit ought to be six or seven Yards wide at least, and should be carried over the tops of the highest Hills that lie within the Compass of any Nobleman's or Gentleman's Design, though it does not extend to the utmost Extremity of it; and from those Eminencies (whereon, if any where, Building or Clumps of Trees ought to be placed) it is that you are to view the whole Design . . .

* Mr. *Bridgman*.

from Volume I, 1718 and 1742

AMongst the several Methods made use of to convey the memorable Actions and great Personages of Antiquity to these Times, this of *Statues* is not the least, being the most publick and durable Memoirs of Virtue, Honour, and Valour . . . I shall not here pretend to give an Historical Account of these illustrious Hero's, nor of their Virtual Attributes and Hieroglyphical Significations, leaving that to the skilful Mythologist; nor yet of their Shape, Lineament, or Articulate and Corporeal Dimensions, that being the Business of the ingenious Statuary. My Intent, in this Place, being to rectifie some Mistakes in their Local Distribution, Magnitude, and general Proportion.

It cann't but be an unpleasant Sight (as common as it is) to view *Jupiter*, *Mars*, *Neptune*, and the rest of the capital Deities of Heaven, misplac'd, and by a meanness of spirit below a good Designer, set perching upon a little Pedestal; one like a Citizen; a second with a Pike in his Hand, like a Foot-Soldier; and the third upon dry Land with a Trident, like a Cart-filler. These are certainly great Diminutions to the Politeness of the Statuary, as they are to the Noble Personages they hieroglyphically represent.

Others, perhaps, err in another respect, by placing *Pan* as a Tutelar God in the Flower-Garden, whilst *Ceres* and *Flora* are the silent Inhabitants of Woods and Groves. To this may be often join'd an Impropriety in the Gesture and Habiliments of these Gods, which ought to differ, as the Actions they are representing do: *Neptune* in the Management of his Sea-Affairs, embracing *Amphitrite*; and *Mars* in his Armorial Array in his Amour with *Venus*; are such Incongruities as the Statuary should always avoid: Since one would be as useless and troublesome a Companion in the guiding and taming his Sea-Horses, as the Warlike Habiliments of the other would be in the Embraces of a Fair Lady.

But to return: *Jupiter* and *Mars* should possess the largest Open Centres and Lawns of a grand Design, elevated upon Pedestal Columnial, and other Architectonical Works, according to the Model of the best Designer, with their immediate Servants and Vassels underneath; *Jupiter* with his *Mercurius*, *Mars* with *Fame*, and the rest of their Attendants; whilst the Niches ought to be fill'd with *Dii Minores* for one, or the Warlike Heroes of Antiquity, aswel as Modern, for the other, every one accoutred and ready to execute the Commands of their great Masters.

Neptune should possess the Centre of the greatest body of Water, (be it either Fountain, Bason, or whatever of that kind) in his Chariot, attended by the *Naiades*, *Tritons*, and other his Sea-Attendants.

Venus ought to be placed among the *Graces, Cupid,* &c. And in all the lesser Centres of a Polygonar Circumscription, it would be proper to place *Apollo* with the *Muses* in the Niches, *Minerva* with the *Liberal Sciences,* &c.

Then *Vulcan* with the *Cyclops* in a Centre of less note, and all the rest of the Deities dispers'd in their particular Places and Order. *Flora, Ceres* and *Pomona,* to their several Charges, and the *Faunes* and *Sylvans,* to the more remote and Rural Centres and Parts of the Wood-work.

If such a Cruel Piece as *Andromeda* fasten'd to a Rock, should be brought into a Garden, it might be proper to place it near the Water, where she might always weep and lament her sad Fate. Thus *Niobe*, &c.

To be more plain: *Venus, Diana, Daphne,* and *Flora,* with their Attendants, may be compleat Furniture for the Flower-Garden; but they ought not to be too small, but bigger than the Life, especially in large Gardens, and elevated upon an accumulation of Architecture or Masonry, (as I have before mention'd) whilst *Mars* and *Neptune* be placed in the larger Centres; *Apollo* amongst the *Muses*; and *Minerva* amongst the *Liberal Sciences,* (as before.) That noble Grace that abundance of these Figures, placed all over our Rural Gardens and Plantations, will afford, is charming to consider . . .

from Volume III, 1718 and 1742

Woods are so much the more beautiful as they are plac'd, or not plac'd on Eminences sloping Hills with Vallies between them, as they are naturally and promiscuously scatter'd and dispers'd over a whole Estate; and it seems to be a great Mistake of those that esteem nothing to be beautiful, but what is regularly planted and distributed out, as are many of Avenues leading to great Houses: Since the Beauty of this Regularity is easily seen at once, and then the Mind is by Nature soon cloy'd of it, but in the other, how pleasingly does it rove uncontroul'd thro' the promiscuous Scenes of a Country. There are others seem to mistake, in thinking none more beautiful, than that that is plac'd thick and close together, as are our common Coppices, but I should rather advise it to be (as already hinted) mix'd with Lawns, Vallies, and rising Hills, that should be always presenting themselves to the Rise of the Beholder, with open Glades, Corn Fields, and Pasture Lands; in this Place a Hillock of Oaks for Shade; in that a hollow and natural Lawn with a Cave or Grott; in one, if possible, a winding Valley between Two rising or sloping Hills of Wood: Here purling Streams; and in another place, Water rowling down not over polish'd Masonry, but over the roughest Frost-work and rugged Stone, cover'd with Moss and other lapidary Excrescencies and Herbs; these agreeable Conveniencies with a little Improvement will without doubt answer the design and employ the thoughts of the most curious Designer.

But however, beautiful Wood and these other Embellishments of Nature are, unless it meets with a skilful hand in the Management, 'tis commonly spoil'd; this I have already spoke to, and so at present contenting my self to caution, that if the Wood is already grown and the House to be built, that great Care be taken in the placing; for that there are Cases, when Wood however beautiful soever in it self may be in a wrong Place, and therefore ought to be cut away or the House so plac'd, that it may be deprived of some distant View; such is the Case when you have blue Hills, a fine Valley, or some noble Lawn, Tower or rising Hills, cloth'd with Wood at a large Distance: These are Beauties so noble, that even grown Wood ought to be cut down to admit an open View to it . . .

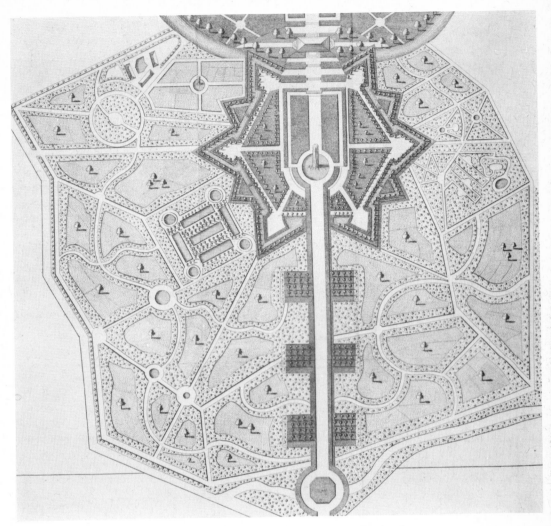

64 'The Manor of Paston divided and planted into Rural Gardens'.
Engraving from Stephen Switzer, *Ichnographia Rustica*, 1718

from Volume II, 1718 and 1742

Tho' since all that pretend to Judgment in Gardening agree, that Variety is
the greatest and most distinguishing Characteristick in any Country-Seat or
Garden, one would think it no very hard Matter, to fix upon one and the same
Method in designing of this beautiful Part of our Business: But I know not
how it comes to pass, People do differ, and that very much; and one seldom
hears of two Persons whose Opinions jump together in any Design, one will
find Fault with what another esteems excellent in its Kind . . . Some there
are that esteem nothing well in a Design, but long, large, wide, regular
Ridings and Walks; and this, in Truth, is right in an open Park or Forest,
where the Owner rides and hunts: But that a Garden-Design for walking in

only, or if thereto we add Magnificence, which, I must own, those long Ridings have, yet it would be a Fault to set too great a Value upon them in a Garden; and for the sake of long level Walks, to level all those little Eminencies and pleasing Labyrinths of Nature: For tho' a few of these Walks are absolutely necessary, in Respect to the Grandeur and general Beauty of a Situation, as the Middle and Side Walk, and a very few Diagonals, yet it is an unpardonable Fault, as we see it almost every where, (let the Expence be what it will) to have scarce any Thing in a whole Design, but carries open Walks; so that be the Garden 40, 50, or 60 Acres, one shall scarce find any private or natural Turn in the whole; if the Wood be grown, down come all the noble Trees that stand in the Way of the Scheme. And this seems to be the greatest Difference in the Opinion of Persons as to Design. And that this is not Fiction, there are a great many Places do testify, particularly that beautiful Wood belonging to the Earl of *Carlisle*, at *Castle-Howard*, where Mr. *London* design'd a Star, which would have spoil'd the Wood; but that his Lordship's superlative Genius prevented it, and to the great Advancement of the Design, has given it that Labyrinth diverting Model we now see it; and it is, at this Time, a Proverb at that Place, *York against London*, in Allusion to the Design of a *Londoner*, and Mr. *London* the Designer . . .

from Volume III, 1718 and 1742

A Description of a beautiful Rural Garden.

BEfore I quit my agreeable and entertaining Subject of Designs in general, I cannot omit giving a particular Description of a *Rural Garden*, which tho' not equally extensive, yet perhaps equally beautiful to most we have in *England*, notwithstanding the happy Possessor bears no higher Character than that of a private Gentleman [i.e. Dyrham].

I have been a great many Pages in treating of Situations, which a Man would always willingly chuse, tho' it is rarely in his Power: I therefore hope this Description will be the more acceptable, as it contains matter of Fact, and is no way chimerical; and when 'tis consider'd, that Nature has a greater Share in the Beauties I am proceeding to, than Art; not but very considerable Sums have been expended to bring these Gardens to that Perfection which I some Years since saw them in, when my Affairs requir'd my Attendance on a Person of the first Rank at the *Bath*.

To describe the Situation of the Seat in general is a Task of Difficulty; the best Account I can give of it in a few Words, is, that 'tis a beautiful Irregularity, here a Dale, there a Mount, here a winding Valley, there a purling Stream, &c. And indeed the Quantity of Water which abounds here, and plentifully supplies the Water-works, is found Fault with by some Persons as an Annoyance to the House, seated low; but without considering the many large and most exquisite contriv'd Drains erected for its Conveyance to distant Ponds.

Some injudicious Persons likewise make an Exception to the Situation of this Seat, not only for its being low and moist; but on Account of its being surrounded on one Side with Hills, so as not to be discern'd 'till you come just upon it; what ever Fault this may be in the Esteem of the Generality of Mankind, I shall not pretend to determine; but I have this to offer in its Favour, that on your Approach to the House from the Hills, you are at once entertain'd with an infinite Variety of beautiful Prospects, the surprizing Pleasure whereof would have been in a great Measure lost by a remote anticipating View. And from the other Side of the House, a fine Vale of a considerable Extent is discover'd even from the first Floor, notwithstanding its being low with Respect to the Northern Side, encompass'd with aspiring Mounts . . . Turning to the left you find a spacious Pavement Walk, the whole Length of the Front of the House and *Green house,* at each End whereof are Paintings in Niches representing Statues.

To this Pavement in the Summer are carry'd Orange-Trees, Lemons, round-headed Bays, &c. in Tubs, and plac'd in Rows, so as to make a most delightful Walk before the whole Front, which is continu'd on the left against the Side of a Terrace-Walk, to the upper Part of the first Parterre: The Parterre is cut into four Quarters of Grass and Gravel, of various Forms, the Borders adjoining to the principal Gravel Walk, leading to the main Door at the Front, being set off with large Pyramid Silver Hollies, Ews, &c. having painted Iron Rods with gilded Nobs for their Support, and the Center-Sides, &c. with round-headed Laurels exactly clipt, Bays, small Pyramid Ews, &c.

Facing the Front of the *Green-house* is a running Canal of clear Water, about a hundred Yards in Length; at the upper End, in an enlarg'd Circle, with a high Head of fine Stone, is a Fountain which casts Water above sixty Foot in Height, and great Variety of small Pipes playing all round, which entirely fill the Circle or Head of the Canal. In this Canal several Sorts of Fish are confin'd, as Trout, Perch, Carp, &c. of a very large Size, and tho' it is deep, yet the Water is so transparent that you may easily discover the scalely Residents, even those of the smallest Dimensions: And this Canal is so very much frequented in the Summer, that the Fish will not be disturb'd at your Approach; but are almost as tame as the Swans, (two whereof continually waft themselves with Grandeur in this Canal) which will not scruple to take an uncommon Feeding from your Hands.

The Situation of the Canal is lower than the Parterre before the Body of the House, separated with Walls; that on the Left making the Parterre a Terrace, and that on the right dividing the Garden from the Park; so that it is as it were a private Garden of it self, and indeed is a most pleasant one in a hot Season: In the Walls on each Side are several Falls of Water, from Pipes and Monsters Heads to Basons, from one Bason to another, which at last empty into Streams appearing like Brooks, and these discharge themselves into the Canal: One of the Walls is fill'd with Fruit-Trees, and the other (the highest) with Ever-Greens; and of each Side the Canal are Walks of Bays, Philireas, &c. in Tubs, and two very large Silver Hollies at the End to grace the Entrance.

The Wall of the Canal is cover'd with a Coping of fine Free Stone, and so are all the Walls belonging to these Gardens. At the upper End of it are about half a dozen Stone Steps, which lead you to the second Parterre: This Parterre is of the whole Breadth of the Garden, and is finely adorn'd with round-headed Standard Laurels, pyramid Ews, &c. with Iron Rods and gilded Nobs; and the two Quarters of it, on each Side the large Walk leading to the Front-Door, are during the Summer set off with Oranges in Tubs, &c. in the Nature of an Orangery: Opposite to the Canal, is an Octagon Fountain of a considerable Extent, the Pipe in the Middle throws a large Stream of Water a very great Height; and round it there are eight large Cases or Heads facing each Side of the Octagon, with a Multitude of small Pipes very close together, which when play'd, make a very good Representation of Pillars of Water.

The End of this Parterre is fenc'd in from the Park with curious Iron Work, on Dwarf-Walls; and on Pillars between the Spikes are fix'd Variety of Heads carv'd out of fine Stone; here's a large Iron Gate beautifully Wrought, and finely painted and gilded, which lets you into the Park; after you have pass'd about twenty Yards on a Gravel Walk in the Park, you come to a noble Cataract or extended Cascade of Water; this Cascade is on a Line with the Octogon Fountain, and the Canal, and all exactly fronting the Door of the *Green-house*; it has, as I remember, near two hundred and fifty Steps to the Top, and as many Falls for the Water to descend, and it is so high, that you have several Seats erected for Resting. At the Bottom there is a large Oval Pond with a Fountain in it; at the Top there is likewise the same, and in the Middle a large and lofty Pedestal, supporting a Neptune cut out in Stone, of large Dimensions, with an exalted Trident in his Hand; a Whale is represented between his Legs, discharging a great Quantity of Water into Basons on the Heads of Tritons, from whence it falls [in] large Sheets to the Pond.

At regular Distances are plac'd several small Pipes or Fountains to the Top of the Cataract, on the Steps which facilitate the Descent of the Water; these Pipes, when they play, seem a Slope-Walk of Fountains; and when the Cataract plays at the same Time, the Weight of the Water, and the Falls are so great, that the Noise very near equals the Billows of a raging Sea, and may be heard at a very great Distance: At the Bottom of the Steps are planted two Thorns encompass'd with Seats, which are arriv'd to a large Stature, and being kept of a round regular Form with frequent Clippings, make a very good Figure: There are small Pipes which twine round the Bodies of these Trees, and appear more like Ivy on the rough Bark, (being painted Green) than leaden Pipes, which on the Turn of a Cock discharge Water from a vast Number of small Nosils in the Head of the Trees, all round as natural as if it rain'd; and in a cloudy Day I have been inform'd, Spectators setting down here to rest themselves, the more these Pipes have play'd, the closer they have embrac'd the Tree for Shelter, supposing it had really rain'd, 'till the Gardener has convinc'd them of their Error, after they had partaken of a sufficient Sprinkling to imprint in their Memories the pleasurable Mistake.

Between this Hill, which gives the Situation for the Cataract, and a Hill in the Park, you have a fine winding Valley of about half a Mile in Length, planted with Horse-Chesnuts; at the upper End is a fine Brake of Wood on the one Side, and on the other a large square Pond; from this Pond a small

Channel is cut for the Water, which after a great many Falls from Cascades, at Length enters another Pond, so that you are never out of the agreeable Noise of a murmuring Stream. Near this Pond, at the Entrance of the Chesnut-Walk, is likewise a third Pond, of a large Extent, having in the Middle a very fine Statue and Fountain.

From hence you come back to the Garden, and mount the Terras-Walks, which are several, one above another, and very beautiful; the first adjoins to the North Side of the House, so that you come from a Closet, one Pair of Stairs, immediately out upon it; and at the End of this, in the Middle of a small Slope-Garden, enclos'd with a lofty Hedge on one Side, and a high Wall on the other, is a small Statue representing *Iris*, from which a Fountain plays, and fills all that Quarter with seeming Rain, to the very great Refreshment of those Persons who frequent the Rooms facing it in a scorching Season: But to return to the Terras's; there are four in Number of a good Length one above another before you arrive at the Top, at the Ends of which you have a Wall to separate them from the Church-yard, beautify'd with fine Paintings in Niches; except it be in one of the broadest, where you have a most commodious Summer-House, answering to a Pigeon-House on t'other Side in the Park. You ascend these Terras-Walks on large square Stone Steps, 'till you come near the Top, when you arrive at very grand and magnificent Steps, cut out in the Form of a half Circle.

When you have ascended these Terras's, the first Thing which offers to your Sight, is a large Stone Statue on a handsome Pedestal, near a Wilderness, and a fine Fountain with plenty of Fish, on Ground of a more exalted Elevation than the Top of the House; from thence you proceed to two Noble Terras-Walks, each above a quarter of a Mile in Length, one for the most Part enclos'd with a very lofty Hedge, kept shorn, and a Wall with Fruit-Trees, making it a solitary Walk, and the other open and expos'd; but planted on one Side with round headed Dwarf Elms, and Firs, and Iron Rails on the other: From this Terras you have a prospect from you of about eight or ten Miles over a rich and fertile Vale, which, by Variety of Woods, Groves, and Meadows, appears like a *Rural Garden* to this stately Mansion. Here you have in View the Avenue to the House, which is full of stately Plantations, and to which you have a regular Descent or Slope planted with Dwarf Fruit-Trees. On the other Side of the grand Avenue are two very large Ponds, almost cover'd with Water-Fowl, and a noble *Dutch* Fountain between, having small Seats and Arbours all round, and Falls of Water, which make the Figure of a Pyramid, by descending from one Bason to another: In the Court-Yard before the House are two large Pedestals with Sphynxes, finely carv'd, and the Stew-Pond; on one Side is the Orchard, and at the End is the Kitchen-Garden.

As you proceed on the Terras Walk, you meet with Niches and Falls of Water, and likewise a Fountain in the Middle; and towards the End you are agreeably surpriz'd with a Flower-Garden on a Slope, to which you are let thro' the Hedge by an undiscover'd Gap; when you come to the End of the Terras, your Prospect is so far enlarg'd, that you see *Welch* Mountains thirty or forty Miles distant: Here you have large arch'd Seats, on which are painted Motto's suitable to their Situation, and a pleasant little Garden laid out into Gravel-Walks, Grass-Plats, &c. from hence you advance to a Mount considerably higher still, in the Middle of a Warren; on the Top of which is a large Seat, call'd a *Windsor* Seat, which is contriv'd to turn round any Way, either for the Advantage of Prospect, or to avoid the Inconveniencies of Wind, the Sun, &c. Here 'tis you have a most entertaining Prospect all round, and you see into several Counties of *England*, as well as into *Wales*.

From this Seat you descend again to a flourishing Wilderness, on an easy Slope, cut out into the utmost Variety of Walks, especially solitary Walks, and beautify'd with Statues: In the Middle there is a delightful square Garden, having four large Seats at the Corners, and a Seat round an aspiring Fir-Tree in the Center, from whence your Prospect terminates in a large old Church, at a very great Distance. I never in my whole Life did see so agreeable a Place for the sublimest Studies, as this is in the Summer, and here are small Desks erected in Seats for that Purpose. On one Side you ascend several Grass-Steps, and come to an artificial Mount, whereon is a large spreading Tree, with a Vane at the Top, and a Seat enclosing it, commanding a most agreeable and entire Prospect of the Vale below; from hence you come down to a very magnificent Arbour, with the Convenience of Water-Works to play round it. Opposite in the Park, on a Hill of equal Elevation, is an Arbour every Way answering this, and compleats the Regularity: From hence you ascend the Mount again, and go by the Lodge and a large Nursery of Trees into the Park, where, on a Hill almost as high as any I have describ'd, is the Spring Head and the Pond, which supplies the Water-Works: It takes up near an Acre of Ground, and at the Head is eighteen or twenty Foot deep; it has an Island in the Middle planted with Trees, contains Variety of the finest Water-Fowl, is well stock'd with most Sorts of Fish; and here you may sail in a Ship on a Mountain . . .

from the Appendix to Volume III, 1742

SO much has been already said as to the Beauty of rural and extensive Gardening, when compared with the stiff *Dutch* Way, which has been for some time exploded, that as to that Part at least, little need be added; and that this was the Method used by the *Romans* of old, the curious Drafts and Accounts of the Ancient Villa's about that once Mistress of the World *Rome*, (published by an ingenious Gentleman lately deceased) fully evince.

This Taste, so truly useful and delightful as it is, has also for some time been the Practice of some of the best Genius's of *France*, under the Title of *La Ferme Ornée*. And that *Great-Britain* is now likely to excel in it, let all those who have seen the Farms and Parks of *Abbs-Court*, *Riskins*, *Dawley-Park*, now a doing, with other Places of the like Nature, declare: In all which it is visible, that the *Roman* Genius, which was once the Admiration of the World, is now making great advances in *Britain* also.

The Plan annex'd to this Appendix . . . is a regulated Epitomy of a much larger Design portraited and lay'd out, by the Right Honourable the

Lord *Bathurst* at *Riskins* near *Colnbrooke,* upon the Plan of the *Ferme Ornée,* and the Villa's of the Ancients; the Lawns round about the House are for the feeding of Sheep, and the insides of the Quarters for sowing of Corn, Turnips, &c. or for the feeding of Cattle.

A is the House.
B The Parterre or Lawn.
C The Menagery.
D The Terrass round the House.
E A Labyrinth.
F The Gardener's House.
G The Melonry.
H The Stable and Stable-Yard.
I Kitchin Garden.
K The Entrance.
L Promiscuous Quarters for Corn, Turnips or feeding of Cattle.
M The Avenue to and from the House.
N An Ah, Ah.
O Parade.

One Thing I would observe in this Plan, that besides the main Walks which go strait diagonal ways, and round the whole Plantation, there are also little private Hedge-Rows or Walks round every Field about six or eight Foot wide, and in some Places they run a-cross the Field where it is large; and particularly at every Angle there is a little piece of Wood in the form of a Labyrinth.

It may be objected against this Design, and all others of this Kind, that it were better the Fields were more square: Which I grant, but then there can be no diagonal Walks, which are very beautiful in any Villa, however not so very necessary but they may be omitted. I must own, that this Draft is but an imperfect Epitomy of the fine Design it is took from, there not being room, in so small a Plate as an Octavo Edition will allow, to make it larger; nor have I room to insert the whole Design: but this I produce, as a small Specimen of what may be done in a larger Case. The foregoing Volumes demonstrate, that I was always a Promoter of this Farm-like Way of Gardening, before it was used by any body, in any place, in *Great-Britain,* and must still think it, that it is not only the most profitable, but the most pleasurable of any Kind of Gardening when the Farm is walled or paled in, as is that of *Abbs-Court,* &c. before mentioned: And when all Roads and Church-ways are removed, and if possible the Tythe agreed for a Reduction to a Modus; I cannot but think that a Farm of 2 or 300 Acres thus employed, (be it even double the Quantity) where the Lawns and Fields are kept free from Ragweed and Thistles, and the Turf well rolled in the Spring, and all Mole-Hills and the Dunging of Cattle kept continually spread about: I cannot, I say, but think that it is really the truest and best Way of Gardening in the World, and such as the politest and best Genius of all Antiquity delighted in.

Lord Perceval, 1st Earl of Egmont
(1683–1748)

The following account from a letter on Hall Barn, Buckinghamshire, preserved among the Egmont MSS. in the British Library, concerns the great garden created in the French taste by the poet, Edmund Waller, between 1651 and 1687 and re-worked between 1715 and 1730 by his grandson and John Aislabie, the grandson's stepfather who went on to create Studley Royal (see p. 237). In 1661 the elder Waller had celebrated St James's Park 'as lately improved by His Majesty' in verses which might well have been used about his own Hall Barn ('young trees upon the banks/Of the new stream appear in even ranks'). In 1724 Lord Perceval obviously saw the French aspect of the gardens ('they put us in mind of those at Versailles'). But he is equally attentive to newer elements, notably the ha-ha, the 'close winding walks', the associative spell of the deep wood and the blurred distinction between garden and wood, from which it is possible to see how the early landscape garden emerged from and alongside the older style. Perceval was perhaps too early to see the fine temple which Colin Campbell or Roger Morris introduced into the landscape in the late 1720s (Plate 65) and which served to confirm its role as mediator between the two forms.

65 Hall Barn, Buckinghamshire. Detail of engraving by Woollett, 1760

from a Letter on Hall Barn, Buckinghamshire (9 August 1724)

Now to give you an account of what we have seen. Fryday morning when we left Beceonsfeild, we went half a mile out of our way to see Hall Barn, M.ʳ Wallers house, a London Box if I may so call a house of 7 windows every way. He was gone a hunting, so we did not go into the house which promised nothing extraordinary, but we spent a full hour and half in viewing the gardens, which you will think are fine when I tell you they put us in mind of those at Versailles. He has 80 Acres in garden & wood, but the last is so managed, as justly to be counted part of the former, for from the parterre you have terraces and gravel'd walks that lead up to and quite thro the wood, in which, several lesser ones cross the principal one of different breadths, but all well gravel'd and for the most part green sodded on the sides. The wood consists of tall beach trees, & thick underwood at least 30 foot high. The narrow winding walks and paths cut in it are innumerable. A woman in full health cannot walk them all, for which reason my wife was carry'd in a windsor chair, like those at Versailles, by which means she lost nothing worth seeing. The walks are terminated by Ha-hah's, over which you see a fine country, and variety of prospects, every time you come to the extremity of the close winding walks that shut out the sun.

Versailles has indeed the advantage in fountains, for there is not one in all this garden, but there are two very noble peices of water full of fish, and handsomely planted & teraced on the sides. In one part of the wood, and in a deep bottom is a place to which one descends with horrour, for it seems the residence of some draggon, but there shines a gleam of light thro the high wood that surrounds & shades it, which recovers the spirits, and makes you sensible a draggon would seek some place still more retired. This place may be call'd the temple of Pan or Silvanus, consisting of several apartments, arches, Corridores &c composed of high thriving Ews, cut very artfully. In the Center of the Inner Circle or Court if I may call it so, stands the figure of a guilt Satyr on a stone pedestal with his finger in his mouth, as if he would have you tread softly, least you should interrupt a bewtifull Hermophrodite near at hand contemplating a flower. I pass over the bowling green & large plantations about the house which are but young, but I must not forget a bench or seat of the famous Edmund Waller's the Poet, which is so reverenced, that old as it is it is never to be removed, but constantly repaired like S.ⁱʳ Francis Drakes ship. The present Waller is his Grand son . . . There is a great deal more still to be done, which will cost a prodigious sum . . .

Daniel Defoe (c. 1661–1731)

Defoe's popular travel book, *A Tour Thro' The Whole Island of Great Britain,* went into nine editions between 1724 and 1778, undergoing revision at the hands of successive editors. The extracts here come from the first edition (1724–6) and the third (1742), which was revised and augmented by another novelist, Samuel Richardson. Defoe's *Tour,* with its sharp journalist eye, is immensely valuable for the glimpses it gives of country estates, many in the course of improvement. Sometimes Defoe notices only that 'the avenues [are] noble, and the gardens perfectly finished' or that Euston Hall has 'all that is pleasant and delightful in nature . . . improv'd by art to every extreme that Nature is able to produce'. At other times his notes are more complete, and we give examples of four such descriptions: the gardens he saw in the 1720s still seem in the French taste, full of 'avenues and vistos' or of 'fountains, canals, vistos, and all the most exquisite pieces of art'. Yet Defoe can also register more natural prospects and admire a 'most beautiful intermixture of wood, and water in the park, and gardens, and grounds adjoining'. By 1742 the augmented *Tour* mirrors the new landscaping tastes, and we provide a further four descriptions of later gardens to indicate the advances in practice as well as theory.

from *A Tour Thro' The Whole Island of
Great Britain* (1724–6 and 1742)

As the Front of [Wanstead] House opens to a long row of Trees, reaching to the Great Road at *Leighton-Stone*; so the Back-Face, or Front, *if that be proper,* respects the Gardens, and with an easy Descent lands you upon the Terras, from whence is a most Beautiful Prospect to the River, which is all form'd into Canals and Openings, to answer the Views from above, and beyond the River, the Walks and Wildernesses go on to such a Distance, and in such a manner up the Hill, as they before went down, that the Sight is lost in the Woods adjoining, and it looks all like one planted Garden as far as the Eye can see . . .

While this was doing, the Gardens [of Hampton Court] were laid out, the Plan of them devised by the King himself [Plate 66]; and especially the Amendments and Alterations were made by the King, or the Queen's particular special Command, or by both; for their Majesties agreed so well in their Fancy, and had both so good Judgment in the just Proportions of Things, which are the principal Beauties of a Garden, that it may be said they both order'd every Thing that was done.

Here the fine Parcel of Limes, which form the Semi-circle on the South Front of the House, by the Iron Gates, looking into the Park, were, by the dextrous Hand of the head Gardener, remov'd, after some of them had been almost thirty Years planted in other Places, tho' not far of. I know the King of *France*, in the Decoration of the Gardens of *Versailles*, had Oaks remov'd, which, by their Dimensions, must have been above an hundred Years old, and yet were taken up with so much Art, and by the Strength of such Engines, by which such a monsterous Quantity of Earth was raised with them, that the Trees could not feel their remove; that is to say, their Growth was not at all hinder'd. This, I confess, makes the Wonder much the less in those Trees at *Hampton-Court* Gardens; but the Performance was not the less difficult or nice, however, in these, and they thrive perfectly well.

While the Gardens were thus laid out, the King also directed the laying the Pipes for the Fountain and *Jette d'Eau's*; and particularly the Dimensions of them, and what Quantity of Water they should cast up, and encreas'd the Number of them after the first Design.

The Ground on the Side of the other Front, has receiv'd some Alterations since the taking down the Water Gallery; but not that Part immediately next the Lodgings: The *Orange* Trees, and fine *Dutch* Bays, are plac'd within the Arches of the Building under the first Floor: so that the lower Part of the House was all one as a Green House for some Time: Here stands advanced, on two Pedestals of Stone, two Marble Vases, or Flower-Pots, of most exquisite Workmanship; the one done by an *Englishman,* and the other by a *German*: 'Tis hard to say which is the best Performance, tho' the doing of it was a kind of Tryal of Skill between them; but it gives us room, without Partiality, to say they were both Masters of their Art.

The Parterre on that Side descends from the Terrass Walk by Steps, and on the Left a Terrass goes down to the Water-side, from which the Garden on the Eastward Front is overlook'd, and gives a most pleasant Prospect.

The fine Scrolls and Bordure of these Gardens were at first edg'd with Box; but on the Queen's disliking the Smell, those Edgings were taken up, but have since been planted again, at least in many Places, nothing making so fair and regular an Edging as Box, or is so soon brought to its Perfection.

On the North Side of the House, where the Gardens seem'd to want skreening from the Weather, or the view of the Chapel, and some Part of the old Building requir'd to be cover'd from the Eye; the vacant Ground, which was large, is very happily cast into a Wilderness, with a Labyrinth, and Espaliers so high, that they effectually take off all that Part of the old Building, which would have been offensive to the Sight. This Labyrinth and Wilderness is not only well design'd, and compleatly finish'd, but is perfectly well kept, and the Espaliers fill'd exactly, at Bottom to the very Ground, and are led up to proportion'd Heights on the Top; so that nothing of that Kind can be more beautiful.

The House itself is every way answerable on the Outside to the beautiful Prospect, and the two Fronts are the largest, and, beyond Comparison, the

66 Hampton Court, Middlesex. Engraving by Highmore and Tinney, *c.* 1745

finest of the Kind in *England*: The great Stairs go up from the second Court of the Palace on the Right Hand, and lead you to the South Prospect...

One cannot be said to have seen any thing that a Man of Curiosity would think worth seeing in this County, and not have been at *Wilton House*; but not the beautiful Building, not the antient Trophy of a great Family, not the noble Scituation, not all the Pleasures of the Gardens, Parks, Fountains, Hare-Warren, or of whatever is Rare; either in Art or Nature are equal to, that yet more glorious Sight, of a noble Princely Palace, constantly filled with its noble and proper Inhabitants; *viz.* the Lord and Proprietor, who is indeed a true *Patriarchal Monarch*, reigns here with an Authority agreeable to all his Subjects (Family); and his reign is made agreeable, by his first practising the most exquisite Government of himself, and then guiding all under him by the Rules of Honour and Vertue; being also himself perfectly Master of all the needful Arts of Family Government; I mean needful to make that Government, both Easy, and Pleasant to those who are under it, and who therefore willingly, and by Choice conform to it.

Here an exhaulted Genius is the Instructor, a glorious Example the Guide, and a Gentle well directed Hand the Governour and Law-giver to the whole;

and the Family like a well govern'd City appears Happy, Flourishing and Regular, groaning under no Grievance, pleas'd with what they Enjoy, and Enjoying every Thing which they ought to be pleas'd with.

Nor is the blessing of this noble Resident extended to the Family only, but even to all the Country round, who in their Degree feel the Effects of the general Beneficence; and where the Neighbourhood, however Poor, receive all the good they can Expect, and are sure to have no Injury, or Oppression.

The Canal before the House lyes Parallel with the Road, and receives into it the whole River *Willey*, or at least is able to do so; it may indeed be said, that the River is made into a Canal; when we come into the Court-Yards before the House there are several peices of Antiquity to enteratain the Curious; as particularly, a noble Column of Porphyry, with a Marble Statue of *Venus* on the Top of it. In *Italy*, and especially at *Rome* and *Naples*, we see a great Variety of fine Columns, and some of them of excellent Workmanship, and Antiquity, and at some of the Courts of the Princes of *Italy* the like is seen; as especially at the Court of *Florence*; but in *England* I do not remember to have seen any thing like this, which as they told me is Two and Thirty Foot high and of excellent Workmanship, and that it came last from *Candia*, but formerly from *Alexandria*, what may belong to the History of it any further, I suppose is not known, at least they could tell me no more of it, who shew'd it me.

On the left of the Court was formerly a large Grotto, and curious Water-Works, and in a House, or Shed, or Part of the Building which open'd with two folding Doors, like a Coach-House, a large Equestrian Statue of one of the Ancestors of the Family in compleat Armour, as also another of a *Roman* Emperor in Brass, but the last time I had the Curiosity to see this House, I mist that Part; so that I suppos'd they were remov'd . . .

Under this Front [of Chatsworth lye the Gardens exquisitely fine, and, to make a clear Vista or Prospect beyond into the flat Country, towards *Hardwick*, another Seat of the same owner, the Duke, to whom what others thought impossible, was not only made practicable, but easy, removed, and perfectly carried away a great Mountain that stood in the way, and which interrupted the Prospect.

This was so entirely gone, that, having taken a strict View of the Gardens at my first being there, and retaining an Idea of them in my Mind, I was perfectly confounded at coming there a second time, and not knowing what had been done; for I had lost the Hill, and found a new Country in view, which *Chatsworth* it self had never seen before.

The House indeed had received Additions, as it did every Year, and perhaps would to this Day, had the Duke liv'd, who had a Genius for such Things beyond the reach of the most perfect Masters, and was not only capable to design, but to finish.

The Gardens, the Water-works, the Cascades, the Statues, Vasa and Painting, tho' they are but very imperfectly described by any of the Writers who have yet named them, and more imperfectly by one Author, who has so lately pretended to View them; yet I dare not venture to mention them here, least, for want of time, and having so long a Journey to go, I should, like those who have gone before me, do it imperfectly, or leave no room to do Justice to other Persons and Places, which I am still to mention. I shall therefore, as I said above, only touch at what others have omitted.

First, 'tis to be observed that on the East Side rises a very high Mountain, on the top of which they dig Mill-stones, and it begins so close to, and so overlooks the House, being prodigiously high, that, should they roll down a pair of those Stones coupled with a wooden Axis, as is the way of drawing them, they would infallibly give a Shock to the Building; yet this Mountain is so planted, and so covered with a Wood of beautiful Trees, that you see no Hill, only a rising Wood, as if the Trees grew so much higher than one another, and was only a Wall of Trees, whose tops join into one another so close, as nothing is seen through them.

Upon the top of that Mountain begins a vast extended Moor or Waste, which, for fifteen or sixteen Miles together due North, presents you with neither Hedge, House or Tree, but a waste and houling Wilderness, over which when Strangers travel, they are obliged to take Guides, or it would be next to impossible not to lose their way.

BUT I must not pass over so slightly the noble Seat of the Right Honourable the Earl of *Burlington* [at Chiswick, Plate 67]; which was a plain, useful House, with a Number of good Offices about it: but as a Part of the old House was destroyed some Years ago, by Fire, his Lordship erected a most beautiful Villa, near to the old House; which for Elegance of Taste, surpasses every thing of its kind in *England*, if not in *Europe*. The Court in Front of the House is of a proportionable Size to the Building, which is gravelled, and kept always very neat. On each Side are Yew Hedges, in Panels, with *Termini*, placed at proper Distance; in Front of which are planted two Rows of Cedars of *Libanus*, which at present have a fine Effect to the Eye, at a small Distance from the House; for the dark Shade of these solemn ever-green Trees occasions a fine Contraste with the elegant white Building which appears between them.

The Ascent to the House is by a noble Flight of Stone Steps, on one Side of which is the Statue of *Inigo Jones*, and on the other that of *Palladio*. The Portico is supported by fine fluted Pillars of the *Corinthian* Order, and the Cornice, Frize, and Architrave are as rich as possible; so that the Front of this Building strikes every Person (tho' not a nice Judge of Architecture) with uncommon Pleasure.

The other Front towards the Garden is plainer, but yet is very bold and grand, having a pleasing Simplicity, as hath also the Side-Front, toward the *Serpentine River*, which is different from the other Two.

The Inside of the House is finished in the highest Taste, the Ceilings being richly gilt and painted; and the Rooms are filled with some of the best Pictures in *Europe*; and tho' the House is small, yet it would take up more Room than can be allowed here, to describe the particular Beauties of it.

The Gardens are also laid out in an elegant Taste. When you descend from the House, you enter on a Lawn of Grass, planted with Clumps of ever-green Trees, between which are two Rows of large Stone Vases. At the Ends next the House are two fine Wolves in Stone, cut by Mr. *Sceidmaker* the famous Statuary: and at the farther End are two large Lions; and to terminate this View are three fine antique Statues, which were dug up in *Adrian*'s Garden at *Rome*, with Stone Seats between each; and on the Back of the Statues is a close Plantation of Ever-greens, which terminates the Prospect.

On the Right-hand, as you go from the House, you look thro' an open Grove of Forest-trees, to the Orangery; which is separated from the Lawn by a Faussee, to secure the Orange-trees from being injured by Persons who are admitted to walk in the Garden; so that they are seen as perfectly, and when the Orange-trees are in Flower, the Scent is diffused over the whole Lawn to the House, as if the Trees were placed on the Lawn.

On the Left-hand you have an easy Slope of Grass down to the Serpentine River, on the Side of which are Clumps of Ever-greens, which make agreeable Breaks to the Eye, between which the Water is seen; and at the farther End is a Peep into an Inclosure, where are an Obelisk and a *Roman* Temple, with Grass Slopes, and a circular Piece of Water in the Middle.

From this Lawn you are led to the Wilderness, through which are three strait Avenues, terminated by three different Buildings; and within the Quarters are Serpentine Walks, thro' which you may walk near a Mile in constant Shade.

On each Side the Serpentine River is a Grass Walk, which follow the Turns of the River; and on the Right-hand of the River is a Building, which is the exact Model of the Portico of *Covent Garden* Church; and on the Left is a Wilderness, which is laid out in regular Walks, with clipp'd Hedges on each Side, which is too mean for the other Parts of the Garden; and it is much to be wondered his Lordship should suffer them to remain in the present Form.

Over the River, in the middle Part, is a *Palladian* Bridge of Wood, which his Lordship crosses in his Coach to come round to the House; for there is a Coach Road thro' the Garden, by which his Lordship passes when he comes from *London*, so that the Earl seldom goes thro' the Town of *Chiswick* to his House.

At the End of the River, next the Road, is a fine Cascade lately erected, which by an Engine to raise the Water, his Lordship proposed to have a constant Fall into the River; but the Engine failing, it is but seldom the Cascade can play, and then but for a short time.

Next the Road his Lordship has raised a Terrace, (with the Earth which came out of the River) from whence you have a Prospect of the adjacent Country; and when the Tide is up, you see the Water of the *Thames*, with the Boats and Barges passing, which greatly enlivens the Prospect. In a Word, there is more Variety in this Garden, than can be found in any other of the same Size in *England*, or perhaps in *Europe* . . .

[Gunnersbury House] is situated near *Ealing*, between the two great Western Roads, and stands on an Eminence, the Ground falling gradually from it to the *Brentford* Road; so that from the Portico in the Back-front of the House, you have an exceeding fine Prospect of the County of *Surrey*, the

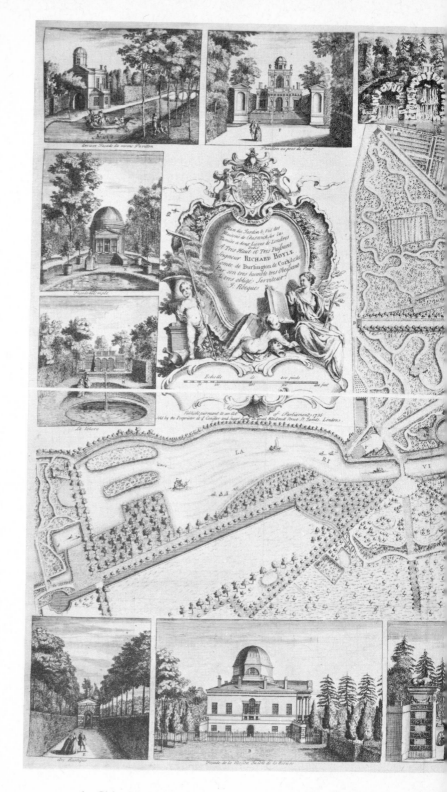

67 Chiswick House, Middlesex. Plan of gardens by Rocque, 1736

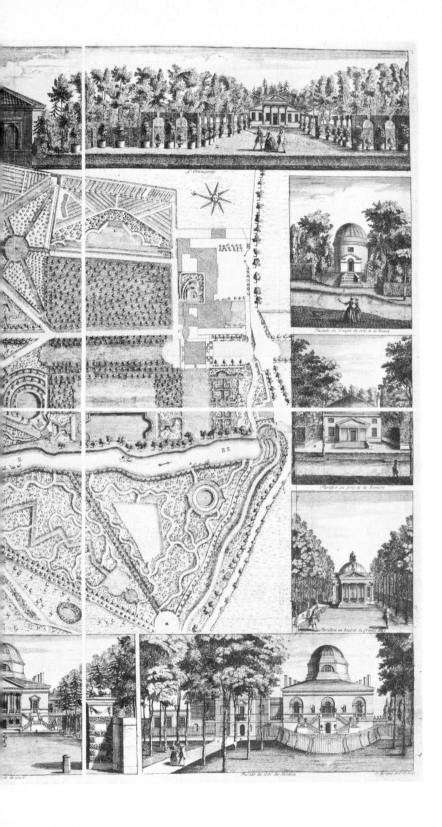

L'Orangerie.

Façade du Temple du côté de la Rivière.

Pavillon au prés de la Rivière.

Pavillon au bout de la Grande.

Façade du Côté du Jardin.

River of *Thames*, and all the Meadows on the Borders for some Miles, as also a good Prospect of *London*, in clear Weather. This House was built by Mr. *Web*, who was Son-in-law to the famous *Inigo Jones*; and indeed the Architecture shews it was contrived by him, or at least by a Scholar of his; for altho' the Building is as plain on the Outside as possible, yet there is a simple Boldness in it, which graces all the Buildings of *Inigo Jones*, rarely to be found in the Works of other Architects . . . Upon going out of the House into the Garden, you come upon a noble Terrace, the whole Width of the Garden, from whence you have a fine Prospect of the neighbouring Country, and on which you may walk dry after the greatest Rains; from this Terrace you descend to the Garden by a noble Flight of Stone Steps, the upper Part of which is concave, and the lower convex, with a noble Stone Balustrade on each Side, as also upon the Coping of the Wall, the Length of the House, which makes a fine Appearance from the Road; but the Gardens are laid out too plain, having the Walls in View on every Side; and at present the Offices are too mean for the House, which I hear the present Possessor intends to alter, in a most elegant Taste, which will render it the finest Seat near *London* . . .

AT *Peckham* is the Seat of the late Lord *Trevor*, which was built in the Reign of King *James* II. by Sir *Thomas Bond*, who was deeply engaged with that unfortunate Prince in his Schemes, and was obliged to quit the Kingdom with him; so the House was plundered by the Populace, and became a Forfeit to the Crown. In the Building and the Gardens, large Sums of Money were expended; for the Whole was executed according to the politest Taste of those Times. The Front of the House stands to the North, having Two Rows of large Elm-trees of a considerable Length before it, thro' which the Tower of *London* appears as a Termination to the Prospect; but on each Side of this Avenue you have a View of *London*, from *Westminster* to *Greenwich*; and at high Water the Masts of the Vessels on the River of *Thames* appear over the Trees and Houses like a Wood, which greatly improves the Prospect. The Fields in Front, and on each Side of the House, being well cultivated, render them very agreeable; and the Town of *Peckham* lies on the Backside of the Gardens, but is shut out from the View by Plantations. The Wilderness indeed was planted too regular, having diagonal Walks intersecting each other, with Hedges on each Side; but this was the Taste which prevailed, when those Gardens were laid out. The Kitchen-garden and the Walls were planted with the choicest Fruit-trees from *France*, and an experienced Fruit-gardener was sent for from *Paris*, to have the Management of them; so that the Collection of Fruits in this Garden has been accounted one of the best in *England*.

A private Gentleman purchased this Seat soon after the Death of the late Lord *Trevor*, and had begun to make very great Alterations, particularly in cutting down Hedges, removing Walls and Buildings, which intercepted the Prospect of the neighbouring Fields; and had the Gentleman lived a few Years longer, he would have intirely altered it to the modern Taste of Gardening, and rendred it a sweet Retirement, considering its Vicinity to *London* . . .

AT *Painshill* near *Cobham* in *Surrey*, is the Seat of the Hon. *Charles*

Hamilton, where is a great Improvement making by inclosing a large Tract of Land designed for a Park, which was most of it so poor as not to produce any thing but *Heath* and *Broom*; but by burning of the *Heath*, and spreading of the Ashes on the Ground, a Crop of *Turneps* was obtained; and by feeding Sheep on the *Turneps*, their Dung became a good Manure to the Land, so that a good Sward of Grass is now upon the Land, where it was judged by most People impossible to get any Herbage. This is the sort of Improvement which was mentioned in *Norfolk*, where Land has been raised from Five Shillings an Acre *per Ann.* to Thirty or Forty Shillings: and were this sort of Husbandry practised in many other Parts of *England*, it would be of great Service to the Publick, and greatly increase the Value of the Lands to the Proprietor . . . The Lands which Mr. *Hamilton* has inclosed, have fine Inequalities; for every 100 Yards there are great Hollows, then rising Grounds again, so that the Prospect is continually changing, as you walk over it; and (if we may guess by what this Gentleman has already done) the Whole will be laid out conformable to the natural Situation of the Ground; and when the Plantations, which are already made, are grown up, it will be a delightful Place; and this upon a Spot of Ground, which lay almost neglected, before this Gentleman became possessed of it; so that whatever is here laid out, will be intirely an Improvement, since without it the Land would have produced very little Rent to the Proprietor. And would the Gentlemen who inclose large Tracts of Land into Parks, follow this Gentleman's Method, of inclosing such Land as is of little Value, and improve it, by making a good Sward upon it, their Estates would be greatly benefited by it.

The House which at present is on this Spot, is very small, being what Mr. *Hamilton* found built on it by his Predecessor; to which he has only added one handsome Room on the Backside, which is elegantly fitted up, and completely furnished with good Pictures: but as there are so many better Situations for a House in the middle of the Park, so it is supposed this Gentleman will erect a new Mansion-house, answerable to the Design of his Plantations.

The River *Mole*, which rises near *Darking*, passes along by the Side of this Park, and in its Course serpents about in so pretty a manner, as that you frequently lose the Sight of it; and by its windings make the Course almost Four Miles within the Compass of this Inclosure. Indeed this River is very narrow, and in dry Weather the Current is exceeding slow, and the Water not well coloured, which, it must be allowed, takes off from its Beauty; yet there is room for great Improvements, by sloping off the Banks, so as to have a better View of the Water; and in many Places by taking away some of the little Projection of the Banks, it may be widened so as to appear considerable at some Distance: which, if done, will add much to the Beauty of the Place.

Near this Place is the House of Mr. *Bridges*, which is built in a very singular Taste, something after the Model of an *Italian Villa*, but very plain on the Outside. The Apartments within seem very commodious, and the principal Rooms are elegantly fitted up, the Ceilings being gilt, and all the Members are richly ornamented: the Offices below are very convenient, and judiciously contrived to answer the Purposes for which they were designed.

But what chiefly struck my Curiosity on seeing it, was a false Story contrived on each Side of the House, taken from the Difference in the Height of the Side-rooms, from those principal Apartments; and these are converted into long Galleries with a small Apartment at one End, which affords a Communication between them. In the *Attick* Story there are very good Lodging-rooms, which are well laid together: so that for the Size of this House, there is hardly any other near *London*, which has more useful and elegant Apartments.

The Situation of the House is on an Eminence, so that it commands the Prospect of the adjacent Fields, which are kept in very exact Order; and there is a Declivity from the House to the River *Mole*, which passes along by the Side of this Gentleman's Garden: and here it appears much more considerable than in any other Part of its Course; for Mr. *Bridges* has taken away so much of the Earth of the Banks, as to make the River, in some Places, Four or Five times broader than it was naturally, so that it makes a handsome Appearance. And by the Side of the Water, he has disposed the Earth into a natural Slope, with a broad Grass-walk, planted with sweet Shrubs on each Side; and at the End of the Walk is a fine Room, which has a View of the Water lengthwise, and is a sweet Retreat in hot Weather, being shaded by large Elm-trees on the South-side, and having the Water on the North and East-sides, which renders it very cool and pleasant. This House is situated about half a Mile from the publick Road to *Portsmouth*, and is so much hid by the Trees near it, as not to be seen until you rise on the Common or Heath beyond *Cobham*, where in several Parts of the Road between that and *Ripley*, you have a fine View of it.

Béat Louis de Muralt (1665–1749)

The following translation of a Swiss view of England appeared in 1726, and it is included for the glimpse it gives of the royal parks. Their air of *rus in urbe* attracted innumerable Londoners, and Walpole reported later in the century that when Queen Caroline spoke of 'shutting up St James's park, and converting it into a noble garden for the palace of that name' and asked his father what it would cost, Sir Robert replied 'only three CROWNS'. Thus began the gradual 'democratization' of those royal demesnes in what is now, in the twentieth century, the heart of London.

from *Letters Describing the Character and Customs of the English and French Nations* (1726)

St. *James's* is another Royal Palace; 'tis old, and very irregular, but convenient and large. There's nothing else to make it agreeable, but the Prospect of the Park, which is near it. Let us get into it, to refresh ourselves a little after the Fatigue of describing the three Royal Palaces.

The Park is a large Extent of Ground with Walks set with Trees all round, which are very agreeable. There's a Canal in the middle edg'd with Trees, where one may see the Ducks swimming; the rest is Meadow, and Pasture for Deer and Cows. Its great Beauty consists in bringing (as it were) the Country into the City. I am inform'd, King *Charles* II. intended to have added more Ornaments to it, and that he had sent for a skillful Person from *Paris* for that Purpose, the same that design'd the Scheme for adorning the *Tuilleries*. After he had taken a narrow View of the Place, he found that its native Beauty, Country Air, and Deserts, had something greater in them, than anything he could contrive, and persuaded the King to let it alone. So the Park remains in the same State, that is, a fine Country-like Place, and is the more agreeable, in my Opinion, because it has neither Art nor Regularity. This is the Place where People go to get rid of the Dirt, Confusion, and Noise of this great City, and where the Ladies in fine Weather display all their Ornaments. They make a fine Appearance, as I have told you before, and their Splendour is the more surprizing, because we imagine 'tis in the Country we see them . . .

Batty Langley (1696–1751)

The title of Langley's work, *New Principles of Gardening*, aptly suggests the scope and treatment of its topic. His awareness of the *new* gardening ideas and his dedication to defining the principles that may govern the art join with his determination to offer detailed practical advice. The passage given here, 'Of the Disposition of Gardens in general', sketches the methods and ideas that he elaborates in the remainder of the volume. He is guided above all by his distaste for 'that abominable Mathematical Regularity and Stiffness' (Plate 68), and is determined patriotically to ensure that his country's very different style comes quickly to rival the Continental ones. Yet his 'noble Idea' of the English garden — the insistence upon irregularity and variety, upon letting the site shape the form and arrangement of the landscape, upon bringing the countryside into the scope of the garden — consorts still with some survivals of various French features (such as basins and canals), and his text is interspersed, though they have been deleted here, with lengthy quotations from Rapin's poem on gardens.

from *New Principles of Gardening* (1728)

ON this very Point depends the whole Beauty or Ruin of a Garden, and therefore every Gentleman should be very cautious therein; I must needs confess, that I have often been surprized to see that none of our late and present Authors did ever attempt to furnish Gentlemen with better Plans and Ideas thereof, than what has hitherto been practised.

The End and Design of a good Garden, is to be both profitable and delightful; wherein should be observed, that its Parts should be always presenting new Objects, which is a continual Entertainment to the Eye, and raises a Pleasure of Imagination.

If the Gentlemen of *England* had formerly been better advised in the laying out their Gardens, we might by this Time been at least equal (if not far superior) to any Abroad.

For as we abound in good Soil, fine Grass, and Gravel, which in many Places Abroad is not to be found, and the best of all Sorts of Trees; it therefore appears, that nothing has been wanting but a noble Idea of the Disposition of a Garden. I could instance divers Places in *England*, where Noblemen and Gentlemens Seats are very finely situated, but wretchedly executed, not only in respect to disproportion'd Walks, Trees planted in improper Soils, no Regard had to fine Views, &c. but with that abominable Mathematical Regularity and Stiffness, that nothing that's bad could equal them.

Now these unpleasant forbidding Sort of Gardens, owe their Deformity to the insipid Taste or Interest of some of our Theorical Engineers, who, in their aspiring Garrets, cultivate all the several Species of Plants, as well as frame Designs for Situations they never saw: Or to some Nursery-Man, who, for his own Interest, advises the Gentleman to such Forms and Trees as will make the greatest Draught out of his Nursery, without Regard to any Thing more: And oftentimes to a Cox-comb, who takes upon himself to be an excellent Draughtsman, as well as an incomparable Gardener; of which there has been, and are still, too many in *England*, which is witness'd by every unfortunate Garden wherein they come. Now as the Beauty of Gardens in general depends upon an elegant Disposition of all their Parts, which cannot be determined without a perfect Knowledge of its several Ascendings, Descendings, Views, &c. how is it possible that any Person can make a good Design for any Garden, whose Situation they never saw?

To draw a beautiful regular Draught, is not to the Purpose; for altho' it makes a handsome Figure on the Paper, yet it has a quite different Effect when executed on the Ground: Nor is there any Thing more ridiculous, and

68 Plate from Batty Langley, *New Principles of Gardening,* 1728

forbidding, than a Garden which is regular; which, instead of entertaining the Eye with fresh Objects, after you have seen a quarter Part, you only see the very same Part repeated again, without any Variety.

And what still greatly adds to this wretched Method, is, that to execute these stiff regular Designs, they destroy many a noble Oak, and in its Place plant, perhaps, a clumsey-bred Yew, Holley, &c. which, with me, is a Crime of so high a Nature, as not to be pardon'd.

There is nothing adds so much to the Pleasure of a Garden, as those great Beauties of Nature, *Hills* and *Valleys*, which, by our *regular Coxcombs*, have ever been destroyed, and at a very great Expence also in Levelling.

For, to their great Misfortune, they always deviate from Nature, instead of imitating it.

There are many other Absurdities I could mention, which those *wretched Creatures* have, and are daily guilty of: But as the preceding are sufficient to arm worthy Gentlemen against such Mortals, I shall at present forbear, and instead thereof, proceed to General Directions for laying out Gardens in a more grand and delightful Manner than has been done before. But first observe,

That the several Parts of a beautiful Rural Garden, are *Walks, Slopes, Borders, Open Plains, Plain Parterres, Avenues, Groves, Wildernesses, Labyrinths, Fruit-Gardens, Flower-Gardens, Vineyards, Hop-Gardens, Nurseries, Coppiced Quarters, Green Openings*, like Meadows: Small Inclosures of *Corn, Cones* of *Ever-Greens*, of *Flowering-Shrubs*, of *Fruit-Trees*, of *Forest-Trees*, and mix'd together: *Mounts, Terraces,* Winding *Valleys, Dales, Purling Streams, Basons, Canals, Fountains, Cascades, Grotto's, Rocks, Ruins, Serpentine Meanders, Rude Coppies, Hay-Stacks, Wood-Piles, Rabbit* and *Hare-Warrens, Cold Baths, Aviaries, Cabinets, Statues, Obelisks, Manazeries, Pheasant* and *Partridge-Grounds, Orangeries, Melon-Grounds, Kitchen-Gardens, Physick* or *Herb-Garden, Orchard, Bowling-Green, Dials, Precipices, Amphitheatres,* &c.

General DIRECTIONS, &c.

I. THAT the grand Front of a Building lie open upon an elegant Lawn or Plain of Grass, adorn'd with beautiful Statues, (of which hereafter in their Place,) terminated on its Sides with open Groves.

II. That grand Avenues be planted from such large open Plains, with a Breadth proportionable to the Building, as well as to its Length of View.

III. That Views in Gardens be as extensive as possible.

IV. That such Walks, whose Views cannot be extended, terminate in Woods, Forests, mishapen Rocks, strange Precipices, Mountains, old Ruins, grand Buildings, &c.

V. That no regular Ever-Greens, &c. be planted in any Part of an open Plain or Parterre.

VI. That no Borders be made, or Scroll-Work cut, in any such Lawn or plain Parterre; for the Grandeur of those beautiful Carpets consists in their native Plainness.

VII. That all Gardens be grand, beautiful, and natural.

VIII. That shady Walks be planted from the End-Views of a House, and terminate in those open Groves that enclose the Sides of the plain Parterre, that thereby you may enter into immediate Shade, as soon as out of the House, without being heated by the scorching Rays of the Sun.

IX. That all the Trees of your shady Walks and Groves be planted with Sweet-Brier, White Jessemine, and Honey-Suckles, environ'd at Bottom with a small Circle of Dwarf-Stock, Candy-Turf, and Pinks.

X. That all those Parts which are out of View from the House, be form'd into Wildernesses, Labyrinths, &c.

XI. That Hills and Dales, of easy Ascents, be made by Art, where Nature has not perform'd that Work before.

XII. That Earths cast out of Foundations, &c. be carried to such Places for raising of Mounts, from which, fine Views may be seen.

XIII. That the Slopes of Mounts, &c. be laid with a moderate Reclination, and planted with all Sorts of Ever-Greens in a promiscuous Manner, so as to grow all in a Thicket; which has a prodigious fine Effect.

In this very Manner are planted two beautiful Mounts in the Gardens of the Honourable Sir *Fisher Tench* at *Low-Layton* in *Essex*.

XIV. That the Walks leading up the Slope of a Mount, have their Breadth contracted at the Top, full one half Part; and if that contracted Part be enclosed on the Sides with a Hedge whose Leaves are of a light Green, 'twill seemingly add a great Addition to the Length of the Walk, when view'd from the other End.

XV. That all Walks whose Lengths are short, and lead away from any Point of View, be made narrower at their further Ends than at the hither Part; for by the Inclination of their Sides, they appear to be of a much greater Length than they really are; and the further End of every long Walk, Avenue, &c. appears to be much narrower than that End where you stand.

And the Reason is, that notwithstanding the Sides of such Walks are parallel to each other, yet as the Breadth of the further End is seen under a lesser Angle, than the Breadth of that Part where you stand, it will therefore appear as if contracted, altho' the Sides are actually parallel; for equal Objects always appear under equal Angles, Q.E.D.

XVI. That the Walks of a Wilderness be never narrower than ten Feet, or wider than twenty five Feet.

XVII. That the Walks of a Wilderness be so plac'd, as to respect the best Views of the Country.

XVIII. That the Intersections of Walks be adorn'd with Statues, large open Plains, Groves, Cones of Fruit, of Ever-Greens, of Flowering Shrubs, of Forest Trees, Basons, Fountains, Sun-Dials, and Obelisks . . .

XIX. That in those serpentine Meanders, be placed at proper Distances, large Openings, which you surprizingly come to; and in the first are entertain'd with a pretty Fruit-Garden, or Paradice-Stocks, with a curious Fountain; from which you are insensibly led through the pleasant Meanders of a shady delightful Plantation; first, into an o[p]en Plain environ'd with lofty Pines, in whose Center is a pleasant Fountain, adorn'd with *Neptune* and his Tritons, &c. secondly, into a Flower-Garden, enrich'd with the most fragrant Flowers and beautiful Statues; and from thence through small Inclosures of Corn, open Plains, or small Meadows, Hop-Gardens, Orangeries, Melon-Grounds, Vineyards, Orchards, Nurseries, Physick-Gardens, Warrens, Paddocks of Deer, Sheep, Cows, &c. with the rural Enrichments of Hay-Stacks, Wood-Piles, &c. . . .

These agreeable surprizing Entertainments in the pleasant Passage thro' a Wilderness, must, without doubt, create new Pleasures at every Turn: And more especially when the Whole is so happily situated, as to be bless'd with small Rivulets and purling Streams of clear Water, which generally admit of the Canals, Fountains, Cascades, &c. which are the very Life of a delightful rural Garden . . .

And to add to the Pleasure of these delightful Meanders, I advise that the Hedge-Rows of the Walks be intermix'd with Cherries, Plumbs, Apples, Pears, Bruxel Apricots, Figs, Gooseberries, Currants, Rasberries, &c. and the Borders planted with Strawberries, Violets, &c.

The most beautiful Forest-Trees for Hedges, are the *English* Elm, the *Dutch* Elm, the Lime-Tree, and Hornbeam: And altho' I have advis'd the Mixing of these Hedges of Forest-Trees with the aforesaid Fruits, yet you must not forget a Place for those pleasant and delightful Flowering-Shrubs, the White Jessemine, Honey-Suckle, and Sweet-Brier.

XX. Observe, at proper Distances, to place publick and private Cabinets, which should (always) be encompass'd with a Hedge of Ever-Greens, and Flowering-Shrubs next behind them, before the Forest-Trees that are Standards.

XXI. Such Walks as must terminate within the Garden, are best finish'd with Mounts, Aviaries, Grotto's, Cascades, Rocks, Ruins, Niches, or Amphitheatres of Ever-Greens, variously mix'd, with circular Hedges ascending behind one another, which renders a very graceful Appearance . . .

XXII. Obelisks of Trellip-Work cover'd with Passion-Flowers, Grapes, Honey-Suckles, and White Jessemine, are beautiful Ornaments in the Center of an open Plain, Flower-Garden, &c.

XXIII. In the Planting of a Wilderness, be careful of making an equal Disposition of the several Kinds of Trees, and that you mix therewith the several Sorts of Ever-Greens; for they not only add a very great Beauty thereunto, by their different Leaves and Colours, in the Summer; but are a great Grace to a Garden in the Winter, when others have stood the Strip of their Leaves.

XXIV. Canals, Fish-Ponds, &c. are most beautiful when environ'd with a Walk of stately Pines, and terminate at each End with a fine Grove of Forest-Trees, or Ever-Greens.

Or, if an extensive Canal terminate at one End in an elegant Piece of Architecture, with a Grove on each Side thereof, and the other end in a Wood, Grove, &c. 'twill have a noble and grand Aspect.

XXV. Groves of Standard Ever-Greens, as Yew, Holly, Box, and Bay-

Trees, are very pleasant, especially when a delightful Fountain is plac'd in their Center.

XXVI. All Grass-Walks should be laid with the same Curvature as Gravel-Walks, and particularly in wet and cold Lands; for, by their being made flat or level from Side to Side, they soon settle into Holes in the Middle, by often walking on, and therein retain Wet, &c. which a circular surfaced Walk resists. The Proportion for the Heights of the Crown, or middle Part of any Grass or Gravel-Walk, is as five is to one, that is, if the Walk be five Foot in Breadth, the Height of the Middle, above the Level of the Sides, must be one Inch; if ten Foot, two Inches; fifteen Foot, three Inches, &c.

XXVII. The Proportion that the Base of a Slope ought to have to its Perpendicular, is as three to one, that is, if the perpendicular Height be ten Feet, its Base must be thirty Feet; and the like of all others.

XXVIII. Distant Hills in Parks, &c. are beautiful Objects, when planted with little Woods; as also are Valleys, when intermix'd with Water, and large Plains; and a rude Coppice in the Middle of a fine Meadow, is a delightful Object.

XXIX. Little Walks by purling Streams in Meadows, and through Corn-Fields, Thickets, &c. are delightful Entertainments.

XXX. Open Lawns should be always in Proportion to the Grandeur of the Building; and the Breadth of Avenues to the Fronts of Edifices, and their own Length also.

The entire Breadth of every Avenue should be divided into five equal Parts: Of which, the Middle, or grand Walk, must be three Fifths; and the Side, or Counter-Walks on each Side one Fifth each. But let the Length of Avenues fall as it will, you must always observe, that the grand Walk be never narrower than the Front of the Building.

The most beautiful and grand Figures for fine large open Lawns, are the Triangle Semicircle, Geometrical Square, Circle or Elipsis, as the Figures A, B, C, D, E.

XXXI. The Circle, Elipsis, Octagon, and mix'd Figures composed of Geometrical Squares, Paralellograms, and Arches of Circles, makes very beautiful Figures for Water, as may be seen in the several Parts of the Designs at the End hereof. But of them all, the Circle is the most grand and beautiful ...

XXXII. In the Planting of Groves, you must observe a regular Irregularity; not planting them according to the common Method like an Orchard, with their Trees in straight Lines ranging every Way, but in a rural Manner, as if they had receiv'd their Situation from Nature itself.

XXXIII. Plant in and about your several Groves, and other Parts of your Garden, good Store of Black-Cherry and other Trees that produce Food for Birds, which will not a little add to the Pleasure thereof ...

XXXIV. Where water is easy to be had, always introduce a Basin or Fountain in every Flower and Fruit-Garden, Grove, and other pleasing Ornaments, in the several private Parts of your rural Garden ...

XXXV. The several Kinds of Forest-Trees make beautiful Groves, as also doth many Ever-Greens, or both mix'd together; but none more beautiful than that noble Tree the *Pine* ...

XXXVI. In the Disposition of the several Parts of Gardens in general, always observe that a perfect Shade be continued throughout, in such a Manner as to pass from one Quarter to another, &c. without being obliged at any Time to pass thro' the scorching Rays of the Sun . . .

XXXVII. There is nothing adds so much to the Beauty and Grandeur of Gardens, as fine Statues; and nothing more disagreeable, than when wrongly plac'd; as *Neptune* on a Terrace-Walk, Mount, &c. or *Pan*, the God of Sheep, in a large Basin, Canal, or Fountain. But to prevent such Absurdities, take the following Directions.

For open Lawns and large Centers:

Mars, God of Battle, with the Goddess *Fame*; *Jupiter*, God of Thunder, with *Venus*, the Goddess of Love and Beauty; and the Graces *Aglaio*, *Thalia*, and *Euphrosyne*; *Apollo*, God of Wisdom, with the nine Muses, *Cleio*, *Melpomene*, *Thalia*, *Euterpe*, *Terpsicoce*, *Erato*, *Calliope Urania*, and *Polymnia*; *Minerva* and *Pallas*, Goddesses of Wisdom, with the seven Liberal Sciences; the three Destinies, *Clotho*, *Lachesis*, and *Atropos*; *Demegorgon* and *Tellus*, Gods of the Earth; *Priapus*, the Garden-God; *Bellona*, Goddess of War; *Pytho*, Goddess of Eloquence; *Vesta*, Goddess of Chastity; *Voluptia*, Goddess of Pleasure; *Atlas*, King of *Mauritania*, a famous Astronomer; *Tysias*, the Inventer of Rhetorick; and *Hercules*, God of Labour.

For Woods and Groves:

Ceres and *Flora*; *Sylvanus*, God, and *Ferona*, Goddess of the Woods; *Actaeon*, a Hunter, whom *Diana* turn'd into a Hart, and was devoured by his own Dogs; *Eccho*, a Virgin rejected of her Lover, pined away in the Woods for Sorrow, where her Voice still remains, answering the Outcries of every Complaint, &c. *Philomela*, a young Maid ravish'd by *Tereus*, who afterwards imprison'd her, and cut out her Tongue; which cruel Action *Progue*, Sister to *Philomela* and Wife to *Tereus*, reveng'd, by killing her own Son *Itis*, whom she had by *Tereus*, and mincing his Flesh, dress'd up a Dish thereof, which she gave her Husband *Tereus* to eat, (unknown to him,) instead of Meat. *Philomela* was afterwards transformed into a Nightingale, and *Itis* into a Pheasant; and lastly, Nuppaeae Fairies of the Woods.

For Canals, Basons, and Fish-Ponds:

Neptune, *Palemon*, *Paniscus*, and *Oceanus*, Gods, and *Dione*, *Melicerta*, *Thetis*, and *Marica*, Goddesses of the Sea; *Salacia* Goddess of Water; *Naiades* Fairies of the Water; and the Syrens *Parthenope*, *Lygia*, and *Leusia*. Niches to be adorn'd with *Dii minores*.

For Fruit-Gardens and Orchards:

Pomona Goddess of Fruit, and the three *Hesperides*, *Eagle*, *Aretusa*, and

Hisperetusa, who were three Sisters that had an Orchard of golden Apples kept by a Dragon, which *Hercules* slew when he took them away.

For Flower-Gardens:

Flora and *Cloris,* Goddesses of Flowers; and also *Venus, Diana, Daphne,* and *Runcina* the Goddess of Weeding.

For the Vineyard:

Bacchus God of Wine.

For Mounts, high Terrace-Walks, &c.

AEolus, God of the Winds and *Orcedes* Fairies of the Mountains.

For Valleys:

The Goddess *Vallonta.*

For private Cabinets in a Wilderness or Grove:

Harpocrates God, and *Agerona* Goddess of Silence, *Mercury* God of Eloquence.

For small Paddocks of Sheep, &c. in a Wilderness:

Morpheus and *Pan* Gods of Sheep; *Pates* the Shepherds Goddess; *Bubona* the Goddess of Oxen; and *Nillo* a famous Glutton, who used himself to carry a Calf every Morning, until it became a large Bull, at which Time he slew it with his Fist, and eat him all in one Day.

For small Enclosures of Wheat, Barley, &c. in a Wilderness:

Robigus a God who preserved Corn from being blasted; *Segesta* a Goddess of the Corn, and *Tutelina* a Goddess, who had the Tuition of Corn in the Fields.

For Ambuscadoes near Rivers, Paddocks, or Meadows:

For those near a Canal or River, *Ulysses,* who first invented the Shooting of Birds; and for those near a Paddock, wherein Sheep, &c. are kept. Cacus slaying by *Hercules.* For *Cacus* being a Shepherd, and a notorious Theif of great Strength and Policy, stole several Sheep and Oxen from *Hercules,* who perceiving his Loss, lay in Ambush, and took *Cacus* in the Fact, for which, with his Club, he knock'd out his Brains.

Lastly, for Places of Banquetting:

The God *Comus*.

Where Bees are kept in Hives:

The God *Aristeus*.

These general Directions, with the preceding deliver'd in the Cultivation of the several Kinds of Fruit and Forest-Trees, Ever-Greens, and Flowering-Shrubs, join'd with the most useful Observations on the several Designs hereunto annex'd, is fully sufficient for any Person whatsoever, to design, lay out, and plant Gardens in general, in a more grand and beautiful Manner than has been done before.

> *And blest is he, who tir'd with his Affairs,*
> *Far from all Noise, all vain Applause, prepares*
> *To go, and underneath some silent Shade,*
> *Which neither Cares nor anxious Thoughts invade,*
> *Does for a while, himself alone possess,*
> *Changing the Town for rural Happiness.*
> *He, when the Sun's hot Steeds to th' Ocean haste,*
> *E'er sable Night the World has overcast,*
> *May from the Hills, the Fields below descry,*
> *At once diverting both his Mind and Eye.*

Robert Castell (d. 1729)

Castell was a member of the circle around Lord Burlington, to whom *The Villas of the Ancients* was dedicated and to whose theories of landscape design it presumably gives expression. Castell bases his study upon the Younger Pliny's famous letters that describe his villas at Tusculum and Laurentum, the most extensive surviving accounts of Roman garden design. Castell translates and provides commentaries upon Pliny's descriptions, and the extract here is taken from one such commentary. The enormous importance of this work is twofold: first, it shows the inspiration which the English Augustan garden derived from Classical literary texts, mediated (one presumes) by encounters with actual villas and gardens in Renaissance Italy, though such is the nature of extrapolation of designs from written accounts that Pliny's letters have been interpreted in various and conflicting ways (see H. Tanzer, *The Villas of Pliny the Younger*, New York 1924); second, Castell's reconstructed plans (Plate 69) enforce his written commentary in suggesting the happy juxtaposition of two sorts of garden styles that characterized both Roman villas and such English estates as Stowe at the time Castell was writing. There was the style that laid out 'Ground and Plantations . . . by the Rule and Line' and the style that imitated the country ('*Imitatio Ruris*'), where there is no visible sign of the 'Skill which is made use of' and where 'natural Forms' of rocks and water and trees are allowed to flourish.

from *The Villas of the Ancients Illustrated* (1728)

Before any Notice be taken of that Part that lay beyond the *Hippodrome*, which is the only *Roman* Garden whose Description is come down to us, it may not be improper to enquire into the first Rise of Gardens, and of what they at first consisted, by which a Judgment may be the better passed on this before us. The Invention of this Art seems to have been owing to the first Builders of *Villas*, who were naturally led to search for the most beautiful Places in which to build them; but as it was hardly possible to meet with any, that within the Compass designed for the Pleasure of the *Villa*, should contain every thing that was compleatly agreeable, it was necessary to supply by Care and Industry whatever was wanting in the natural Face of the Country: but at first they aimed at nothing further than the Disposition of their Plantations, for by the small Knowledge we can arrive at, in the Gardens of the first Ages, they seem to have been no more than select, well-water'd Spots of Ground, irregularly producing all sorts of Plants and Trees, grateful either to the Sight, Smell, or Taste, and refreshed by Shade and Water:

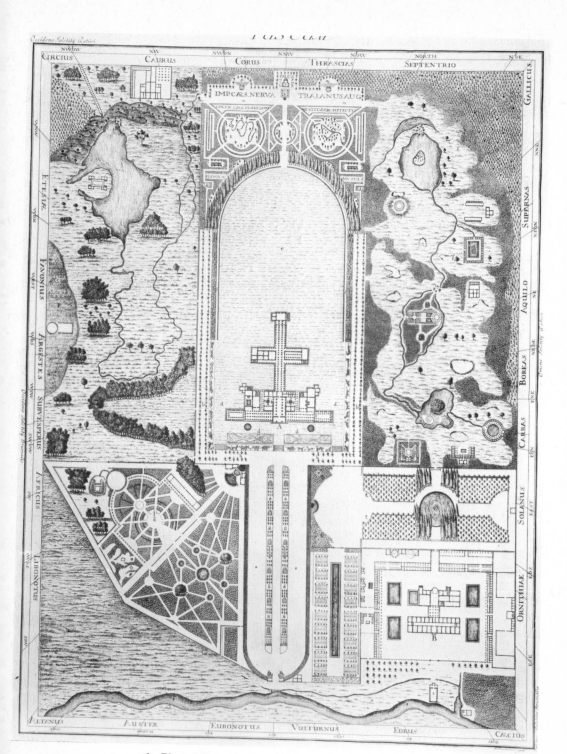

69 Plan of Tusculum from Robert Castell, *The Villas of the Ancients Illustrated*, 1728

Their whole Art consisting in little more than in making those Parts next their *Villas* as it were accidentally produce the choicest Trees, the Growth of various Soils, the Face of the Ground suffering little or no Alteration; the Intent of Gardens being within a fixt Compass of Ground, to enjoy all that Fancy could invent most agreeable to the Senses. But this rough Manner, not appearing sufficiently beautiful to those of a more regular and exact Taste, set them upon inventing a Manner of laying out the Ground and Plantations of Gardens by the Rule and Line, and to trim them up by an Art that was visible in every Part of the Design. By the Accounts we have of the present Manner of Designing in China, it seems as if from the two former Manners a Third had been formed, whose Beauty consisted in a close Imitation of Nature; where, tho' the Parts are disposed with the greatest Art, the Irregularity is still preserved; so that their Manner may not improperly be said to be an artful Confusion, where there is no Appearance of that Skill which is made use of, their *Rocks*, *Cascades*, and *Trees*, bearing their natural Forms. In the Disposition of *Pliny's* Garden, the Designer of it shews that he was not unacquainted with these several Manners, and the Whole seems to have been a Mixture of them all Three. In the *Pratulum* Nature appears in her plainest and most simple Dress; such as the first Builders were contented with about their *Villas*, when the Face of the Ground it self happened to be naturally beautiful. By the Care used in regulating the turning and winding Walks, and cutting the Trees and Hedges into various Forms, is shewn the Manner of the more regular Gardens; and in the *Imitatio Ruris*, he seems to hint at the third Manner, where, under the Form of a beautiful Country, *Hills*, *Rocks*, *Cascades*, *Rivulets*, *Woods*, *Buildings*, &c. were possibly thrown into such an agreeable Disorder, as to have pleased the Eye from several Views, like so many beautiful Landskips; and at the same time have afforded at least all the Pleasures that could be enjoy'd in the most regular Gardens. The main Body of this Garden was disposed after the Second of these three Manners; through its winding Paths One as it were accidentally fell upon those Pieces of a rougher Taste, that seem to have been made with a Design to surprize those that arrived at them, through such a Scene of Regularities, which (in the Opinion of some) might appear more beautiful by being near those plain Imitations of Nature, as Lights in Painting are heightened by Shades. The Intent of this Garden (besides pleasing the Eye, being to afford Shade and Coolness in the hotter Season of the Year) required it to be well stockt with Trees and Water; which last we may suppose took its seeming natural Course through the rougher Parts of the Garden, and in the regular appeared in a more artful Disposition; as did also the Trees, which both here and in those Parts on the *South* Side, or Front of the *Villa*, were cut into unwarrantable Forms, if the Ornaments of Gardens are allow'd to be only Imitations of Nature's Productions; for it cannot be supposed that Nature ever did or will produce Trees in the Form of Beasts, or Letters, or any Resemblance of Embroidery, which Imitations rather belong to the Statuary, and Workers with the Needle than the Architect; and tho' pleasing in those Arts, appear monstrous in this. Tho' it is plain that this Manner of adorning Gardens was not at that Time a new Invention, since as has been observed in the former

Part of this Work, *Varro* in his Description of his *Ornithon*, mentions the *Parterre* that lay near it: And this Custom was got to such a Head in the Time of *Pliny*, that the Gardeners, from clipping and laying out every thing by the Line, and turning Trees and Hedges into various Forms, were called *Topiarii*; and it is easy to think that in Compliance to the Fashion, the Architect of this *Villa*, tho' we see he knew better, was induced to make use of those Ornaments. As to the several Names, which were formed by the Box-Hedges of this Garden, we cannot be certain of any but One; which was that of the Master.

James Thomson (1700–48)

Another associate of the Burlington circle, Thomson, began issuing his poems on the four seasons with *Winter* in 1726; the first complete text, with fine illustrations by William Kent, appeared in 1730. A greatly revised and enlarged version of the poem appeared in 1744, and the text of these extracts is of that date: however, all but the first paragraph of the first extract had appeared in 1730, as had the first paragraph of the second. Lord Lyttelton's Hagley Park, which figures in the second selection, was where Thomson revised his poem and is thus an appropriate addition to the text of *Spring* in 1744. *The Seasons*, uneven as poetry, is nevertheless an important account of some early eighteenth-century attitudes towards landscape. The first passage here celebrates 'The Negligence of *Nature*' both in the open countryside and in the 'finish'd Garden'. Yet his eye for the former is inevitably conditioned by his education — by his reading of Virgil ('the *Mantuan* Swain'), by his taste for painting and the assumption that a poet may imitate a painter's art, by his enthusiasm for Locke's psychological ideas — and it is not always easy to adjudicate how 'pure' is his taste for unadorned scenery. Thomson probably represents very accurately that subtle attitude of the early landscape gardenists towards a nature whose beauties are discovered in and yet also brought to perfection only by means of Art. It is an attitude, however, that is quick to despise French gardens:

> . . . those disgraceful piles of wood and stone;
> Those parks and gardens, where, his haunts betrimm'd,
> And Nature by presumptuous Art oppress'd,
> The woodland Genius mourns.   (*Liberty* V)

The English garden, by contrast, is a space of freedoms. Lord Lyttelton in the second extract is seen in his park, at liberty to choose from among various paths and scenery according to his mood. Both passages reveal Thomson's exploration of the connections between the external world of nature and the internal world of human mind and imagination: this was a theme of increasing importance. Among *The Seasons'* many ambitions, the celebration of the rise of the landscape garden figures prominently, and several other passages, including one on Stowe, could have been chosen. Kent's illustrations (Plate 70) provide an apt commentary upon the poem — the deep, Claudian prospect into the country from some landscape decorated with buildings; the pastoral colouring of shepherds; the involvement of spectators in a thorough appreciation of the visual and scientific aspects of nature (see Kent's figure pointing us into the scene); even Thomson's occasional invocation of Baroque personifications is mirrored in Kent's descending deities.

70 Illustration by Kent and Tardieu of *Spring* from Thomson's *The Seasons*, 1730

from *The Seasons* (1730)

There let the Classic Page thy Fancy lead
Thro' rural Scenes; such as the *Mantuan* Swain
Paints in immortal Verse and matchless Song:
Or catch thy self the Landskip, gliding swift
Athwart Imagination's vivid Eye:
Or by the vocal Woods and Waters lull'd,
And lost in lonely Musing, in a Dream,
Confus'd, of careless Solitude, where mix
Ten thousand wandering Images of Things,
Soothe every Gust of Passion into Peace,
All but the Swellings of the soften'd Heart,
That waken, not disturb the tranquil Mind.

    BEHOLD yon breathing Prospect bids the Muse
Throw all her Beauty forth. But who can paint
Like Nature? Can Imagination boast,
Amid it's gay Creation, Hues like her's?
Or can it mix them with that matchless Skill,
And lose them in each other, as appears
In every Bud that blows? If Fancy then
Unequal fails beneath the pleasing Task;
Ah what shall Language do? Ah where find Words
Ting'd with so many Colours; and whose Power,
To Life approaching, may perfume my Lays
With that fine Oil, those aromatic Gales,
That inexhaustive flow continual round? . . .

    SEE, where the winding Vale her lavish Stores,
Irriguous, spreads. See, how the Lilly drinks
The latent Rill, scarce oozing thro' the Grass,
Of Growth luxuriant; or the humid Bank,
In fair Profusion, decks. Long let us walk,
Where the Breeze blows from yon extended Field
Of blossom'd Beans. *Arabia* cannot boast
A fuller Gale of Joy than, liberal, thence
Breathes thro' the Sense, and takes the ravish'd Soul.
Nor is the Mead unworthy of thy Foot,
Full of fresh Verdure, and unnumber'd Flowers,
The Negligence of *Nature*, wide, and wild;
Where, undisguis'd by mimic *Art*, she spreads
Unbounded Beauty to the roving Eye.

Here their delicious Task the fervent Bees,
In swarming Millions, tend. Around, athwart,
Thro' the soft Air, the busy Nations fly,
Cling to the Bud, and, with inserted Tube,
Suck it's pure Essence, it's etherial Soul.
And oft, with bolder Wing, they soaring dare
The purple Heath, or where the Wild-thyme grows,
And yellow load them with the luscious Spoil.

 AT length the finish'd Garden to the View
It's Vistas opens, and it's Alleys green.
Snatch'd thro' the verdant Maze, the hurried Eye
Distracted wanders; now the bowery Walk
Of Covert close, where scarce a speck of Day
Falls on the lengthen'd Gloom, protracted sweeps;
Now meets the bending Sky, the River now
Dimpling along, the breezy-ruffled Lake,
The Forest darkening round, the glittering Spire,
Th' etherial Mountain, and the distant Main . . .

   In these green Days [i.e. of Spring],
Reviving Sickness lifts her languid Head;
Life flows afresh; and young-ey'd Health exalts
The whole Creation round. Contentment walks
The sunny Glade, and feels an inward Bliss
Spring o'er his Mind, beyond the Power of Kings
To purchase. Pure Serenity apace
Induces Thought, and Contemplation still.
By swift degrees the Love of Nature works,
And warms the Bosom; till at last sublim'd
To Rapture, and enthusiastic Heat,
We feel the present DEITY, and taste
The Joy of GOD to see a happy World.

 THESE are the Sacred Feelings of thy Heart,
Thy Heart inform'd by Reason's purest Ray.
O LYTTELTON, the Friend! thy Passions thus
And Meditations vary, as at large,
Courting the Muse, thro' HAGLEY-PARK you stray,
Thy *British Tempe*! There along the Dale,
With Woods o'er-hung, and shag'd with mossy Rocks,
Whence on each hand the gushing Waters play,
And down the rough Cascade white-dashing fall,
Or gleam in lengthen'd Vista thro' the Trees,
You silent steal; or sit beneath the Shade
Of solemn Oaks, that tuft the swelling Mounts

Thrown graceful round by Nature's careless Hand,
And pensive listen to the various Voice
Of rural Peace: the Herds, the Flocks, the Birds,
The hollow-whispering Breeze, the Plaint of Rills,
That, purling down amid the twisted Roots
Which creep around, their dewy Murmurs shake
On the sooth'd Ear. From these abstracted oft,
You wander through the Philosophic World;
Where in bright Train continual Wonders rise,
Or to the curious or the pious Eye.
And oft, conducted by Historic Truth,
You tread the long Extent of backward Time:
Planning, with warm Benevolence of Mind,
And honest Zeal unwarp'd by Party-Rage,
Britannia's Weal; how from the venal Gulph
To raise her Virtue, and her Arts revive.
Or, turning thence thy View, these graver Thoughts
The Muses charm: while, with sure Taste refin'd,
You draw th' inspiring Breath of antient Song;
Till nobly rises, emulous, thy own.
Perhaps thy lov'd LUCINDA shares thy Walk,
With Soul to thine attun'd. Then Nature all
Wears to the Lover's Eye a Look of Love;
And all the Tumult of a guilty World,
Tost by ungenerous Passions, sinks away.
The tender Heart is animated Peace;
And as it pours it's copious Treasures forth,
In vary'd Converse, softening every Theme,
You, frequent-pausing, turn, and from her Eyes,
Where meeken'd Sense, and amiable Grace,
And lively Sweetness dwell, enraptur'd, drink
That nameless Spirit of etherial Joy,
Inimitable Happiness! which Love,
Alone, bestows, and on a favour'd Few.
Meantime you gain the Height, from whose fair Brow
The bursting Prospect spreads immense around;
And snatch'd o'er Hill and Dale, and Wood and Lawn,
And verdant Field, and darkening Heath between,
And Villages embosom'd soft in Trees,
And spiry Towns by dusky Columns mark'd
Of rising Smoak, your Eye excursive roams:
Wide-stretching from the *Hall*, in whose kind Haunt
The *Hospitable Genius* harbours still,
To Where the broken Landskip, by Degrees,
Ascending, roughens into ridgy Hills;
O'er which the *Cambrian* Mountains, like far Clouds
That skirt the blue Horizon, doubtful, rise.

Sir John Clerk of Penicuik, Bt (1676–1755)

The second baronet of Penicuik, near Edinburgh, had travelled widely in Italy at the end of the seventeenth century and among the gardens and estates of England before he completed his poem on 'The Country Seat' in the late 1720s. It records his instructions on building and planting in verse as vigorous and individual as some of the ideas. The work obviously benefited from his travels, his reading about 'Antient Paradise' (he subscribed to Castell's *Villas of the Ancients*), his acquaintance among patrons and designers in England, and his own practical competence as an estate manager. The poem discusses three types of country seat — the house of state, the place of convenience and use, and the 'little villa', perhaps like his own Mavisbank House, Midlothian (Plate 71). Though he does not propose three different and answering styles of garden, he is adamant that the relationship of house and landscape be thoroughly considered. Matters of proportion and scale seem as important for Sir John Clerk, and for other professors of the English garden, as the need for variety. In other respects, too, he places himself among the leaders of the landscape movement: by his exclamation, ' 'Tis a beauty to see things natural'; by his attention to what Pope called the 'Genius of the Place' and the calling in of the country; by his fundamental belief in a garden's appeal to the *mind*, where mental variousness and diversity is matched by richly versatile designs. If he attends to Classical precedents and mythology (one suspects that his suggestion, 'every beauteous Villa should be placed/In open view of Neptune's wide extended Realms', echoes Pliny's praise of his seaside villa at Laurentum), he is also ready to adapt the Classical traditions to the exigencies of British climate. The text of his poem is from a manuscript of 1731 in the Clerk Papers in the Scottish Record Office.

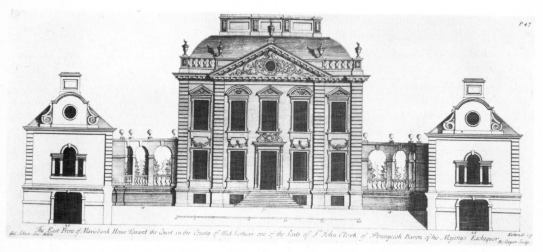

71 Mavisbank, Midlothian. Engraving from *Vitruvius Scoticus*, 1810

from 'The Country Seat' (1731)

Tho every beauteous Villa should be placd
In open view of Neptunes wide extended Realms;
Yet shun his Borders with your utmost Care.
Here noise and Tumult reign, for winds and waves
Insult the Shore and with united Force
Seem bent to ruine once again the World.
Here liquid mountains rising to the Sky
Disclose the gloomy Caverns of the Deep
Unknown Rocks with Banks of sinking Sands
And certain Death in many dreadfull Shapes.
Here Ships distressd and many wrecks appear
The Shatter'd Fortunes of the mariner;
Piratick Ambuscades affright the Shoar,
And piercing winds the tender Plants devour.
Yet at some Certain Points the Sea will yeild,
A noble Prospect to the neighb'ring Fields;
There Noise will Cease and [N]eptunes awfull frowns
Are he[l]d in Distance. All his Kingdom seems
A peacefull Lake, or beauteous azure Plain.
So there are Pictures done with utmost art,
Which must at proper Distances be seen;
For when their bold rough Strokes are brought too nigh,
They lose their Beauty and offend the Eye.

Still other harsh and frightfull objects be
Which not a little grace a Country-Seat;
If only brought within the Bounds of Sight.
Deep rapid Rivers, wide extended Lakes
High tow'ring Rocks and noisy Cataracts.
Such Rivers from a thousand urns pour forth
A Constant Deludge; all their flowry Banks
Sapt and deformd appear; no animal
However urgd by violent Heat or Thirst
Dares to attempt the raging turbid Flood.
Thus with uncertain Channell on they roll
Unless where rugged Rocks their Force withstand.
Lakes from afar will charm the Eye and seem
Huge Silver Mirrors set in verdant frames.
But come we nearer, feeble nature shrinks
To find them hideous Gulphs with perilous Banks.

Rocks with tumultous Noise will eccho forth
Loud Peals of Thunder from the Cataract.
But yet all these tho natures spots and stains,
Or of the delugd world the dire Remains,
With wondrous beauty variegate the Plains.

Would you be equally beyond the reach
Of inundations, and tempestuous Storms,
Choose not a Seat too lofty nor too low,
But on a River's Bank or downy Plain
That gently slopes to the meridian Sun.
Let many lofty Trees with Spreading Tops
Defend you from the Cold of Northern Blasts.
Let here and there be seen some little Hills
Fit Pasture for your harmless bleating Flocks.
Let all the Fields in view be checquerd round
With flowry meadows Groves and plenteous Springs,
Or Rivulets descending from the higher Grounds.
These Countries which are level, low and plain,
Have no Variety to entertain
The busy mind, but always are the Same . . .

Come now ye rural Deities and show
What Forms will beautify the neighb'ring Plains.
The verdant Banks, and meads, that so they may
With never fading Charms allure our Eyes.
Stretch out the Lines of every Avenue
With spreading trees in many stately Rowes;
Display the Parterres and the Shady Walks
The sloping Greens, the Ponds and water-works.
The fruitfull orchard and the mazy Grove
Where billing Birds may meet in fond Caress.
Where every Goddess and their train
A clear and Secret Bathing Place may find.
Where Flora with a Knot of gaudy Flowrs
May dress her lovely head, and in the Shades
Vertumnus and Pomona breath their Loves.
And thus unseen, may all the heav'nly Powrs
Adorn the Solitude of rural Bowrs.

That Avenue will most delight the Sight
That on some beauteous object shapes its way.
Such is a temple, whose high towring Spire
Divides the ho'vring Clouds, and seems to be
A lofty Pillar to support the Heavns.
This lovely Prospect may your busy mind
With usefull Speculations entertain;

Consider first, that all you do enjoy
Is owing to the God, whose awfull Shrine
These sacred walks enclose, and where
With thankfull Heart you often should resort.
And if that here your Fathers lye entombd,
Your stately house and pleasant fields at last,
With other Charms of Life you must forego,
And this way travel to the shades below.

Another noble Prospect may be deem'd
That of the great Metropolis or Town;
Where Noise and Tumult you delight to shun.
Her gilded spires reflect the beamy Ray
On each surrounding Field, and with a glance
Try to recall the fled Inhabitants.
Far from all churlish Habits she returns
With usury the Favours she receives,
And to the active Patriot always gives.
Her loud harmonious Bells a warning give
To shun such powerfull draughts of rural Joy
As may intoxicate the lazy Mind.
She calls as Cincinnatus left his Plough,
So we our chief Delights should not pursue
But for our Countrys sake our Cares renew.

Around the Fabrick spread the wide Parterre
Like to a verdant Mantle edgd with Gold,
Or an embroyderd Carpet all perfumd
With Indian Sweets, here with a mystick mien
Let Nature in the Pride of blooming Flowrs
Triumphant sit, and all the Gardiners Toils
Direct with matchless grace, here let her show
How wild & shapless Fields may be adornd
With easy Labour and without Constraint.
How each neglected Corner, each Defect
May by a little art converted be
To Beauties, that may please the nicest Eye.
Forbear then all these trifling mazy knotts
Of Shrubs and Flowrs that crowd the flagrant Scene.
Nature enjoyns all Cost and Toil to Spare
Which mar the Prospect or obstruct the Air.

Gardens must always some Proportion bear
To e'vry kind of Structure which they grace.
For tho' no Rule is fixd, the Man of Taste
May cause each Discord slide in Harmony.
What tho' a Royal Garden should contain

In every single Plot a spacious Field,
Yet more confind dimensions may Content
The Master of a humble Edifice.
Likewise a due Proportion must be kept
Between the Charge of laying out your Grounds
In pompous order and their due Repairs.
A small neat Garden claims to be preferrd
To those of larger Size with Shabby Mien,
Where nothing but disorder can be seen.

Variety is what we next admire
In every Garden; hence the various Forms
Of gravely Terrasses and verdant Slopes,
Fountains and Statues, Cataracts and Grots,
The airy, open, and the coverd walks;
With other objects rising to our View
Which for their Multitude seem always new.

But every Beauty ceases when compard
With what we in the fragrant orchard find.
Here vegetable Life displays her Charms
In radiant Colours and in sprightly Dress
The Summer's Queen unfolds her juicy Stores
In such ambrosial Fruits, all coverd [o'er]
With spangled Rinds of purple and of Gold.
Would you with double Pleasure taste the Bliss,
Which fair Pomona courteously bestows,
Then learn with Skill to use the Pruning Hook,
The Spade and Rake with other Garden Tools
To make the Ground Submissive to your Will.
With your own hands insert the fruitfull Bud,
And by the Knife let every Tree be taught
Its proper Order, where to shoot or spread,
Or in what Shape to raise its beauteous Head.

Thus have the greatest monarchs of the world
Employd their Time, and seemd alike to prize
The royal Scepter and the humble Spade.
Thus mighty Cyrus with a Gardiner's Care
Bestowd his peacefull Intervals of War.
Soon as the world itself a Being had
To Man the great all seeing Pow'r injoynd
With a laborious Hand to dress the Ground.
Now of all Grounds the Orchard claims the Praise
As most ressembling Antient Paradise.

Next may some little Plotts be laid aside
To be the Parents of all reptile Fruits,
The milky Herb and ev'ry wholsome Root:
Tis here the virtuous and the wise may know,
How Health and vigour best may be preservd,
By mod'rate Labour free from anxious cares.
How Mortals in the Golden Age were fed,
Till they like Savage Beasts began to stray,
And on their Fellow Creatures learnd to prey.

Whether in Orchard, or in Kitchen Grounds,
Nature requires the Gardiners helping Hand,
Yet never force her with unkindly art.
She with a Mother's tender Care bestows
On ev'ry Region all such Fruits and Herbs
As most are fitted for th' Inhabitants.
But Philosophic Gardiners Still may try
How far the Golden Orange or the Vine,
Will bear the British Soil and humid Air.
The curious Botanist may likewise raise
With artificial Warmth exotick Plants.
But those who are on true Improvements bent
Must with our Nat'ral Products be content.

Let copious Streams from all the neighb'ring Hills
In tubes or Channells roll their lucid streams
Thro' all your Garden Plotts and Valley Grounds.
Those with perpetual Verdure crown the Spring,
Enliven every Plant & every Tree,
Charming in various Shapes the wandring Eye.
Some Streams by Sportive jetts are thrown aloft
And mixt in Air; some with united Force
Like thund'ring Torrents from the highest Rocks
Rush headlong down and fill the beauteous Lakes.
You who take Pleasure in aquatick Schemes,
Avoid Canals or Ponds of any Form,
Where living Fountains never show their Heads;
But stagnant lye from latent sources fed.
Such with their balefull steams infect the Air
And are but awkward ornaments at best.
But if low Fields or silent Brooks deny
Their friendly Aid to deck the limpid Plain,
What Nature gives, receive; Dianas self
With her fair Nymphs máy bath their snowy Limbs,
In silver Lakes, for want of Chrystal Springs.

Proportion ev'ry Fountain to the Stream
Which gives it Life. [T]is monstrous to behold
A vast large Bason, which no water fills
But what a little paltry jett bestows.
The Fountains margin should not much extend
Beyond what may the falling drops Contain.
And the cheif Beauty of a Fountain is
When gushing Waters flow in plenteous Streams.
But where the same are wanting, we must try
If Groupes of Sculpture can defects supply.

Whether with stony wall, or thorny hedge
You fence your Garden round, be always sure
To keep each lovely Object still in Sight:
But shun the artless Practise to expose
Your Fields at once to any Single View.
At ev'ry Step new objects must arise
And all your Fields and Garden Plots be Such
As may not only please our wand'ring Eyes
But feed luxuriant Fancy with Surprize.

Distinguish well what suits a foreign Clime,
And what to British Air and Soil belongs.
In this our Isle some Fruits perfection owe
To walls of Brick, but others more inur'd
To blust'ring winds and Rains, on Standards grow.
Nor multiply your walks, nor scrup'lous be
To rear up some in ev'ry proper Place.
These Garden Plots can never fail to please
Which most abound with sweet and fragrant flowers,
Where all the Fountains are with Torrents fed,
And all the Walls with painted Fruits are Clad.

Whatever Charms in rural Life are known,
These most Conspicuous are in woods & Groves,
Where Solitude no bold Intruder finds.
Then thro' the bushy Trees and lonesome Shades,
Nature in all her several windings trace;
Search out the Beautys which unfinishd lye
And let assisting Art compleat the Scene.
If from a neighb'ring Rock a Spring descends
There let a Fountain grace a shady Grove:
And where uncommon moisture steeps the ground
Convert the place into a Lake or Pond.
If any opening gives a Prospect round
Of distant Fields there place a Seat or Bow'r.
Which may defend from Heat & sudden Rain

And heighten into Transports all your Views.
If spacious Plains shall intersect a Wood
Let there your Flocks and nimble Deer be fed,
The milky Kine, or Beeves, or gen'rous Steeds;
Thus while we wander thro' the mazy Ground
Surprising objects will regale our View,
And rural Bliss in full Perfection shew.

Now stop my Muse your bold and arduous flight,
And dare no more the vast Pierian Height;
On Escas Flowry Bank there is a Grove,
Where the harmonious Thrush repeats his Love;
There I'll observe the Precepts you indite,
But never any more attempt to write;
Some may perhaps amidst the num'rous Throng,
Of Swains, attentive listen to your Song.
And from your gen'ral Rules instruction take,
What Edifice to raise or Gardens make:
But other are, on whom those Rules you waste,
For Goths will always have a Gothic Taste.

Alexander Pope (1688–1744)

Pope's place in this chronology is determined by his most celebrated public statement of gardening principles in the verse epistle to Lord Burlington; it is preceded,
though, by his early essay of 1713 from *The Guardian*, in which he attacks the
fashion for topiary, and by a long account of Lord Digby's gardens at Sherborne in
Dorset in a letter to Martha Blount, tentatively dated 1724. Pope exercised a
doubly strong influence over the course of garden history: by his published pro-
nouncements, and by his private example. His own gardens at Twickenham (see
pp. 247ff.) were justly famous during his lifetime, not least because he alluded to them
in his satires and in his private correspondence; he is also known to have advised
friends and acquaintances on their garden projects. The second extract provides a
vivid illustration of this world of private elysiums and landscaping enthusiasms: it
shows how adept Pope was at exploring and understanding a complicated garden
and how subtly he responded to its more geometrical elements (Plate 72) as well as
its 'natural' scenes. *The Guardian* paper, the first extract, establishes Pope's awareness of Classical precedents; but he can dissociate himself from the taste for
topiary, which Pliny at least professed (see Castell, p. 187), in order to launch his
witty attack upon its chronic abuse among his contemporaries. The third extract
combines his delight in, and skill with, satire and his generous approbation of
gardens like Stowe (Plates 73 and 74). Despite various attempts to identify Timon's
Villa (the Duke of Chandos's Cannons House and Walpole's Houghton Hall have
been candidates), it is more likely to have been an imaginary and composite image
of current absurdities in design. While Pope's contribution to the landscape movement cannot be minimized, it will be noticed that the principles of design enuncia-
ted in the letter to Burlington have already been encountered in earlier texts
(Switzer, for example); what the *Epistle* achieves, above all, is a memorable and
incisive vision of what many lesser writers struggled to express.

Essay from *The Guardian* (1713)

I Lately took a particular Friend of mine to my House in the Country, not
without some Apprehension that it could afford little Entertainment to a
Man of his Polite Taste, particularly in Architecture and Gardening, who
had so long been conversant with all that is beautiful and great in either.
But it was a pleasant Surprize to me, to hear him often declare, he had found
in my little Retirement the Beauty which he always thought wanting in the
most celebrated Seats, or if you will Villa's, of the Nation. This he described
to me in those Verses with which *Martial* begins one of his Epigrams:

72 Detail of engraving from Salomon Kleiner, *Vera et Accurata Delineatio Omnium Templorum et Coenobiorum*, 1724 et seq.

Baiana nostri Villa, Basse, Faustini,
Non otiosis ordinata myrtetis,
Viduaque platano, tonsilique buxeto,
Ingrata lati spatia detinet campi,
Sed rure vero, barbaroque laetatur.[*]

THERE is certainly something in the amiable Simplicity of unadorned Nature, that spreads over the Mind a more noble sort of Tranquility, and a loftier Sensation of Pleasure, than can be raised from the nicer Scenes of Art.

THIS was the Taste of the Ancients in their Gardens, as we may discover from the Descriptions are extant of them. The two most celebrated Wits of the World have each of them left us a particular Picture of a Garden; wherein those great Masters, being wholly unconfined, and Painting at Pleasure, may be thought to have given a full Idea of what they esteemed most excellent in this way. These (one may observe) consist intirely of the useful Part of Horticulture, Fruit-Trees, Herbs, Water, &c. The Pieces I am speaking of are *Virgil*'s Account of the Garden of the old *Corycian*, and *Homer*'s of that of *Alcinous*. The first of these is already known to the *English* Reader, by the excellent Versions of Mr. *Dryden* and Mr. *Addison*. The other having never been attempted in our Language with any Elegance, and being the most beautiful Plan of this sort that can be imagined, I shall here present the Reader with a Translation of it.

[* Bassus, the country seat of our friend Faustinus at Baia, does not spread over the fields unfruitfully in rows of idle myrtle, vineless plane trees, plantations of fancy clipped boxwood. It rejoices in the true rustic, the untrimmed farm.]

The Gardens of *Alcinous*, from *Homer's Odyss*.

Close to the Gates a spacious Garden lies,
From Storms defended and inclement Skies:
Four Acres was th' allotted Space of Ground,
Fenc'd with a green Enclosure all around.
Tall thriving Trees confest the fruitful Mold;
The red'ning Apple ripens here to Gold,
Here the blue Figg with luscious Juice o'erflows,
With deeper Red the full Pomegranate glows,
The Branch here bends beneath the weighty Pear,
And verdant Olives flourish round the Year.
The balmy Spirit of the Western Gale
Eternal breaths on Fruits untaught to fail:
Each dropping Pear a following Pear supplies,
On Apples Apples, Figs on Figs arise:
The same mild Season gives the Blooms to blow,
The Buds to harden, and the Fruits to grow.
   Here order'd Vines in equal Ranks appear,
With all th' United Labours of the Year.
Some to unload the fertile Branches run,
Some dry the black'ning Clusters in the Sun,
Others to tread the liquid Harvest join,
The groaning Presses foam with Floods of Wine.
Here are the Vines in early Flow'r descry'd,
Here Grapes discolour'd on the Sunny Side,
And there in Autumn's *richest Purple dy'd.*
   Beds of all various Herbs, for ever green,
In beauteous Order terminate the Scene.
   Two plenteous Fountains the whole Prospect crown'd;
This thro' the Gardens leads its Streams around,
Visits each Plant, and waters all the Ground:
While that in Pipes beneath the Palace flows,
And thence its Current on the Town bestows;
To various Use their various Streams they bring,
The People one, and one supplies the King.

SIR *William Temple* has remark'd, that this Description contains all the justest Rules and Provisions which can go toward composing the best Gardens. Its Extent was four *Acres*, which, in these times of Simplicity, was look'd upon as a large one, even for a Prince: It was inclos'd all round for Defence; and for Conveniency join'd close to the Gates of the Palace.

HE mentions next the Trees, which were Standards, and suffered to grow to their full height. The fine Description of the Fruits that never failed, and the eternal Zephyrs, is only a more noble and poetical way of expressing the continual Succession of one Fruit after another throughout the Year.

THE *Vineyard* seems to have been a Plantation distinct from the *Garden*;

as also the *Beds of Greens* mentioned afterwards at the Extremity of the Inclosure, in the Nature and usual Place of our *Kitchen Gardens*.

THE two Fountains are disposed very remarkably. They rose within the Inclosure, and were brought by Conduits or Ducts, one of them to Water all Parts of the Gardens, and the other underneath the Palace into the Town, for the Service of the Publick.

HOW contrary to this Simplicity is the modern Practice of Gardening; we seem to make it our Study to recede from Nature, not only in the various Tonsure of Greens into the most regular and formal Shapes, but even in monstrous Attempts beyond the reach of the Art it self: We run into Sculpture, and are yet better pleas'd to have our Trees in the most awkward Figures of Men and Animals, than in the most regular of their own.

> *Hinc & nexilibus videas e frondibus hortos,*
> *Implexos late muros, & Moenia circum*
> *Porrigere, & latas e ramis surgere turres;*
> *Deflexam & Myrtum in Puppes, atque area rostra:*
> *In buxisque undare fretum, atque e rore rudentes.*
> *Parte alia frondere suis tentoria Castris;*
> *Scutaque spiculaque & jaculantia citria Vallos.*[*]

I believe it is no wrong Observation, that Persons of Genius, and those who are most capable of Art, are always most fond of Nature, as such are chiefly sensible, that all Art consists in the Imitation and Study of Nature. On the contrary, People of the common Level of Understanding are principally delighted with the Little Niceties and Fantastical Operations of Art, and constantly think that *finest* which is least Natural. A Citizen is no sooner Proprietor of a couple of Yews, but he entertains Thoughts, of erecting them into Giants, like those of *Guild-hall*. I know an eminent Cook, who beautified his Country Seat with a Coronation Dinner in Greens, where you see the Champion flourishing on Horseback at one end of the Table, and the Queen in perpetual Youth at the other.

FOR the benefit of all my loving Country-men of this curious Taste, I shall here publish a Catalogue of Greens to be disposed of by an eminent Town-Gardiner, who has lately applied to me upon this Head. He represents, that for the Advancement of a politer sort of Ornament in the Villa's and Gardens adjacent to this great City, and in order to distinguish those Places from the meer barbarous Countries of gross Nature, the World stands much in need of a Virtuoso Gardiner who has a Turn to Sculpture, and is thereby capable of improving upon the Ancients of his Profession in the Imagery of Ever-greens, My Correspondent is arrived to such Perfection, that he cuts

[* Here you see a garden enclosed with plaited boughs, vast woven walls, battlements stretching all around, and big towers of greenery rising; myrtles tortured into ship shapes, poops and prows, waves billowing out of boxwood and cordage formed of dew; elsewhere tented encampments of foliage, shields, javelins, and a palisade of darting cedars.]

Family Pieces of Men, Women or Children. Any Ladies that please may have their own Effigies in Myrtle, or their Husbands in Horn beam. He is a Puritan Wag, and never fails, when he shows his Garden, to repeat that Passage in the Psalms, *Thy Wife shall be as the fruitful Vine, and thy Children as Olive Branches round thy Table*. I shall proceed to his Catalogue, as he sent it for my Recommendation.

ADAM and *Eve* in Yew; *Adam* a little shatter'd by the fall of the Tree of Knowledge in the great Storm; *Eve* and the Serpent very flourishing.

THE Tower of *Babel*, not yet finished.

St. GEORGE in Box; his Arm scarce long enough, but will be in a Condition to stick the Dragon by next *April*.

A *green Dragon* of the same, with a Tail of Ground-Ivy for the present.

N.B. *These two not to be Sold separately*.

EDWARD the *Black Prince* in Cypress.

A *Laurustine* Bear in Blossom, with a Juniper Hunter in Berries.

A Pair of Giants, *stunted*, to be sold cheap.

A Queen *Elizabeth* in Phylyraea, a little inclining to the Green Sickness, but of full growth.

ANOTHER Queen *Elizabeth* in Myrtle, which was very forward, but Miscarried by being too near a Savine.

AN old Maid of Honour in Wormwood.

A topping *Ben Johnson* in Lawrel.

DIVERS eminent Modern Poets in Bays, somewhat blighted, to be disposed of a Pennyworth.

A Quick-set Hog shot up into a Porcupine, by its being forgot a Week in rainy Weather.

A Lavender Pig with Sage growing in his Belly.

NOAH's *Ark* in Holly, standing on the Mount; the Ribs a little damaged for want of Water.

A Pair of *Maidenheads* in Firr, in great forwardness.

Letter to Martha Blount (*c.* 1724)

Madam, — I promisd you an account of Sherborne, before I had seen it, or knew what I undertook. I imagind it to be one of those fine old Seats of which there are Numbers scatterd over England. But this is so peculiar and its Situation of so uncommon a kind, that it merits a more particular description.

The House is in the form of an H. The body of it, which was built by Sir Walter Rawleigh, consists of four Stories, with four six-angled Towers at the ends. These have since been joind to four Wings, with a regular Stone Balustrade at the top & four towers more than finish the building. The Windows & Gates are of a yellow Stone throughout, and one of the flatt Sides toward the Garden has the wings of a newer Architecture with beautiful Italian Window-frames done by the first Earl of Bristol, which, if they were joind in the middle by a Portico covering the Old Building, would be a noble Front. The design of such an one I have been amusing myself with drawing, but tis a question whether my Lord Digby will not be better amus'd than to execute it. The finest room is a Salon 50 ft. long, & a Parlor hung with very excellent Tapistry of Rubens, which was a present from the King of Spain to the E. of Bristol in his Ambassy there.

This stands in a Park, finely crownd with very high Woods, on all the tops of the Hills, which form a great Amfitheatre sloping down to the house. On the Garden Sides the Woods approach close, so that it appears there with a thick Line & Depth of Groves on each hand, & so it shows from most parts of the Park. The Gardens are so Irregular, that tis very hard to give an exact idea of 'em but by a Plan. Their beauty rises from this Irregularity, for not only the Several parts of the Garden itself make the better Contraste by these sudden Rises, Falls, and Turns of ground; but the Views about it are lett in, & hang over the Walls, in very different figures and aspects. You come first out of the house into a green Walk of Standard Lymes with a hedge behind them that makes a Colonnade, thence into a little triangular wilderness, from whose Centre you see the town of Sherborne in a valley, interspersd with trees. From the corner of this you issue at once upon a high green Terras the whole breadth of the Garden, which has five more green Terras's hanging under each other, without hedges, only a few pyramid yews & large round Honisuckles between them. The Honisuckles hereabouts are the largest & finest I ever saw. You'l be pleasd when I tell you the Quarters of the above mentiond little Wilderness are filld with these & with Cherry trees of the best kinds all within reach of the hand. At the ends of these Terras's run two long Walks under the Side walls of the Garden which communicate with the other Terras's that front these opposite. Between, the Vally is layd level and divided into two regular Groves of Horse chestnuts, and a Bowling-green in the middle of about 180 foot. This is bounded behind with a Canall, that runs quite across the Groves & also along one Side, in the form of a T. Behind this, is a Semicircular Berceau, and a Thicket of mixed trees that compleats the Crown of the Amfitheatre which is of equal extent with the Bowling-green. Beyond that runs a natural River thro green banks of turf, over which rises another Row of Terras's, the first supported by a slope Wall planted with Vines (So is also the Wall that bounds the channel of the river.) A second & third appeard above this, but they are to be turnd into a Line of Wilderness with wild winding walks for the convenience of passing from one side to the other in Shade, the heads of whose trees will lye below the uppermost Terras of all, which compleats the Garden and over-looks both that & the Country. Even above the wall of this the natural Ground rises, & is crownd with several venerable Ruins of an Old Castle, with Arches & broken views, of which I must say more hereafter.

When you are at the left corner of the Canal and the Chestnut groves in the bottome, you turn of a sudden under very old trees into the deepest Shade. One walk winds you up a Hill of venerable Wood over-archd by nature, & of a vast height, into a circular Grove, on one side of which is a close high Arbour, on the other a sudden open Seat that overlooks the

Meadows & river with a large distant prospect. Another walk under this hill winds by the River side quite coverd with high Trees on both banks, over hung with Ivy, where falls a natural Cascade with never-ceasing murmurs. On the opposite hanging of the Bank (which is a Steep of 50 ft) is plac'd, with a very fine fancy, a Rustick Seat of Stone, flaggd and rough, with two Urns in the same rude taste upon pedestals, on each side: from whence you lose your eyes upon the glimmering of the Waters under the wood, & your ears in the constant dashing of the waves. In view of this, is a Bridge that crosses this Stream, built in the same ruinous taste: the Wall of the Garden hanging over it, is humourd so as to appear the Ruin of another Arch or two above the bridge. Hence you mount the Hill over the Hermits Seat (as they call it) describd before, & so to the highest Terras, again.

On the left, full behind these old Trees, which make this whole Part inexpressibly awful & solemn, runs a little, old, low wall, beside a Trench, coverd with Elder trees & Ivyes; which being crost by another bridge, brings you to the Ruins, to compleat the Solemnity of the Scene. You first see an old Tower penetrated by a large Arch, and others above it thro which the whole Country appears in prospect, even when you are at the top of the other ruins, for they stand very high, & the Ground slopes down on all sides. These venerable broken Walls, some Arches almost entire of 30 or 40 ft deep, some open like Portico's with fragments of pillars, some circular or inclosd on three sides, but exposd at top, with Steps which Time has made of disjointed Stones to climb to the highest points of the Ruin: These I say might have a prodigious Beauty, mixd with Greens & Parterres from part to part, and the whole Heap standing as it does on a round hill, kept smooth in green turf, which makes a bold Basement to show it. The open Courts from building to building might be thrown into Circles or Octagons of Grass or flowers, and even in the gaming Rooms you have fine trees grown, that might be made a natural Tapistry to the walls, & arch you over-head where time has uncoverd them to the Sky. Little paths of earth, or sand, might be made, up the half-tumbled walls; to guide from one View to another on the higher parts; & Seats placd here and there, to enjoy those views, which are more romantick than Imagination can form them. I could very much wish this were done, as well as a little Temple built on a neighboring round Hill that is seen from all points of the Garden & is extremely pretty. It would finish some Walks, & particularly be a fine Termination to the River to be seen from the Entrance into that Deep Scene I have describd by the Cascade where it would appear as in the clouds, between the tops of some very lofty Trees that form an Arch before it, with a great Slope downward to the end of the said river.

What should induce my Lord D. the rather to cultivate these ruins and do honour to them, is that they do no small honour to his Family; that Castle, which was very ancient, being demolishd in the Civil wars after it was nobly defended by one of his Ancestors in the cause of the King. I would sett up at the Entrance of 'em an Obelisk, with an inscription of the Fact: which would be a Monument erected to the very Ruins; as the adorning & beauti- fying them in the manner I have been imagining, would not be unlike the

AEgyptian Finery of bestowing Ornament and curiosity on dead bodies. The Present Master of this place (and I verily believe I can ingage the same for the next Successors) needs not to fear the Record, or shun the Remembrance of the actions of his Forefathers. He will not disgrace them, as most Modern Progeny do, by an unworthy Degeneracy, of principle, or of Practise. When I have been describing his agreable Seat, I cannot make the reflection I've often done upon contemplating the beautiful Villa's of Other Noblemen, raisd upon the Spoils of plunderd nations, or aggrandiz'd by the wealth of the Publick. I cannot ask myself the question, 'What Else has this man to be lik'd? what else has he cultivated or improv'd? What good, or what desireable thing appears of him, without these walls? I dare say his Goodness and Benevolence extend as far as his territories; that his Tenants live almost as happy & contented as himself; & that not one of his Children wishes to see this Seat his owne. I have not lookd much about, since I was here: All I can tell you of my own knowledge is, that going to see the Cathedral in the town hard by, I took notice as the finest things, of a noble Monument and a beautiful Altar-piece of Architecture; but if I had not inquird in particular, he nor his, had ever told me that both the one & the other was erected by Himself: The next pretty thing that catchd my eye was a neat Chappel for the use of the Towns-people, (who are too numerous for the Cathedral) My Lord modestly told me, he was glad I lik't it, because it was of his own architecture.

I hope this long letter will be some Entertainment to you, I was pleased not a little in writing it; but don't let any Lady from hence imagine that my head is so full of any Gardens as to forget hers. The greatest proof I could give her to the contrary is, that I have spent many hours here in studying for hers, & in drawing new plans for her. I shall soon come home, & have nothing to say when we meet, having here told you all that has pleas'd me: But Wilton is in my way, & I depend upon that for new matter. Believe me ever yours, with a sincerity as old-fashiond, and as different from Modern Sincerity, as This house, this family, & these ruins, are from the Court, & all its Neighbourhood. Dear Madam, Adieu.

from *An Epistle to Lord Burlington* (1731)

Oft have you hinted to your Brother Peer,
A certain Truth, which many buy too dear:
Something there is, more needful than Expence,
And something previous ev'n to Taste — 'Tis *Sense*;
Good Sense, which only is the Gift of Heav'n,
And tho' no Science, fairly worth the Seven.
A Light, which in *yourself* you must perceive;
Jones and *Le Nôtre* have it not to give.

forms that make remember Genius of the place

To build, to plant, whatever you intend,
To rear the Column, or the Arch to bend,
To swell the Terras, or to sink the Grot;
In all, let *Nature* never be forgot.
Consult the *Genius* of the *Place* in all,
That tells the Waters or to rise, or fall,
Or helps th' ambitious Hill the Heav'ns to scale,
Or scoops in circling Theatres the Vale,
Calls in the Country, catches opening Glades,
Joins willing Woods, and varies Shades from Shades,
Now breaks, or now directs, th' intending Lines;
Paints as you plant, and as you work, *Designs*.

sense part and the order of the whole

Begin with *Sense*, of ev'ry Art the Soul,
Parts answ'ring Parts, shall slide into a Whole,
Spontaneous Beauties all around advance,
Start, ev'n from *Difficulty*, strike, from *Chance*;
Nature shall join you; *Time* shall make it grow
A Work to wonder at — perhaps a STOW.

Without it, proud *Versailles!* thy Glory falls,
And *Nero*'s Terrasses desert their Walls:
The vast *Parterres* a thousand hands shall make,
Lo! *Bridgman* comes, and floats them with a *Lake*:
Or cut wide *Views* thro' Mountains to the Plain,
You'll wish your Hill, and shelter'd Seat, again.

Behold *Villario*'s ten-years Toil compleat,
His *Quincunx* darkens, his Espaliers meet,
The Wood supports the Plain; the Parts unite,
And strength of Shade contends with strength of Light;
His bloomy Beds a waving Glow display,
Blushing in bright Diversities of Day,
With silver-quiv'ring Rills maeander'd o'er —
— Enjoy them, you! *Villario* can no more;
Tir'd of the Scene Parterres and Fountains yield,
He finds at last he better likes a Field.

Thro' his young Woods how pleas'd *Sabinus* stray'd,
Or sate delighted in the thick'ning Shade,
With annual Joy the red'ning Shoots to greet,
And see the stretching Branches long to meet!
His Son's fine Taste an op'ner *Vista* loves,
Foe to the *Dryads* of his Father's Groves,
One *boundless Green* or *flourish'd Carpet* views,
With all the mournful Family of *Yews*;
The thriving Plants ignoble Broomsticks made
Now sweep those Allies they were born to shade.

Yet hence the *Poor* are cloth'd, the *Hungry* fed;
Health to himself, and to his Infants *Bread*
The Lab'rer bears; What thy hard Heart denies,
Thy charitable Vanity supplies.
Another Age shall see the golden Ear
Imbrown thy Slope, and nod on thy Parterre,
Deep Harvests bury all thy Pride has plann'd,
And laughing *Ceres* re-assume the Land.

At *Timon*'s *Villa* let us pass a Day,
Where all cry out, 'What Sums are thrown away!
So proud, so grand, of that stupendous Air,
Soft and *Agreeable* come never there.
Greatness, with *Timon*, dwells in such a Draught
As brings all *Brobdignag* before your Thought:
To compass this, his Building is a Town,
His Pond an Ocean, his Parterre a Down;
Who but must laugh the Master when he sees?
A puny Insect, shiv'ring at a Breeze!
Lo! what huge Heaps of Littleness around!
The Whole, a labour'd Quarry above ground!
Two *Cupids* squirt before: A Lake behind
Improves the keenness of the Northern Wind.
His *Gardens* next your Admiration call,
On ev'ry side you look, behold the Wall!
No pleasing Intricacies intervene,
No artful Wilderness to perplex the Scene:
Grove nods at Grove, each Ally has a Brother,
And half the Platform just reflects the other.
The suff'ring Eye inverted Nature sees,
Trees cut to Statues, Statues thick as Trees,
With here a Fountain, never to be play'd,
And there a Summer-house, that knows no Shade.
Here *Amphitrite* sails thro' Myrtle bow'rs;
Then *Gladiators* fight, or die, in flow'rs;
Un-water'd see the drooping Sea-horse mourn,
And Swallows roost in *Nilus*' dusty Urn. . . .

In you, my *Lord*, Taste sanctifies Expence,
For Splendor borrows all her Rays from Sense.
You show us, *Rome* was glorious, not profuse,
And pompous Buildings once were things of use.
Just as they are, yet shall your noble Rules
Fill half the Land with *Imitating Fools*,
Who random Drawings from your Sheets shall take,
And of one Beauty many Blunders make;
Load some vain Church with old Theatric State;

Turn Arcs of Triumph to a Garden-gate;
Reverse your Ornaments, and hang them all
On some patch'd Doghole ek'd with Ends of Wall,
Then clap four slices of Pilaster on't,
And lac'd with bits of Rustic, 'tis a Front:
Shall call the Winds thro' long Arcades to roar,
Proud to catch cold at a *Venetian* door;
Conscious they act a true *Palladian* part,
And if they starve, they starve by Rules of Art.

Gilbert West (1703–56)

Not merely is *Stowe, The Gardens of the Right Honourable Richard Viscount Cobham* one of the earliest poems entirely devoted to the description of an English estate, it is the first of many publications on Stowe. West was the nephew of Viscount Cobham and he obviously brings to his account a sympathetic and a tutored eye. He pictures and meditates upon the features of the gardens, bringing out the evocative quality of the monuments and their reflection of Classical mythology, national pride or local sentiment. West's verses, with their explanatory footnotes, afford valuable evidence to the historian of the gardens concerning the authorship of various temples and (in lines 55–8) the advanced planning of the Elysian Fields in 1732. The poem also indicates that at Stowe the visitor experiences both the old-fashioned geometrical garden (lines 368–75, for example) and the rural landscape (lines 85–8, 234–41 and 354–67); the two are juxtaposed, as Castell assumed they were in Pliny's villas, but it is the second which seems to dominate.

Stowe, The Gardens of the Right Honourable Richard Viscount Cobham (1732)

TO Thee, great Master of the vocal String,
O *Pope*, of *Stowe*'s Elyzian Scenes I sing:
That *Stowe*, which better far thy Muse divine
Commands to live *in one distinguish'd Line.
Yet let not thy superior Skill disdain
The friendly Gift of this *Poetick Plan*.
The same presiding Muse alike inspires
The *Planter*'s Spirit and the *Poet*'s Fires,
Alike, unless the Muse propitious smile,
Vain is the *Planter*'s, vain the *Poet*'s Toil,
All great, all perfect Works from *Genius* flow,
The *British Iliad* hence, and hence the Groves of *Stowe*.

* See Epistle to the Earl of *Burlington*.

*To guardian *Phoebus* the first Strains belong,
(And may th' auspicious Omen bless the Song)
To *Phoebus*, and th' attendant Virgin Train,
That o'er each Verse, each learned Science reign,
And round embellishing the gay *Parterre*,
Unite their sacred Influences here.
Here *Congreve*, welcome Guest, oft chear'd the Days,
With friendly Converse, or poetick Lays.
Here *Lyttleton* oft spreads his growing Wing,
Delighted in these Shades to rove and sing.
And Thou, where *Thames* impels his silver Flood,
Quitting the Care of thy own rising Wood,
Oft, as thy Breast, with pleasing Rapture glow'd,
Hast here, O *Pope*, avow'd th' inspiring God.
In a green Niche's over-arching Shrine,
Each tuneful Goddess shrouds her Form divine.
Beneath, in the wide Area's middle Space,   [Plate 61]
A jetting Fount its chrystal Flood displays.
In whose clear Face again reflected shine
Pierian Phoebus, and the Virgin Nine.
Here too for ever bloom †th' *Aonian* Bays,
Ordain'd the Meed of tuneful Poets Lays.
In seemly Order *They* on either Hand,
Alternate in the verdant Arches stand:
Alternate glitt'ring with the gilded Vase,
On either Hand the verdant Arches blaze.
Here, odorous Flowers perfume the vital Gale,
‡And here *Hesperian* Oranges exhale.
Transported hence the Summer-hearth they grace,
And shine, collected in the *China* Vase;
Or on the *Sunday*'s consecrated Morn,
Select in Nosegays the fair Breast adorn.

Lead thro' the §Circle, Virgins, lead me on,
Where, guided by the still-revolving Sun,
The faithful Dial counts the fleeting Hour,
Lead to the Church's venerable Tower:
Which like the life-producing Plant of Old,
That flourish'd once in *Eden*'s blessed Mould,
In the mid-Garden placed, its sacred Head
Uprears, embosom'd in aspiring Shade:
And blest with Vertue, like that wond'rous Tree,
Confers on Mortals Immortality.

* Statues of *Apollo*, the *Nine Muses*, and the *Liberal Arts* and *Sciences* placed round the *Parterre*.
† Bay-Trees and gilt Vases, placed alternately in the Arches of the Archade.
‡ The Orangerie.
§ The Sun-Dial Parlour.

[55]   Hence thro' the Windings of the mazy Wood
Descending, lo! the *Octagon*'s clear Flood,
And rustick *Obelisk*'s aerial Height,
Burst in one sudden View upon the Sight.
*_Batavian_ Poplars here in ranks ascend;
Like some high Temple's arching Isles extend
The taper Trunks, a living Colonnade;
Eternal Murmur animates the Shade.
Above, †two *Dorick* Edifices grace
An elevated *Platform*'s utmost Space;
From whence, beyond the Brook that creeps below,
Along yon beauteous Hill's green sloping Brow,
The Garden's destin'd Boundaries extend,
Where *Cobham*'s pleasing Toils, tho' late, shall end,
Beneath the far-stretch'd *Lake*'s capacious Bed,
Receives the loud, praecipitate *Cascade*;
And tufted Groves along the verdant Side,
Cast their deep Shadows o'er the silver Tide:
The silver Tide (where yonder high-rais'd Mound
Forms the wide-floating *Lake*'s extremest Bound)
In secret Channels thro' the swelling Hill,
Gives Force and Motion to th' impulsive Wheel;
Whose constant Whirl, the spouting Jets supplies,
And bids aloft th' unwilling Waters rise.
Fair on the Brow, a spacious Building stands,
Th' applauded Work of *Kent*'s judicious Hands:
The spreading Wings in arched Circles bend,
And rustick Domes each arched Circle end.
Thence back returning, thro' the narrow Glade,
See, where the ‡*Ruin* lifts its mould'ring Head!
[85]   Within, close-shelter'd from the peering Day,
Satyrs and Fauns their wanton Frolicks play.
While sad *Malbecco* in the secret Cell,
Hears each rude Monster §'ring his Matin's Bell.'

     Where yon high Firs display their darksome Green,
And mournful Yews compose a solemn Scene,
Around thy Building, *Gibbs*, ‖a sacred Band

* The Abeal Walk.
† Two Pavilions built by *Sir J. Vanbrugh*.
‡ The Ruin, painted on the Inside with the Story of *Malbecco*, out of *Spencer*'s *Fairy Queen*, Book 3. Canto 10.
§ An Hemystick of *Spencer*.
‖ *Alluding to the Inscription on the Building*.
  Hic Manus, ob Patriam pugnando Vulnera passi;
  Quique pii Vates, & Phoebo digno locuti;
  Inventas aut qui Vitam excoluere per Artes;
  Quique sui memores alios fecere merendo.   Virg. Lib. 6.

73 Stowe, Buckinghamshire. Drawing by Jacques Rigaud, *c.* 1733, of the
'View from *Gibbs*'s *Building*'

Of Princes, Patriots, Bards, and Sages stand: [Plate 73]
Men, who by Merit purchas'd lasting Praise,
Worthy each *British* Poet's noblest Lays:
Or bold in Arms for Liberty they stood,
And greatly perish'd for their Country's Good:
Or nobly warm'd with more than mortal Fire,
Equal'd to *Rome* and *Greece* the *British* Lyre:
Or Human Life by useful Arts refin'd,
Acknowledg'd Benefactors of Mankind.

Thou first *Elizabeth*, Imperial Maid,
By freeborn Subjects willingly obey'd;
Foe to the Tyranny of *Spain*, and *Rome*,
Abroad respected, and belov'd at home,
Beneath the friendly Shelter of thy Throne
Each Art of Peace with useful Lustre shone:
Industrious Commerce courted every Gale,
And spread in distant Worlds her fearless Sail.
Encourag'd Science rear'd her laurel'd Head,

And all the pleasing Train of Muses led.
Lo! *Verulam* and *Shakespear* near Thee stand,
Rais'd by thy Smiles to grace this happy Land:
Both dear to *Phoebus*, sacred both to Fame,
With Princes here an equal Rank they claim;
This with the richest Stores of Learning fraught,
That by indulgent Nature only taught.
All hail! auspicious Queen, thy Praise shall live
(If Worth like thine Eternity can give)
When no proud Bust th' Imperial Wreath shall bear,
And Brass and Marble waste to Dust and Air.

O! that like Thee, succeeding Kings had strove,
To build their Empire on their Peoples Love!
That taught by thy Example they had known,
That only Justice can support a Throne!
Then had not *Britain* wanted *Hambden's* Hand,
Weak and oppressive Counsels to withstand:
Nor had the Patriot, on his native Plain,
Dy'd for the Laws he struggled to maintain.
Behold his Bust with Civick Honours grac'd,
Nearest to thine, immortal *Nassau* plac'd,
To thine, great *William*, whose protecting Sword,
That *Liberty*, for which *He* fell, restor'd.

Next *Locke*, who in defence of Conscience rose,
And strove religious Rancour to compose:
Justly opposing every human Test,
Since GOD alone can judge who serves him best.

But what is he, in whom the heav'nly Mind
Shines forth distinguish'd and above Mankind?
This, this is *Newton*; *He*, who first survey'd
The Plan, by which the Universe was made:
Saw Nature's simple, yet stupendous Laws,
And prov'd th' Effects, tho' not explain'd the Cause.

Thou too, bold *Milton*, whose immortal Name,
Thy Country dares to match with *Homer's* Fame;
Whose tow'ring Genius vast and unconfin'd,
Left ev'n the Limits of the World behind;
Thro' Hell, thro' Chaos, and infernal Night,
Ascending to the Realms of purest Light;
Or else on Earth, in *Eden's* happy Grove,
With Peace, with Bliss conversing, and with Love:
Here art thou plac'd, these blooming shades among,
Second to those alone thy Muse has sung.

74 Stowe, Buckinghamshire. Drawing by Jacques Rigaud, *c.* 1733, of the
'View of the *Queen's Theatre* from the *Rotunda*'

    *An ancient Wood (upon whose topmost Bough
High-waving croaks the unauspicious Crow)
From hence its venerable Gloom extends,
Where, rivalling its lofty Height, ascends
The pointed Pyramid: This too is thine,
Lamented *Vanbrugh!* This thy last Design.
†Among the various Structures, that around,
Form'd by thy Hand, adorn this happy Ground,
This, sacred to thy Memory shall stand:
Cobham, and grateful Friendship so command.

Nysean Bacchus next the Muse demands;
To Him, in yon high Grove, a ‡*Temple* stands;
Where *British* Oaks their ancient Arms display,

* The Rook-Spinny.
† Alluding to the Inscription, Inter Plurima Hortorum horunce AEdificia a Johanne
Vanbrugh Equite designata Hanc Pyramidem illius Memoriae sacram esse voluit
COBHAM.
‡ The rustick Temple, built by Sir *J. Vanbrugh*.

Impervious to the Sun's unclouded Ray,
There, half-conceal'd, it rears its Rustick Head;
The painted Walls mysterious *Orgies spread.
A jolly Figure on the Cieling reels,
Whose every Nerve the potent Goblet feels:
His Vine-bound Brows bespeak him God of Wine,
The Cheeks, and swelling Paunch, O! —— are thine.
—— (not unknown to *Phoebus* is the Name)
Once felt the Fervour of a softer Flame;
When heedless Fortune shot the sudden Dart,
And unexpected Rapture seiz'd his Heart.
My faithful Verse this Secret shall reveal,
Nor —— himself shall blame the mirthful Tale.

A cool Recess there is, not far away,
Sacred to Love, to Mirth, and rural Play.
Hither oftimes the youthful Fair resort,
To cheat the tedious Hours with various Sport.
Some mid the *Nine-pins* marshall'd Orders roll,
With Aim unerring the impetuous *Bowl*.
Others, whose Souls to loftier Objects move,
Delight the *Swing*'s advent'rous Joys to prove:
While on each side the ready Lovers stand,
The flying Cord obeys th' impulsive Hand.
As on a Day contending Rivals strove,
By manly Strength to recommend their Love;
Toss'd to and fro, up flew the giddy Fair,
And scream'd, and laugh'd, and play'd in upper Air.
The flutt'ring Coats the rapid Motion find,
And One by One admit the swelling Wind:
At length the last, white, subtle Veil withdrew,
And those mysterious Charms expos'd to view —
What Transport then, O —— possess'd thy Soul!
Down from thy Hand, down dropt the idle *Bowl*:
As for the skilful *Tip* prepar'd he stood,
And Hopes and Fears alarm'd th' expecting Croud.
Sudden to seize the beauteous Prey he sprung;
Sudden with Shrieks the ecchoing Thicket rung.
Confounded and abash'd, the frighted Maid,
(While rising Blushes ting'd her Cheeks with red)
Fled swift away, more rapid than the Wind,
And left the treach'rous *Swing*, and —— behind,
Down the smooth Lawn she flew with eager Haste,
And near thy †Obelisk, O *Coucher*, pass'd:

* Rites and Revels of *Bacchus*.
† An Obelisk, in Memory of *Robin Coucher*.

As on the wounded Stone thy Name she view'd,
The well-known Name her every Fear renew'd;
And strait, in dreadful Vision, to her Eyes
She sees another Priest and Lover rise.
Nor cou'd thy gentle Mind her Fears assuage,
Nor honest Heart, that knew nor Guile nor Rage;
But with redoubled speed away she fled,
And sought the Shelter of the closer Shade;
Where in thick Covert, to her weary Feet,
*A Private Grotto promis'd safe Retreat:
Alas! too private, for too safely there
The fierce Pursuer seiz'd the helpless Fair;
The Fair he seiz'd, while round him all the Throng
Of laughing *Dryads*, *Hymenaeals* sung:
Pronubial *Juno* gave the mystick Sign,
And *Venus* nodded from †her neighb'ring Shrine.   [Plate 74]
The Grotto, conscious of the happy Flame,
From this auspicious Deed derives its *Name*.

    Here future Lovers, when in Troops they come,
Venus, to visit thy distinguish'd Dome,
As thro' this consecrated Shade they pass,
Shall offer to the Genius of the Place.

[234]   Shift now the closer Scene: and view around,
With various Beauties the wide Landskip crown'd.
Here level Glades extend their length'ning Lines,
There in just Order the deep *Quincunce* shines.
Here chrystal Lakes reflect contiguous Shades,
There distant Hills uplift their azure Heads.
Round the free ‡*Lawn* here gadding Heifers stray,
And frisking Lambs in sportive Gambols play.
There murmur to the Wind Groves ever-green,
And inter-mingled Buildings rise between:
The Sun declin'd with milder Glory burns,
And the fair Piece with various Light adorns.
Lo! in the *Centre* of this beauteous *Scene*,
Glitters beneath her §*Dome* the *Cyprian Queen*:

---

* The Randibus.
† The Rotunda.
‡ A large Field encompass'd with the Garden.
§ The Rotunda, on Pillars of the *Ionic* Order, with an Altar of blue Marble, and gilded Statue of the *Venus* of *Medicis*.

Not like to her, whom ancient *Homer* prais'd,
To whom a thousand sacred Altars blaz'd:
When simple Beauty was the only Charm,
With which each tender Nymph and Swain grew warm:
But, yielding to the now-prevailing Taste,
In *Gold*, for modern Adoration, drest.
For her the *Naiads*, in their watry Bed,
Amid the level Green *a Mirror spread;
Along whose terrass'd Banks the shelt'ring Wood,
Defends from ruder Winds th' unruffled Flood.

 Beyond, a sylvan †*Theatre* displays
Its circling Bosom to the Noon-tide Rays.
In Shade, o'er Shade, the slopeing Ranks ascend,
And tall *Abeals* the steep Gradation end.
Here to the Sun the glossy *Laurels* shine,
There wave the darker Honours of the *Pine*.

 High on a Pedestal, whose swelling Base,
To Heav'n itself aspiring Columns raise,
Shines the great Part'ner of *Augustus*' Bed,
The guardian Goddess of the noble Shade.
Beneath, in order ranged on either hand,
Attendant Nymphs and Swains rejoycing stand.

 But cou'd the Muse presume her lowly Pray'r
Might win attentien from the Royal Ear,
Here shou'd those Princely Stars, that dawning smile,
With kindly Lustre on *Britannia*'s Isle,
Fair Constellation! in one Blaze unite,
Aiding with filial Beams their Mother's Light.
Here shou'd Imperial CAROLINE be seen,
The glorious Rival of the ‡*Phrygian Queen*,
Who 'mid the thousand Altars that around,
Blaz'd in old *Rome*'s *Pantheon*, high enthron'd,
With Pride survey'd the venerable Dome,
Fill'd with the heav'nly Off-spring of her Womb.

 And see! where, elevated far above,
§A Column overlooks yon nodding Grove;

---

* The Rotunda Pond.
† The Queen's Theatre, with Her Majesty's Statue erected on four Columns.
‡ *Cybele*, Mother of the Gods.
§ The King's Pillar and Statue.

On which, the Scene of Glory to compleat,
Deck'd with the Ensigns of Imperial State,
Stands the great Father, *George*, whose equal Sway,
With Joy *Britannia*'s happy Realms obey.
Thence round, he views the cultivated Plain,
That smiling speaks the Blessings of his Reign.
Thus, o'er their Planets radiant Suns preside,
By Heav'n's fixt Laws their various Courses guide;
And shedding round Benevolence divine,
Bless'd by depending Worlds, indulgent shine.

    Deep in this close, umbrageous, wild Recess,
Where the sweet Songsters of the feather'd Race,
Warble their native Musick thro' the Shade;
*A solitary Building hides its Head.
This peaceful Fabrick, for Repose design'd,
Close Valves defend from penetrating Wind;
And the thick Under-wood's combining Boughs,
On every Side a verd'rous Wall compose.
Nigh, sound the quiv'ring Poplars in the Air,
Like falling Waters murm'ring from afar.
Here, where their quiet unmolested Reign
The Gods of Sleep and Solitude maintain;
Whether soft Slumbers close thy languid Eyes,
Or Thought be lost in pleasing *Réveries*,
From yon sage †*Motto* learn thy self to spare,
And bid adieu to unavailing Care.
Let not the Censures of the Wise dismay;
But where they own clear Reason leads the Way,
Her pleasing Dictates uncontroll'd pursue,
Thy Dreams, may be as good as Theirs, perhaps as true.

    Forsaking now the Covert of the Maze,
Along the broader Walk's more open space,
Pass we to where a sylvan Temple spreads
Around the *Saxon Gods*, its hallow'd Shades.

    Hail! Gods of our renown'd Fore-Fathers, hail!
Ador'd Protectors once of *England*'s Weal.
Gods, of a Nation, valiant, wise, and free,
Who conquer'd to establish *Liberty*!
To whose auspicious Care *Britannia* owes
Those Laws, on which she stands, by which she rose.

* The Sleeping-House.
† Cum Omnia sint in incerto fave Tibi.

Still may your Sons that noble Plan pursue,
Of equal Government prescrib'd by you.
Nor e'er indignant may you blush to see,
The Shame of your corrupted Progeny!

First radiant *Sunna* shews his beamy Head,
Mona to Him, and scepter'd *Tiw* succeed;
Tiw, ancient Monarch of remotest Fame,
Who led from *Babel*'s Tow'rs the *German* Name.
And warlike *Woden*, fam'd for martial Deeds,
From whom great *Brunswick*'s noble Line proceeds.
Dread *Thuner* see! on his Imperial Seat,
With awful Majesty, and kingly State
Reclin'd! at his Command black Thunders roll,
And Storms and fiery Tempests shake the Pole.
With various Emblem next fair *Friga* charms,
Array'd in female *Stole* and manly Arms.
Expressive *Image* of that Double Soul,
Prolifick Spirit that informs the Whole;
Whose Genial Power throughout exerts its Sway,
And Earth, and Sea, and Air, its Laws obey.
Last of the Circle hoary *Seatern* stands;
Instructive Emblems fill his mystick Hands.
In this a Wheel's revolving Orb declares
The never-ending Round of rolling Years,
That holds a Vessel fill'd with fading Flowers
And Fruits collected by the ripening Hours.
Be warn'd from hence, ye Fair Ones! to improve
The transitory Minutes made for Love,
E're yet th' inexorable Hand of *Time*
Robs of its bloomy Sweets your lovely Prime.

[354]   Lo, *Nelson*'s airy Seat, whose rising Sides
Obscuring Fir, and shining Laurel hides!
Here in sweet Contrast Rural Scenes display'd
Around their native wilder Beauties spread.
The tufted Woodland's, where the Hunter's Horn
Oft wakes with chearful Note the drowzy Morn;
The Brook that glitters in the Vale below,
And all the rising Lawn's enlightned Brow,
*In lowly Huts adown whose shelving Side.
From Storms secure the peaceful Hinds reside:
The spacious *Park*, within whose circling Pale,
The bounding Deer at large imprison'd dwell;
And feed in social Herds along the Glade,

* The Village of *Dadford*.

Or lonely seek the solitary Shade.
[368] Far o'er the level Green, in just array,
Long Rows of Trees their adverse Fronts display.
So when two Nations, fierce in Arms, prepare
At one decisive Stroke to end the War,
In seemly Order, e'er the Battle joins,
The marshal'd Hosts extend their threat'ning Lines,
And Files to Files oppos'd await the Word,
That gives a Loose to the destroying Sword.

High on a Mount, amid a verdant Field,
Where intermitted Lines wide opening yield;
Where from their plenteous Urns the watry Gods
Pour o'er the green expanse their limpid Floods,
Behold the *good old King* in Armour clad,
Triumphant Wreaths his sacred Temples shade.
And in his gracious Aspect shine exprest,
The manly Beauties of his gentle Breast;
His Mind, sincere, benevolent and great,
Nor aw'd by *Danger*, nor with *Pow'r* elate;
For *Valour* much, but more for *Justice* known,
Brave in the Field, and *Good* upon the Throne.

†An ample Arch, beneath whose spacious Round,
The massy Valves on turning Hinges sound,
Opens its hospitable Bosom wide;
Thro' which at large the rolling Chariots glide.
On swelling Bastions here ‡*Two* Buildings rise,
(While far beneath the low-sunk Valley lies;
Where, or in one broad Lake the Waters spread,
Or draw their humid Trains along the Mead)
Of *These*, a Shelter from the scorching Rays,
One in the Garden spreads his rustick Base:
One in the Park, an habitable Frame,
The Household *Lares*, and *Penates* claim.

But shall the Muse approach the Pile, assign'd
Once, for a Mansion to her much-lov'd Friend,
And not bestow one sad, one tuneful Tear,

---

* Equestrian Statue of *George* I. at the Head of the Canal, with this Inscription,
   In medio mihi Caesar erit,
  Et viridi in Campo Signum de Mamore ponam
  Propter Aquam.   *Virg.*
† The great Entrance into the Park, and approach to the House along the Garden Wall.
‡ Two Buildings, call'd *Boycut Buildings*, on each side the Entrance. One in the
Garden, the other in the Park was intended for a House for Colonel *Speed*, deceas'd.

Unhappy *Speed!* on thy untimely Bier?
Here, had not hasty Fate our Hopes deceiv'd,
In sweet Retirement tranquil had'st thou liv'd;
And pass'd with him, whose Friendship did ingage
In Arms thy Youth, In Peace thy weary Age.
Faithful Companion of his toilsome Days,
He led *Thee* on in Glory's noble Chace!
Faithful Companion of his calm Retreat,
Here had he destin'd thy delightful Seat.
Here too the Muse had joy'd to see thee blest,
Of every Hope, of every Wish possest;
Had sung, with Friendship and Affection mov'd,
Thy honest Heart by all esteem'd and lov'd;
And to thy living Worth that Tribute paid,
Which sorrowing now she offers to thy Shade.

Anonymous

The landscape of Castle Howard (Plate 75) provides, according to Horace Walpole, 'the greatest scenes of rural magnificence'; he might also have added that it was among the earliest of English landscape gardens. Its creation and the associations which the scenes were intended to provoke are recounted in this poem, *Castle Howard*, addressed to Charles, 3rd Earl of Carlisle, possibly by Lady Irwin, his daughter, and published around 1733. The poem has been used in fragments before (notably by Christopher Hussey in *English Gardens and Landscapes 1700–1750*), but it deserves more extensive quotation. It is, in the first place, much more specific than similar poems on English gardens — an almost contemporary effusion on Studley Royal, published in Thomas Gent's *The Ancient and Modern History of the Loyal Town of Rippon* (1733), is composed of generalities that would apply to virtually any garden. The precision of *Castle Howard* allows fascinating insights into the Augustan habits of mind that were called into play by a garden; yet, as the poet claims,

> All that Luxurious Fancy can invent,
> What Poets feign, what Painters represent;
> Not in Imagination here we trace,
> Realities adorn this happy Place.

Though there are occasional phrases that make one wonder whether the writer had read Pope's *Epistle to Lord Burlington* of 1731, the verses are as fresh and candid a view of Castle Howard as the landscape scenery itself is unique and superb.

from *Castle Howard* (c. 1733)

> From ev'ry Place you cast your wand'ring Eyes,
> You view gay Landskips, and new Prospects rise,
> There a Green Lawn bounded with Shady Wood,
> Here Downy Swans sport in a Lucid Flood.
> Buildings the proper Points of View adorn,
> Of *Grecian*, *Roman* and *Egyptian* Form.
>
> These interspers'd with Woods and Verdant Plains,
> Such as possess'd of old th' *Arcadian* Swains.
> Hills rise on Hills; and to complete the Scenes,

Like one continu'd Wood th' Horizon seems.
This in the main describes the Points of View,
But something more is to some Places due . . .

Lead through the Park, where Lines of Trees unite,
And Verd'rous Lawns the bounding Deer delight:
By gentle Falls the docile Ground descends,
Forms a fair Plain, then by Degrees ascends.
These Inequalities delight the Eye,
For Nature charms most in Variety.
When ev'r her gen'ral Law by Arts effac'd,
It shows a Skill, but proves a want of Taste.
O'r all Designs Nature shou'd still preside;
She is the cheapest, and most perfect Guide.

Far in the Park there lies a spacious Vale.
Form'd to inspire a soft Poetick Tale.
On ev'ry Side with shady Wood 'tis bound,
A Maiden Verdure covers all the Ground.
Hither Saint *Hubert* secretly repairs,

75 Castle Howard, Yorkshire. Painting by Hendrik de Cort, *c.* 1790–1810

And hears the eager Hunters Vows and Pray'rs.
The flying Deer by sad Experience feels,
The cruel Hounds, close at his tremb'ling Heels,
In silent Tears his last Distress he shows,
Then falls *Actaeon* like to bloody Foes.

Here other Woods and Lawns demand a Place,
Which well an abler Poets Theme wou'd grace:
But such unnumbered Beauties bless this Seat,
'Twere endless on each diff'rent Charm to treat.
Hipocrates has some where justly said,
That Arts are long, and Nature's Debt soon paid.
Cou'd we the certain Apothem reverse;
Were Arts soon learn'd, and distant was the Herse,
Then wou'd unrival'd *Carlisle*'s Genius shine,
Who has so early form'd this great Design:
But Fate has fix'd the Limits of our Stay,
And while I write, Time gently glides away.

East from the House a beaut'ous Down there lies,
Where Art with Nature emulating vyes:
Not smoother Surface boast the *Tempean* Plains,
Tho' sung by Poets in immortal Strains:
Not finer Verdure can young *Flora* bring,
Tho' she commands an ever blooming Spring.
Upon this Plain a Monument appears [the Pyramid],
Sacred to Piety and filial Tears.
Here to his Sire did grateful *Carlisle* raise,
A certain Record a more lasting Praise,
Than Volumes writ in Honour to his Name;
Those often die, being made the Sport of Fame:
The Moth, the Worm, and Envy, them annoy,
But Time can only Pyramids destroy.

Beyond this Down a Building rears its Head [the Mausoleum],
Sacred to the immortal Vert'ous dead.
The name of *Carias* noted King it bears,
Made famous by his faithful Consort's Tears.
Nor was the Structure *Artemisia* rais'd,
With greater Justice more deserv'dly prais'd.
Tho' that a Wonder was by Ancients deem'd,
This by the Moderns is not less esteem'd.
More difficult to please, and more perverse,
Judging more rashly, tho' they know much less.
Here *Carlisle* will thy sacred *Manes* repose,
This solemn Place thy Ashes will enclose.
How it will please thy gentle Shade to view,

Some Ages hence, Oh, may my Prophecy prove true!
Descending from thy Line a gen'rous Race,
Fit to adorn the Camp, or Court to Grace:
Who, after having gain'd deserv'd Applause,
For having bravely serv'd their Country's Cause,
Shall to Ambition rural Joys prefer,
And fix their Happiness and Pleasure here.
So when the *Trojan* Prince, with glad Surprize,
Survey'd the Hero's who shou'd from him rise,
All Dangers and all Labours he despis'd,
So much his noble Progeny he priz'd;
Only to future Prospects cou'd attend,
Since from his Line the *Caesars* shou'd descend.

The Garden now demands my humbly Lays,
Which merits a more worthy pen shou'd praise.
So far extended, and so great the Space,
Magnificence in ev'ry part we trace.
Before the House you view a large *Parterre*,
Not crouded with the Trifles brought from far:
No Borders, Alleys, Edgings spoil the Scene,
'Tis one unvary'd piece of Pleasing Green:
No starv'd Exoticks here lament their Fate,
Fetter'd and bound like Pris'ners of State:
Or as *Diogenes* in Tub confin'd,
Wishing like him th'enlivening Sun to find.
'Tis ornamented by the Sculpture's Hand,
Here Statues, Obilisks, and Vases stand.
Beyond 'tis circled by a pleasant Grove,
Rais'd from the Family of constant Love:
No boist'rous Storms, nor an inclement Sky,
Which tender Leaves, and springing Buds destroy,
Affect the Sombre Shade you here enjoy;
Perpetual Verdure all the Trees disclose,
Which like true Love no Change of Seasons knows . . .

A noble Terrass lies before the Front,
By which into a Paradise you mount [Ray Wood].
Not greater Beauty boasts th'*Idalian* Grove,
Tho' that is sacred to the Queen of Love.
Such stately Trees encircle ev'ry view,
As never in Dodanas Forest grew.
Here the smooth Beach and rev'rend Oak entwine,
And form a Temple for the Pow'rs Divine:
So Ages past from ancient Bards we've heard,
When Men the Deity in Groves rever'd.
A Tow'ring Wood superior in its Kind,

Was to the Worship of the God's assign'd:
While *Plebian* Trees, which lowly Shade produce,
Were held unworthy of this Sacred Use.
Here Broad Meander Walks, each Way surprize;
And if Variety's a Charm we prize,
That Charm this Grove can in Perfection boast,
As Art in copying Nature pleases most.
Gardens of diff'rent Forms delight the Eye,
From whence a beaut'ous Country we discry:
And sure, if any Place deserves to claim,
This Wood with Justice *Belvidere* we name.
Statues at proper Views enrich the Scene,
Here chaste *Diana* and the *Paphian* Queen,
Tho' Opposites in Fame, tho' Rivals made
Contented stand under one common Shade.
Such Harmony of Soul this Place inspires,
All furious Passions, and all fierce Desires
Are here becalm'd, and Gentleness succeds,
The certain Parent whence Content proceeds.
Who wou'd not then prefer this pleasing Bow'r,
Since Life is fleeting, and the present Hour
Is all that Fate has put into our Pow'r?
To Riches, Grandeur, Fame, Ambition's Pleas,
Since Peace of Mind gives greater Joy than these . . .

Robert Morris (1701–54)

Morris read his lectures on architecture to a Society for the Improvement of Arts and Sciences, about which little is known, during the first half of the 1730s. The extracts here, from his eleventh and twelfth (delivered in 1734), are taken from the collected edition published in 1759 after his death. Morris was the theorist among British Neo-Palladians: he had expounded the virtues of Roman architecture in his *Essay in Defence of Ancient Architecture* (1728) and traced its influence through Palladio and Scamozzi. In his lectures he is much concerned with the idea of the villa, both architecturally and as an integral part of larger landscape compositions; in this he is probably publicizing the theories of his kinsman, Roger Morris, and Roger's collaborator, Henry Herbert, 9th Earl of Pembroke, who together designed Marble Hill (Plate 24). The extracts concern Robert Morris's proposals for 'little *Fabricks* erected in the Gardens of some NOBLE *Patron* of Arts'; their uses, as he says, are many, but one to which he continually returns is the promotion of a 'Chain of Thought' which in one carefully designed situation 'opens to the Mind a vast Field to entertain the Tongue or Pen of a Philosopher, to plunge into the deep Recesses of Nature' (Plate 76).

76 Garden temple. Drawing, perhaps by Roger Morris, ?1730s

from *Lectures on Architecture* (1734)

The Design before us affords a Delicacy of Taste and Invention to appropriate a Spot analogous to its Decoration. It is of the *Corinthian Order*,
dress'd with such *Ornaments* and *Garnishing* as are necessary to perfect the
Composition. Here the ARCHITECT must be supply'd by an artificial
Scene to entertain his Fancy: He must, by agreeable Images of rural Beauties,
furnish himself with what is *useful*, and adapted to the design, so joining
ART and NATURE together to render the Scene the more delightful.

The first thing to be consider'd, is the Use to which this Design is
proposs'd to be apply'd, it being intended for Pleasure as well as a Retirement
in some Garden, or agreeable decorated Spot. Few Conveniencies are wanting,
therefore I suppose it only as a Summer-house a little remote from some
noble *Villa*; and the Building I would place in some *Avenue* leading thereto.
It is HERE in the *cooler Hours* of Reflection, a Man might retire, to contemplate the important *Themes* of *Human Life*; recluse from gay Fancies, he
might secrete himself, not envying the more External Grandeur of Power,
or despising the humbler, or lower Class of Beings, to whom Providence or
Fortune hath been less auspicious. In the silent Recesses of Life, are more
noble and *felicitous* Ideas, and which more immediately concern our Attention . . .

REFLECTIONS of this kind [on the geography and climate of the world],
are the Growth of Retirement to a contemplative *Genius*; and the *Design*
before us, decorated with those Embelishments, requires a Situation capable
of raising such elevated *Ideas*. I shall therefore suppose it erected in the
Center of a *Wood*, and each Front to have an Opening or *Vista* only the
breadth of the Building. If it were on a little Ascent it would be better, and
more advantageous for Prospect. Not far remote from the back Front I
would choose a *Rivulet* or *Canal*. The Woods I would plant with low *Trees*
or *Bushes*, with little *Vista's* and private Walks; and those left wild and
unprun'd, that at Noon-day they should receive only Light enough to
distinguish the *Blaze* of *Day* from *Evening Shade*, there the Chorus of the
Birds would afford new Pleasures, and by dispersing Seats, &c. among the
Walks, would greatly add to its Beauty.

WITHOUT the Woods I would have *Meadows* strew'd with various
Flowers, which being dispers'd among those of the *Earth's* natural Produce,
would render the Glebe more delightful to behold. If the *River* ran through
it, and was disposed into multitudes of little Streams, 'twould still add to its
Beauty, and make the Ground *more fertile*; 'twould diversify the Scene, and
by a Chain of rising Hills beyond, to terminate the View, would make a
beautiful Landscape. In one part of the Wood I propose a *Grotto*, and in it
a *Bath*. This should be placed in the most unfrequented Part, surrounded

with *Ever-greens*, and the Access to it by a declining spiral Walk, to terminate in a circular *Theatre*, about 10 ft. below the Surface of the Garden. This, by *subterranean* Aqueducts, might be supply'd by the Rivulet, and *artificially* dispers'd among *craggy, mossy Rocks*, form'd by a skilful Hand, which would be a pleasing Scene to gratify the curious Eye and Ear. The little murmuring Rills of Water, trickling down in disorder'd Streams, would create a kind of *melancholly musical Tone*, not altogether unpleasant.

STILL to render the Retirement compleat, the Walks should be a con-tinued *Verdure*, and so planted, that some of them should always afford perpetual Shade. The *timorous Hare* should be protected from the Artifice of *ensnaring Men*; and the Birds possess perpetual *Freedom* without *Annoy-ance*. Here a *Mind* innocently employ'd by its *Starts* and *Sallies*, and its Excursions into *philosophic Depths*, by a Propensity to Solitude, always meets with Entertainment. Every Sprig of *Grass* may afford a multitude of fine Thoughts, to employ the Imagination; and by a Genius turn'd to *microscopical* Speculations, a Way is open'd to entertain the Fancy with unbounded Reflections . . .

FROM an Eminence thus situate [the attics] many agreeable Views might be had to distant Objects, which would afford an amusing Entertainment in the Sereneness of a declining Sun and calm Air, when Nature seems lull'd into a kind of pleasing REVERIE. As this Profile before us is to terminate a Walk in a Garden, I propose, in the Course of these *Lectures*, to delineate some little Temple or Building, with its Plan, suited to this purpose. The ancient *Romans* planted their Plots in this *rural* manner; and their *Temples*, dedicated to their peculiar GODS, were dispersed among the *Groves* and *Woods*, which Art or Nature had made, with *Vistas* to them, or some more secret Approach, to which, for the most part, *Devotion* or *Luxury* led the Master of the *Villa* to retire to. In such Retreats the *Roman* Senators were wont to taste the Pleasures of Retirement, to unbend their Minds from the more weighty Concerns of their Commonwealth; till, perhaps, satiated with too great an Excess of Indolence, and *ennervated* by Luxury, succeeding Tyrants claim'd a Superiority over them, and by degrees they lost their LIBERTY. — Then their noble *Palaces*, their magnificent and beautiful *Villa*'s, their delicious Situations were wrested from them, and at length the whole Empire became a Seat of *wild Desolation*.

YET still their Arts survive, and we may boast of many noble Genius's with suitable Fortunes, who are Copiers of those fam'd *Romans*; *Cato* and *Pliny*, *Varro* and *Columella*, with their Villa's decorated in as *beautiful, rural*, or *magnificent* a manner as those of the Ancients. — But choice of different Situations must much diversify the intended Pile . . .

MY Three preceding Designs, of this second part of my *Lectures*, have been dispos'd chiefly to a *Rural* and *Pleasant* Soil, I propose in this to change the Scene for one more *Robust* and Rustick, a Design capable of sustaining the Storms and tempestuous Inclemency of the Elements; it being plain, and the *Plan* fitted by its Strength and Contrivance to withstand the Injuries of Winds and Weather . . .

THIS Design I would propose to place on the Summit of a HILL, a long-extended Vale to the principal Front; and not far remote from the declining Verge of the HILL, I would have a navigable River: WINDSOR, or GREENWICH, or RICHMOND, or SHOOTER'S-HILL, afford a Scene something like this; and the Profile before us being intended for the chief Front, I would propose it for a *South* Aspect to the *Vale* below, bounded only by the declining *Horizon*.

WITH the Variety of Woods and Meadows, and different Views of the River, I would wish to have some beautifully situated *Villa's*, interspersed with little *Villages* and *Towns*; in the Scene some Views should be to Pastures cover'd with Flocks of Sheep, from thence to Fields of Corn, in which the ripening Harvests would afford Delight to the Eye ...

I WOULD have no Garden laid out by Art, but such only as Nature it self produc'd; the Vale below would afford all the Pleasures of a distant View. I would have a little Spot sufficient to serve the House with Fruits and Herbage ...

FROM one end of a *Building*, thus form'd in *Plan*, and a Situation, a View half rural, the other half a rocky *Wild*, or open to the Sea, would afford a delightful Variety, a pleasant Landscape. And from each Front, so many different Views might be had, in every Season of the Year, as would render the Spot always agreeable; and if Business required a Residence in some populous *Town* or *City*, half that Pleasure might be there enjoy'd, by having several Views of those Landscapes at different Seasons, taken by a skilful Hand, at the *Villa* it self. This would renew the Felicity, to see a beautiful Vale with all the fineness of a *rural Scene* from one Front, and a *Building* capable of being erected at such a Point of Sight; and to the other, the well-designed Picture would disclose to View, all the Horrors of *romantick Precipices*, or the Inclemency of the Elements in a *Tempest*.

Philip Yorke, 2nd Earl of Hardwicke
(1720–90)

Philip Yorke visited the gardens that John Aislabie had created at Studley Royal in September 1744 (Plate 77). The record he kept of his visit includes an early example of the Chinese taste, which Chambers was to exploit in the following decades. Not that Studley, which Christopher Hussey has called 'one of the most spectacular scenic compositions in England', presents much of a Chinese feeling today. The extension of the grounds to incorporate the ruins of Fountains Abbey (Plate 32), about which Yorke writes, was achieved in 1768; but before that date the 'venerable Pile' was obviously considered the proper visual and effective complement to the whole composition: it contributed, according to a poet of the 1730s, a full repertoire of Gothic and picturesque sentiment to the more gentle character of the rest of Aislabie's domain:

> Where Prayers were read, and pious Anthems sung,
> Now Heaps of Rubbish the Apartments throng.
> Up roofless Walls the clasping Ivy creeps,
> Where many a Bird of Prey in Safety sleeps:
> Or finds in dreary Caves a kind Retreat,
> And broods on Rapine in her gloomy Seat.

Yorke's 'Journal of What I Observed Most Remarkable in a Tour into the North' was published by the Bedfordshire Historical Record Society in 1968, and our text is taken from this edition.

from 'A Journal of What I Observed Most Remarkable in a Tour into the North' (1744)

Spent 6 hours in riding over Mr. Aislabie's park at Studley. The natural beauties of this place are superior to anything of the kind I ever saw, and improved with great taste both by the late and present owner. The extent of the whole is 710 acres, of which about 150 are reckoned into the garden, and the river Scheld, which runs through the ground, covers (as they told us) 23 of them. It is impossible from a single survey, however well conducted, to conceive oneself or give a stranger an adequate idea of Studley. Imagine rocks covered with wood, sometimes perpendicularly steep and craggy, at others descending in slopes to beautiful lawns and parterres, water thrown into 20 different shapes — a canal, a basin, a lake, a purling stream, now

77 Studley Royal, Yorkshire. Engraving by Anthony Walker, 1758, of the
banqueting house and round temple

gliding gently through the plain, now foaming and tumbling in a cascade
down 8 or 10 steps. In one place it is finely turned through the middle arch
of a rough stone bridge. The buildings are elegant and well suited to the
ground they stand upon. The temple of Venus is at the head of a canal in the
midst of a thick wood; that of Hercules on another spot not less delightful.
A Gothic tower overlooks the park and gardens from the summit of a rock.
Mr. Aislabie designs to erect a Chinese house of a pyramidical form, with a
gallery encircling every story, upon the point of a ridge which encloses on
each hand a valley finely wooded and washed by a rivulet. One side is formed
into a number of small terraces interspersed with rocks, which makes a
Chinese landscape. You have besides several agreeable views of Ripon, the
adjacent country, and Fountains Abbey; and what seems almost peculiar to
Studley is that the same object, taken at a different point of view, is sur-
prisingly diversified and has all the grace of novelty.

   The ruins of the Abbey lie just without the enclosure of the park. They
are in the possession of a Roman Catholic gentleman, who has refused very
large offers from the late Mr. Aislabie. They would indeed have been a noble
addition to the beauties of his place. This monastery was seated in a romantic
vale, and, when entire, spread over 5 or 6 acres. Its remains are remarkably

well preserved and make a very venerable magnificent appearance. The church, which is 200 yds. long, wants little but its roof to be as perfect as ever; the tower, contrary to the usual manner, rises at the north end. The hall is 36 yds. by 15; the dormitory, supported by cloisters, 106 yds. At the end of them runs the Scheld under 4 arches. There are besides the ruins of the kitchen, a granary or common parlour over it, the abbot's lodge, and the principal gateway — all very distinguishable and entire. Over the west window of the church is a bird standing on a tun, probably the device of the builder or founder, and a date which is 1444 or 1449.

Joseph Warton (1722–1800)

An intriguingly early glimpse of the reaction against the landscape garden, Warton's poem, *The Enthusiast*, subtitled *The Lover of Nature*, rejects the artifice of a garden like Stowe and opts for the wilder countryside beyond the ha-ha. Warton was something of a radical in matters of literary as well as gardenist taste: his essays on Pope, published in instalments in 1756 and 1782, argued that the more exuberant genius of Thomas Gray's *The Bard* touched deeper chords of the imagination than Pope's poetry. The attitudes of *The Enthusiast* anticipate those literary scepticisms about English Augustanism; like Gray's bard, he claims to prefer 'some Pine-topt Precipice' to a landscape designed by William Kent. Ironically, Warton's sense of 'real' nature outside a garden is derived substantially from paintings, notably by artists like Salvator Rosa, and from landscapes like the gorge of the Anio, or Aniene, at Tivoli (Plate 78), both of which provided inspiration for the landscape garden.

78 Gaspard Dughet (called Poussin), 'View of Tivoli', c. 1645–8

Joseph Warton (1722–1800)

from *The Enthusiast* (1744)

YE green-rob'd *Dryads*, oft' at dusky Eve
By wondering Shepherds seen, to Forests brown,
To unfrequented Meads, and pathless Wilds,
Lead me from Gardens deckt with Art's vain Pomps.
Can gilt Alcoves, can Marble-mimic Gods,
Parterres embroider'd, Obelisks, and Urns
Of high Relief; can the long, spreading Lake,
Or Vista lessening to the Sight; can *Stow*
With all her *Attic* Fanes, such Raptures raise,
As the Thrush-haunted Copse, where lightly leaps
The fearful Fawn the rustling Leaves along,
And the brisk Squirrel sports from Bough to Bough,
While from an hollow Oak the busy Bees
Hum drowsy Lullabies? The Bards of old,
Fair Nature's Friends, sought such Retreats, to charm
Sweet *Echo* with their Songs; oft' too they met,
In Summer Evenings, near sequester'd Bow'rs,
Or Mountain-Nymph, or Muse, and eager learnt
The moral Strains she taught to mend Mankind.
As to a secret Grot *AEgeria* stole
With Patriot *Numa*, and in silent Night
Whisper'd him sacred Laws, he list'ning sat
Rapt with her virtuous Voice, old *Tyber* leant
Attentive on his Urn, and husht his Waves.

Rich in her weeping Country's Spoils *Versailles*
May boast a thousand Fountains, that can cast
The tortured Waters to the distant Heav'ns;
Yet let me choose some Pine-topt Precipice
Abrupt and shaggy, whence a foamy Stream,
Like *Anio*, tumbling roars; or some bleak Heath,
Where straggling stand the mournful Juniper,
Or Yew-tree scath'd; while in clear Prospect round,
From the Grove's Bosom Spires emerge, and Smoak
In bluish Wreaths ascends, ripe Harvests wave,
Herds low, and Straw-rooft Cotts appear, and Streams
Beneath the Sun-beams twinkle — The shrill Lark,
That wakes the Wood-man to his early Task,
Or love-sick *Philomel*, whose luscious Lays

Sooth lone Night-wanderers, the moaning Dove,
Pitied by listening Milkmaid, far excell
The deep mouth'd Viol, the Soul-lulling Lute,
And Battle-breathing Trumpet. Artful Sounds!
That please not like the Choristers of Air,
When first they hail th' Approach of laughing *May*.
[Can Kent design like Nature? Mark where Thames
Plenty and pleasure pours through Lincoln's meads;
Can the great artist, though with taste supreme
Endued, one beauty to this Eden add?
Though he, by rules unfetter'd, boldly scorns
Formality and Method, round and square
Disdaining, plans irregularly great.]
Creative *Titian*, can thy vivid Strokes,
Or thine, O graceful *Raphael*, dare to vie
With the rich Tints that paint the breathing Mead?
The thousand-colour'd Tulip, Violet's Bell
Snow-clad and meek, the Vermil-tinctur'd Rose,
And golden Crocus?

[*Note:* The lines above within square brackets were added in later editions.]

William Shenstone (1714–63)

The following interview between Shenstone and Thomson in 1746, published in the *Edinburgh Magazine* of 1800, provides a valuable glimpse of how *cognoscenti* actually responded to a garden. Shenstone's garden at The Leasowes (Plates 79 and 80) was among the most notable gardens of the mid-century and its creator's 'Unconnected Thoughts on Gardening' among the most important writings (see pp. 289 ff.). This interview reveals not only the social pastimes (and crudities) for which a garden provided space, but also its poetic or associationist role: Shenstone and his guests discussing how to improve the 'idea' of Virgil's Grove; Pope proposing to create the image of a Gothic cathedral among the trees of a garden. Thomson's remarks further suggest that to his ability to read pictures in landscape he has also added an appreciation of the importance of movement *through* a garden, the three- even four-dimensional experience of submitting to scenery. His account of Lord Lyttelton in the second extract from *The Seasons* (see pp. 194–5) also described this experience.

79 The Leasowes, Shropshire. Aquatint by H. F. James and Stadler of the priory and house, *c.* 1800

'Account of an Interview between Shenstone and Thomson' (1746)

MR William Lyttelton and Mr Thomson, Author of the Seasons, found me reading a pamphlet in one of my niches at the Leasowes. Mr Lyttelton introduced his friend by saying he had undertaken to shew that gentleman all the beauties of the country, and thought he could not complete his promise without giving him a view of my situation. Thomson burst out in praise of it, and appeared particularly struck with the valley and brook by which he had passed, as they came the foot-way from Hales Owen. After some little stay in the house, we passed into the green behind the house. Thomson wished the garden to be extended, so as to include the valley on the left hand; not considering that I meant no regular garden, but to embellish my whole farm. The French, it appears, have their [P]*arque ornèe*; and why is not *Ferme ornée* as good an expression? He was much pleased upon observing how finely the back landskip was bounded. I took him to a seat near my upper pool, where he immediately mentioned Farmer's Hill as the principal beauty of the place. He seemed pleased also with the study on the bank of the water, since removed. As we were returning, Mr L. told me, "that I might not perhaps know that gentleman, tho' he was assured I was perfectly well acquainted with him in his writings. That it was Mr Thomson." My behaviour was a little awkward, and better calculated to express the satisfaction I took in the honour he did me, than to give him any idea either of my understanding or politeness. Being limited in point of time, and conscious of an hare upon the spit at Hagley, he could not stay to see my upper wood: "You have nothing to do (says he) but to dress Nature. Her robe is ready made; you have only to caress her; love her; kiss her; and then — descend into the valley." Coming out into the court before the house, he mentioned Clent and Waw-ton Hill as the two bubbies of Nature: then Mr L. observed the nipple, and then Thomson the fringe of Uphmore wood; till the double entendre was work'd up to a point, and produced a laugh. Thomson observed the little stream running across my gate, and hinted that he should avail himself of that also. We now passed into Virgil's Grove. What a delightful place, says he, is this for a person of a poetical genius. I don't wonder you're a devotee to the Muses. — This place, says Mr L. will *improve* a poetical genius. — Aye, replied Mr T. and a poetical genius will improve this place. I should think of nothing farther. Your situation detains us beyond the time appointed. How very valuable were this stream at Hagley! — I told him my then intention of building a model of Virgil's Tomb; which, with the Obelisk and a number of mottoes selected from Virgil, together with the pensive idea belonging to the place, might vindicate, or at least countenance, the appellation I had given it. Thomson assented to my notion of taste in gardening (that of contracting Nature's

80 The Leasowes, Shropshire. Etching by Hearne and Pouncy of
the river and bridge, 1792

beauties, altho' he somewhat misquoted me, and did not understand the
drift of my expression. Collecting, or collecting into a smaller compass, and
then disposing without crowding the several varieties of Nature, were perhaps
a better account of it, than either was expressed by his phrase or mine.)
He denominated my Virgil's Grove there Le Vallon occlus. — Sombre,
says Mr L. — No, not sombre occlus. — This must evidently be the idea
of Petrarch's Valclusa. He recommended a walk *up* that valley from Virgil's
Grove. Mr Pitt (the Secretary) had done the same before. He was wishing
at my Upper Pond to turn the water into a running stream. I mentioned the
inconvenience; to obviate which, he proposed a bridge. I went with him to
Hale's Mills. Thomson asked if I had seen many places laid out in the
modern way? — No — Asked if I had seen Chiswick? — Yes. — He
mentioned it as a sublime thing in the true Venetian taste. He supposed me
to come often to town; and desired to wait on me at Richmond, Mr L.
commending Richmond prospects, he said they were only too rich in villas.
He begged a pinch of snuff; and, on passing by the Abetes, near the Mill
Pool, mentioned that Pope had a scheme in his head of planting trees to
resemble a Gothic Cathedral. Hearing the Dam there was made by the

245

Monks, O! says he, this is God-dam, the wit of which I could not see. I directed them to scape Hales town, and to go up the lane by the pool side, not without an eye to the pleasing figure my house makes across that pool; where Mr L. advised me to have a boat, and was much struck with the appearance it must have from my wood. Here Mr Thomson shaking hands with me, we all parted, *omnes omnia bona dicentes, et laudentes fortunam meam.*

The year after I met Mr Thomson, as I returned from Church, at Hales Mill, in a hired two-wheeled chaise, with a black horse and a white one length wise. We accosted each other with much cordiality, and he promised earnestly to come and see me (as he *had* done the year before,) when I expected a longer visit. But 'twas then, as I remember, that the park improvements there engrossed the family's attention, and Mr T. could not be spared from any projects of that sort.

August 27, 1748. — The very week he was again expected at Hagley appeared this paragraph in the Birmingham paper: "This morning, at four, died, of a violent fever, at his house in Kewlane, the celebrated Mr James Thomson, Author of the Seasons, &c." I have heard he waited too long for the return of his friend Dr Armstrong, and did not chuse to employ any other physician.

He had nothing of the Gentleman in his person or address. But he made amends for the deficiency by his refined sense and spirited expression; and, as I remember, a manner of speaking not unlike his friend Quin. He did not talk a great deal or fluently; but, after pauses of reflection, produced something or other that accounted for his delay.

Anonymous

The following account of Pope's own garden just three years after his death appeared in *The General Magazine* of Newcastle in January 1748; it was discovered and published by Professor Maynard Mack some years ago. The letter speaks admirably for itself, especially if read in conjunction with the plan of Pope's garden (Plate 81) published by his gardener, John Searle. What Pope created for his retreat at Twickenham from 1719 onwards became something of a legend by his death, and the pilgrims and tourists visiting the garden and grotto (from which vandals began to prise the geological specimens as souvenirs) steadily increased. The visitor from Newcastle is, happily, more discriminating and provides a knowledgeable and sensitive description. Pope's house was torn down in 1807 by Baroness Sophia Charlotte Howe, who is said to have been incensed by the stream of visitors; the grotto (Plate 82) alone survives today, a sad remnant of what so delighted this visitor in 1747.

'An Epistolary Description of the Late Mr. Pope's House and Gardens at Twickenham' (1747)

THO' now I have liv'd in *London* two Months, I have not been able to steal more than one Day from constant Attendance to the Business which brought me up; but that however, was made a most pleasant one, by an entertaining Ramble into the Country along with a few agreeable Companions. Nothing can excel the fine Views and Scenes about this great Town: Every Thing within the Compass of Art and Nature is carried to the highest Pitch: The Hills and Lawns, Woods and Fields, are cultivated and displayed to the utmost of Skill and Industry; and such a Multitude of elegant Seats and Villas rising on all Sides, amaze a new Spectator with their various Design and Grandeur. But it is not my present Purpose to entertain you with a general Description of this rich Country: I have a Particular in view, that I know will be infinitely more acceptable to your Taste and Curiosity. We set out early in the Morning, and made choice of the Road along the South Banks of the *Thames*, which leads to *Richmond*, where we proposed to bait; but arriving there before Noon, we found Time enough upon our Hands to ride up as far as *Twit'nam* and return to Dinner. You will instantly guess our Intention was to visit the Residence of the late Mr *Pope*: This indeed was our Design; and as we approach'd it, I could not help being agitated, with a kind of glowing Ardour, flutt'ring at my Heart, often revolving these Lines,

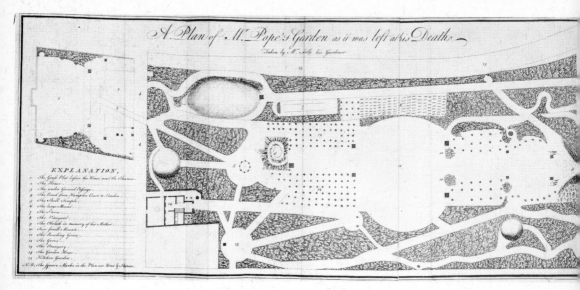

81 Pope's villa, Twickenham. Plan of the garden from John Searle,
'A Plan of Mr. Pope's Garden as it was left at his Death', 1745

"Come let us trace the matchless Vale of *Thames*,
"Fair winding, where the Muses us'd to haunt,
"In *Twit'nam's* Bowers, and for their POPE implore
"The healing God." —

They are a little alter'd, from *Thompson's* Seasons; and you who know how
infinitely fond I am of Mr *Pope's* Poetry, will not wonder at my being seiz'd
on this Occasion, with a Gust of Enthusiasm; nor that I tell you I enter'd
the Gardens with a warm Offering of Respect and Reverence. And now, Sir,
I will give you the best Description of the Place that I can draw from the
cursory View which our Time allow'd us to take of it.

   Twickenham is a delightful Village, situated about a North Country Mile
above *Richmond*, on the opposite Side of the River. Mr *Pope's* House stands
in the South-west End of the Village; the Area of the Ground is a gentle
Declivity most agreeably sloping to the *Thames*, which here exactly answers
Denham's inimitable Description of it.

"Tho' deep yet clear, tho' gentle yet not dull;
"Strong without Rage, without o'erflowing full.

Between the River and the House ascends a Parterre or Piece of Grass,
near Square; on the uppermost Verge of which is the House, fronting the
River, and backing against the Wall of the high Road which leads thro' the
Town of *Twit'nam*, and passes behind the House: On the other Side of this
Road, still easily ascending further from the *Thames*, lie the Gardens, whose

Bounds are of an irregular Form, not encompassed with Walls, but Hedges, containing (I think) not much over or under two Acres of Ground. This gives you a general Notion of the whole, and its Situation: and, to be more particular, I shall trace over as many of the Parts as occur to me, beginning again at the Bottom of the Plan, where the lingring *Thames* glides softly by, and washes the Margin of the green Parterre; at the Head of which, as it were niched into a rising Mound, or Bank, stands the House; not of so large or magnificent a Structure, as a lightsome Elegance and neat Simplicity in its Contrivance. It is at present neither inhabited nor furnished; but shut up and silent, as that great Genius which lately resided in it. The Sides of the Court, or Parterre, are bounded by deep Thickets of Trees, Hedges, and various Evergreens and Shrubs, ascending in a wild, but delightful Slope, beginning with these of the humblest Growth, and gradually rising, end with lofty Elms and other Forest Trees. This Grass plot is join'd to the Garden by a subterraneous Passage, or Cavern; which entering the House below the Middle of the Front, and passing cross under the high Road, opens into a Wilderness Part of the Garden. Over the Front Entrance into this Grotto lies a balustraded Platform, and serves the Building both as a Vestible and Portico; for a Balcony projecting from the middle Window of the second Story, and supported by Pillars resting upon the Platform, makes so much of it resemble a Portico; but the Platform extending without these Pillars, becomes more a Vestible: Add to this, the Window opening into the Balcony being crowned with a Pediment, gives the several Parts an Air of one Figure, or whole, and adds an inexpressible Grace to the Front. Mr *Pope*, you may observe, in a Letter to Mr *Blount*, says, that in forming the subterraneous Way and Grotto, he there found a Spring of the clearest Water, which fell in a perpetual Rill that eccho'd thro' the Cavern Day and Night: The Discovery of this rilling Fountain was a fortunate Accident to Mr *Pope*, whose Taste was so admirably suited to give a Thing of that kind the happiest Turn of poetical Improvement; as you will presently see. The Grotto is an irregular Vault and Passage, open at both Extremities, and further illuminated by two Windows to the Front: In passing it along, we are presented with many Openings and Cells, which owe their Forms to a Diversity of Pillars and Jambs, ranged after no set Order or Rule, but aptly favouring the particular Designs of the Place: They seem as roughly hew'd out of Rocks and Beds of mineral Strata, discovering in the Fissures and angular Breaches, Variety of Flints, Spar, Ores, Shells, &c. among which the Stream issuing from the Spring of Water is distributed to a Diversity of Purposes: Here it gurgles in a gushing Rill thro' fractur'd Ores and Flints; there it drips from depending Moss and Shells; here again, washing Beds of Sand and Pebbles, it rolls in Silver Streamlets; and there it rushes out in Jets and Fountains; while the Caverns of the Grot incessantly echo with a soothing Murmur of aquatick Sounds. To multiply this Diversity, and still more increase the Delight, Mr *Pope's* poetick Genius has introduced a kind of Machinery, which performs the same Part in the Grotto that supernal Powers and incorporeal Beings act in the heroick Species of Poetry: This is effected by disposing Plates of Looking glass in the obscure Parts of the Roof and Sides of the Cave, where a sufficient Force of Light is wanting to discover the Deception, while the other Parts, the Rills, Fountains, Flints, Pebbles, &c. being duly illuminated, are so reflected by the various profited Mirrors, as, without exposing the Cause, every Object is multiplied, and its Position represented in a surprizing Diversity. Cast your Eyes upward, and you half shudder to see Cataracts of Water precipitating over your Head, from impending Stones and Rocks, while saliant Spouts rise in rapid Streams at your Feet: Around, you are equally surprized with flowing Rivulets and rolling Waters, that rush over airey Precipices, and break amongst Heaps of ideal Flints and Spar. Thus, by a fine Taste and happy Management of Nature, you are presented with an undistinguishable Mixture of Realities and Imagery. In passing out of the Grotto we enter into a Wilderness, and have in view directly before us a Rotundo, or kind of Temple, entirely compos'd of Shells, and consisting wholly of a Cupola, or Dome, supported upon rustick Columns, so as to leave it open every Way to the surrounding Garden. From the Grotto to the Temple we ascend along a Walk in the natural Taste, being rather strew'd than pav'd with Flints and Pebbles, inclos'd with Thickets, and over-arch'd with wild and interwoven Branches of Trees[.] From the Temple, this sylvan Arcade, together with the Passage of the Grotto, make a sort of continued Tube, thro' which a small Expanse of the *Thames* is beheld as in a Perspective, making a beautiful remote Appearance; where Vessels that pass up and down the River, suddenly glance on the Eye, and again vanish from it in a Moment. Before I lose Sight of the Grotto, I must not omit taking Notice of an Inscription from *Horace*, placed over the Entrance from the Garden.

— *Secretum iter, et fallentis semita vitae.*

An *English* Translation of this, equally poetical, elegant, and concise, I think is hardly possible: By attempting it, I have greatly fallen short in the last respect,

A hid Recess, where Life's revolving Day,
In sweet Delusion gently steals away.

I would next give you some particular Idea of the Garden, but am afraid I shall fail most of all in this Part of my Attempt: for that free natural Taste, and unaffected Simplicity, which presides every where in the Plan, wanders so much from all common Forms and stated Fashions, that a Wood or a Forest doth not deviate much more from Rule: It is not here,

That — Grove nods at Grove, each Alley has a Brother,
    And half the Platform just reflects the other,
But — Pleasing Intricacies intervene,
    And artful Wildness to perplex the Scene.

Near the Bounds of the Garden, the Trees unite themselves more closely together, and cover the Hedges with a thick Shade, which prevents all prying

82 Pope's grotto, Twickenham. Sketch, perhaps by Lady Burlington, ?1730s

from without, and preserves the Privacy of the interior Parts. These Wilderness-Groves are either Quincunces, or cut thro' by many narrow serpentine Walks; and as we recede from the Boundary and approach towards the Center, the Scene opens and becomes less entangled; the Alleys widen, the Walks grow broader, and either terminate in small green Plots of the finest Turf, or lead to the Shell Temple. The Middle of the Garden approaches nearest to a Lawn or open Green, but is delightfully diversified with Banks and Hillocks; which are entirely cover'd with Thickets of Lawrel, Bay, Holly, and many other Evergreens and Shrubs, rising one above another in beautiful Slopes and Inter-mixtures, where Nature freely lays forth the Branches, and disports uncontroul'd; except what may be entirely prun'd away for more Decency and Convenience to the surrounding Grass-plots, for no Shear-work or Tonsure is to be found in all the Scene. Towards the South side of the Garden is a Plantation of Vines curiously disposed and dress'd; it adjoins the Wilderness, and is in the same Taste, but opener to the Sun, and with more numerous interveening Paths. Among the Hillocks on the upper Part of the open Area, rises a Mount much higher than the rest, and is composed of more rude and indigested Materials; it is covered with Bushes and Trees of a wilder Growth, and more confused Order, rising as it were out of Clefts of Rocks, and Heaps of rugged and mossy Stones; among which a narrow intricate Path leads in an irregular Spiral to the Top; where is placed a Forest Seat or Chair, that may hold three or four Persons at once, overshaded with the Branches of a spreading Tree. From this Seat we face the Temple, and overlook the various Distribution of the Thickets, Grass plots, Alleys, Banks, &c. Near this Mount lies the broadest Walk of the Garden, leading from the Center to the uppermost Verge; where, upon the gentle Eminence of a green Bank, stands an Obelisk, erected by Mr *Pope* to the Memory of his Mother: It is a plain Stone Pillar resting upon a Pedestal: and the Plynth of the Pillar bears this Inscription on its four Sides, beginning with that which faces the Walk.

AH EDITHA!

MATRUM OPTIMA.

MULIERUM AMANTISSIMA.

VALE.

As this Obelisk terminates the longest Prospect of Mr *Pope's* Garden, it shall also put a Period to my Description; which is not of a Place that bears the high Air of State and Grandeur, and surprizes you with the vastness of Expence and Magnificence; but an elegant Retreat of a Poet strongly inspired with the Love of Nature and Retirement; and shews you, with respect to these Works, what was the Taste of the finest Genius that this or any other Age has produced. I cannot conclude my Epistle better, than with a few Lines from the great Master himself, which contain his own Remarks upon his Situation at *Twit'nam*.

> To Virtue only and her Friends a Friend,
> The World besides may murmur or commend.
> Know, all the distant Din that World can keep,
> Rolls o'er my Grotto and but soothes my Sleep.
> There my Retreat, the best Companions grace,
> Chiefs out of War, and Statesmen out of Place.
> There ST JOHN mingles with my friendly Bowl,
> The Feast of Reason, and the Flow of Soul.
> And HE, whose Lightning pierc'd th' *Iberian* Lines,
> Now forms my Quincunx, and now ranks my Vines:
> Or tames the Genius of the stubborn Plain,
> Almost as quickly as he conquer'd *Spain*.

Envy must own, I live among the Great,
No Pimp of Pleasure, and no Spy of State;
With Eyes that pry not, Tongue that ne'er repeats,
Fond to spread Friendships, but to cover Heats;
To help who want, to forward who excel,
This all who know me, know; who love me, tell;
And who unknown defame me, let them be
Scribblers or Poets, alike are Mob to me.

In South Sea Days not happier, when surmis'd
The Lord of Thousands, than if now excis'd:
In Forests planted by a Father's Hand,
Than in five Acres now of rented Land;
Content with Little, I can piddle here
On Brocoli and Mutton round the Year;
But ancient Friends (tho' poor, or out of Play)
That touch my Bell, I cannot turn away.
'Tis true no Turbots dignify my Boards,
But Gudgeons, Flounders, what my *Thames* affords.
To *Hounslow-Heath* I point, and *Bansted-Down*,
Thence comes your Mutton, and these Chicks my own:
From yon old Walnut Tree a Shower shall fall,
And Grapes, long-lingring on my only Wall . . .
Fortune not much of humbling me can boast,
Tho' double-tax'd, how little have I lost?
My Life's Amusements have been just the same,
Before and after standing Armies came.
My Lands are sold, my Father's House is gone;
I'll hire another's; is not that my own?
And your's my Friends? thro' whose free opening Gate
None comes too early, none departs too late.
For I (who hold sage *Homer*'s Rule the best)
Welcome the coming, speed the going Guest.
"Pray Heav'n it'last! (cries *Swift*) as you go on!
"I wish to God this House had been your own:
"Pity! to build without a Son or Wife:
"Why, you'll enjoy it only all your Life" . . .
Well, if the Use be mine, can it concern one,
Whether the Name belong to P[o]pe or *Vernon*?
What's Property? dear *Swift*! you see it alter
From you to me, from me to *Peter Walter* . . .
Shades that to *Ba[co]n* could Retreat afford
Are now the Portion of a booby Lord:
And *Hemsley*, once proud *Buckingham*'s Delight,
Slides to a Scriv'ner, or a City Knight.
Let Lands and Houses have what Lords they will,
Let us be fix'd, and our own Masters still.

William Gilpin (1724–1804)

This *Dialogue upon the Gardens . . . at Stow* is valuable both for its documentation of Stowe and for its early indications of Gilpin's picturesque tastes (see pp. 337 ff.). He visited Lord Cobham's gardens in 1747 and published his *Dialogue* anonymously the following year; there were further editions in 1749 and 1751. The three extracts here clearly reveal Gilpin's central concerns. At the Rotunda his two characters debate rival ideas of landscape style: Callophilus, as his name implies, loves the beauty of natural scenes that have been arranged by art; Polypthon expresses his eponymous ill-will by rejecting the decorations of art and by affirming (as he does more lyrically in the second passage) a penchant for natural beauties. In the Elysian Fields they concur, however, in 'reading' this example of 'moral gardening', and though Polypthon enjoys the 'satire' of the temples he still waxes enthusiastic about northern scenery outside gardens. Both visitors to Stowe enjoy the painterly suggestions of Stowe's landscape, finding *landskips* at every turn; both testify to the mental and emotional responses that places like Stowe elicit from visitors. The third extract, which concludes the *Dialogue*, makes each of those reactions quite clear; in addition, it announces an early occasion of Gilpin's finding that a scene struck him 'beyond the power of thought . . . and every mental operation is suspended. In this pause of intellect, this deliquirium of the soul, an enthusiastic sensation of pleasure over spreads it.' (*Three Essays*, 1792.) As a young man at Stowe, Gilpin displays the two habits that characterize his later picturesque writings: a delight in tracing the formal, abstract patterns of a landscape, and a fascination with his imaginative involvement.

from *A Dialogue upon the Gardens of the Right Honourable the Lord Viscount Cobham at Stow in Buckinghamshire* (1748)

Calloph. I am admiring the fine View from hence: So great a Variety of beautiful Objects, and all so happily disposed, make a most delightful Picture. Don't you think this Building too is a very genteel one, and is extremely well situated? These Trees give it an agreeable, cool Air, and make it, I think, as elegant a Retreat for the Enjoyment of a Summer's Evening, as can well be imagined. — But it is mere trifling to sit here: Let us walk towards the Rotunda. — This little Alley will carry us to *Dido's* Cave.

Polypth. Dido's Cave! why 'tis built of hewn Stone! Here she is however, and her *pious* Companion along with her.

Calloph. Those two Cupids joining their Torches, I never see but I admire extremely: they are very finely painted.

Polypth. I think they are indeed. But let us be a little complaisant, and not interrupt these kind Lovers too long. I want to see this Rotunda.

Calloph. There then you have it: I hope you cannot complain of an heavy Building here. I do not know any Piece of Stonework in the whole Garden that shews itself to more Advantage than this does, or makes a more beautiful Figure in a Variety of fine Views from several Parts of the Garden: Several Parts of the Garden likewise return the Compliment, by offering a great many very elegant Prospects to it. There you have an Opening laid out with all the Decorations of Art; a spacious Theatre; the Area floated by a Canal, and peopled with Swans and Wild-ducks: Her late Majesty is the principal Figure in the Scene, and around her a merry Company of Nymphs and Swains enjoying themselves in the Shade.

Polypth. I must confess I cannot very much admire —

Calloph. Come; none of your Cavils. — Observe how this View is beautifully contrasted by one on the opposite Side of a different kind; in which we are almost solely obliged to Nature. You must know I look upon this as a very noble Prospect! The Field is formed by that Semi-circle of Trees into a very grand Theatre. The Point of Sight is centred in a beautiful manner by the Pyramid, which appears to great Advantage amongst those venerable Oaks: Two or three other Buildings, half hid amongst the Trees, come in for their Share in the Prospect, and add much to the Beauty of it.

Polypth. I agree with you entirely; nor do I think this other View inferior to it. That Variety of different Shades amongst the Trees; the Lake spread so elegantly amongst them, and glittering here and there thro' the Bushes, with the Temple of *Venus* as a Termination to the View, make up a very beautiful Landskip.

Calloph. Here is a Vista likewise very happily terminated by the Canal, and the Obelisk rising in the Midst of it. There is another close View likewise towards *Nelson's* Seat.

Polypth. Upon my Word, we have a Variety of very elegant Prospects centred in this Point. I could sit here very agreeably a little longer . . .

Polypth. Pray, what Building is that before us? I cannot say I dislike the Taste it is designed in. It seems an Antique.

Calloph. It is the Temple, Sir, of Ancient Virtue; the Place I am now conducting you to. You will meet within it a very illustrious Assembly of great Men; the wisest Lawgiver, the best Philosopher, the most divine Poet, and the most able Captain, that perhaps ever lived.

Polypth. You may possibly, Sir, engage yourself in a Dispute, by fixing your Epithets in such an absolute manner; there are so many Competitors in each of these Ways, that altho' Numbers may be called truly eminent, it will be a difficult matter to fix Pre-eminence upon any.

Calloph. You will hardly, I fancy, dissent from me, when I introduce you to these great Heroes of Antiquity: There stands *Lycurgus*; there *Socrates*;

there *Homer*; and there *Epaminondas*. Illustrious Chiefs, who made Virtue their only Pursuit, and the Welfare of Mankind their only Study; in whose Breasts mean Self-interest had no Possession. To establish a well-regulated Constitution; to dictate the soundest Morality, to place Virtue in the most amiable Light; and bravely to defend a People's Liberty, were Ends which neither the Difficulty in overcoming the Prejudices, and taming the savage Manners of a barbarous State; the Corruptions of a licentious Age, and the Ill-usage of an invidious City; neither the vast Pains of searching into Nature, and laying up a Stock of Knowledge sufficient to produce the noblest Work of Art; nor popular Tumults at Home, and the most threatning Dangers Abroad, could ever tempt them to lose Sight of, or in the least abate that Ardency of Temper with which they pursued them.

Polypth. A noble Panegyric upon my Word! why, Sir, these great Spirits have inspired you with the very Soul of Oratory. However, in earnest, I confess your Encomium is pretty just; and I am apt to believe that if any of those worthy Gentlemen should take it into his Head to walk from his Nitch, it would puzzle the World to find his Equal to fix in his Room. — That old Ruin, I suppose, is intended to contrast with this new Building.

Calloph. Yes, Sir, it is intended to contrast with it not only in the Land-skip, but likewise in its Name and Design. Walk a little nearer, and you will see its Intention.

Polypth. I can see nothing here to let me into its Design, except this old Gentleman; neither can I find any thing extraordinary in him, except that he has met with a Fate that he is entirely deserving of, which is more than falls to the Share of every worthless Fellow.

Calloph. Have you observed how the Statue is decorated?

Polypth. O! I see the whole Design: A very elegant Piece of Satyr, upon my Word! This pompous Edifice is intended, I suppose, to represent the flourishing Condition, in which ancient Virtue still exists; and those poor shattered Remains of what has never been very beautiful (notwithstanding, I see, they are placed within a few Yards of a Parish-church) are designed to let us see the ruinous State of decayed modern Virtue. And the Moral is, that Glory founded upon true Worth and Honour, will exist, when Fame, built upon Conquest and popular Applause, will fade away. This is really the best thing I have seen: I am most prodigiously taken with it.

Calloph. I intend next to carry you to a Scene of another kind. I am going to shew you the Grotto, a Place generally very taking with Strangers. — I thought that Piece of Satyr would catch your Attention: I hope likewise you will be as well pleased here. This Gate will carry us into the romantic Retire-ment. What do you think of this Scene?

Polypth. Why really, Sir, it is quite a Novelty: This Profusion of Mirrors has a very extraordinary Effect: The Place seems divided into a thousand beautiful Apartments, and appears fifty times as large as it is. The Prospects without are likewise transferred to the Walls within: And the Sides of the Room are elegantly adorned with Landskips, beyond the Pencil of *Titian*; with this farther Advantage, that every View, as you change your Situation, varies itself into another Form, and presents you with something new.

Calloph. Don't you think that serpentine River, as it is called, is a great Addition to the Beauty of the Place?

Polypth. Undoubtedly it is. Water is of as much Use in a Landskip, as Blood is in a Body; without these two Essentials, it is impossible there should be Life in either one or the other. Yet methinks it is a prodigious Pity that this stagnate Pool should not by some Magic be metamorphosed into a crystal Stream, rolling over a Bed of Pebbles. Such a quick Circulation would give an infinite Spirit to the View. I could wish his Lordship had such a Stream at his Command; he would shew it, I dare say, to the best Advantage, in its Passage thro' the Gardens. But we cannot *make* Nature, the utmost we can do is to *mend* her. — I have heard a *Scotch* Gentleman speak of the River, upon which the Town of *Sterling* stands, which is as remarkable a Meander as I have ever heard of. From *Sterling* to a little Village upon the Banks of this River, by Land it is only four Miles, and yet if you should follow the Course of the Water, you will find it above twenty. — There is an House likewise that stands upon a narrow Isthmus of a Peninsula, formed by this same River, which is mighty remarkable: The Water runs close to both Ends of it, and yet if you sail from one to the other, you will be carried a Compass of four Miles. — Such a River winding about this Place, would make it a Paradise indeed!

As we are got into the North, I must confess I do not know any Part of the Kingdom that abounds more with elegant natural Views: Our well-cultivated Plains, as you observed before, are certainly not comparable to their rough Nature in point of Prospect. About three Years ago I rode the Northern Circuit: The Weather was extremely fine; and I scarce remember being more agreeably entertained than I was with the several charming Views exhibited to me in the northern Counties. Curiosity indeed, rather than Business, carried me down: And as I had my Time pretty much to myself, I spent it in a great measure in hunting after beautiful Objects. Sometimes I found myself hemmed within an Amphitheatre of Mountains, which were variously ornamented, some with scattered Trees, some with tufted Wood, some with grazing Cattle, and some with smoaking Cottages. Here and there an elegant View likewise was opened into the Country. — A Mile's riding, perhaps, would have carried me to the Foot of a steep Precipice, down which thundered the whole Weight of some vast River, which was dashed into Foam at the Bottom, by the craggy Points of several rising Rocks: A deep Gloom overspread the Prospect, occasioned by the close Wood that hung round it on every Side. — I could describe to you a Variety of other Views I met with there, if we *here* wanted Entertainment in the Way of Landskip. One, however, I cannot forbear mentioning, and wishing at the same time that his Lordship had such Materials to work with, and it could not be but he would make a most noble Picture. — The Place I have in view is upon the Banks of the River *Eden* (which is indeed one of the finest Rivers I ever saw). I scarce know a fitter Place for a Genius in this Way to exert itself in. There is the greatest Variety of garnished Rocks, shattered Precipices, rising Hills, ornamented with the finest Woods, thro' which are opened the most elegant Vales that I have ever met with: Not to mention the most enchanting Views up and down the River, which winds itself in such a manner as to shew its Banks to the best Advantage, which, together with very charming Prospects into the Country, terminated by the blue Hills at a Distance, make as fine a Piece of Nature, as perhaps can any where be met with . . .

Polypthon, notwithstanding the sour Humour he had given so many Evidences of in his Walk, began now to relent, and could talk of nothing but the agreeable Entertainment that had been afforded him. Sometimes he would run out into the highest Encomiums of the many beautiful Terminations of the several Walks and Vistas; and observe how many Uses each Object served, and in how many different Lights it was made to vary itself. "For Instance, says he, the Pavilion you shewed me from the Temple of "*Venus,* terminates that Terrace in a very grand Manner; and makes likewise "a very magnificent Appearance, where it corresponds with another of the "same Form, at the Entrance into the Park: Yet the same Building, like a "Person acquainted with the World, who can suit his Behaviour to Time and "Place, can vary itself upon occasion into a more humble Shape, and when "viewed thro' a retired Vista, can take upon it the lowly Form of a close "Retreat." — When he had enlarged pretty copiously upon this Subject, he would next launch out into the highest Praises of the vast Variety of Objects that was every where to be met with: "Men of all Humours, says he, will here "find something pleasing and suited to their Taste. The thoughtful may meet "with retired Walks calculated in the best Manner for Contemplation: The "gay and chearful may see Nature in her loveliest Dress, and meet Objects "corresponding with their most lively Flights. The romantic Genius may "entertain itself with several very beautiful Objects in its own Taste, and "grow wild with Ideas of the inchanted kind. The disconsolate Lover may "hide himself in shady Groves, or melancholy wander along the Banks of "Lakes and Canals; where he may sigh to the gentle Zephyrs; mingle his "Tears with the bubbling Water; or where he may have the best Oppor- "tunity, if his Malady be grown to such an Height, of ending his Despair, and "finishing his Life with all the Decency and Pomp of a Lover in a Romance. "In short, says he, these Gardens are a very good Epitome of the World: "They are calculated for Minds of every Stamp, and give free Scope to "Inclinations of every kind: And if it be said that in some Parts they too "much humour the debauched Taste of the Sensualist, it cannot be denied "on the other hand, but that they afford several very noble Incitements to "Honour and Virtue." — But what beyond all other things seemed most to please him, was the amicable and beautiful Conjunction of *Art* and *Nature* thro' the whole: He observed that the *former* never appeared stiff, or the *latter* extravagant.

Upon many other Topicks of Praise *Polypthon* run out with great Warmth. *Callophilus* seemed surprized, and could not forbear asking him, By what means his Opinions became so suddenly changed? "Why, says he, Sir, I have "said nothing now that contradicts any thing I said before. I own I met with "two or three Objects that were not entirely to my Taste, which I am far "from condemning for that Reason; tho' if I should, it is nothing to the

"purpose, because I am now taking a Survey of the whole together; in which
"Light I must confess I am quite astonished with the View before me.
"Besides, I hate one of your wondering Mortals, who is perpetually breaking
"out into a Note of Admiration at every thing he sees: I am always apt to
"suspect his Taste or his Sincerity. It is impossible that all Genius's can
"alike agree in their Opinions of any Work of Art; and the Man who never
"*blames,* I can scarce believe is qualified to *commend.* Besides, finding fault
"now and then, adds Weight to Commendation, and makes us believed to be
"in earnest. However, notwithstanding what you may think of my frequent
"Cavils, I assure you, with the greatest Sincerity, I never before saw anything
"of the kind at all comparable to what I have here seen: I shall by no means
"close this Day with a *Diem perdidi;* nor would the *Roman* Emperor himself,
"I believe, have made the Reflection if he had spent his condemned Hours in
"this Place."

By this time the Gentlemen were come to the Gate, thro' which *Polypthon*
assured his Friend he passed with the greatest Reluctance, and went growling
out of this delightful Garden, as the Devil is said to have done out of Paradise.

Henry Fielding (1707–54)

The philosophical and moral overtones of the new landscape garden are evident in Fielding's use of it as an apt setting for Squire Allworthy. Natural benevolence and a peaceful disposition are announced by his name, his actions and his estate: 'owing less to Art than to Nature' confirms, as Shaftesbury had taught (see pp. 122 ff.), the instinctive human goodness in its owner as well as the perfect, apparently spontaneous ordering of his garden. If, as is thought, Allworthy's character is based upon that of Ralph Allen, then, as F. Holmes Dudden has suggested, his landscape is probably drawn from Allen's Prior Park, near Bath (what is added being the view towards Glastonbury from Tor Hill). Allen was a great friend of Pope, who called him the 'noblest man in England', and an intimate member of his gardenist circle: Allen sent innumerable stones to help decorate Pope's grotto, and Pope in his turn stayed at Prior Park (Plate 83).

from *Tom Jones* (1749)

THE *Gothick* Stile of Building could produce nothing nobler than Mr. *Allworthy's* House. There was an Air of Grandeur in it, that struck you with Awe, and rival'd the Beauties of the best *Grecian* Architecture; and it was as commodious within, as venerable without.

It stood on the South-east Side of a Hill, but nearer the Bottom than the Top of it, so as to be sheltered from the North-east by a Grove of old Oaks, which rose above it in a gradual Ascent of near half a Mile, and yet high enough to enjoy a most charming Prospect of the Valley beneath.

In the midst of the Grove was a fine Lawn sloping down towards the House, near the Summit of which rose a plentiful Spring, gushing out of a Rock covered with Firs, and forming a constant Cascade of about thirty Feet, not carried down a regular Flight of Steps, but tumbling in a natural Fall over the broken and mossy Stones, till it came to the bottom of the Rock; then running off in a pebly Channel, that with many lesser Falls winded along, till it fell into a Lake at the Foot of the Hill, about a quarter of a Mile below the House on the South Side, and which was seen from every Room in the Front. Out of this Lake, which filled the Center of a beautiful Plain, embellished with Groupes of Beeches and Elms, and fed with Sheep, issued a River, that for several Miles was seen to meander through an amazing Variety of Meadows and Woods, till it emptied itself into the Sea, with a large Arm of which, and an Island beyond it, the Prospect was closed.

83 Prior Park, Somerset. Engraving by Anthony Walker, 1750

On the right of this Valley opened another of less Extent, adorned with several Villages, and terminated by one of the Towers of an old ruined Abbey, grown over with Ivy, and Part of the Front which remained still entire.

The left Hand Scene presented the View of a fine Park, composed of very unequal Ground, and agreeably varied with all the Diversity that Hills, Lawns, Wood and Water, laid out with admirable Taste, but owing less to Art than to Nature, could give. Beyond this, the Country gradually rose into a Ridge of wild Mountains, the Tops of which were above the Clouds.

Part Three

The Progress of
Gardening

Richard Pococke (1704–65)

An Irish cleric, at his death the Bishop of Meath, Pococke's most interesting feature is his passion for travel. The following extracts record some of his many excursions to English country seats during his various visits from Ireland in the 1750s. He sees the water garden at Bramham and notices the missed opportunity for a serpentine stream; at 'St Giles Wimborn' his notes bring the landscape pictures collected by *amateurs* into a proper juxtaposition with the gardens modelled upon them, though he also observes evidence inside and out of the Chinese taste; in Surrey, the next extract, he records both an early taste for Italianate statuary and the modern one for Gothic ruins, often alongside Palladian buildings; his succinct account of The Leasowes follows next, and finally his visits to Bulstrode (note the interest in British archaeological remains) and to Woburn Farm. With his taste for 'natural' landscapes, it is not perhaps surprising that the journals of the travels also evince some enthusiasm for the Lake District and Snowdonia. Our text of 'Travels Through England' is taken from the manuscript version in the British Library.

from 'Travels Through England' (1750–7)

4 August 1750

From Newtown Kime I went two miles to the village of Bramham, & a mile further to Mʳ Fox's Bramham house, late Ld Bingleys, whose heiress he married; — it is a handsome house & offices built of hewn stone, — but it is on account of the improvements abroad that this place is resorted to; — behind the house are walks with very high hedges on each side, & a terrace goes round great part of the improvement fenced with a ha ha wall; — one comes round to a Dorick building like the front of a Temple & then to a Gothick building not quite finished, & so one descends to the water, from which there is an avenue to the house, & another up to a round Ionick Temple, something in imitation of the Temple of Hercules at Tivoli: There are two or three basons of water, which fall into a larger, & that falls by a Cascade twenty feet into another bason, from which there is a valley, that might be improved into a fine serpentine River; — There is a considerable ascent to the aforesaid temple, — & from that are three or four visto's cut, one of which is terminated by a Dorick building, something like the Portico of Covent garden Church: — & to the west of the garden in the Park is a thatched house, to which the family sometimes go for variety & take some refreshments . . .

6 October 1754

I went two miles to St Giles Wimborn commonly called St Giles, where Lord Shaftsbury has a seat; — In a saloon are pictures of the family: In another large room lately finished in a very elegant manner are some fine pictures of Gaspar Poussin, Claud Lorain & others & one of Nicholas Poussin, the story of the Levite & the Harlot. In another large room are family pictures, as that of the first Lord Shaftsbury who was Chancellor, & four daughter[s] of the present Lords Grandfather, each having the emblems of one of the four elements, with Latin poetry under them relating to those subjects: There is a sleeping apartment on this floor, & I observed some Chinese figures made with shells in China. The Gardens are very beautifully laid out, in a serpentine river, pieces of water, Lawns, & c: & very gracefully adorn'd with wood. One first comes to an Island in which there is a Castle, then near the water is a Gateway with a tower on each side, & passing between two waters, there is a fine Cascade from the one to the other, a thatch'd house, a round pavilion on a Mount, Shake Spears house, in which is a small statue of him & his works in a Glass case; & in all the houses & seats are books in hanging Glass cases. There is a pavilion between the waters, and both a Chinese and stone-bridge over them. I saw here a sea duck which lays in rabbits burrows, from which they are call'd Burrow ducks, & are something like the shell drake. There is a most beautifull Grotto finished by Mr Castles of Marybone; — It consists of a winding walk and an antiroom. These are mostly made of Rockspar & c: adorn'd with Moss: In the inner room is a great profusion of most beautiful shells, petrifications and fine polished pebbles, and there is a chimney to it which is shut up with doors covered with shells in such a manner as that it does not appear. The Park also is very delightful, and there is a building in it . . .

27 November 1754

I . . . passed near More Park Mr Temples (wch place I did not view, but am well informd that in the house & garden are several small statues busts reliefs & c of the Arundel Collection. & under the dial in the garden was interrd the heart of Sr Wm Temple according to his will. The cave in the park cut out of the sandy rock near Waverley Abbey is singularly beautifull) in about half a mile I came to Waverley Abbey on the river Wey, it was founded in 1128 by William Gifford Bishop of Winchester for Cistercian Monks being the first in England of that order. The Estate was Mr Aislabies, who built the house & made the plantations & other improvements. it was then Mr Childs & now belongs to Mr Hunter son of the Governor. The house is a fine piece of Architecture of Campbell's, on one of Palladio's designs; — Mr Hunter has added wings to it, joyn'd by a Gallery adorned on the outside with Pilasters, the grand front of the house is to the Garden, which is laid out in lawn, wood, & winding walks near the river. The ruins of the monastery add no small beauty to it; the church is much destroy'd. A building which seems to have been the Refectory is pretty entire, except that one end is down . . .

24 September 1756

I view'd the ruins of Halesowen Abbey, commonly call'd the Manor: there remains of the large church only one of the north windows of the chancel, & two of the south Cross Isle, all plain narrow windows with the mitred Arch: To the south are six narrow windows with the same kind of arch but of a finer Gothic Workmanship. This might be part of the Refectory. I return'd from this place to Halesowen & observ'd on each side of a rivlet a rocky bed which produces a blew kind of fire stone as I take it to be. I went a mile to Mʳ Shenston's situated on the side of a rising ground facing to the south. We were led first towards the bottom of the west side & going into a shady walk, we saw a Cascade, the water of which passes through a narrow bed into a pond below, which might be improv'd to great advantage; we then came round to the South, & after passing some seats, we came through an Arcade made of roots, which opened surprizingly on a water that falls down in many breaks, & is seen through the wood which has a most charming effect: ascending up the hill, still round the skirts of the farm, which is all meadow, we came to a seat, which commands a fine view, & coming on the north side, we descended to a fine piece of water, & ascending again we came to a shady walk in a straight line, but uneven at bottom it is about a furlong in length with a building at the end; we then went into an open walk commanding a glorious view of the country & of Dudley, as well as the town of Halesowen we return'd & descended to a wood & came to a steep descent, & were all of a sudden surpriz'd with a beautiful Cascade, tumbling down a precipice, & two or three more as the river winds round, a bridge, & different views of water, as of the same river all down to the large piece of water before describ'd, which appears as part of it. From this the descent is through a lawn to the house. There are urns in several parts, on which & on most of the seats are inscriptions, mostly of the Latin poets, & some inscrib'd to the memory of his friends, as an urn to Somerville, who writ the Chace, and a seat to Thompson the Poet . . .

28–9 April 1757

Pass'd through Uxbridge seeing the late judge Talbots a very pretty place to the right, & going in the Oxford road, we had Mʳ Ways to the right, near the road to Chesham & Rickmansworth, pass'd by the Aylesbury road & came four miles to Gerards Cross, at the Park wall of Bulstrode, the Duke of Portlands, which I came to see. This was the seat of the first Earl of Portland. The ground & plantations of the park are very fine, on an eminence to the left is a British Camp. There was a long avenue to the house which was taken away & a kitchen gardens near it is removed; to the left was a lawn to which there was a steep descent of several feet, all which is now forming into grass with a gentle descent; behind the house is a wood with walks through it & round it; & a parterre is forming in one part & in another a shrubbery. At the further end of it is a canal covered with wild ducks; from this there is a descent to the left, to the Dairy & menagerie, in which several sorts of birds & fowls are kept & breed, particularly Chinese Pheasants of both kinds.

The Dairy is adorn'd with a Chinese front, as a sort of open Summer house, & about it are some pieces of water, for the different water Poultry. In the same vale is the kitchen garden lately wall'd in & planted, in which are all sorts of contrivances for ripening fruits...

On the 29th I went from Bulstrode by Fulmere & then by Langley Park, where the Duke of Marlborough has built a very handsome new house of hewn stone, with four fronts & five windows in the principal fronts & 7 on each side. We came into the Bath road a mile to the west of Colnbrook & going through that place turn'd to the right & came to Stanes, where the Coln falls into the Thames, we went to Chertsey, & then about two miles further to Mr Southcotes within a mile of Weybridge. This is the first improvement in the Farm kind, & is esteem'd the most elegant, in England. It consists of walks to the left, first round two meadows on rather high ground and then round another on low ground, on the right side of them, through the further side of which a canal is made from the poultry house, which is in form of a temple, & extends towards the Thames. These walks are adorn'd not only with plantations of wood but with spots & beds of flowering shrubs & other flowers, to fill up angles & other shrubs to diversifie the scene; from the end next the house and behind it is a piece of water form'd like a river over which there is a bridge that leads to several small fields mostly of corn & some meadows with walks & plantations round them. This was the first beginning of the farm.

Joseph Spence (1699–1768)

Spence was Professor of Poetry and, later, of Modern History at Oxford; he is famous, above all, for his record of the conversations and ideas of his many friends and acquaintances which were collected in *Observations, Anecdotes, and Characters of Books and Men*. First published in 1820, it was yet known and widely quoted during the eighteenth century. It is especially valuable to the garden historian for its compendium of remarks on landscaping by Pope, several of which have been quoted in our Introduction. A much augmented and annotated edition appeared in 1966, edited by James M. Osborn, and it is from this that the first extract is taken. Spence summarized 'some general rules' about landscape design, and we may take it that they rehearse not only his own ideas but those also of friends like Pope. The second extract comes from a manuscript among the Newcastle Papers at Yale University, where an account of Henry Hoare's landscape at Stourhead in Wiltshire (Plate 84) is copied into a letter from Spence to the Duke of Newcastle.

Letter to the Rev. Mr Wheeler (on gardening) (1751)

Dear Sir,

When you set me to write about gardening, you set me upon a thing that I love extremely; but as to any large tract of ground, there is no saying anything in particular without being upon the spot; and having considered it well and often. Some general rules one might mention, but, after all, nine parts in ten depend upon the application. Yet I will just mention some that I followed myself.

The first and most material is to consult the Genius of the place. What is, is the great guide as to what ought to be. The making a fine plan for any place unknown is like Bays's saying 'that he had made an excellent simile, if he did but know how to apply it'. To study the ground thoroughly, one should not only take a view of the whole and all its parts, and consider the laying of it in general, and all its beauties and advantages or inconveniences and impediments, in particular, but also walk all round it in the line without your own bounds; to see what beauties may be added by breaking through your outline.

2dly To fix the principal point of view for the whole plan, and any secondary points of view that may be of consequence in the disposition of the parts.

3dly To follow Nature. Gardening is an imitation of 'Beautiful Nature', and therefore should not be like works of art. Wherever art appears, the gardener has failed in his execution. Our old gardens were formed by the rule and square, with a perpetual uniformity and in a manner more fit for architecture than for pleasure-grounds. Nature never plants by the line, or in angles. I have lately seen thirty-six prints of a vast garden belonging to the present emperor of China: there is not one regular walk of trees in the whole ground, they seem to exceed our late best designers in the natural taste almost as far as those do the Dutch taste, brought over into England in King William's time. As to angles, I have such a mortal aversion to them, that was I to choose a motto for myself as a pretender to gardening, it should be, 'Mutat quadrata rotundis.' I should almost ever prefer serpentizing walks to straight ones, and round off the corners of groves instead of pointing them.

4^{ly} To assist or correct the general character of the ground, if deficient or displeasing. Thus if your ground be all dry, a winding stream should be brought into it, if possible; if not, pieces of water, with alders and weeping willows and other aquatics about them, dashed here and there, at proper distances from each other. If the ground be all flat, one should make risings and inequalities in it: very small swellings will help it much if properly placed, and natural irregular risings (or mounts) where any particular object or pleasing prospect is to be caught, etc.

5^{ly} To correct or conceal any particular object that is disagreeable.

6^{ly} To open a view to whatever is particularly agreeable.

7^{ly} To manage your plantations in such a manner that you may be led to some striking object, or change, unexpectedly: in which case not only the change or object, but the surprise itself is pleasing.

84 Stourhead, Wiltshire. Drawing by Fredrik Magnus Piper, 1779

8^ly To conceal the bounds of your grounds everywhere, if possible. This is done by grove-works, sunk fences (the best of which is the *chevaux de frise*) and what they call invisible fences, as being but little discernible to the eye. If you have sheep to keep and enliven the lawn, movable fences are the best, if any necessary, and of all such fences I should prefer what they call the Palladian rail, or wattles, in the following form:

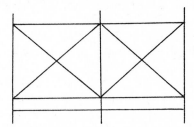

The fence most common in the Emperor of China's garden (of which eighteen prints are very soon to be published at London) is a good deal of this kind, and none of them are at all like those ridiculous things called Chinese rails, and which are got now so much in fashion in town as well as in the country.

9^ly To unite the different parts of your garden gently together.

10 To contrive the outparts so, as to unite well with the country round about them.

11 To mix useful things even in the ornamental parts, and something of ornament even in the useful parts.

12 To make objects that are too near seem farther off: which is done by shewing more of the intermediate ground and narrowing your view to them more and more as it recedes from you.

13 To draw distant objects nearer to you and make them seem part of your work: which is done by hiding the intermediate length of ground and planting what may fall in and unite, to the eye, with such distant objects.

14 To study variety in all things, as nothing without it can be pleasing. Inequality of ground, mixture of land and water, opposition of lights and shades, or grove and open, breaking the lines of trees, interspersing different sorts of trees in each grovette, placing trees of different greens and flowers of different colours by one another, etc. — Mr. Kent always used to stake out his grovettes before they planted, and to view the stakes every way, to see that no three of them stand in a line: to which another, as necessary rule may be added: that in all smaller plantations one should never set above three or four trees of the same sort together.

15 To observe the different friendships and enmities of different colours, and to place the most friendly ones next each other.

16 In the mixing of lights and shades, to let the former have the prevalence, or, in other words, to give the whole a joyous air rather than a melancholy one. In this again the Chinese seem very much to exceed our pleasure-ground makers. They have scarce any such thing as close or thick groves in any of their near views: they fling them all on some of the hills at a distance.

All that I have laid out here so particularly (and perhaps a great deal more) is included by Mr. Pope in two lines, where in speaking of gardens he says:

He gains all Ends, who pleasingly confounds,
Surprises, varies, and conceals the bounds:

and in conversation, I have heard him include it in one single word, Variety.

These are all the general rules that I can recollect at present, but you ask me too what I have done to my own ground in particular [Byfleet, in Surrey]. This might be answered in four words: I found it all confined, gloomy, regular and flat, I have made it appear less flat, quite irregular, light and open.

If you desire a yet more particular account, take it as follows.

My whole domain is not above 16 or 17 acres. The acre next the house consists of a garden with a grove in the midst of it, a kitchen garden hid behind a fruit-wall, and a piece of nursery-ground concealed in the same manner. 'Tis fenced from the sheep that feed just beyond it by a winding brook, instead of a wall which formerly stood there and used to say to the eye, 'Hitherto shall thou look and no farther.' The grass-field that spreads itself next to it, of about four acres, is dashed here and there with trees, with a dark clump towards the middle of it and two unequal openings or lawns (which with the scattered trees give it a parkish look) and a winding walk of sand runs all round it. Between this sand-walk and the hedge-rows I have scattered large flowers, flowering-shrubs, and evergreens in several places, so that this is a half-garden. The rest of my fields, which spread on wider all along beyond these, have the winding walk continued all round them, with here and there a rising, to take off the cornerings, and these risings are chiefly planted with lauristenas, laurels, and three or four different sorts of firs, which makes this farther part look like fields, only a little improved. By the help of these walks I can go all round my little territory in half an hour after a shower of rain, without being wet: for the sand dries soon and is much easier hoed and kept clean than gravel, besides its being much cheaper, especially to me: for, God help us, we live in the neighbourhood of one of the most dreary, sandy heaths in Europe.

In the midst of this abominable heath rises a large hill, on which Julius Caesar is said to have encamped before he passed from this country through the Thames into Middlesex. The make of the camp is still very visible and spreads in its greatest length to the north-east of us. All the hither line of it I have planted here and there with clumps of firs, which in a few years will make it part of my garden: for the tops of the trees in my garden-grove unite (to the eye) with the trees in my hedgerows, and both of them will hereafter unite with the trees on the hill: so that they will make as it were one continued wood, and at the same time hide all that barren side of the hill from me.

To the south and the south-west, we have a very beautiful run of hills at ten or twelve miles distance, and to the south-east four or five very pretty ones, about a mile off. You may be sure I was as ready to open a view to all these as I was to shut out the other, though I have not cut my hedges down all the way; but perhaps here for [a] hundred or hundred and fifty feet, and then left it uncut for fifty, and so of the rest. The nearer ones too, I have planted with clumps of firs and other trees.

The greatest misfortune of my ground was its being one flat. Toward the house I have helped it a little, by raising little knoles and terraces; so placed that whichever way you look, the eye will meet with some rising. But my greatest assistance was the opening the view to these hills, for as they lay semicircularly about me, when you take a view of the whole, my flat ground looks like half the arena of an amphi-theatre, and in that light has rather a good look than a bad one.

I have said nothing of a walk that I have planted (not in regular lines, but scatteringly) for half a mile, from the bridge that leads into our village to the church, and another of about the same length half way to one of the best neighbours in the world.

Won't you say that all these are great works for such a little man as I am in all respects, to engage in and finish before I was quite three years old in this place, and that I am a very fortunate man to have others join me in such odd undertakings? Yet this too has happened: the good neighbour I mentioned has planted his half mile to meet my plantation, and another gentleman has carried on the plantations on the hills round us in a much ampler and nobler manner than I ever intended. If one was to measure the farthest points that are already planted from east to west, I dare say it would be a line of near four miles, as these from north to south would, I believe, be three and a half; and supposing a circle drawn all round them, it would contain a much larger quantity of ground than the city of Geneva and all the contiguous land belonging to that state.

from a Letter to the Duke of Newcastle (on Stourhead) (1765)

You go to the Grotto first thro' a dark walk, where you often catch little pieces of the water thro' the bottoms of the trees, then Open a little way again: & then a [2nd] dark walk, which rises to a rustic Arch & from that begins to descend toward the Grotto. When you are at this Arch, You see a thick wood to a good hight [rising] before you; a low . . . laurel — arching over the path, which hides all the Front of the Grot, except a part of the top to the lefthand: & a little on to the same side, is a lump or two of Stones, with Harts-tongue, Fern, & much periwinkle, growing on & between them. When under the laurel-arch, you first discover the entrance to the Grot, at about 16 f before you; & thence go thorough a close archt passage of 14 f into the Principal circular Room, of 20 f Diameter. Here there is an Opening, coverable with a sort of Curtain when you chose it, which gives a View to the Lake on the left hand; & the Nymph sleeping over a little Cascade is on your right; the light falls in often very pleasingly upon her from an unseen side window above. There is also an opening . . . in the center of the Dome or roof; in one view shewing some of the wood above, & in another the sky. You go out of this room thro' a second archt passage as the former, into An open of 12 f long, before Stour's Cave; where he sits retired within, with his Urn always running with a very pure water. That little opening gives you a View of the Lake to the left, & has a rustic sort of staircase on the right. The steps are of unequal width, & broken in front; they rise winding; & are 23 in number. The Grot is hid here too, on the top of the stairs; & there is a Seat, & Peep to some pretty objects on & near ye Lake. You descend hence to a soft & pleasing Scenary, which leads you to the Pantheon.

This is partly taken from the famous temple of the same name. The Vestibule, after the Portico, serves to prepare the eye for the moderate light, & sight of the Objects [set] in the Rotund wch is only lighted from above. The Walls, are of a Blossom, or rather light broken-purple, color; (Mr Hoare;) the Dome, Entablature, & Ornaments, generally white; only the Pedestals are of different color'd Marbles: the Floor, is Bremen-Stone, darken'd with Log-wood. The Statues are mixt; Hercules in the midst, an Emperess (with the attributes of Juno, & Ceres) next him: & so, of the rest. There are also relievo's over the Statues; & the very backs of ye Seats are painted with other releivo's in chiaro scuro by Mr Hoar.

You . . . [walk along the side of the Lake to] the Temple of Apollo; taken partly from the Temple at Tivoli, & partly from a Temple to the Sun at Balbeck. There are 12 Corinthian Columns; and Niches for Eleven Statues: & the 12 Signs of the Zodiac are to be over these statues & the door. The Door exactly faces the Palladian Bridge; & from it you take in all the great Beauties of the place. It is to be lighted from the top of the Dome. Guido's Aurora, enlarged by the Seasons following the Chariot of Apollo, & Night flying from before her, is to be painted round the inside walls by Mr Hoar. When you sit deep within the Temple, you wou'd think it was built close by the Lake, & when you walk round the Latter below, you are almost continually entertained by the Reflection of it, in the water.

Francis Coventry (d. 1759)

The World was the most influential and successful periodical since *The Spectator*. Floated in 1753 by an important bookseller, Robert Dodsley, and supported by a company of amateur and professional talent, which included Horace Walpole, Joseph Warton and Lord Chesterfield, *The World* adopted the role of witty and ironical commentator upon contemporary foibles and fashions. In its sixth number it remarked caustically upon the excessive zeal of gardeners after Kent:

Clipt hedges, avenues, regular platforms, strait canals have been for some time very properly exploded. There is not a citizen who does not take more pains to torture his acre and half into irregularities, than he formerly would have employed to make it as formal as his cravat. Kent, the friend of nature, was the Calvin of this reformation, but like the other champion of truth, after having routed tinsel and trumpery, with the true zeal of a founder of a sect he pushed his discipline to the deformity of holiness: not content with banishing symmetry and regularity, he imitated nature even in her blemishes, and planted dead trees and mole-hills, in opposition to parterres and quincunxes.

The extract from the fifteenth number maintains the satire against *villas* and against the modish absurdities of total dedication to serpentine lines (see Plate 85), which Hogarth had championed the same year in *The Analysis of Beauty*.

from *The World*, No. 15 (1753)

Thus our present artists in GARDENING far exceed the wildness of nature, and pretending to improve on the plans of Kent, distort their ground into irregularities the most offensive that can be imagined. A great comic painter has proved, I am told, in a piece every day expected, that the line of beauty is an S: I take this to be the unanimous opinion of all our professors of horticulture, who seem to have the most idolatrous veneration for that crooked letter at the tail of the alphabet. Their land, their water must be serpentine; and because the formality of the last age ran too much into right lines and parallels, a spirit of opposition carries the present universally into curves and mazes.

 IT was questioned of some old mathematician, a great bigot to his favourite science, whether he would consent to go to heaven in any path that was not triangular? It may, I think, with equal propriety be questioned of a modern GARDENER, whether he would consent to go thither in any path that is not

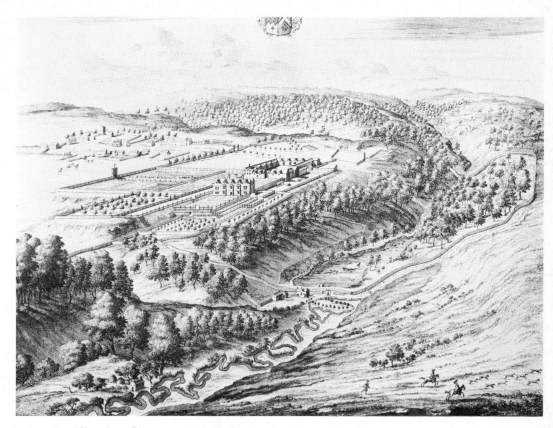

85 Miserden, Gloucestershire. Engraving by Kip and Knyff, *c. 1720*

serpentine? Nothing on earth, at least, can please out of that model; and there is reason to believe that paradise itself would have no charms for one of these gentlemen, unless its walks be disposed into labyrinth and maeander. In serious truth, the vast multitude of grotesque little villa's, which grow up every summer within a certain distance of London, and swarm more especially on the banks of the Thames, are fatal proofs of the degeneracy of our national taste. With a description of one of these whimsical nothings, and with a few previous remarks upon the owner of it, I shall conclude this paper.

SQUIRE Mushroom, the present worthy possessor of Block-hill, was born at a little dirty village in Hertfordshire, and received the rudiments of his education behind a writing-desk, under the eye of his father, who was an attorney at law. It is not material to relate, by what means he broke loose from the bondage of parchment, or by what steps he rose from primaeval meanness and obscurity to his present station in life. Let it be sufficient to say, that at the age of forty he found himself in possession of a considerable fortune. Being thus enriched, he grew ambitious of introducing himself to the world as a man of taste and pleasure; for which purpose he put an edging of silver lace on his servants waistcoats, took into keeping a brace of whores, and resolved to have a VILLA. Full of this pleasing idea, he purchased an old farm-house, not far distant from the place of his nativity, and fell to building and planting with all the rage of taste. The old mansion immediatly shot up into Gothic spires, and was plaistered over with stucco; the walls were notched into battlements; uncouth animals were set grinning at one another over the gate-posts, and the hall was fortified with three rusty swords, five brace of pistols, and a *Medusa*'s head staring tremendous over the chimney. When he had proceeded thus far, he discovered in good time that his house was not habitable; which obliged him to add two rooms entirely new, and entirely incoherent with the rest of the building. Thus while one half is designed to give you the idea of an old Gothic edifice, the other half presents to your view Venetian windows, slices of pilaster, balustrades, and other parts of Italian architecture . . .

BUT the triumph of his genius was seen in the disposition of his gardens, which contain every thing in less than two acres of ground. At your first entrance, the eye is saluted with a yellow serpentine river, stagnating through a beautiful valley, which extends near twenty yards in length. Over the river is thrown a bridge, *partly in the chinese manner*, and a little ship with sails spread and streamers flying, floats in the midst of it. When you have passed this bridge, you enter into a grove perplexed with errors and crooked walks; where having trod the same ground over and over again, through a labyrinth of horn-beam hedges, you are led into an old hermitage built with roots of trees, which the squire is pleased to call St. Austin's cave. Here he desires you to repose yourself, and expects encomiums on his taste; after which a second ramble begins through another maze of walks, and the last error is much worse than the first. At length, when you almost despair of ever visiting daylight any more, you emerge on a sudden into an open and circular area, richly chequered with beds of flowers, and embellished with a little fountain playing in the center of it. As every folly must have a name, the squire informs you, that *by way of whim* he has christened this place *little Marybon*; at the upper end of which you are conducted into a pompous, clumsy and gilded building, said to be a temple, and consecrated to Venus; for no other reason which I could learn, but because the squire riots here sometimes in vulgar love with a couple of orange-wenches, taken from the purlieus of the playhouse.

TO conclude, if one wished to see a coxcomb expose himself in the most effectual manner, one would advise him to build a VILLA; which is the *chef-d'oeuvre* of modern impertinence, and the most conspicuous stage which Folly can possibly mount to display herself to the world.

Samuel Richardson (1689-1761)

Richardson was another friend of Ralph Allen at Prior Park (see Fielding, p. 260) and the editor of Defoe's *Tour* in 1742. This paragraph from his third novel, *The History of Sir Charles Grandison*, describes the estate at Grandison Hall, which contains — as Edward Malins has suggested — several of Brown's most characteristic features. Though Richardson obviously uses the landscape for symbolic purposes — it mirrors Sir Charles's high character and fine appearance, just as Miss Lucy Selby's sentimentality is reflected in her account of it — the description also allows us to see more accurately perhaps than in *Tom Jones* an average gentleman's seat and park of the 1750s (Plate 86).

from *The History of Sir Charles Grandison*
(1753-4)

'THIS large and convenient house is situated in a spacious park; which has several fine avenues leading to it.

'On the north side of the park, flows a winding stream, that may well be called a river, abounding with trout and other fish; the current quickened by a noble cascade, which tumbles down its foaming waters from a rock, which is continued to some extent, in a kind of ledge of rock-work rudely disposed.

'The park itself is remarkable for its prospects, lawns, and rich-appearing clumps of trees of large growth; which must therefore have been planted by the ancestors of the excellent owner; who, contenting himself to open and enlarge many fine prospects, delights to preserve, as much as possible, the plantations of his ancestors; and particularly thinks it a kind of impiety to fell a tree, that was planted by his father.

'On the south side of the river, on a natural and easy ascent, is a neat, but plain villa, in the rustic taste, erected by Sir Thomas; the flat roof of which presents a noble prospect. This villa contains convenient lodging-rooms; and one large room in which he used sometimes to entertain his friends.

'The gardener's house is a pretty little building. The man is a sober diligent man, he is in years: Has a housewifely good creature of a wife. Content is in the countenances of both: How happy must they be!

'The gardens, vineyard, &c. are beautifully laid out. The orangery is flourishing; every-thing indeed is, that belongs to Sir Charles Grandison; alcoves, little temples, seats, are erected at different points of view: The orchard, lawns, and grass-walks, have sheep for gardeners; and the whole being bounded only by sunk fences, the eye is carried to views that have no bounds.

'The orchard, which takes up near three acres of ground, is planted in a peculiar taste. A neat stone bridge in the centre of it, is thrown over the river: It is planted in a natural slope; the higher fruit-trees, as pears, in a semicircular row, first; apples at further distances next; cherries, plumbs, standard apricots, &c. all which in the season of blossoming, one row gradually lower than another, must make a charming variety of blooming sweets to the eye, from the top of the rustic villa, which commands the whole.

'The outside of this orchard, next the north, is planted with three rows of trees, at proper distances from each other; one of pines; one of cedars; one of Scotch firs, in the like semicircular order; which at the same time that they afford a perpetual verdure to the eye, and shady walks in the summer, defend the orchard from the cold and blighting winds.

'This plantation was made by direction of Sir Thomas, in his days of fancy. We have heard that he had a poetical, and, consequently, a fanciful taste.'

86 Arthur Devis, 'Sir George and Lady Strickland in the Grounds of Boynton Hall, Yorkshire', 1751

John Shebbeare ('Battista Angeloni')
(1709–88)

For his two-volume collection of letters, published in 1755, and again in 1756, Shebbeare adopts the popular eighteenth-century *persona* of a foreign visitor to England — in this case, an Italian — sending home descriptions of typical scenes and customs abroad for the entertainment and edification of his countrymen. That Shebbeare should therefore devote a letter to landscaping (taken here from the 1755 edition) is significant in suggesting how established the phenomenon and taste were by mid-century. Chiefly a political journalist, Shebbeare perhaps tries to make some slight political capital in the first paragraph out of English superiority; but he continues with a clear account of the variety and irregularity of the English garden. It is an interesting result of this new taste that Italian Renaissance gardens come to be considered as unsatisfactory as the French and for the same reasons; yet their variety had once, for such writers as Wotton (see p. 48), been as exciting a mirror of human variousness as the new English landscapes. What Shebbeare is typical in emphasizing is the associationist and sentimental habits of mind that began to dominate the eighteenth century. His criticism of cluttered estates announces the vogue for gardens with fewer temples, statues and such artifacts and, as Brown was beginning to provide (Plate 87), for more play with the formal elements of grass, water and trees.

from *Letters on the English Nation*, letter to the
Rev. Father Filippo Bonini in Rome (1755)

IF the Italians were the first improvers of gardens, and plantations, the French have excelled us, and the English carried the taste of that embellishment much higher, than it has appeared either in our country, or in France.

THEY have excluded that regularity of plan which makes the design of all gardens in every other part of Europe, and following those ideas which are characteristic of some sensation relating to human nature, have made a garden in England a sensible consideration, and adapted it to all states which are incident to human minds in general.

THE gay and airy temper finds the open and chearful spots of light, which are acceptable to that disposition, and the melancholy mood finds the solitary and shady grove, by the side of which slowly creeps along the brook, complaining softly amongst the pebbles.

IN the English gardens there is infinite variety without regularity, agreeable to the face of nature that diversifies all, and not according to the ancient and present taste of France and Italy, which disposes a garden like a human

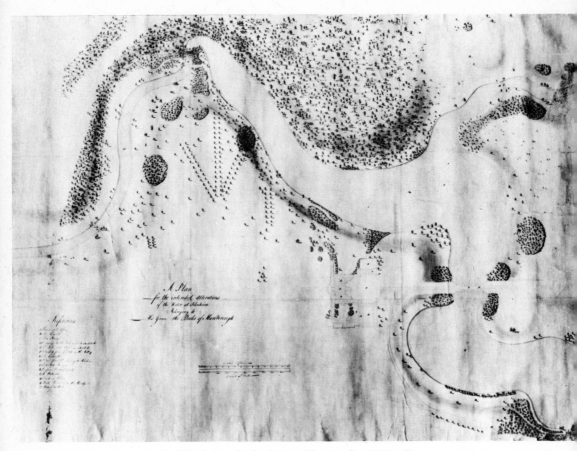

87 Blenheim, Oxfordshire. Plan by Capability Brown, *c.* 1765

creature, and carries the image of self into all its designs, with alleys answering alleys, like legs to legs, and arms to arms, and the great walk in the middle for the trunk of the body.

A MANNER of disposing things very natural to the mind of that man, which cannot divest itself of such interesting ideas as self, and yet very unnatural with respect to that which these dispositions ought to resemble.

THE *jet d'eau* is quite out of fashion in this kingdom; the cascade, and falling streams bubbling amongst rocks, the winding river without regularity of figure, or strait parallel lines, make the water-works of this country.

IN truth, it is always unnatural to see water rising into the air, contrary to its original tendency.

THIS, however contrary it may be to pure taste, I think in some countries may be allowed of, such as in the summer's days in our native land, when the sultry air is fanned by the motion of the water in the *jets d'eau*, and the refreshing sense of coolness imparted at once to the feeling, seeing, and hearing; for the two last senses have the ideas of coolness imparted to them, by the sight and sound of water.

IN this island, where intense heat is seldom known, and when it happens is of short duration, there does not seem to be the same necessity of violating the native propensity of water, to obtain a greater pleasure by it, than can otherwise be had.

HOWEVER, this simplicity and grandeur of taste in gardening, which has produced many fine plantations in this kind, is at present suffering with that of all other things; the caracatura and minute are again prevailing in too many places.

THE citizen who visits his rural retirement close to the road, thronged with coaches, carts, waggons, chaises, and all kinds of carriages, which differs from London only in this, that in winter it rains smoke in the city, and in summer dust in the country, must have his plantation of an acre diversified with all that is to be found in the most extensive garden of some thousand acres; here must be temples to every goddess as well as Cloacina, woods, waters, lawns, and statues, which being thus contrived to contain so many things, is in fact, nothing at all, and that which might be something by being but one, is entirely lost by being intended to be so many; one wonders how so many things can be crammed into so small a place, as we do at the whole furniture of a room in a cherry stone; it is a scene for fairies.

THIS is but the old taste of shaped flower-knots in box, cut yews, and clipt hedges, in another edition, which has no more taste than the former.

PERHAPS there is not a thing upon the face of the earth truer than the belief that taste is the general possession of all men; I mean every man assumes it to himself, tho' he denies it to his neighbour, by which it is at once universal in one view, and non-existent in another.

THERE is however, some analogy between man and all his designs of this kind; the true taste in gardens is formed on what we feel in ourselves, at the sight of different scenes in nature; a garden without this meaning in its disposition cannot please long; novelty indeed, will beget some delight in the beginning, but without scenes which correspond to all situations of our minds, it soon becomes flat and irksome.

TO design a garden well, the person must study the ground on which he intends to plant, the nature of those parts thro' which the water flows, and what use can be made of the woods already grown; from considerations of this kind, taste may communicate characters to different parts, and adapt the whole to that variety of passions and sensations, which distinguish the human heart.

THIS requires much imagination; it is not sufficient to remember what was seen at any one place; to follow that exactly would be impossible, or if it could be done, the whole would be one piece of plagiarism.

THE art lies in selecting the most striking objects, which have affected the mind with any kind of passion or sensation, and then by recalling those ideas, give a combination to these objects which has never yet been seen in nature, and yet which the eye of a judge will agree to be natural when put together.

THIS, tho' it may seem a task of no great difficulty, is yet much more so than may be at first imagined; for tho' many people remember what they have seen, yet very few in nature have the power of uniting the parts of various subjects, so as to make one whole that shall be striking, characteristic and affecting.

IT is in the combination of visible objects, so as that they may affect the mind with any passion, pleasing or displeasing sensation, as it is in that of combining sounds, which may affect us with similar feelings.

IN the latter, the tones which accompany the expressions of tenderness, grief, rage, or other passions, must be distinguished and combined, so as to characterize an air either complaining, soft, or angry, which is much the same kind of genius, with that of combining the objects of sight in light and shade, open and obscure, creating horror or delight, indulging love or sorrow.

AS there are few musicians who have excelled in all parts of a grand composition, so there are few who have succeeded in the planning and designing gardens.

ONE master in music is excellent in composing the first violin of a concerto, and meagre in all the rest; others in their favourite instruments with the like imperfections; Corelli fills all, and makes the whole piece one simple and united sound of various instruments, each sustaining and sustained.

IN gardening also, one designer plans the gay part, and fails in the serious; he trills along a little stream with elegance and propriety, and brobdignags the expanse of water and almost makes a new deluge; Kent, the best designer in this way, is the Corelli of gardeners, as may be seen wherever he has followed his own inclination, in the gardens he has designed.

Alas! the bane of men of fine and elegant taste, and the cause of its sudden decline, is the belief in every rich man who has an inclination to build, or plant, that he has a taste equal to his wealth, and to the undertaking, and a right to obtrude his opinion on the most accomplished judge, in architecture and gardening: this epistle I fear is too much in the didactic strain, when I recollect to whom I am writing, to you whose taste in these arts is certainly just and elegant, from what you have shewn in poetry their sister.

William Chambers (1723–96)

Ever since such early writers as Temple and Addison (see pp. 96 and 138) held up the Chinese '*Sharawadgi*' as an example to English taste, it was inevitable that gardenists would want to know more about their predecessors. Information was provided by the engravings of the Italian Father Matteo Ripa of the Imperial palace and gardens at Jehol, one hundred and fifty miles north-east of Peking; these were known to Lord Burlington in the 1720s and his copy of them survives in the British Library. A famous French work on Chinese gardens by J. D. Attiret (1747) was translated by Joseph Spence in 1752 as *A Particular Account of the Emperor of China's Gardens*. The attempt to provide designs after the Chinese for home consumption was made in such works as William and John Halfpenny's *Rural Architecture in the Chinese Taste* of 1750, and in less predictable places, as Thomas Lightoler's *The Gentleman and Farmer's Architect* (1762), where are found plans for Chinese farmhouses and facades 'to place before disagreeable objects'. William Chambers, who twice visited China, made three distinct contributions to this vogue for Chinese landscape: in 1757 he published the volume from which this extract is taken — though offered as 'Of the Art of Laying Out Gardens Among the Chinese', it is as much a re-affirmation of the English principles of landscaping in the light of the Oriental example. Chinese gardeners, he says in a revealing phrase, are 'like the European painters': an inspiration and support for English practice. In the late 1750s Chambers was invited to improve and embellish the gardens at Kew: his designs, which include the pagoda, were published as *Plans, Elevations, Sections, and Perspective Views of the Gardens and Buildings at Kew in Surry* in 1763 (Plate 88). His third contribution, *A Dissertation on Oriental Gardening* of 1772, has its place as much in the picturesque debates as in the history of the Chinese taste and is preserved in that context later in this book (pp. 318 ff.).

from *Designs of Chinese Buildings, Furniture, Dresses, Machines, and Utensils* (1757)

THE gardens which I saw in China were very small; nevertheless from them, and what could be gathered from Lepqua, a celebrated Chinese painter, with whom I had several conversations on the subject of gardening, I think I have acquired suficient knowledge of their notions on this head.

NATURE is their pattern, and their aim is to imitate her in all her beautiful irregularities. Their first consideration is the form of the ground, whether it be flat, sloping, hilly, or mountainous, extensive, or of small compass, of a dry or marshy nature, abounding with rivers and springs, or liable to a scarcity of water; to all which circumstances they attend with great care, chusing such dispositions as humour the ground, can be executed with the least expence, hide it's defects, and set it's advantages in the most conspicuous light.

As the Chinese are not fond of walking, we seldom meet with avenues or spacious walks, as in our European plantations: the whole ground is laid out in a variety of scenes, and you are led, by winding passages cut in the groves, to the different points of view, each of which is marked by a seat, a building, or some other object.

THE perfection of their gardens consists in the number, beauty, and diversity of these scenes. The Chinese gardeners, like the European painters, collect from nature the most pleasing objects, which they endeavour to combine in such a manner, as not only to appear to the best advantage separately, but likewise to unite in forming an elegant and striking whole.

THEIR artists distinguish three different species of scenes, to which they give the appellations of pleasing, horrid, and enchanted. Their enchanted scenes answer, in a great measure, to what we call romantic, and in these they make use of several artifices to excite surprize. Sometimes they make a rapid stream, or torrent, pass under ground, the turbulent noise of which strikes the ear of the new-comer, who is at a loss to know from whence it proceeds: at other times they dispose the rocks, buildings, and other objects that form the composition, in such a manner as that the wind passing through the different interstices and cavities, made in them for that purpose, causes strange and uncommon sounds. They introduce into these scenes all kinds of extraordinary trees, plants, and flowers, form artificial and complicated ecchoes, and let loose different sorts of monstrous birds and animals.

IN their scenes of horror, they introduce impending rocks, dark caverns, and impetuous cataracts rushing down the mountains from all sides; the trees are ill-formed, and seemingly torn to pieces by the violence of tempests; some are thrown down, and intercept the course of the torrents, appearing as if they had been brought down by the fury of the waters; others look as if shattered and blasted by the force of lightning; the buildings are some in ruins, others half-consumed by fire, and some miserable huts dispersed in the mountains serve, at once to indicate the existence and wretchedness of the inhabitants. These scenes are generally succeeded by pleasing ones. The Chinese artists, knowing how powerfully contrast operates on the mind, constantly practise sudden transitions, and a striking opposition of forms, colours, and shades. Thus they conduct you from limited prospects to extensive views; from objects of horrour to scenes of delight; from lakes and rivers to plains, hills, and woods; to dark and gloomy colours they oppose such as are brilliant, and to complicated forms simple ones; distributing, by a judicious arrangement, the different masses of light and shade, in such a manner as to render the composition at once distinct in it's parts, and striking in the whole.

Where the ground is extensive, and a multiplicity of scenes are to be introduced, they generally adapt each to one single point of view: but where it is limited, and affords no room for variety, they endeavour to remedy this defect, by disposing the objects so, that being viewed from different points, they produce different representations; and sometimes, by an artful disposition, such as have no resemblance to each other.

IN their large gardens they contrive different scenes for morning, noon, and evening; erecting, at the proper points of view, buildings adapted to the recreations of each particular time of the day: and in their small ones (where, as has been observed, one arrangement produces many representations) they dispose in the same manner, at the several points of view, buildings, which, from their use, point out the time of day for enjoying the scene in it's perfection.

As the climate of China is exceeding hot, they employ a great deal of water in their gardens. In the small ones, if the situation admits, they frequently lay almost the whole ground under water; leaving only some islands and rocks: and in their large ones they introduce extensive lakes, rivers, and canals. The banks of their lakes and rivers are variegated in imitation of nature; being sometimes bare and gravelly, sometimes covered with woods quite to the water's edge. In some places flat, and adorned with flowers and shrubs; in others steep, rocky, and forming caverns, into which part of the waters discharge themselves with noise and violence. Sometimes you see meadows covered with cattle, or rice-grounds that run out into the lakes, leaving between them passages for vessels; and sometimes groves, into which enter, in different parts, creeks and rivulets, sufficiently deep to admit boats; their banks being planted with trees, whose spreading branches, in some places, form arbours, under which the boats pass. These generally conduct to some very interesting object; such as a magnificent building, places on the top of a mountain cut into terrasses; a casine situated in the midst of a lake; a cascade; a grotto cut into a variety of apartments; an artificial rock; and many other such inventions.

Their rivers are seldom streight, but serpentine, and broken into many irregular points; sometimes they are narrow, noisy, and rapid, at other times deep, broad, and slow. Both in their rivers and lakes are seen reeds, with other aquatic plants and flowers, particularly the *Lyen Hoa*, of which they are very fond. They frequently erect mills, and other hydraulic machines, the motions of which enliven the scene: they have also a great number of vessels of different forms and sizes. In their lakes they intersperse islands; some of them barren, and surrounded with rocks and shoals; others enriched with every thing that art and nature can furnish most perfect. They likewise form artificial rocks; and in compositions of this kind the Chinese surpass all other nations. The making them is a distinct profession; and there are at Canton, and probably in most other cities of China, numbers of artificers constantly employed in this business. The stone they are made of comes from the southern coasts of China. It is of a bluish cast, and worn into irregular forms by the action of the waves. The Chinese are exceeding nice in the choice of this stone; insomuch that I have seen several Tael given for a bit no bigger than a man's fist, when it happened to be of a beautiful form and lively colour. But these select pieces they use in landscapes for their apartments: in gardens they employ a coarser sort, which they join with a bluish cement, and form rocks of a considerable size. I have seen some of these exquisitely fine, and such as discovered an uncommon elegance of taste in the contriver. When they are large they make in them caves and grottos, with openings, through which you discover distant prospects. They cover them, in different places, with trees, shrubs, briars, and moss; placing on their tops little temples, or other buildings, to which you ascend by rugged and irregular steps cut in the rock.

WHEN there is a sufficient supply of water, and proper ground, the Chinese never fail to form cascades in their gardens. They avoid all regularity in these works, observing nature according to her operations in that mountainous country. The waters burst out from among the caverns, and windings of the rocks. In some places a large and impetuous cataract appears; in others are seen many lesser falls. Sometimes the view of the cascade is intercepted by trees, whose leaves and branches only leave room to discover the waters, in some places, as they fall down the sides of the mountain. They frequently throw rough wooden bridges from one rock to another, over the steepest part of the cataract; and often intercept it's passage by trees and heaps of stones, that seem to have been brought down by the violence of the torrent.

IN their plantations they vary the forms and colours of their trees; mixing such as have large and spreading branches, with those of pyramidal figures, and dark greens, with brighter, interspersing among them such as produce flowers; of which they have some that flourish a great part of the year. The Weeping-willow is one of their favourite trees, and always among those that border their lakes and rivers, being so planted as to have it's branches hanging over the water. They likewise introduce trunks of decayed trees, sometimes erect, and at other times lying on the ground, being very nice about their forms, and the colour of the bark and moss on them.

VARIOUS are the artifices they employ to surprize. Sometimes they lead you through dark caverns and gloomy passages, at the issue of which you are, on a sudden, struck with the view of a delicious landscape, enriched with every thing that luxuriant nature affords most beautiful. At other times you are conducted through avenues and walks, that gradually diminish and grow rugged, till the passage is at length entirely intercepted, and rendered impracticable, by bushes, briars, and stones: when unexpectedly a rich and extensive prospect opens to view, so much the more pleasing as it was less looked for.

ANOTHER of their artifices is to hide some part of a composition by trees, or other intermediate objects. This naturally excites the curiosity of the spectator to take a nearer view; when he is surprised by some unexpected scene, or some representation totally opposite to the thing he looked for. The termination of their lakes they always hide, leaving room for the imagination to work; and the same rule they observe in other compositions, wherever it can be put in practice.

THOUGH the Chinese are not well versed in opticks, yet experience has taught them that objects appear less in size, and grow dim in colour, in proportion as they are more removed from the eye of the spectator. These discoveries have given rise to an artifice, which they sometimes put in practice. It is the forming prospects in perspective, by introducing buildings,

88 Plate from William Chambers, *Plans, Elevations, Sections, and Perspective Views of the Gardens and Buildings at Kew in Surry,* 1763

vessels, and other objects, lessened according as they are more distant from the point of view; and that the deception may be still more striking, they give a greyish tinge to the distant parts of the composition, and plant in the remoter parts of these scenes trees of a fainter colour, and smaller growth, than those that appear in the front or fore-ground; by these means rendering what in reality is trifling and limited, great and considerable in appearance.

THE Chinese generally avoid streight lines; yet they do not absolutely reject them. They sometimes make avenues, when they have any interesting object to expose to view. Roads they always make streight; unless the unevenness of the ground, or other impediments, afford at least a pretext for doing otherwise. Where the ground is entirely level, they look upon it as an absurdity to make a serpentine road: for they say that it must either be made by art, or worn by the constant passage of travellers; in either of which cases it is not natural to suppose men would chuse a crooked line when they might go by a streight one.

WHAT we call clumps, the Chinese gardeners are not unacquainted with; but they use them somewhat more sparingly than we do. They never fill a whole piece of ground with clumps: they consider a plantation as painters do a picture, and groupe their trees in the same manner as these do their figures, having their principal and subservient masses.

THIS is the substance of what I learnt during my stay in China, partly from my own observation, but chiefly from the lessons of Lepqua: and from what has been said it may be inferred, that the art of laying out grounds, after the Chinese manner, is exceedingly difficult, and not to be attained by persons of narrow intellects. For though the precepts are simple and obvious, yet the putting them in execution requires genius, judgment, and experience; a strong imagination, and a thorough knowledge of the human mind. This method being fixed to no certain rule, but liable to as many variations, as there are different arrangements in the works of the creation.

William Shenstone (1714-63)

Shenstone's most famous achievement was, not any of his writings, but his land-scape at The Leasowes (Plates 79 and 80). Though Horace Walpole found it insipid, and though it led Dr Johnson rather ponderously to dismiss landscape gardening as but an 'innocent amusement', The Leasowes was a creation that 'trusts to nature and simple sentiment' (Gray's rather disparaging comment on Shenstone's verse). And those same commitments are rehearsed in his notes upon landscape gardening, where he theorizes along lines that he put into practice at The Leasowes. Shenstone's main delight in a garden was its associationist potential, its appeal to the imagination, its promotion of ideas. At The Leasowes the visitor encountered memorial urns, dedicated to his friends, a grotto with a Latin inscription that invoked the Nereids, a grove named in memory of Virgil. In Shenstone's 'Unconnected Thoughts on Gardening' (first published in the second volume of *The Works in Verse and Prose, of William Shenstone, Esq.* in 1764) there is a constant emphasis upon ways to involve the mind in the exploration of a garden. Another insistence, that was to appeal to the picturesque theorists later in the century, was upon 'the irregularity of surface' that ruins or large oaks present to the sight. For the rest, 'Unconnected Thoughts' are the received ideas from a half-century of landscape theories coloured by Shenstone's very personal commitment to his own garden.

'Unconnected Thoughts on Gardening' (1764)

GARDENING may be divided into three species — kitchen-gardening — parterre-gardening — and landskip, or picturesque-gardening: which latter is the subject intended in the following pages — It consists in pleasing the imagination by scenes of grandeur, beauty, or variety. Convenience merely has no share here; any farther than as it pleases the imagination.

PERHAPS the division of the pleasures of imagination, according as they are struck by the great, the various, and the beautiful, may be accurate enough for my present purpose: why each of them affects us with pleasure may be traced in other authors. See Burke, Hutchinson, Gerard. The theory of agreeable sensations, &c.

THERE seems however to be some objects which afford a pleasure not reducible to either of the foregoing heads. A ruin, for instance, may be neither new to us, nor majestick, nor beautiful, yet afford that pleasing melancholy which proceeds from a reflexion on decayed magnificence. For this reason an able gardiner should avail himself of objects, perhaps not very striking; if they serve to connect ideas, that convey reflexions of the pleasing kind.

OBJECTS should indeed be less calculated to strike the immediate eye, than the judgment or well-formed imagination; as in painting.

IT is no objection to the pleasure of novelty, that it makes an ugly object more disagreeable. It is enough that it produces a superiority betwixt things in other respects equal. It seems, on some occasions, to go even further. Are there not broken rocks and rugged grounds, to which we can hardly attribute either beauty or grandeur, and yet when introduced near an extent of lawn, impart a pleasure equal to more shapely scenes? Thus a series of lawn, though ever so beautiful, may satiate and cloy, unless the eye passes to them from wilder scenes; and then they acquire the grace of novelty.

VARIETY appears to me to derive good part of it's effect from novelty; as the eye, passing from one form or color, to a form or color of a different kind, finds a degree of novelty in it's present object which affords immediate satisfaction.

VARIETY however, in some instances, may be carried to such excess as to lose it's whole effect. I have observed ceilings so crammed with stucco-ornaments; that, although of the most different kinds, they have produced an uniformity. A sufficient quantity of undecorated space is necessary to exhibit such decorations to advantage.

GROUND should first be considered with an eye to it's peculiar character: whether it be the grand, the savage, the sprightly, the melancholy, the horrid, or the beautifull. As one or other of these characters prevail, one may some-what strengthen it's effect, by allowing every part some denomination, and then supporting it's title by suitable appendages — For instance, The lover's walk may have assignation seats, with proper mottoes — Urns to faithfull lovers — Trophies, garlands, &c. by means of art.

WHAT an advantage must some Italian seats derive from the circumstance of being situate on ground mentioned in the classicks? And, even in England, wherever a park or garden happens to have been the scene of any event in history, one would surely avail one's self of that circumstance, to make it more interesting to the imagination. Mottoes should allude to it, columns, &c. record it; verses moralize upon it; and curiosity receive it's share of pleasure.

IN designing a house and gardens, it is happy when there is an oppor-tunity of maintaining a subordination of parts; the house so luckily placed as to exhibit a view of the whole design. I have sometimes thought that there was room for it to resemble an epick or dramatick poem. It is rather to be wished than required, that the more striking scenes may succeed those which are less so.

Taste depends much upon temper. Some prefer Tibullus to Virgil, and Virgil to Homer — Hagley to Persfield, and Persfield to the Welsh moun-tains. This occasions the different preferences that are given to situations — A garden strikes us most, where the grand, and the pleasing succeed, not intermingle, with each other.

I BELIEVE, however, the sublime has generally a deeper effect than the merely beautiful.

I USE the words landskip and prospect, the former as expressive of home scenes, the latter of distant images. Prospects should take in the blue distant hills; but never so remotely, that they be not distinguishable from clouds. Yet this mere extent is what the vulgar value.

LANDSKIP should contain variety enough to form a picture upon canvas; and this is no bad test, as I think the landskip painter is the gardiner's best designer. The eye requires a sort of ballance here; but not so as to encroach upon probable nature. A wood, or hill, may ballance a house or obelisk; for exactness would be displeasing. We form our notions from what we have seen; and though, could we comprehend the universe, we might perhaps find it uniformly regular; yet the portions that we see of it, habituate our fancy to the contrary.

THE eye should always look rather down upon water: Customary nature makes this requisite. I know nothing more sensibly displeasing than Mr. T—'s flat ground betwixt his terras and his water.

IT is not easy to account for the fondness of former times for strait-lined avenues to their houses; strait-lined walks through their woods; and, in short, every kind of strait-line; where the foot is to travel over, what the eye has done before. This circumstance, is one objection. Another, somewhat of the same kind, is the repetition of the same object, tree after tree, for a length of way together. A third is, that this identity is purchased by the loss of that variety, which the natural country supplies every where; in a greater or less degree. To stand still and survey such avenues, may afford some slender satisfaction, through the change derived from perspective; but to move on continually and find no change of scene in the least attendant on our change of place, must give actual pain to a person of taste. For such an one to be condemned to pass along the famous vista from Moscow to Petersburg, or that other from Agra to Lahor in India, must be as disagreeable a sentence, as to be condemned to labour at the gallies. I conceived some idea of the sensation he must feel, from walking but a few minutes, immured, betwixt Lord D—'s high-shorn yew-hedges; which run exactly parallel, at the distance of about ten feet; and are contrived perfectly to exclude all kind of objects whatsoever.

WHEN a building, or other object has been once viewed from its proper point, the foot should never travel to it by the same path, which the eye has travelled over before. Lose the object, and draw nigh, obliquely.

THE side-trees in vistas should be so circumstanced as to afford a probability that they grew by nature.

RUINATED structures appear to derive their power of pleasing, from the irregularity of surface, which is VARIETY; and the latitude they afford the imagination, to conceive an enlargement of their dimensions, or to recollect any events or circumstances appertaining to their pristine grandeur, so far as concerns grandeur and solemnity. The breaks in them should be as bold and abrupt as possible, — If mere beauty be aimed at (which however is not their chief excellence) the waving line, with more easy transitions, will become of greater importance — Events relating to them may be simulated by numberless little artifices; but it is ever to be remembered, that high hills and sudden descents are most suitable to castles; and fertile vales, near wood and water, most imitative of the usual situation for abbeys and religious houses; large oaks, in particular, are essential to these latter.

> Whose branching arms, and reverend height
> Admit a dim religious light.

A cottage is a pleasing object partly on account of the variety it may introduce; on account of the tranquillity that seems to reign there; and perhaps, (I am somewhat afraid) on account of the pride of human nature.

> Longi alterius spectare laborem.

In a scene presented to the eye, objects should never lie so much to the right or left, as to give it any uneasiness in the examination. Sometimes, however, it may be better to admit valuable objects even with this disadvantage. They should else never be seen beyond a certain angle. The eye must be easy, before it can be pleased.

No mere slope from one side to the other can be agreeable ground: The eye requires a balance — i.e. a degree of uniformity: but this may be otherwise effected and the rule should be understood with some limitation.

> — Each alley has it's brother,
> And half the plat-form just reflects the other.

LET us examine what may be said in favour of that regularity which Mr. Pope exposes. Might he not seemingly as well object to the disposition of an human face, because it has an eye or cheek, that is the very picture of it's companion? Or does not providence who has observed this regularity in the external structure of our bodies and disregarded it within, seem to consider it as a beauty? The arms, the limbs, and the several parts of them correspond, but it is not the same case with the thorax and the abdomen. I believe one is generally sollicitous for a kind of ballance in a landskip, and, if I am not mistaken, the painters generally furnish one: A building for instance on one side, contrasted by a group of trees, a large oak, or a rising hill on the other. Whence then does this taste proceed, but from the love we bear to regularity in perfection? After all, in regard to gardens, the shape of ground, the disposition of trees, and the figure of water, must be sacred to nature; and no forms must be allowed that make a discovery of art.

ALL trees have a character analogous to that of men: Oaks are in all respects the perfect image of the manly character: In former times I should have said, and in present times I think I am authorized to say, the British one. As a brave man is not suddenly either elated by prosperity, or depressed by adversity, so the oak displays not it's verdure on the sun's first approach; nor drops it, on his first departure. Add to this it's majestic appearance, the rough grandeur of it's bark, and the wide protection of it's branches.

A LARGE, branching, aged oak, is perhaps the most venerable of all inanimate objects.

URNS are more solemn, if large and plain; more beautiful, if less and ornamented. Solemnity is perhaps their point, and the situation of them should still cooperate with it.

BY the way, I wonder that lead statues are not more in vogue in our modern gardens. Though they may not express the finer lines of an human body, yet they seem perfectly well calculated, on account of their duration, to embellish landskips, were they some degrees inferior to what we generally behold. A statue in a room challenges examination, and is to be examined critically as a statue. A statue in a garden is to be considered as one part of a scene or landskip; the minuter touches are no more essential to it, than a good landskip painter would esteem them were he to represent a statue in his picture.

APPARENT art, in it's proper province, is almost as important as apparent nature. They contrast agreeably; but their provinces ever should be kept distinct.

WHERE some artificial beauties are so dexterously managed that one cannot but conceive them natural, some natural ones so extremely fortunate than [sic] one is ready to swear they are artificial.

CONCERNING scenes, the more uncommon they appear, the better, provided they form a picture, and include nothing that pretends to be of nature's production, and is not. The shape of ground, the site of trees, and the fall of water, nature's province. Whatever thwarts her is treason.

ON the other hand, buildings and the works of art, need have no other reference to nature than that they afford the ευσεμνον with which the human mind is delighted.

ART should never be allowed to set a foot in the province of nature, otherwise than clandestinely and by night. Whenever she is allowed to appear here, and men begin to compromise the difference — Night, gothicism, confusion and absolute chaos are come again.

TO see one's urns, obelisks, and waterfalls laid open; the nakedness of our beloved mistresses, the naiads, and the dryads, exposed by that ruffian winter to universal observation; is a severity scarcely to be supported by the help of blazing hearths, chearful companions, and a bottle of the most grateful burgundy.

THE works of a person that builds, begin immediately to decay; while those of him who plants begin directly to improve. In this, planting promises a more lasting pleasure, than building; which, were it to remain in equal perfection, would at best begin to moulder and want repairs in imagination. Now trees have a circumstance that suits our taste, and that is annual variety. It is inconvenient indeed, if they cause our love of life to take root and flourish with them; whereas the very sameness of our structures will, without the help of dilapidation, serve to wean us from our attachment to them.

IT is a custom in some countries to condemn the characters of those (after death) that have neither planted a tree, nor begat a child.

THE taste of the citizen and of the mere peasant are in all respects the same. The former gilds his balls; paints his stonework and statues white; plants his trees in lines or circles; cuts his yew-trees four-square or conic; or gives them, what he can, of the resemblance of birds, or bears, or men; squirts up his rivulet in jetteaus; in short, admires no part of nature, but her ductility: exhibits every thing that is glaring, that implies expence, or that effects a surprize because it is unnatural. The peasant is his admirer.

IT is always to be remembered in gardening that sublimity or magnificence, and beauty or variety, are very different things. Every scene we see in nature is either tame and insipid; or compounded of those. It often happens that the same ground may receive from art; either certain degrees of sublimity and magnificence, or certain degrees of variety and beauty; or a mixture of each kind. In this case it remains to be considered in which light they can be rendered most remarkable, whether as objects of beauty, or magnificence. Even the temper of the proprietor should not perhaps be wholly disregarded: for certain complexions of soul will prefer an orange tree or a myrtle, to an oak or cedar. However this should not induce a gardiner to parcel out a lawn into knots of shrubbery; or invest a mountain with a garb of roses. This would be like dressing a giant in a sarsenet gown, or a saracen's head in a brussels night-cap. Indeed the small and circular clumps of firs, which I see planted upon some fine large swells, put me often in mind of a coronet placed on an elephant or camel's back. I say a gardiner should not do this, any more than a poet should attempt to write of the king of Prussia in the style of Philips. On the other side, what would become of Lesbia's sparrow should it be treated in the same language with the anger of Achilles?

Gardiners may be divided into three sorts, the landskip gardiner, the parterre gardiner, and the kitchen gardiner, agreeably to our first division of gardens.

I HAVE used the word landskip-gardiners; because in pursuance of our present taste in gardening, every good painter of landskip appears to me the most proper designer. The misfortune of it, is, that these painters are apt to regard the execution of their work, much more than the choice of subject.

THE art of distancing and approximating, comes truly within their sphere: the former by the gradual diminution of distinctness, and of size; the latter by the reverse. A strait lined avenue that is widened in front, and planted there with ewe trees, then firs, then with trees more and more s[h]ady, till they end in the almond-willow, or silver osier; will produce a very remarkable deception of the former kind; which deception will be encreased, if the nearer dark trees, are proportionable and truly larger than those at the end of the avenue that are more s[h]ady.

To distance a building, plant as near as you can to it, two or three circles of different coloured greens — Ever-greens are best for all such purposes — Suppose the outer one of holly, and the next of laurel, &c. The consequence will be that the imagination immediately allows a space betwixt these circles and another betwixt the house and them; and as the imagined space is indeterminate, if your building be dim-coloured, it will not appear inconsiderable. The imagination is a greater magnifier than a microscopic glass. And on this head, I have known some instances, where by shewing intermediate ground, the distance has appeared less, than while an hedge or grove concealed it.

HEDGES, appearing as such, are universally bad. They discover art in nature's province.

TREES in hedges partake of their artificiality, and become a part of them. There is no more sudden, and obvious improvement, than an hedge removed, and the trees remaining; yet not in such manner as to mark out the former hedge.

WATER should ever appear, as an irregular lake, or winding stream.

Islands give beauty, if the water be adequate; but lessen grandeur through variety.

IT was the wise remark of some sagacious observer, that familiarity is for the most part productive of contempt. Graceless offspring of so amiable a parent! Unfortunate beings that we are, whose enjoyments must be either checked, or prove destructive of themselves. Our passions are permitted to sip a little pleasure; but are extinguished by indulgence, like a lamp over-whelmed with oil. Hence we neglect the beauty with which we have been intimate; nor would any addition it could receive, prove an equivalent for the advantage it derived from the first impression. Thus negligent of graces that have the merit of reality, we too often prefer imaginary ones that have only the charm of novelty: And hence we may account, in general, for the prefer-ence of art to nature, in our old fashioned gardens.

ART, indeed, is often requisite to collect and epitomize the beauties of nature; but should never be suffered to set her mark upon them: I mean in regard to those articles that are of nature's province; the shaping of ground, the planting of trees, and the disposition of lakes and rivulets. Many more particulars will soon occur, which, however, she is allowed to regulate, somewhat clandestinely, upon the following account — Man is not capable of comprehending the universe at one survey. Had he faculties equal to this, he might well be censured for any minute regulations of his own. It were the same, as if, in his present situation, he strove to find amusement in contriving the fabrick of an ant's nest, or the partitions of a bee-hive. But we are placed in the corner of a sphere; endued neither with organs, nor allowed a station, proper to give us an universal view; or to exhibit to us the variety, the orderly proportions, and dispositions of the system. We perceive many breaks and blemishes, several neglected and unvariegated places in the part; which, in the whole would appear either imperceptible, or beautiful. And we might as rationally expect a snail to be satisfied with the beauty of our par-terres, slopes, and terrasses — or an ant to prefer our buildings to her own orderly range of granaries, as that man should be satisfied, without a single thought that he can improve the spot that falls to his share. But, though art be necessary for collecting nature's beauties, by what reason is she authorized to thwart and to oppose her? Why, fantastically endeavor to humanize those vegetables, of which nature, discreet nature, thought it proper to make trees? Why endow the vegetable bird with wings, which nature has made momen-tarily dependent upon the soil? Here art seems very affectedly to make a display of that industry, which it is her glory to conceal. The stone which represents an asterisk, is valued only on account of it's natural production: Nor do we view with pleasure the laboured carvings and futile diligence of Gothic artists. We view with much more satisfaction some plain Grecian fabric, where art, indeed, has been equally, but less visibly, industrious. It is thus we, indeed, admire the shining texture of the silk-worm; but we loath the puny author, when she thinks proper to emerge; and to disgust us with the appearance of so vile a grub.

BUT this is merely true in regard to the particulars of nature's province; wherein art can only appear as the most abject vassal, and had, therefore, better not appear at all. The case is different where she has the direction of buildings, useful or ornamental; or, perhaps, claims as much honor from temples, as the deities to whom they are inscribed. Here then it is her interest to be seen as much as possible: And, though nature appear doubly beautiful by the contrast her structures furnish, it is not easy for her to confer a benefit which nature, on her side, will not repay.

A RURAL scene to me is never perfect without the addition of some kind of building: Indeed I have known a scar of rock-work, in great measure, supply the deficiency.

IN gardening it is no small point to enforce either grandeur or beauty by surprize; for instance, by abrupt transition from their contraries — but to lay a stress upon surprize only; for example, on the surprize occasioned by an aha! without including any nobler purpose; is a symptom of bad taste, and a violent fondness for mere concetto.

GRANDEUR and beauty are so very opposite, that you often diminish the one as you encrease the other. Variety is most a-kin to the latter, simplicity to the former.

SUPPOSE a large hill, varied by art, with large patches of different-colored clumps, scars of rock, chalk quarries, villages, or farm-houses; you will have, perhaps, a more beautiful scene, but much less grand than it was before.

IN many instances, it is most eligible to compound your scene of beauty and grandeur — Suppose a magnificent swell arising out of a well-variegated valley; it would be disadvantageous to encrease it's beauty, by means destructive to it's magnificence.

THERE may possibly, but there seldom happens, any occasion to fill up valleys, with trees or otherwise. It is for the most part the gardener's business to remove trees, or ought that fills up the low ground; and to give, as far as nature allows, an artificial eminence to the high.

THE hedge-row apple-trees in Herefordshire afford a most beautiful scenery, at the time they are in blossom: But the prospect would be really grander, did it consist of simple foliage. For the same reason, a large oak (or beech) in autumn, is a grander object than the same in spring. The sprightly green, is then obfuscated.

SMOOTHNESS and easy transitions are no small ingredient in the beautiful; abrupt and rectangular breaks have more of the nature of the sublime. Thus a tapering spire is, perhaps, a more beautiful object than a tower, which is grander.

MANY of the different opinions relating to the preference to be given to seats, villas, &c. are owing to want of distinction betwixt the beautiful and the magnificent. Both the former and the latter please; but there are imaginations particularly adapted to the one, and to the other.

MR. ADDISON thought an open uninclosed champain country, formed the best landskip. Somewhat here is to be considered. Large unvariegated, simple objects have the best pretensions to sublimity; a large mountain, whose sides are unvaried with objects, is grander than one with infinite variety: But then it's beauty is proportionably less.

HOWEVER, I think a plain space near the eye gives it a kind of liberty it loves: And then the picture, whether you chuse the grand or beautiful, should be held up at it's proper distance. Variety is the principal ingredient in beauty; and simplicity is essential to grandeur.

OFFENSIVE objects, at a proper distance, acquire even a degree of beauty: For instance, stubble, fallow ground.

Anonymous

The Rise and Progress of the Present Taste in Planting Parks, Pleasure Grounds, Gardens, Etc., a verse history of English gardening, was written in an era that welcomed the fact that 'the charms of art decay,/And lovely Nature re-assumes her sway', and from a point of view that applauds 'Capability' Brown's achievements. Yet as the first section of the extract immediately reveals, 'lovely Nature' has still to be lent the skills and energies of landscape designers who are urged to 'conceal ... every blemish' and to *assemble* anthologies of nature's best features. It is, in fact, 'too busy Art' that is rejected. And the poem concludes with an apostrophe to Brown and Brown's patron, Charles, 9th Viscount Irwin of Temple Newsam, to whom the anonymous author dedicates his verses. Yet it is a clue to the subtleties of these aesthetic debates that the poet who lauds the 'charms of nature' can still praise in Brown's designs the meeting of painterly and literary talents. Brown began work at Temple Newsam, near Leeds, in 1765, only two years before the poem was published, which explains why the lake had not reached its full size at the time of writing. A painting that does show the finished landscape (Plate 89) also reveals the derivative painterly habits — recollections of Claude, Wootton and Wilson — through which 'nature' was regarded: it is a visual document that throws light on the poem's views of natural scenery mediated by a similar artistic self-consciousness.

89 Temple Newsam, Yorkshire. Painting by M. A. Rooker, *c.* 1767

from *The Rise and Progress of the Present Taste in
Planting Parks, Pleasure Grounds, Gardens, Etc.* (1767)

O study Nature! and with thought profound,
Previous to laying out with taste your ground:
O mark her beauties as they striking rise,
Bid all her adventitious charms surprize!
Eye all her shining, all her shadowy grace,
And to conceal them every blemish trace:
Yet there's a happiness that baffles Art,
In showing Nature *great* in every part,
Which chiefly flows from mingled lights and shades,
In lawns, and woods, hills, rivers, rocks and glades;
For only happy's that assemblage made,
Where force of light contends with force of shade.
But when too busy Art destroys each grace,
And shades with ornaments her lovely face,
We abdicated beauty eye with pain,
And Art presides, where Nature ought to reign . . .

But you, my Lord, at Templenewsham find,
The charms of Nature gracefully combin'd,
Sweet waving hills, with woods and verdure crown'd,
And winding vales, where murmuring streams resound:
Slopes fring'd with Oaks *which* gradual die away,
And all around romantic scenes display.
Delighted still along the Park we rove,
Vary'd with Hill and Dale, with Wood and Grove:
O'er velvet Lawns what noble Prospects rise,
Fair as the Scenes, that Reuben's hand supplies!
But when the Lake shall these sweet Grounds adorn,
And bright expanding like the eye of Morn,
Reflect whate'er above its surface rise,
The Hills, the Rocks, the Woods, and varying Skies,
Then will the wild and beautiful combine,
And Taste and Beauty grace your whole Design.

But your great Artist, like the source of light,
Gilds every Scene with beauty and delight;
At Blenheim, Croome, and Caversham we trace
Salvator's Wildness, Claud's enlivening grace,
Cascades and Lakes as fine as Risdale drew,

While Nature's vary'd in each charming view.
To paint his works wou'd Pousin's Powers require,
Milton's sublimity, and Dryden's fire:
For both the Sister Arts in him combin'd,
Enrich the great ideas of his mind;
And these still brighten all his vast designs,
For here the Painter, there the Poet shines!
With just contempt he spurns all former rules,
And shows true Taste is not confin'd to schools.
He barren tracts with every charm illumes,
At his command a new Creation blooms;
Born to grace Nature, and her works complete,
With all that's beautiful, sublime and great!
For him each Muse enwreathes the Lawrel Crown,
And consecrates to Fame immortal Brown.

Thomas Whately (d. 1772)

Written in 1765, five years before publication in London and in Dublin (from which version our text is taken), *Observations on Modern Gardening* was translated into French within the year and reached a fifth English edition by 1793. Whately (or sometimes Whateley) proposed for the art of landscape gardening what had often been accomplished for painting — namely, a treatise on its aims, methods and achievements: what Roger de Piles, for example, had done in France at the end of the seventeenth century or Jonathan Richardson's *Essay on the Theory of Painting* in England during the early eighteenth. In fact, Whately claims in the Introduction that 'Gardening . . . is as superior to landskip painting, as a reality to a representation', a remark which does much to illuminate the endeavours of 'Capability' Brown. Whately's comprehensive survey of gardenist ideas and techniques together with Walpole's *History* of the art, published in the same year, marks the maturity of the English landscape garden in theory as Brown's work did in practice. The first extracts from *Observations* concern groves and the handling of water, where Whately's characteristic (and Brownian) attention to formal composition of natural elements is made clear: as examples of each he describes Claremont and Wotton in Buckinghamshire respectively. The final extracts treat of ruins and 'character', the idea that informs all his analyses of scenery. 'Character' is the shaping and colouring of a particular section of a landscape in order to 'affect our imaginations and our sensibility'; as another passage from Whately's book, quoted in our Introduction (see p. 38), reveals, this associationism is designed to function fluidly and expressively, without the more studied and '*emblematical*' forms of the early Augustan garden.

from *Observations on Modern Gardening* (1770)

But the surface and the outline are not the only circumstances to be attended to. Though a grove be beautiful as an object, it is besides delightful as a spot to walk or to sit in; and the choice and the disposition of the trees for effects *within*, are therefore a principal consideration. Mere irregularity alone will not please; strict order is there more agreeable than absolute confusion: and some meaning better than none. A regular plantation has a degree of beauty; but it gives no satisfaction, because we know that the same number of trees might be more beautifully arranged. A disposition, however, in which the lines only are broken without varying the distances, is less natural than any; for though we cannot find strait lines in a forest, we are habituated to them in the hedge-rows of fields; but neither in wild nor in cultivated nature do we ever see trees equi-distant from each other: that regularity belongs to art alone. The distances therefore should be strikingly different: the trees should gather into groupes, or stand in various irregular lines, and describe several figures: the intervals between them should be contrasted both in shape and in dimensions: a large space should in some places be quite open; in others the trees should be so close together, as hardly to leave a passage between them; and in others as far apart as the connexion will allow. In the forms and the varieties of these groupes, these lines, and these openings, principally consists the interior beauty of a grove.

The force of them is most strongly illustrated at Claremont; where the walk to the cottage, though destitute of many natural advantages, and eminent for none; though it commands no prospect; though the water below it is a trifling pond; though it has nothing, in short, but inequality of ground to recommend it; is yet the finest part of the garden: for a grove is there planted, in a gently-curved direction, all along the side of a hill, and on the edge of a wood, which rises above it. Large recesses break it into several clumps, which hang down the declivity; some of them approaching, but none reaching quite to the bottom. These recesses are so deep, as to form great openings in the midst of the grove; they penetrate almost to the covert; but the clumps being all equally suspended from the wood; and a line of open plantation, though sometimes narrow, running constantly along the top; a continuation of grove is preserved, and the connexion between the parts is never broken. Even a groupe, which near one of the extremities stands out quite detached, is still in stile so similar to the rest, as not to lose all relation. Each of these clumps is composed of several others still more intimately united: each is full of groupes, sometimes of no more than two trees; sometimes of four or five; and now and then in larger clusters: an irregular waving line, issuing from some little croud, loses itself in the next; or a few scattered trees drop in a more distant succession from the one to the other. The intervals, winding here like a glade, and widening there into broader openings, differ in extent, in figure, and direction; but all the groupes, the lines, and the intervals are collected together into large general clumps, each of which is at the same time both compact and free, identical and various. The whole is a place wherein to tarry with secure delight, or saunter with perpetual amusement . . .

In considering the subjects of gardening, ground and wood first present themselves; water is the next, which, though not absolutely necessary to a beautiful composition, yet occurs so often, and is so capital a feature, that it is always regretted when wanting; and no large place can be supposed, a little spot can hardly be imagined, in which it may not be agreeable; it accommodates itself to every situation; is the most interesting object in a landskip, and the happiest circumstances in a retired recess; captivates the eye at a distance, invites approach, and is delightful when near; it refreshes an open exposure; it animates a shade; chears the dreariness of a waste, and enriches the most crouded view: in form, in style, and in extent, may be made equal to the greatest compositions, or adapted to the least: it may spread in a calm expanse, to sooth the tranquillity of a peaceful scene; or hurrying along a devious course, and splendour to a gay, and extravagance to a romantic, situation. So various are the characters which water can assume, that there is scarcely an idea in which it may not concur, or an impression which it cannot enforce: a deep stagnated pool, dank and dark with shades which it dimly reflects, befits the seat of melancholy; even a river, if it be sunk between two dismal banks, and dull both in motion and colour, is like a hollow eye which deadens the countenance; and over a sluggard, silent stream, creeping heavily along all together, hangs a gloom, which no art can dissipate, nor even the sun-shine disperse. A gently murmuring rill, clear and shallow, just gurgling, just dimpling, imposes silence, suits with solitude, and leads to meditation: a brisker current, which wantons in little eddies over a bright sandy bottom, or babbles among pebbles, spreads chearfulness all around: a greater rapidity, and more agitation, to a certain degree are animating; but in excess, instead of wakening, they alarm the senses; the roar and the rage of a torrent, its force, its violence, its impetuosity, tend to inspire terror; that terror, which, whether as cause or effect, is so nearly allied to sublimity . . .

Water is so universally and so deservedly admired in a prospect, that the most obvious thought in the management of it, is to lay it as open as possible; and purposely to conceal it, would generally seem a severe self-denial: yet so many beauties may attend its passage through a wood, that larger portions of it might be allowed to such retired scenes, than are commonly spared from the view; and the different parts in different stiles would then be fine contrasts to each other. If the water at Wotton were all exposed, a walk of near two miles along the banks would be of a tedious length, from the want of those changes of the scene, which now supply through the whole extent a succession of perpetual variety. That extent is so large as to admit of a division into four principal parts, all of them great in stile and in dimensions; and differing from each other both in character and situation. The two first are the least; the one is a reach of a river, about the third of a mile in length, and of a competent breadth, flowing through a lovely mead, open in some places to views of beautiful hills in the country, and adorned in others with clumps of trees, so large, that their branches stretch quite across, and form a high arch over the water. The next seems to have been once a formal basin, encompassed with plantations; and the appendages on either side still retain some traces of regularity; but the shape of the water is free from them; the size is about fourteen acres; and out of it issue two broad collateral streams, winding towards a large river, which they are seen to approach, and supposed to join. A real junction is however impossible, from the difference of the levels; but the terminations are so artfully concealed, that the deception is never suspected; and when known, is not easily explained. The river is the third great division of the water; a lake into which it falls is the fourth. These two do actually join; but their characters are directly opposite; the scenes they belong to are totally distinct; and the transition from the one to the other is very gradual; for an island near the conflux, dividing the breadth, and concealing the end of the lake, moderates for some way the space; and permitting it to expand but by degrees, raises an idea of greatness, from uncertainty accompanied with encrease. The reality does not disappoint the expectation; and the island, which is the point of view, is itself equal to the scene; it is large, and high above the lake; the ground is irregularly broken; thickets hang on the sides; and towards the top is placed an Ionic portico, which commands a noble extent of water, not less than a mile in circumference, bounded on one side with wood, and open on the other to two sloping lawns, the least of an hundred acres, diversified with clumps, and bordered by plantations: yet this lake, when full in view, and with all the importance which space, form, and situation can give, is not more interesting than the sequestered river, which has been mentioned as the third great division of the water. It is just within the verge of a wood, three quarters of a mile long, every where broad, and its course is such as to admit of infinite variety, without any confusion. The banks are cleared of underwood; but a few thickets still remain; and on one side an impenetrable covert soon begins; the interval is a beautiful grove of oaks, scattered over a green-swerd of extraordinary verdure. Between these trees and these thickets the river seems to glide gently along, constantly winding, without one short turn, or one extended reach, in the whole length of the way. This even temper in the stream suits the scenes through which it passes; they are in general of a very sober cast; not melancholy, but grave; never exposed to a glare; never darkened with gloom; nor by strong contrasts of light and shade exhibiting the excess of either; undisturbed by an extent of prospects without, or a multiplicity of objects within, they retain at all times a mildness of character, which is still more forcibly felt when the shadows grow faint as they lengthen; when a little rustling of birds in the spray, the leaping of the fish, and the fragrancy of the woodbine, denote the approach of evening; while the setting sun shoots its last gleams on a Tuscan portico, which is close to the upper basin, but which from a seat near this river is seen at a distance, through all the obscurity of the wood, glowing on the banks, and reflected on the surface of the water. In another still more distinguished spot is built an elegant bridge, with a colonade upon it, which not only adorns the place where it stands, but is also a picturesque object to an octogon building near the lake, where it is shewn in a singular situation, over-arched, encompassed, and backed with wood, without any appearance of the water beneath. This building in return is also an object from the bridge; and a Chinese room, in a little island just by, is another; neither of them are considerable; and the others which are visible are at a distance; but more or greater adventitious ornaments are not required in a spot so rich as this in beauties peculiar to its character. A profusion of water pours in from all sides round upon the view; the opening of the lake appears; a glimpse is caught of the upper basin; one of the collateral streams is full in sight; and the bridge itself is in the midst of the finest part of the river; all seem to communicate the one with the other; though thickets often intercept, and groupes perplex the view, yet they never break the connection between the several pieces of water; each may still be traced along large branches, or little catches, which in some places are over-shadowed and dim; in others glisten through a glade, or glimmer between the boles of trees in a distant perspective; and in one, where they are quite lost to the view, some arches of a stone bridge, but partially seen among the wood, preserve their connection. However interrupted, however varied, they still appear to be parts of one whole, which has all the intricacy of number, and the greatness of unity; the variety of a stream, and the quantity of a lake; the solemnity of a wood, and the animation of water . . .

To this great variety must be added the many changes which may be made by the means of *ruins*; they are a class by themselves, beautiful as objects, expressive as characters, and peculiarly calculated to connect with their appendages into elegant groupes: they may be accommodated with ease to irregularity of ground, and their disorder is improved by it; they may be intimately blended with trees and with thickets, and the interruption is an advantage; for imperfection and obscurity are their properties; and to carry the imagination to something greater than is seen, their effect. They may for any of these purposes be separated into detached pieces; contiguity is not necessary, nor even the appearance of it, if the relation be preserved; but straggling ruins have a bad effect, when the several parts are equally considerable. There should be one large mass to raise an idea of greatness, to attract the others about it, and to be a common centre of union to all: the smaller pieces then mark the original dimensions of one extensive structure; and no longer appear to be the remains of several little buildings.

All remains excite an enquiry into the former state of the edifice, and fix the mind in a contemplation on the use it was applied to; besides the characters expressed by their style and position, they suggest ideas which would not arise from the buildings, if entire. The purposes of many have ceased; an abbey, or a castle, if complete, can now be no more than a dwelling; the memory of the times, and of the manners, to which they were adapted, is preserved only in history, and in ruins; and certain sensations of regret, of veneration, or compassion, attend the recollection: nor are these confined to the remains of buildings which are now in disuse; those of an old mansion raise reflections on the domestic comforts once enjoyed, and the ancient hospitality which reigned there. Whatever building we see in decay, we naturally contrast its present to its former state, and delight to ruminate on the comparison. It is true that such effects properly belong to real ruins; but they are produced in a certain degree by those which are fictitious; the impressions are not so strong, but they are exactly similar; and the representation, though it does not present facts to the memory, yet suggests subjects to the imagination: but in order to affect the fancy, the supposed original design should be clear, the use obvious, and the form easy to trace; no fragments should be hazarded without a precise meaning, and an evident connection; none should be perplexed in their construction, or uncertain as to their application. Conjectures about the form, raises doubts about the existence of the ancient structure; the mind must not be allowed to hesitate; it must be hurried away from examining into the reality, by the exactness and the force of the resemblance . . .

Another species of character arises from direct *imitation*; when a scene, or an object, which has been celebrated in description, or is familiar in idea, is represented in a garden. Artificial ruins, lakes, and rivers, fall under this denomination; the air of a seat extended to a distance, and scenes calculated to raise ideas of Arcadian elegance, or of rural simplicity, with many more which have been occasionally mentioned, or will obviously occur, may be ranked in this class; they are all representations; but the materials, the dimensions, and other circumstances, being the same in the copy and the original, their effects are similar in both; and if not equally strong, the defect is not in the resemblance; but the consciousness of an imitation, checks that train of thought which the appearance naturally suggests; yet an over-anxious sollicitude to disguise the fallacy is often the means of exposing it; too many points of likeness sometimes hurt the deception; they seem studied and forced; and the affectation of resemblance destroys the supposition of a reality. A hermitage is the habitation of a recluse; it should be distinguished by its solitude, and its simplicity; but if it is filled with crucifixes, hour-glasses, beads, and every other trinket which can be thought of, the attention is diverted from enjoying the retreat to examining the particulars; all the collateral circumstances which agree with a character, seldom meet in one subject; and when they are industriously brought together, though each be natural, the collection is artificial.

The peculiar advantages which gardening has over other imitative arts, will not, however, support attempts to introduce, they rather forbid the introduction of characters, to which the space is not adequate. A plain simple field, unadorned but with the common rural appendages, is an agreeable opening; but if it is extremely small, neither a hay-stack, nor a cottage, nor a stile, nor a patch, nor much less all of them together, will give it an air of reality. A harbour on an artificial lake is but a conceit: it raises no idea of refuge or security; for the lake does not suggest an idea of danger; it is detached from the large body of water; and yet is in itself but a poor incon-siderable basin, vainly affecting to mimick the majesty of the sea. When imitative characters in gardening are egregiously defective in any material circumstance, the truth of the others exposes and aggravates the failure.

But the art of gardening aspires to more than imitation: it can create *original* characters, and give expressions to the several scenes superior to any they can receive from allusions. Certain properties, and certain dispositions, of the objects of nature, are adapted to excite particular ideas and sensations: many of them have been occasionally mentioned; and all are very well known: they require no discernment, examination, or discussion, but are obvious at a glance; and instantaneously distinguished by our feelings. Beauty alone is not so engaging as this species of character; the impressions it makes are more transient and less interesting; for it aims only at delighting the eye, but the other affects our sensibility. An assemblage of the most elegant forms in the happiest situations is to a degree indiscriminate, if they have not been selected and arranged with a design to produce certain expres-sions; an air of magnificence, or of simplicity, of chearfulness, tranquillity, or some other general character, ought to pervade the whole; and objects pleasing in themselves, if they contradict that character, should therefore be excluded; those which are only indifferent must sometimes make room for such as are more significant; many will often be introduced for no other merit than their expression; and some which are in general rather disagreeable, may occasionally be recommended by it. Barrenness itself may be an accept-able circumstance in a spot dedicated to solitude and melancholy.

The power of such characters is not confined to the ideas which the objects immediately suggest; for these are connected with others, which insensibly lead to subjects, far distant perhaps from the original thought, and related to it only by a similitude in the sensations they excite. In a prospect, enriched and enlivened with inhabitants and cultivation, the attention is caught at first by the circumstances which are gayest in their season, the bloom of an orchard, the festivity of a hay-field, and the carols of harvest-home; but the chearfulness which these infuse into the mind, expands afterwards to other objects than those immediately presented to the eye; and we are thereby disposed to receive, and delighted to pursue, a variety of pleasing ideas, and every benevolent feeling. At the sight of a ruin, reflections on the change, the decay, and the desolation before us, naturally occur; and they introduce a long succession of others, all tinctured with that melancholy which these have inspired: or if the monument revive the memory of former times, we do not stop at the simple fact which it records, but recollect many more coaeval circumstances, which we see, not perhaps as they were, but as they are come down to us, venerable with age, and magnified by fame; even without the assistance of buildings, or other adventitious circumstances, nature alone furnishes materials for scenes, which may be adapted to almost every kind of expression; their operation is general, and their consequences infinite: the mind is elevated, depressed, or composed, as gaiety, gloom, or tranquillity, prevail in the scene; and we soon lose sight of the means by which the character is formed; we forget the particular objects it presents; and giving way to their effects, without recurring to the cause, we follow the track they have begun, to any extent, which the disposition they accord with will allow: it suffices that the scenes of nature have a power to affect our imagination and our sensibility; for such is the constitution of the human mind, that if once it is agitated, the emotion often spreads far beyond the occasion; when the passions are roused, their course is unrestrained; when the fancy is on the wing, its flight is unbounded; and quitting the inanimate objects which first gave them their spring, we may be led by thought above thought, widely differing in degree, but still corresponding in character, till we rise from familiar subjects up to the sublimest conceptions, and are rapt in the contemplation of whatever is great or beautiful, which we see in nature, feel in man, or attribute to divinity.

William Mason (1725–97)

Mason was a Yorkshire clergyman, amateur painter, dramatist, poet and garden designer. These two last interests combined to produce the four books of *The English Garden*, 'a long and tedious poem', according to the authors of *Oxfordshire* (The Buildings of England, 1974). It rehearses the by now familiar ambitions and achievements of the English gardenists and the rise of the landscape garden to the Brownian perfection which Mason admired. In the fourth book he tells of the flower garden that he created in 1772 at Nuneham Courtenay, near Oxford, for Viscount Nuneham, later the 2nd Earl Harcourt: it is with this that the extract deals. This flower garden shows Mason at his most interesting (even though the verses do not particularly rise to the occasion), and its combination of sentiment and floral informality announces one nineteenth-century outcome of the landscape gardening movement. The garden comprised 'Bowers, statues, inscriptions, busts, temples'. Paul Sandby, who painted it (Plate 90), thought it 'one of the most delightful scenes that the power of imagination can form or fancy paint'. Lord Harcourt told Sandby that the inscriptions and busts were 'so essential a part of the decorations that if they do not principally constitute the beauty of the garden, at least they make that beauty perceived and felt'. One important inscription came from Rousseau, who had stayed at Nuneham: '*Si l'auteur de la nature est grand dans les grandes choses, il est très grand dans les petites.*' A bust of Rousseau was added to the garden before 1778. Thus Mason's design for Lord Harcourt (who features in the poem as Alcander) contrives a novel marriage between the sentiments for nature, which Rousseau voiced in *La Nouvelle Héloïse*, and the play with nature's forms and colours that characterizes the designs of Brown, who was to shape the riverside landscape at Nuneham in 1779. Much survives today of both Brown's landscape and Mason's flower garden.

from *The English Garden* (1772–81)

As thro' a neighb'ring Grove, where antient beech
Their awful foliage flung, ALCANDER led
The pensive maid along. "Tell me," she cry'd,
"Why, on these forest features all-intent,
"Forbears my friend some scene distinct to give
"To Flora and her fragrance? Well I know
"That in the general Landscape's broad expanse
"Their little blooms are lost; but here are glades,
"Circled with shade, yet pervious to the sun,

90 Mason's flower garden at Nuneham Courtenay, Oxfordshire.
View by Paul Sandby from *The Virtuosi's Museum*, 1778

"Where, if enamell'd with their rainbow-hues,
"The eye would catch their splendor: turn thy Taste,
"Ev'n in this grassy circle where we stand,
"To form their plots; there weave a woodbine Bower,
"And call that Bower NERINA'S." At the word
ALCANDER smil'd; his fancy instant form'd
The fragrant scene she wish'd; and Love, with Art
Uniting, soon produc'd the finish'd whole.

Down to the South the glade by Nature lean'd;
Art form'd the slope still softer, opening there
Its foliage, and to each Etesian gale
Admittance free dispensing; thickest shade
Guarded the rest. — His taste will best conceive
The new arrangement, whose free footsteps, us'd
To forest haunts, have pierc'd their opening dells,

Where frequent tufts of sweetbriar, box, or thorn,
Steal on the green sward, but admit fair space
For many a mossy maze to wind between.
So here did Art arrange her flow'ry groups
Irregular, yet not in patches quaint,
But interpos'd between the wand'ring lines
Of shaven turf which twisted to the path.
Gravel or sand, that in as wild a wave
Stole round the verdant limits of the scene;
Leading the Eye to many a sculptur'd bust
On shapely pedestal, of Sage, or Bard,
Bright heirs of fame, who living lov'd the haunts
So fragrant, so sequester'd. Many an Urn
There too had place, with votive lay inscrib'd
To Freedom, Friendship, Solitude, or Love.

   And now each flow'r that bears transplanting change,
Or blooms indigenous, adorn'd the scene:
Only NERINA'S wish, her woodbine bower,
Remain'd to crown the whole. Here, far beyond
That humble wish, her Lover's Genius form'd
A glittering Fane, where rare and alien plants
Might safely flourish. . .

Horace Walpole (1717–97)

Walpole's essay on the *History of the Modern Taste in Gardening* was written in the years prior to 1770, printed with his *Anecdotes of Painting in England* the following year, but not published until 1780. The *History* was issued separately in 1785. The text used below is from the second edition, issued with additions in 1782. Unlike Thomas Whately, whose *Observations* he mentions, Walpole was concerned to trace the *history* of English landscape gardening, and he figures therefore among those pioneers who tried to order the arts and establish a critical and scholarly survey of their fortunes (see Lawrence Lipking, *The Ordering of the Arts in Eighteenth-Century England*, Princeton, N.J. 1970). There had been other attempts to sketch garden history — the poem of 1767 (see pp. 299 f.), George Mason's *Design in Gardening* (1768) and the first book of William Mason's *The English Garden* (1772): but Walpole's was the most influential and its control over subsequent historians continues to be enormous. He stressed the literary inspiration (notably Milton) for the landscape garden and the emphatic role of the ha-ha in releasing

91 Paul Sandby, 'View of Strawberry Hill, Twickenham', *c.* 1774

the garden into the fields beyond. He is, however, somewhat tendentious in his discussion of William Kent, neither allowing his predecessors among professional gardeners much credit, nor recognizing that before Kent gradual inroads were made against what he called the 'preposterous inconveniences' of older gardens, nor even guessing that the 'absurd magnificence of Italian' villas might have stimulated Kent as much as Italian paintings. This said, his estimate of Kent's art is still the best we have and is accordingly given here. Walpole's authority as a garden historian is based upon his first-hand researches, his experience of many contemporary gardens, which are discussed in his *Journals of Visits to Country Seats* (see the *Publications of the Walpole Society*, vol. XVI, 1928) and in his voluminous correspondence. From this have been selected two letters to precede the passage on Kent: the first describes his own estate at Strawberry Hill, Twickenham (Plate 91), and is addressed to Sir Horace Mann in Italy; the second, to Richard Bentley, recounts a visit to Hagley: both were written in 1753. The texts are taken from the *Yale Edition of Horace Walpole's Correspondence*, edited by Wilmarth S. Lewis.

from a Letter to Sir Horace Mann (June 1753)

I COULD not rest any longer with the thought of your having no idea of a place of which you hear so much, and therefore desired Mr Bentley to draw you as much idea of it, as the post would be persuaded to carry from Twickenham to Florence. The enclosed enchanted little landscape then is Strawberry Hill; and I will try to explain so much of it to you as will help to let you know whereabouts we are, when we are talking to you, for it is uncomfortable in so intimate a correspondence as ours, not to be exactly master of every spot where one another is writing or reading or sauntering. This view of the castle is what I have just finished, and is the only side that will be at all regular. Directly before it is an open grove, through which you see a field which is bounded by a serpentine wood of all kind of trees and flowering shrubs and flowers. The lawn before the house is situated on the top of a small hill, from whence to the left you see the town and church of Twickenham encircling a turn of the river, that looks exactly like a seaport in miniature. The opposite shore is a most delicious meadow, bounded by Richmond Hill which loses itself in the noble woods of the park to the end of the prospect on the right, where is another turn of the river and the suburbs of Kingston as luckily placed as Twickenham is on the left; and a natural terrace on the brow of my hill, with meadows of my own down to the river, commands both extremities. Is not this a tolerable prospect? You must figure that all this is perpetually enlivened by a navigation of boats and barges, and by a road below my terrace, with coaches, post-chaises, wagons and horsemen constantly in motion, and the fields speckled with cows, horses and sheep.

from a Letter to Richard Bentley (September 1753)

. . . As I got into Worcestershire, I opened upon a landscape of country which I prefer even to Kent, which I had reckoned the most beautiful county in England: but this, with all the richness of Kent, is bounded with mountains. Sir George Lyttelton's house is immeasurably bad and old: one room at the top of the house, which was reckoned a *conceit* in those days, projects a vast way into the air . . . You might draw, but I can't describe the enchanting scenes of the park: it is a hill of three miles, but broke into all manner of beauty; such lawns, such wood, rills, cascades, and a thickness of verdure quite to the summit of the hill, and commanding such a vale of towns and meadows, and woods extending quite to the Black Mountains in Wales, that I quite forgot my favourite Thames! — Indeed, I prefer nothing to Hagley but Mount Edgecumbe. There is extreme taste in the park: the seats are not the best, but there is not one absurdity. There is a ruined castle, built by Miller, that would get him his freedom even of Strawberry: it has the true rust of the Barons' Wars. Then there is a scene of a small lake with cascades falling down such a Parnassus! with a circular temple on the distant eminence; and there is such a fairy dale, with more cascades gushing out of rocks! and there is a hermitage, so exactly like those in Sadeler's prints, on the brow of a shady mountain, stealing peeps into the glorious world below! and there is such a pretty well under a wood, like the Samaritan woman's in a picture of Nicolò Poussin! and there is such a wood without the park, enjoying such a prospect! and there is such a mountain on t'other side of the park commanding all prospects, that I wore out my eyes with gazing, my feet with climbing, and my tongue and my vocabulary with commending!

from *The History of the Modern Taste in Gardening* (1771–80)

I call a sunk fence the leading step, for these reasons. No sooner was this simple enchantment made, than levelling, mowing and rolling, followed. The contiguous ground of the park without the sunk fence was to be harmonized with the lawn within; and the garden in its turn was to be set free from its prim regularity, that it might assort with the wilder country without. The sunk fence ascertained the specific garden, but that it might not draw too obvious a line of distinction between the neat and the rude, the contiguous out-lying parts came to be included in a kind of general design: and when nature was taken into the plan, under improvements, every step that was made, pointed out new beauties and inspired new ideas. At that moment appeared Kent, painter enough to taste the charms of landscape, bold and opinionative enough to dare and to dictate, and born with a genius to strike out a great system from the twilight of imperfect essays. He leaped the fence, and saw that all nature was a garden. He felt the delicious contrast of hill and valley changing imperceptibly into each other, tasted the beauty of the gentle swell, or concave scoop, and remarked how loose groves crowned an easy eminence with happy ornament, and while they called in the distant view between their graceful stems, removed and extended the perspective by delusive comparison.

Thus the pencil of his imagination bestowed all the arts of landscape on the scenes he handled. The great principles on which he worked were perspective, and light and shade. Groupes of trees broke too uniform or too extensive a lawn; evergreens and woods were opposed to the glare of the champain, and where the view was less fortunate, or so much exposed as to be beheld at once, he blotted out some parts by thick shades, to divide it into variety, or to make the richest scene more enchanting by reserving it to a farther advance of the spectator's step. Thus selecting favourite objects, and veiling deformities by screens of plantation, sometimes allowing the rudest waste to add its foil to the richest theatre, he realised the compositions of the greatest masters in painting. Where objects were wanting to animate his horizon, his taste as an architect could bestow immediate termination. His buildings, his seats, his temples, were more the works of his pencil than of his compasses. We owe the restoration of Greece and the diffusion of architecture to his skill in landscape.

But of all the beauties he added to the face of this beautiful country, none surpassed his management of water. Adieu to canals, circular basons, and cascades tumbling down marble steps, that last absurd magnificence of Italian and French villas. The forced elevation of cataracts was no more. The gentle stream was taught to serpentize seemingly at its pleasure, and where discontinued by different levels, its course appeared to be concealed by thickets properly interspersed, and glittered again at a distance where it might be supposed naturally to arrive. Its borders were smoothed, but preserved their waving irregularity. A few trees scattered here and there on its edges sprinkled the tame bank that accompanied its maeanders, and when it disappeared among the hills, shades descending from the heights leaned towards its progress, and framed the distant point of light under which it was lost, as it turned aside to either hand of the blue horizon.

Thus dealing in none but the colours of nature, and catching its most favourable features, men saw a new creation opening before their eyes. The living landscape was chastened or polished, not transformed. Freedom was given to the forms of trees; they extended their branches unrestricted, and where any eminent oak, or master beech had escaped maiming and survived the forest, bush and bramble was removed, and all its honours were restored to distinguish and shade the plain. Where the united plumage of an ancient wood extended wide its undulating canopy, and stood venerable in its darkness, Kent thinned the foremost ranks, and left but so many detached and scattered trees, as softened the approach of gloom and blended a chequered light with the thus lengthened shadows of the remaining columns.

Succeeding artists have added new master-strokes to these touches; perhaps improved or brought to perfection some that I have named. The introduction of foreign trees and plants, which we owe principally to Archibald duke of Argyle, contributed essentially to the richness of colouring so peculiar to our modern landscape. The mixture of various greens, the contrast of forms between our forest-trees and the northern and West-Indian firs and pines, are improvements more recent than Kent, or but little known to him. The weeping-willow and every florid shrub, each tree of delicate or bold leaf, are new tints in the composition of our gardens. The last century was certainly acquainted with many of those rare plants we now admire. The Weymouth pine has long been naturalized here; the patriarch plant still exists at Longleat. The light and graceful acacia was known as early; witness those ancient stems in the court of Bedford-house in Bloomsbury-square; and in the bishop of London's garden at Fulham are many exotics of very ancient date. I doubt therefore whether the difficulty of preserving them in a clime so foreign to their nature did not convince our ancestors of their inutility in general; unless the shapeliness of the lime and horse-chesnut, which accorded so well with established regularity, and which thence and from their novelty grew in fashion, did not occasion the neglect of the more curious plants.

But just as the encomiums are that I have bestowed on Kent's discoveries, he was neither without assistance or faults. Mr. Pope undoubtedly contributed to form his taste. The design of the prince of Wales's garden at Carlton-house was evidently borrowed from the poet's at Twickenham. There was a little of affected modesty in the latter, when he said, of all his works he was most proud of his garden. And yet it was a singular effort of art and taste to impress so much variety and scenery on a spot of five acres. The passing through the gloom from the grotto to the opening day, the retiring and again assembling shades, the dusky groves, the larger lawn, and the solemnity of the termination at the cypresses that lead up to his mother's tomb, are managed with exquisite judgement; and though lord Peterborough assisted him

To form his quincunx and to rank his vines,

those were not the most pleasing ingredients of his little perspective.

I do not know whether the disposition of the garden at Rousham, laid out for general Dormer, and in my opinion the most engaging of all Kent's works, was not planned on the model of Mr. Pope's, at least in the opening and retiring shades of Venus's vale. The whole is as elegant and antique as if the emperor Julian had selected the most pleasing solitude about Daphne to enjoy a philosophic retirement.

That Kent's ideas were but rarely great, was in some measure owing to the novelty of his art. It would have been difficult to have transported the style of gardening at once from a few acres to tumbling of forests: and though new fashions like new religions, (which are new fashions) often lead men to the most opposite excesses, it could not be the case in gardening, where the experiments would have been so expensive. Yet it is true too that the features in Kent's landscapes were seldom majestic. His clumps were puny, he aimed at immediate effect, and planted not for futurity. One sees no large woods sketched out by his direction. Nor are we yet entirely risen above a too great frequency of small clumps, especially in the elbows of serpentine rivers. How common to see three or four beeches, then as many larches, a third knot of cypresses, and a revolution of all three! Kent's last designs were in a higher style, as his ideas opened on success. The north terras at Claremont was much superior to the rest of the garden.

A return of some particular thoughts was common to him with other painters, and made his *hand* known. A small lake edged by a winding bank with scattered trees that led to a seat at the head of the pond, was common to Claremont, Esher and others of his designs. At Esher,

> Where Kent and Nature vied for Pelham's love,

the prospects more than aided the painter's genius—they marked out the points where his art was necessary or not; but thence left his judgement in possession of all its glory.

Having routed *professed* art, for the modern gardener exerts his talents to conceal his art, Kent, like other reformers, knew not how to stop at the just limits. He had followed nature, and imitated her so happily, that he began to think all her works were equally proper for imitation. In Kensington-garden he planted dead trees, to give a greater air of truth to the scene—but he was soon laughed out of this excess. His ruling principle was, that *nature abhors a strait line*—His mimics, for every genius has his apes, seemed to think that she could love nothing but what was crooked. Yet so many men of taste of all ranks devoted themselves to the new improvements, that it is surprizing how much beauty has been struck out, with how few absurdities. Still in some lights the reformation seems to me to have been pushed too far. Though an avenue crossing a park or separating a lawn, and intercepting views from the seat to which it leads, are capital faults, yet a great avenue cut through woods, perhaps before entering a park, has a noble air, and

> Like footmen running before coaches
> To tell the inn what Lord approaches,

announces the habitation of some man of distinction. In other places the total banishment of all particular neatness immediately about a house, which is frequently left gazing by itself in the middle of a park, is a defect. Sheltered and even close walks in so very uncertain a climate as ours, are comforts ill exchanged for the few picturesque days that we enjoy: and whenever a family can purloin a warm and even something of an old fashioned garden from the landscape designed for them by the undertaker in fashion, without interfering with the picture, they will find satisfactions on those days that do not invite strangers to come and see their improvements.

Part Four

*Picturesque Taste
and the Garden*

William Chambers (1723–96)
and William Mason (1725–97)

Chambers' earliest contribution to the vogue for Chinese gardening has already been presented (see pp. 283 ff.). His *Dissertation on Oriental Gardening*, while it offers a good deal more information about Oriental designs, is just as importantly a vigorous contribution to an English gardenist debate that reached its peak in the 1790s. Chambers argues for more variety, including the horrid and terrible, in a landscape in order to provide for what in 1757 he had called 'a strong imagination' and a more 'thorough' repertoire of 'the human mind'. His dislike of Brown, apart from considerable personal animus, was because his designs were too insipid and his landscape too limited in the range and intensity of their mental involvement. Chinese motifs had certainly added strangeness to a landscape — Chambers himself at Kew (Plate 88) and William Kent in his illustrations to *The Faerie Queene* (Plate 92) had both invoked them. The extracts here from the *Dissertation* document both Chambers' dislike of 'insipid and vulgar' landscapes which 'differ very little from common fields' and his personal brand of picturesque designs by which the 'strongest feelings . . . of the human mind . . . are excited': these range from a grandeur of avenues and straight lines to the sublime and horrid, like the territory of any contemporary Gothic novel, through a veritable Disneyland of exotic devices. The most famous riposte to Chambers' *Dissertation* came from William Mason (see following extract) in his *Heroic Epistle*, of which fourteen editions were necessary in four years: part parody of Chinese absurdities in English gardens and protest at their unsuitable associationist tactics, part political squib directed at the Tory establishment (Chambers was Comptroller General of His Majesty's Works). Walpole saw Mason's satire as a chastisement of tyrannical attempts to corrupt English liberties (of which the early English garden was an expression) and as a re-affirmation of Whig Enlightenment principles. If Mason succeeded in having the *Dissertation* ridiculed in England, it nevertheless proved a popular and influential book in Europe, where it did much to define the idea of *le jardin anglo-chinois*.

from *A Dissertation on Oriental Gardening* (1772)

Though the Chinese artists have nature for their general model, yet are they not so attached to her as to exclude all appearance of art; on the contrary, they think it, on many occasions, necessary to make an ostentatious shew of their labour. Nature, say they, affords us but few materials to work with. Plants, ground and water, are her only productions: and though both the forms and arrangements of these may be varied to an incredible degree, yet have they

92 Illustration by Kent of 'Guyon leaves the Palmer and Crosses the
Idle Lake with Phedria' from Spenser's *Faerie Queene*, 1751

but few striking varieties, the rest being of the nature of changes rung upon
bells, which, though in reality different, still produce the same uniform kind
of jingling; the variation being too minute to be easily perceived.

Art must therefore supply the scantiness of nature; and not only be
employed to produce variety, but also novelty and effect: for the simple
arrangements of nature are met with in every common field, to a certain
degree of perfection; and are therefore too familiar to excite any strong
sensations in the mind of the beholder, or to produce any uncommon degree
of pleasure.

It is indeed true that novelty and variety may both be attained by transplanting the peculiarities of one country to another; by introducing rocks,
cataracts, impending woods, and other parts of romantic situations, in flat
places; by employing much water where it is rare; and cultivated plains,
amidst the rude irregularities of mountains: but even this resource is easily
exhausted, and can seldom be put in practice, without a very great expence.

The Chinese are therefore no enemies to strait lines; because they are,
generally speaking, productive of grandeur, which often cannot be attained
without them: nor have they any aversion to regular geometrical figures,
which they say are beautiful in themselves, and well suited to small compositions, where the luxuriant irregularities of nature would fill up and embarrass
the parts they should adorn. They likewise think them properest for flower
gardens, and all other compositions, where much art is apparent in the
culture; and where it should therefore not be omitted in the form.

Their regular buildings they generally surround with artificial terrasses, slopes, and many flights of steps; the angles of which are adorned with groupes of sculpture and vases, intermixed with all sorts of artificial water-works, which, connecting with the architecture, serve to give it consequence, and add to the gaiety, splendor, and bustle of the scenery.

Round the main habitation, and near all their decorated structures, the grounds are laid out with great regularity, and kept with great care: no plants are admitted that intercept the view of the buildings; nor no lines but such as accompany the architecture properly, and contribute to the general good effect of the whole composition: for they hold it absurd to surround an elegant fabric with disorderly rude vegetation; saying, that it looks like a diamond set in lead; and always conveys the idea of an unfinished work. When the buildings are rustic, the scenery which surrounds them is wild; when they are grand, it is gloomy; when gay, it is luxuriant: in short, the Chinese are scrupulously nice in preserving the same character through every part of the composition; which is one great cause of that surprizing variety with which their works abound.

They are fond of introducing statues, busts, bas-reliefs, and every production of the chisel, as well in other parts of their Gardens, as round their buildings; observing, that they are not only ornamental, but that by commemorating past events, and celebrated personages, they awaken the mind to pleasing contemplation, hurrying our reflections up into the remotest ages of antiquity: and they never fail to scatter antient inscriptions, verses, and moral sentences, about their grounds; which are placed on large ruinated stones, and columns of marble, or engraved on trees and rocks; such situations being always chosen for them, as correspond with the sense of the inscriptions; which thereby acquire additional force in themselves, and likewise give a stronger expression to the scene . . .

Such is the common scenery of the Chinese Gardens, where the ground has no striking tendency to any particular character. But where it is more strongly marked, their artists never fail to improve upon its singularities; their aim is to excite a great variety of passions in the mind of the spectator; and the fertility of their imaginations, always upon the stretch in search of novelty, furnishes them with a thousand artifices to accomplish that aim.

The scenes which I have hitherto described, are chiefly of the pleasing kind: but the Chinese Gardeners have many sorts, which they employ as circumstances vary; all which they range in three separate classes; and distinguish them by the appellations of the pleasing, the terrible, and the surprizing.

The first of these are composed of the gayest and most perfect productions of the vegetable world; intermixed with rivers, lakes, cascades, fountains, and water-works of all sorts: being combined and disposed in all the picturesque forms that art or nature can suggest. Buildings, sculptures, and paintings are added, to give splendor and variety to these compositions; and the rarest productions of the animal creation are collected; to enliven them: nothing is forgot that can either exhilerate the mind, gratify the senses, or give a spur to the imagination.

Their scenes of terror are composed of gloomy woods, deep vallies inaccessible to the sun, impending barren rocks, dark caverns, and impetuous cataracts rushing down the mountains from all parts. The trees are ill formed, forced out of their natural directions, and seemingly torn to pieces by the violence of tempests: some are thrown down, and intercept the course of the torrents; others look as if blasted and shattered by the power of lightening: the buildings are in ruins; or half consumed by fire, or swept away by the fury of the waters: nothing remaining entire but a few miserable huts dispersed in the mountains, which serve at once to indicate the existence and wretchedness of the inhabitants. Bats, owls, vultures, and every bird of prey flutter in the groves; wolves, tigers and jackalls howl in the forests; half-famished animals wander upon the plains; gibbets, crosses, wheels, and the whole apparatus of torture, are seen from the roads; and in the most dismal recesses of the woods, where the ways are rugged and overgrown with weeds, and where every object bears the marks of depopulation, are temples dedicated to the king of vengeance, deep caverns in the rocks, and descents to subterraneous habitations, overgrown with brushwood and brambles; near which are placed pillars of stone, with pathetic descriptions of tragical events, and many horrid acts of cruelty, perpetrated there by outlaws and robbers of former times: and to add both to the horror and sublimity of these scenes, they sometimes conceal in cavities, on the summits of the highest mountains, founderies, lime-kilns, and glass-works; which send forth large volumes of flame, and continued columns of thick smoke, that give to these mountains the appearance of volcanoes.

Their surprizing, or supernatural scenes, are of the romantic kind, and abound in the marvellous; being calculated to excite in the minds of the spectators, quick successions of opposite and violent sensations. Sometimes the passenger is hurried by steep descending paths to subterraneous vaults, divided into apartments, where lamps, which yield a faint glimmering light, discover the pale images of antient kings and heroes, reclining on beds of state; their heads are crowned with garlands of stars, and in their hands are tablets of moral sentences: flutes, and soft harmonious organs, impelled by subterraneous waters, interrupt, at stated intervals, the silence of the place, and fill the air with solemn melody.

Sometimes the traveller, after having wandered in the dusk of the forest, finds himself on the edge of precipices, in the glare of day-light, with cataracts falling from the mountains around, and torrents raging in the depths beneath him; or at the foot of impending rocks, in gloomy vallies, overhung with woods, on the banks of dull moving rivers, whose shores are covered with sepulchral monuments, under the shade of willows, laurels, and other plants, sacred to Manchew, the genius of sorrow.

His way now lies through dark passages cut in the rocks, on the side of which are recesses, filled with colossal figures of dragons, infernal fiends, and other horrid forms, which hold in their monstrous talons, mysterious, cabalistical sentences, inscribed on tables of brass; with preparations that yield a constant flame; serving at once to guide and to astonish the passenger: from time to time he is surprized with repeated shocks of electrical impulse, with showers of artificial rain, or sudden violent gusts of wind, and instantaneous explosions of fire; the earth trembles under him, by the power of confined air; and his ears are successively struck with many different sounds, produced by the same means; some resembling the cries of men in torment; others the roaring of bulls, and howl of ferocious animals, with the yell of hounds, and the voices of hunters; others are like the mixed croaking of ravenous birds; and others imitate thunder, the raging of the sea, the explosion of cannon, the sound of trumpets, and all the noise of war.

His road then lies through lofty woods, where serpents and lizards of many beautiful sorts crawl upon the ground, and where innumerable monkies, cats and parrots, clamber upon the trees, and intimidate him as he passes; or through flowery thickets, where he is delighted with the singing of birds, the harmony of flutes, and all kinds of soft instrumental music: sometimes, in this romantic excursion, the passenger finds himself in extensive recesses, surrounded with arbors of jessamine, vine and roses, where beauteous Tartarean damsels, in loose transparent robes, that flutter in the air, present him with rich wines, mangostans, ananas, and fruits of Quangsi; crown him with garlands of flowers, and invite him to taste the sweets of retirement, on Persian carpets, and beds of camusath skin down . . .

European artists must not hope to rival Oriental splendor; yet let them look up to the sun, and copy as much of its lustre as they can, circumstances will frequently obstruct them in their course, and they may often be prevented from soaring high: but their attention should constantly be fixed on great objects; and their productions always demonstrate, that they knew the road to perfection, had they been enabled to proceed on the journey.

Where twining serpentine walks, scattering shrubs, digging holes to raise mole-hills, and ringing never-ceasing changes on lawns, groves and thickets, is called Gardening, it matters little who are the Gardeners; whether a peasant or a Poussin; whether a child in sport, or a man for hire: the meanest may do the little there is to be done, and the best could reach no farther. But wherever a better style is adopted, and Gardens are to be natural, without resemblance to vulgar Nature; new without affectation, and extraordinary without extravagance; where the spectator is to be amused, where his attention is constantly to be kept up, his curiosity excited, and his mind agitated by a great variety of opposite passions; there Gardeners must be men of genius, experience and judgement; quick in perception, rich in expedients, fertile in imagination, and thoroughly versed in all the affections of the human mind.

An Heroic Epistle to Sir William Chambers (1773)

KNIGHT of the Polar Star! by Fortune plac'd,
To shine the Cynosure of British taste;
Whose orb collects, in one refulgent view,
The scatter'd glories of Chinese Virtù;
And spread their lustre in so broad a blaze,
That Kings themselves are dazzled, while they gaze.
O let the Muse attend thy march sublime,

And, with thy prose, caparison her rhyme;
Teach her, like thee, to gild her splendid song,
With scenes of Yven-Ming, and sayings of Li-Tsong;
Like thee to scorn Dame Nature's simple fence;
Leap each Ha Ha of truth and common sense;
And proudly rising in her bold career,
Demand attention from the gracious ear
Of Him, whom we and all the world admit,
Patron supreme of science, taste, and wit.
Does Envy doubt? Witness ye chosen train!
Who breathe the sweets of his Saturnian reign;
Witness ye H*lls, ye J*ns*ns, Sc*ts, S*bb*s,
Hark to my call, for some of you have ears.
Let D**d H*e, from the remotest North,
In see-saw sceptic scruples hint his worth;
D**d, who there supinely deigns to lye
The fattest Hog of Epicurus' sty;
Tho' drunk with Gallic wine, and Gallic praise,
D**d shall bless Old England's halcyon days;
The mighty Home bemir'd in prose so long,
Again shall stalk upon the stilts of song;
While bold Mac-Ossian, wont in Ghosts to deal,
Bids candid Smollet from his coffin steal;
Bids Mallock quit his sweet Elysian rest,
Sunk in his St. John's philosophic breast,
And, like old Orpheus, make some strong effort
To come from Hell, and warble *truth at Court*.
   There was a time, "in Esher's peaceful grove,
"When Kent and Nature vy'd for Pelham's love[">],
That Pope beheld them with auspicious smile,
And own'd that Beauty blest their mutual toil.
Mistaken Bard! could such a pair design
Scenes fit to live in thy immortal line?
Hadst thou been born in this enlighten'd day,
Felt, as we feel, Taste's oriental ray,
Thy satire sure had given them both a stab,
Called Kent a Driveller, and the Nymph a Drab.
For what is Nature? Ring her changes round,
Her three flat notes are water, plants, and ground;
Prolong the peal, yet spite of all your clatter,
The tedious chime is still ground, plants, and water.
So, when some John his dull invention racks,
To rival Boodle's dinners, or Almack's,
Three uncouth legs of mutton shock our eyes,
Three roasted geese, three butter'd apple-pies.
   Come then, prolific Art, and with thee bring
The charms that rise from thy exhaustless spring;

To Richmond come, for see, untutor'd Brown
Destroys those wonders which were once thy own.
Lo, from his melon-ground the peasant slave
Has rudely rush'd, and levell'd Merlin's Cave;
Knock'd down the waxen Wizzard, seiz'd his wand,
Transform'd to lawn what late was Fairy land;
And marr'd, with impious hand, each sweet design
Of Stephen Duck, and good Queen Caroline.
Haste, bid yon livelong Terras re-ascend,
Replace each vista, straighten every bend;
Shut out the Thames; shall that ignoble thing
Approach the presence of great Ocean's King?
No! let Barbaric glories feast his eyes,
August Pagodas round his palace rise,
And finish'd Richmond open to his view,
"A work to wonder at, perhaps a" Kew.

Nor rest we here, but, at our magic call,
Monkies shall climb our trees, and lizards crawl;
Huge dogs of Tibet bark in yonder grove,
Here parrots prate, there cats make cruel love;
In some fair island will we turn to grass
(With the Queen's leave) her elephant and ass.
Giants from Africa shall guard the glades,
Where hiss our snakes, where sport our Tartar maids;
Or, wanting these, from Charlotte Hayes we bring,
Damsels alike adroit to sport and sting.

Now to our lawns of dalliance and delight,
Join we the groves of horror and affright;
This to atchieve no foreign aids we try,
Thy gibbets, Bagshot! shall our wants supply;
Hounslow, whose heath sublimer terror fills,
Shall with her gibbets lend her powder mills.
Here too, O King of Vengeance, in thy fane,
Tremendous Wilkes shall rattle his gold chain;
And round that fane on many a Tyburn tree,
Hang fragments dire of Newgate-history;
On this shall H⋆ll⋆d's dying speech be read,
Here B—te's confession, and his wooden head;
While all the minor plunderers of the age
(Too numerous far for this contracted page)
The R⋆g⋆ys, Mungos, B⋆ds⋆ws there,
In straw-stufft effigy, shall kick the air.
But say, ye powers, who come when Fancy calls,
Where shall our mimic London rear her walls?
That Eastern feature, Art must next produce,
Tho' not for present yet for future use;
Our sons some slave of greatness may behold,

Cast in the genuine Asiatic mould:
Who of three realms shall condescend to know
No more than he can spy from Windsor's brow;
For Him that blessing of a better time,
The Muse shall deal awhile in brick and lime;
Surpass the bold ΑΔΕΛΦΙ in design,
And o'er the Thames fling one stupendous line
Of marble arches, in a bridge, that cuts
From Richmond Ferry slant to Brentford Butts.
Brentford with London's charms will we adorn;
Brentford, the bishoprick of Parson Horne.
There at one glance, the royal eye shall meet
Each varied beauty of St. James's Street;
Stout T٭lb٭t there shall ply with hackney chair,
And Patriot Betty fix her fruit-shop there.
Like distant thunder, now the coach of state
Rolls o'er the bridge, that groans beneath its weight.
The Court have crost the stream; the sports begin;
Now N٭٭l preaches of rebellion's sin:
And as the powers of his strong pathos rise,
Lo, brazen tears fall from Sir Fl٭٭r's eyes.
While skulking round the pews, that babe of grace,
Who ne'er before at sermon shew'd his face,
See Jemmy Twitcher shambles; stop! stop thief!
He's stol'n the E٭ of D٭nb٭h's handkerchief.
Let B٭rr٭t٭n arrest him in mock fury,
And M٭٭d hang the knave without a jury.
But hark the voice of battle shouts from far,
The Jews and Macaroni's are at war:
The Jews prevail, and, thund'ring from the stocks,
They seize, they bind, they circumcise C٭s F٭.
Fair Schw٭٭٭n smiles the sport to see,
And all the Maids of Honour cry Te! He!
    Be these the rural pastimes that attend
Great B٭nsw٭k's leisure: these shall best unbend
His royal mind, whene'er, from state withdraw'n,
He treads the velvet of his Richmond lawn;
These shall prolong his Asiatic dream,
Tho' Europe's balance trembles on it's beam.
And thou, Sir William! while thy plastic hand
Creates each wonder, which thy Bard has plann'd,
While, as thy art commands, obsequious rise
Whate'er can please, or frighten, or surprize,
O! let that Bard his Knight's protection claim,
And share, like faithful Sancho, Quixote's fame.

Joseph Heely (fl. 1770s)

Heely's popular letters on three famous gardens are as leisurely and rambling as visits to the gardens themselves would have been. Since Hagley and The Leasowes are touched upon enough in this anthology, it is Enville (Plate 93), the seat of the Earl of Stamford, that is represented here. There was a thatched cottage, 'with its little circular lawn in front' and 'graceful clustering trees that verge the area, and form a perfect canopy over the building', a chapel dedicated to Shenstone, a shepherd's lodge in the Gothic taste, a rotunda in the Classical, an octagonal boat house and a Gothic billiard room presided over by busts of Homer and Cicero ('Ev'n in an ornament its place remark' was Pope's advice, rather neglected in this case). It is all eloquent of the landscape taste applied with delightfully personal aplomb. Heely responds well to these idiosyncratic features as well as to the compositional skills and design of its succeeding scenes; he surrenders himself with an earnest thoroughness to their various effects, noting in particular the distinctions between sublime and beautiful which Burke had established in 1756 and which came to be applied to different parts of a landscape garden.

from *Letters on the Beauties of Hagley,
Envil, and The Leasowes* (1777)

A large circuitous sheet of water, extends itself over an ample body of ground, in the midst of thousand natural charms, that description, I fear, will give you but a very faint idea of. The eye commonly fixes first on the object that is the greatest novelty, or the most apparently striking. In this gay, accomplished scene, perhaps that object is a cascade, well broken, fierce, and picturesque; tumbling down several distinct falls, and under a rude, grotesque arch of rock, emptying itself into a part of the pool, worn into a sort of creek by the violence of the torrent. I think I never saw so fine an effect from light and shade, as is here produced by the gloom of ever-greens and other trees, and the peculiar brightness of the foaming water—nor ever remember to have seen a place better, or more naturally adapted for a cascade than this, rolling down a narrow valley, covered with thicket, and within the bosom of so glorious a wood.

Above this cascade, in the midst of forest drapery, perspectively rises a small dusky antique building, in an elevated situation, far beyond the water falls, and on the brow of the shrubby dingle, while lower on the left, the eye is led to a farm-house, half hid, and peeping above the trees; from whence opens an extensive lawn running down to the lake, adorned with single trees, some groupes, and a thin compartment of grove on its extremity; a boundary exceedingly pleasing, and what is a very lively contrast to the bold and animated scenery on the other side the water falls.

The ample forest that mantles the roving precipitate hills there, wreathes about their brows, stealing sometimes down their gay sides, clad in the gayest verdure; again, sweeping up to a fanciful building called a gothic gateway, which it gracefully embosoms; from whence the polished lawn spreads down to the pool, stretching towards the house, and loses itself within a detached grove of ancient oaks, and elms.

The boat-house from whence this landscape is taken, is an octagon, prettily ornamented within by festoons of flowers, and medallions in stucco. A curious sliding window, that opens to the water, adorned with painted glass in whimsical groupes of grotesque figures, is certainly very ornamental; but this stained glass, amusing as it is to the generality of people, excludes, when the window is shut, a variety of objects infinitely more interesting . . .

While I mused within these bowers, attentive to the variety about me, I could not help wishing the heads of the banks were more closely bushed, particularly on the opposite side, as it would encourage an opacous cast, which I cannot but think is now wanting, and what is indisputably a necessary accompaniment: places that are meant to be sequestered, and gloomy, never can be rendered too much so; nor ought any point to be visible, but what favours the character: the very dashing of the water only, sufficiently convinces me, that whatever taste may add about it, should be analogous, such as a close united shade, uncouth rudeness, scars of rock, ivy twisted trees, and cavernous banks.

Thus a little higher, between the different plunges of the cascades, you will find every thing, by a proper attention, conformable, natural, and expressive; instanced particularly in a single plank only, thrown across the stream — this, though I believe but little noticed, is one of those graceful objects that make themselves great from their simplicity, and even meanness.

Nothing can be more engaging than the walk from the seat, to the outside of this romantic spot — the impetuous torrent of one cascade rushing down a chasm near your foot — another seen at a distance through the trees, pouring over rocks its whitened foam; and as you stand on my favourite plank, looking down the sloping channel edged with laurels, the boat-house, over the broad lake, will hold you long in admiration of its beauty, and picturesque situation — turning to the cascade behind you, and then to its troubled water below, you have other feelings — it is true, nothing was ever better formed to create surprize, and pleasure; but at the same time one cannot help being affected with a sort of terror, standing in the very midst of an incessant roar of water, and seeing it break with such resistless fury — I declare I considered myself as a victim devoted to its rage, and expected every moment, upon some sudden burst, to be washed, without any kind of ceremony, down the torrent, into the dreary hollow below.

After emerging from this inimitable scene, the path winds precipitately by the reservoirs, which I wish were better hid, into a wild and gloomy copse,

93 Enville, Shropshire. Detail of aquatint by H. F. James,
Dodd and Cartwright, *c.* 1800

where you meet with a commodious cold bath, to which soon after succeeds a
scene entirely pastoral; composed of a farm-house, fold, fields of rich herbage, stored with cattle; a straggling bed of alders, hazles, willows, and a
green hanging meadow, surrounded by woody declivities . . .

I long lingered here in much pleasure, and left it with reluctance, to
pierce the interior part of the wood; where, in a cool and welcome shade,
under the spreading arms of a large oak, I found a bench that faced a deep dip
of thicket covered ground; over which, on a steep knole, fringed by the
stately forest, a rotundo stands uncommonly attractive.

There is nothing more desirable, or eases the eye so much as a break, now
and then, to a lawn, or to some fanciful object, in the midst of a gloomy and
extensive wood — a fine opportunity of this sort, here offers to take in both;
and that in great beauty, only by extirpating the underwood, in a manner to
shew the inequality of the ground, and the object more distinctly — were
this properly executed, no scene in the whole domain, would have a finer
effect.

I now walked along a path, whose sides are so thickly interwoven with
trees, copse wood, and bushes — so impervious — that no opening is left for
a sun-beam to chear the solitary way.

In passing from the bench under the oak, I found but little variation,
except in the ground, which again forms itself into a very steep hill, luxur-
iantly mantled as before. Here you will find another path inclining to the
right, which instead of pursuing, as it leads only to the rotundo, I mounted the
hill, and found soon after, the forest give way to a beautiful and capacious
plain, at once the glory, and the pride of Envil — the transition does not
surprize, but it fills the eye as it reposes on the slanting hill covered with
numerous groups of sheep, with ineffable pleasure.

Every step I took, quickened my expectation — the distant country broke upon me by degrees, till at length the grand circle was held up in all its magnificence — Those pathetic lines of Milton, as I slowly wandered along the broad sublime level, in admiration of the splendid prospect, wrought on my feelings, and I could not help repeating aloud, "These are thy glorious works, &c." . . .

Envil cannot be called a park, nor can it very consistently be called a farm. It partakes of all the principal divisions of gardening, and may be equally distinguished in the light of park, garden, farm, and riding — yet were it confined to the first only, on some considerations, it might be thought more in character, and more relative. A palace and a park ought ever to be inseparable: the one naturally calls for the other; and when united by the powers of genius, in all the luxuriance of the splendid and the beautiful — I mean that splendor and beauty, which is built upon the principles of simplicity — both appear evidently perfect.

Should the park scheme ever take effect, which I have been informed has been thought on, Envil, pleasing as it is at present, would, I doubt not, be rendered much more so, and derive such advantages in the change of character, as to shine indisputably one of the most accomplished places to be met with — once more.

Vicesimus Knox (1752–1821)

Included in the author's *Essays Moral and Literary* (two volumes, 1778 and 1779), the following unstrenuous meditation in the benevolent tradition of Shaftesbury considers man's predisposition to be pleased by gardens. Like the Vicar of Wakefield, who usually sat with his family 'to enjoy an extensive landscape in the calm of the evening', Knox indulges a mild pastoralism ('Rural scenes . . . are all capable of exciting the gently agreeable emotions') that continued to attach itself to a taste for landscape gardens. His invocation of 'a picturesque imagination', too, has a vaguely sentimental air, as yet unaffected by the attempts of Gilpin, Price and Knight to schematize and make it more rigorous.

'On the Pleasures of a Garden' (1779)

NOT he alone is to be esteemed a benefactor to mankind, who makes an useful discovery; but he also, who can point out and recommend an innocent pleasure. Of this kind are the pleasures arising from the observation of nature; and they are highly agreeable to every taste uncorrupted by vicious indulgence.

There will always be many in a rich and civilized country, who, as they are born to the enjoyment of competent estates, engage not in business civil or professional. But the restless mind must either find or make an object. Pleasure, therefore, becomes, to the unemployed, a serious pursuit. Whatever is its essence, and whatever the declaimer may urge against it, pleasure will be sought by all who possess the liberty of election. It becomes then incumbent on the moralist, not only to urge the performance of duty, but to exhibit objects that please without enervating the mind, and gratify desire without corrupting the principles.

Rural scenes, of almost every kind, are delightful to the mind of man. The verdant plain, the flowery mead, the meandering stream, the playful lamb, the warbling of birds, are all capable of exciting the gently agreeable emotions. But the misfortune is, that the greater part are hurried on in the career of life with too great rapidity to be able to give attention to that which solicits no passion. The darkest habitation in the dirtiest street of the metropolis, where money can be earned, has greater charms, with many, than the groves of Hagley.

Yet the patron of refined pleasure, the elegant Epicurus, fixed the seat of his enjoyment in a garden. He thought a tranquil spot, furnished with the united sweets of art and nature, the best adapted to delicate repose. And even the severer philosophers of antiquity were wont to discourse in the shade of a spreading tree, in some cultivated plantation.

It is obvious, on intuition, that nature often intended solely to please the eye. She decorates the flowret, that springs beneath our feet, in all the perfection of external beauty. She has clothed the garden with a constant succession of various hues. Even the leaves of the tree undergo a pleasing vicissitude. The fresh verdure they exhibit in the spring, the various shades they assume in summer, the yellow and russet tinge of autumn, and the nakedness of winter, afford a constant pleasure to a picturesque imagination. From the snow-drop to the moss-rose, the flower-garden displays an infinite variety of shape and colour. The taste of the florist has been ridiculed as trifling; yet, surely, without reason. Did nature bring forth the tulip and the lily, the rose and the honeysuckle, to be neglected by the haughty pretender to superior reason? To omit a single social duty for the cultivation of a polyanthus, were ridiculous as well as criminal; but to pass by the beauties lavished before us, without observing them, is no less ingratitude than stupidity. A bad heart finds little amusement but in a communication with the active world where scope is given for the indulgence of malignant passions; but an amiable disposition is commonly known by a taste for the beauties of the animal and the vegetable world.

The northern countries of Europe are not the best adapted to the natural delights of rural scenery. Our vernal seasons, which the poets celebrate in all the luxuriance of description, are commonly rendered cold and uncomfortable, by the long continuance of an eastern wind. Our poets borrowed their ideas of a spring from the poets of Italy, who collected theirs from nature. A genial day in April, is among us the subject of general congratulation. And, while the lilac blossoms, and the laburnum drops its golden clusters, the shivering possessor of them is constrained to seek warmth at the side of his chimney. Yet, from the temperature of our climate we derive a beauty unknown in the gardens of a warmer country. Few objects are more pleasing than the smooth lawn; but the soft verdure, which constitutes its beauty, is not to be found in more southern climates. It is certainly true, that the rarity of our truly vernal weather, like that of other delights, increases the pleasure of it; and it is probable, for this reason, that an Englishman, notwithstanding his complaints against his atmosphere, enjoys the pleasures of a garden in their full perfection. A fine day, says Temple, is a kind of sensual pleasure; but surely it would cease to be such, if every day were fine.

A practical attention to a garden, by many, is esteemed degrading. It is true, that pastoral and agricultural manners, if we may believe the dignified descriptions of Virgil, are greatly degenerated. The employments of shepherds and husbandmen are now mean and sordid. The care of the garden is left to a peasant. Nor is it unreasonable to assign the work, which wearies without amusement, to those, who are sufficiently amused by the prospect of their wages. But the operations of grafting, of inoculating, of pruning, of transplanting, are curious experiments in natural philosophy; and, that they are pleasing as well as curious, those can testify, who remember what they felt on seeing their attempts succeed.

Among the employments suitable to old age, Cicero has enumerated gardening. It requires no great exertion of mind or body; and its satisfactions are of that kind which please without agitation. Their beneficial influence on health, is an additional reason for an attention to them at an age when infirmities abound.

In almost every description of the seats of the blessed, ideas of a garden seem to have predominated. The word Paradise itself is synonymous with garden. The fields of Elysium, that sweet region of poesy, are adorned with all that imagination can conceive to be delightful. Some of the most pleasing passages of Milton are those in which he represents the happy Pair engaged in cultivating their blissful abode. Poets have always been delighted with the beauties of a garden. Lucan is represented by Juvenal as reposing in his garden. Virgil's Georgics prove him to have been captivated with rural scenes; though, to the surprise of his readers, he has not assigned a book to the subject of a garden. Our Shenstone made it his study; but, with all his taste and fondness for it, he was not happy in it. The captivating scenes which he created at the Leasowes, afforded him, it is said, little pleasure in the absence of spectators. The truth is, he made the embellishment of his grounds, which should have been the amusement of his life, the business of it; and involved himself in such troubles, by the expences it occasioned, as necessarily excluded tranquil enjoyment.

It is the lot of few to possess territories like his, sufficiently extensive to constitute an ornamented farm. Still fewer are capable of supporting the expence of preserving it in good condition. But let not the rich suppose they have appropriated the pleasures of a garden. The possessor of an acre, or a smaller portion, may receive a real pleasure, from observing the progress of vegetation, even in a culinary plant. A very limited tract, properly attended to, will furnish ample employment for an individual. Nor let it be thought a mean care; for the same hand that raised the cedar, formed the hyssop on the wall. Even the orchard, cultivated solely for advantage, exhibits beauties unequalled in the shrubbery; nor can the green-house produce an appearance to match the blossom of the apple and the almond.

Amusement reigns, says Dr. Young, man's great demand. Happy were it, if the amusement of managing a garden were more generally relished. It would surely be more conducive to health, and the preservation of our faculties to extreme old age, were that time which is now devoted to the dice and to the card-table, spent in the open air, and in active employment.

Thomas Jefferson (1743–1826)

While the finer points of picturesque gardening were debated in England, its gardens were the object of visits and admiration by increasing numbers of foreign tourists. One of the most distinguished of these was the future third President of the United States, Thomas Jefferson, who had drafted the Declaration of Independence, adopted in 1776. For part of his tour Jefferson was accompanied by John Adams. Jefferson was always 'devoted to the garden' and to the improvement and maintenance of his estates and of the American landscape generally. He used Whately's *Observations* (see pp. 301 ff.) as his guide in England, where he was obviously greatly impressed by what he saw: he wrote to a friend back home that English gardening 'is the article in which [that country] surpasses all the earth. I mean their pleasure gardening. This, indeed, went far beyond my ideas.' The effects of his visit became visible in the landscaping of his grounds at Monticello, in Virginia, notably in plans for a *ferme ornée* and for 'lawns and clumps of Trees, the lawns opening so as to give advantageous catches of prospect'. The manuscript of Jefferson's tour of English gardens is in the Swem Library of the College of William and Mary at Williamsburg, Virginia.

'Memorandums Made on a Tour to Some of the Gardens in England' (1786)

Memorandums made on a tour to some of the gardens in England described by Whateley in his book on gardening. while his descriptions in point of style are models of perfect elegance and classical correctness, they are as remarkeable for their exactness. I always walked over the gardens with his book in my hand, examined with attention the particular spots he described, found them so justly characterised by him as to be easily recognized, and saw with wonder that his fine imagination had never been able to seduce him from the truth. my enquiries were directed chiefly to such practical things as might enable me to estimate the expence of making and maintaining a garden in that style. my journey was in the months of March & April 1786.

Cheswick. Belongs to D. of Devonshire. a garden about 6. acres; the Octagonal dome has an ill effect, both within & without; the garden shews still too much of art; an obelisk of very ill effect. another in the middle of a pond useless.

Hampton court. old fashioned. — clipt yews grown wild.

Twickenham. Pope's original garden $3\frac{1}{2}$ a^s Sr Wm Stanhope added $1\frac{1}{2}$ acre.

333

this is a long narrow slope, grass & trees in the middle, walk all round. *Now S*. *Wellbore Ellis's.* obelisk at bottom of Pope's garden as monument to his mother. inscription. Ah! Editha matrum optuma, mulierum amantissima, Vale. the house about 30. yds. from the Thames; the ground shelves gently to the water side. on the back of the house passes the street, & beyond that the garden. the grotto is under the street, & goes out level to the water. in the center of the garden a mound with a spiral walk round it. a rookery.

Esher place. the house in a bottom near the river. on the other side the ground rises pretty much. the road by which we come to the house forms a dividing line in the middle of the front. on the right are heights, rising one beyond & above another, with clumps of trees. on the farthest a temple. a hollow filled up with a clump of trees, the tallest in the bottom, so that the top is quite flat. on the left the ground descends. clumps of trees. the clumps on each hand balance finely. a most lovely mixture of concave & convex. the garden is of about 45. a^s besides the park which joins. belongs to Lady Francis Pelham.

Claremont. Ld Clive's. nothing remarkeable.

Paynshill. mr. Hopkins. 323. acres. garden & park all in one. well described by Whateley. grotto said to have cost 7000.£. Whateley says one of the bridges is of stone. but both are now of wood. the lower 60.f. high. there is too much evergreen. the Dwelling house built by Hopkins. ill situated. he has not been there in 5. years. he lived there 4. years while building the present house. it is not finished. it's architecture is incorrect. a Doric temple beautiful.

Woburn. belongs to Ld Peters. Ld Loughborough is the present tenant for 2. lives. 4. people to the farm. 4. to the pleasure garden. 4. to the kitchen garden. all are intermixed, the pleasure garden being merely a highly ornamented walk through & round the divisions of the farm & kitchen garden.

Caversham. sold by Ld Cadogan to Maj^r Marsac. 25. a^s of garden, 400. a^s of park, 6. a^s of kitchen garden. a large lawn, seperated by a sunk fence from the garden, appears to be part of it. a straight broad gravel walk passes before the front & parallel to it, terminated on the right by a Doric temple, & opening at the other end on a fine prospect. this straight walk has an ill effect. the lawn in front, which is pasture, well disposed with clumps of trees.

Wotton. now belongs to the M. of Buckingham, son of George Grenville. the lake covers 50. a^s the river 5. a^s the bason 15. a^s the little river 2. a^s = 72. a^s of water. the lake & great river are on a level. they fall into the bason 5.f. below, & that again into the little river 5.f. lower. these waters lie in form of an L. the house is in middle of open side, front[ing] the angle. a walk goes round the whole, 3. miles in circumference, & containing with it about 300. a^s sometimes it passes close to the water, sometimes so far off as to leave large pasture ground between it & water. but 2. hands to keep the pleasure grounds in order. much neglected. the water affords 2000. brace of carp a year. there is a Palladian bridge of which I think Whateley does not speak.

Stowe. belongs to the M. of Buckingham, son of G. Grenville, & who takes it from Ld Temple. 15. men & 18. boys employed in keeping pleasure grounds. within the walk are considerable portions separated by inclosures & used for pasture. the Egyptian pyramid is almost entirely taken down by the late

Ld Temple, to erect a building there, in commemoration of mr. Pitt. but he died before beginning it and nothing is done to it yet. the grotto, and two rotundas are taken away. there are 4. levels of water, receiving it one from the other. the bason contains 7. a^s the lake below that 10. a^s Kent's building is called the temple of Venus. the inclosure is entirely by ha! ha! at each end of the front line there is a recess like the bastion of a fort. in one of these is the temple of Friendship. in the other the temple of Venus. they are seen the one from the other, the line of sight passing, not thro' the garden, but through the country parallel to the line of the garden. this has a good effect. in the approach to Stowe, you are brought a mile through a straight avenue, pointing to the Corinthian arch & to the house, till you get to the Arch. then you turn short to the right. the straight approach is very ill. the Corinthian arch has a very useless appearance, inasmuch as it has no pretension to any destination. instead of being an object from the house, it is an obstacle to a very pleasing distant prospect. the Graecian valley being clear of trees, while the hill on each side is covered with them, is much deepened to appearance.

Leasowes. in Shropshire. — now the property of mr Horne by purchase. 150. a^s within the walk. the waters small. this is not even an ornamented farm. it is only a grazing farm with a path round it. here & there a seat of board, rarely any thing better. architecture has contributed nothing. the obelisk is of brick. Shenstone had but 300.£ a year, & ruined himself by what he did to

94 Hagley, Worcestershire. Engraving by Smith and Vivares, 1749

this farm. it is said that he died of the heart-aches which his debts occasioned him. the part next the road is of red earth; that on the further part grey. the 1st & 2^d cascades are beautiful. the landscape at N°. 18. & prospect at 32. are fine. the walk through the wood is umbrageous & pleasing. the whole arch of prospect may be of 90°. many of the inscriptions are lost.

Hagley. [Plate 94] now Ld Wescot. 1000. a^s no distinction between park & garden. both blended, but more of the character of garden 8. or 9. labourers keep it in order. between 2. & 300. deer in it. some few of them red deer. they breed sometimes with the fallow. this garden occupying a descending hollow between the Clent & Witchbury hills, with the spurs from those hills, there is no level in it for a spacious water. there are therefore only some small ponds. from one of these there is a fine cascade; but it can only be occasionally, by opening the sluice. this is in a small, dark, deep hollow, with recesses of stone in the banks on every side. in one of these is a Venus pudique, turned half round as if inviting you with her into the recess. there is another cascade seen from the Portico or the bridge. the castle is triangular, with a round tower at each angle, one only entire; it seems to be between 40. & 50. f. high. the ponds yield a great deal of trout. the walks are scarcely gravelled.

Blenheim. 2500. a^s of which 200. is garden, 150. water, 12. kitchen garden, & the rest park. 200. people employed to keep it in order, & to make alterations & additions. about 50. of these employed in pleasure grounds. the turf is mowed once in 10. days. in summer. about 2000. fallow deer in the park, & 2. or 3000. sheep. the palace of H.2. was remaining till taken down by Sarah, widow of the 1st D. of Marlborough. it was on a round spot levelled by art, near what is now water & but a little above it. the island was a part of the high road leading to the palace. Rosamond's bower was near where is now a little grove about 200. yards from the palace. the well is near where the bower was; the water here is very beautiful, & very grand. the cascade from the lake a fine one. except this the garden has no great beauties. it is not laid out in fine lawns and woods, but the trees are scattered thinly over the ground, & every here & there small thickets of shrubs, in oval raised beds, cultivated, & flowers among the shrubs. the gravelled walks are broad, art appears too much. there are but a few seats in it, & nothing of architecture more dignified. there is no one striking position in it. there has been a great addition to the length of the river since Whateley wrote.

Enfield chase. one of the 4. lodges. garden about 60. a^s originally by Ld Chatham, now in the tenure of Dr Beaver, who married the daughter of mr. Sharpe. the lease lately renewed. not in good repair. the water very fine. would admit of great improvement by extending walks. &c. to the principle water at the bottom of the lawn.

Moor Park. the lawn about 30. a^s a piece of ground up the hill of 6. a^s — a small lake. — clumps of Spruce firs. — surrounded by walk. separately inclosed. destroys unity. the property of mr Rous, who bought of Sr Thomas Dundas. the building superb. the principle front a Corinthian portico of 4 columns. in front of the wings a colonnade, Ionic, subordinate. back front a terras, 4. Corinthian pilasters. pulling down wings of buildings. removing deer. wants water.

William Gilpin (1724-1804)

Gilpin's visit to Stowe in 1747 (see p. 254) inaugurated his application of picturesque principles to landscape gardens. But his first use of the term 'picturesque' occurs in the *Essay on Prints* (1768), where it is defined as 'that kind of beauty which would look well in a picture'. The word had been used before mainly to imply *graphic* or *pictorial*, but by 1801 a supplement to Johnson's *Dictionary* allowed a range of meanings which include what is pleasing to the eye, what strikes the viewer as singular or appeals to him with the force of a painting, what is expressible in painting or would either afford a good subject for a painted landscape or help in conceiving one. Gilpin's publications had assisted enormously in extending this definition. Encouraged by Thomas Gray and William Mason, he brought out his first picturesque tour in 1782, *Observations on the River Wye, and Several Parts of South Wales &c. Relative Chiefly to Picturesque Beauty*; others followed — that on the Lake District in 1786, on the Highlands in 1789 — until the final, posthumously published volume of 1809. It cannot be claimed that Gilpin initiated this vogue for travel in search of picturesque experience, but he did extend its popularity, thereby educating the sight of innumerable readers, and he did attempt to provide it with firm principles. The three originators of picturesque travel as a genre of writing were probably Thomas Gray, whose published letters of 1775 included his remarks on a tour to the Lakes; Arthur Young, whose *Tours* began to appear in 1768 and although ostensibly concerned with agriculture devoted much space to 'picturesque elegance'; and

95 William Gilpin, watercolour, late 1780s

Dr John Brown. This last's famous letter on the Lakes was widely known even before its publication in 1768: it argued that the 'full perfection' of the scenery around Keswick 'would require the united powers of Claude, Salvator and Poussin'. In the same landscapes Gray made frequent use of his Claude-glass, a convex mirror on darkened ground in which scenery appeared as if painted and therefore, one deduces, much more agreeable. That Gilpin shared these predilections is immediately apparent in the oval plates to his volumes which present landscapes as rather generalized compositions (see Plate 95). His delight in picturesque scenery corresponds to, because it has grown out of, his absorption in tracing surprises, variety and distant discoveries in a painted or engraved landscape. The extract here relates to park scenery, that ambiguous territory between the 'polished' or beautiful gardens near the house and the rough or picturesque (the terms are identical for Gilpin) scenes beyond. Gilpin, as the final sentence makes clear, prefers the latter. But what draws him to the former is its *composition*; for he considered Nature's great defect to be in the ordering of her elements, which could be remedied equally by the landscape gardener or the picturesque traveller who was encouraged to re-assemble the various features of a scene into a more pleasing whole.

from *Remarks on Forest Scenery* (1791)

FROM *clumps* we naturally proceed to *park-scenery*, which is generally composed of *combinations of clumps*, interspersed with lawns. It is seldom composed of any large district of wood; which is the characteristic of forest-scenery.

The park, which is a species of landscape little known, except in England, is one of the noblest appendages of a great house. Nothing gives a mansion so much dignity as these home demeisns; nor contributes more to mark it's consequence. A great house, in a course of years, naturally acquires space around it. A noble park therefore is the natural appendage of an ancient mansion.

To the size, and grandeur of the house, the park should be proportioned. *Blenheim-castle* with a paddock around it; or a small villa in the middle of Woodstock-park, would be equally out of place.

The house should stand nearly in the centre of the park; that is, it should have ample room about it on every side. Petworth-house, one of the grandest piles in England, loses much of it's grandeur from being placed at the extremity of the park, where it is elbowed by a church-yard.

The *exact spot* depends intirely on the ground. There are grand situations of various kinds. In general, houses are built first; and parks are added afterwards by the occasional removal of inclosures. A great house stands most nobly on an elevated knoll, from whence it may overlook the distant country; while the woods of the park skreen the regularity of the intervening cultivation. Or it stands well on the side of a valley, which winds along it's front; and is adorned with wood, or a natural stream hiding, and discovering itself among the clumps at the bottom of the vale. Or it stands with dignity, as Longleat does, in the centre of demeisns, which shelve gently down to it on every side. — Even on a dead flat I have seen a house draw beauties around it. At the seat of the late Mr. Bilson Legge, (now lord Stawel's) in the middle of Holt-forest, a lawn unvaried by a single swell, is yet varied with clumps of different forms, receding behind each other, in so pleasing a manner, as to make an agreeable scene.

By these observations I mean only to shew, that in whatever part of a park a house may have been originally placed, it can hardly have been placed so awkwardly, but that, in some way or other, the scenery may be happily adapted to it. There are some situations indeed so very untoward, that scarce any remedy can be applied: as when the front of a house immediately urges on a rising ground. But such awkward situations are rare; and in general, the variety of landscape is such, that it may almost always be brought in one form, or other, to serve the purposes of beauty. The many improvements of the ingenious Mr. Brown, in various parts of England, bear witness to the truth of these observations. — The beauty however of park-scenery is undoubtedly *best* displayed on a *varied surface* — where the ground swells, and falls — where hanging lawns, skreened with wood, are connected with vallies — and where one part is continually playing in contrast with another.

As the park is an appendage of the house, it follows, that it should participate of it's neatness, and elegance. Nature, in all her great walks of landscape, observes this accommodating rule. She seldom passes abruptly from one mode of scenery to another; but generally connects different species of landscape by some third species, which participates of both. A mountainous country rarely sinks immediately into a level one; the swellings and heavings of the earth, grow gradually less. Thus as the house is connected with the country through the medium of the park; the park should partake of the neatness of the one, and of the wildness of the other.

As the park is a scene either planted by art, or, if naturally woody, artificially improved, we expect a beauty, and contrast in it's *clumps,* which we do not look for in the wild scenes of nature. We expect to see it's lawns, and their appendages, contrasted with each other, in shape, size, and disposition; from which a variety of artificial scenes will arise. We expect, that when trees are left standing as *individuals,* they should be the most beautiful of their kind, elegant and well-balanced. We expect, that all offensive trumpery, and all the rough luxuriance of undergrowth, should be removed; unless where it is necessary to thicken, or connect a scene; or hide some staring boundary. In the wild scenes of nature we have grander exhibitions, but greater deformities, than are generally met with in the works of art. As we seldom meet with these sublime passages in improved landscape; it would be unpardonable if any thing disgusting should appear.

In the park-scene we wish for no expensive ornament. Temples, Chinese-bridges, obelisks, and all the laboured works of art, suggest inharmonious ideas. If a bridge be necessary, let it be elegantly plain. If a deer-shed, or a keeper's lodge be required; let the fashion of each be as simple, as it's use. Let nothing appear with ostentation, or parade. — Within restrictions however of this kind we mean not to include piles of *superior grandeur*. Such a palace as Blenheim-castle distributes it's greatness far and wide. There, if the bridge be immense, or the obelisk superb, it is only what we naturally expect. It is the chain of ideas properly carried on, and *gradually lost*. My remarks regard only such houses, as may be rich indeed, and elegant; but have nothing in them of *superior magnificence*.

One ornament of this kind, I should be inclined to allow; and that is a handsome gate at the entrance of the park: but it should be proportioned in richness, and elegance to the house; and should also correspond with it in stile. It should raise the first impression of what you are to expect. Warwick-castle requires a mode of entrance very different from lord Scarsdale's at Kettlestone; and Burleigh-house, very different from both. The park-gate of Sion-house is certainly elegant; but it raises the idea of a stile of architecture, which you must drop, when you arrive at the house.

The road also through the park should bear the same proportion. It should be spacious, or moderate, like the house it approaches. Let it wind: but let it not take any deviation, which is not well accounted for. To have the convenience of winding along a valley, or passing a commodious bridge, or avoiding a wood, or a piece of water, any traveller would naturally wish to deviate a little; and obstacles of this kind, if necessary, must be interposed. Mr. Brown was often very happy in creating these artificial obstructions.

From every part of the approach, and from the ridings, and favourite walks about the park, let all the boundaries be secreted. A view of paling, tho in some cases it may be picturesque, is in general disgusting.

If there be a *natural* river, or a real ruin in the scene, it may be a happy circumstance: let the best use be made of it: but I should be cautious in advising the *creation* of either. At least, I have rarely seen either ruins, or rivers well manufactured. Mr. Brown, I think, has failed more in river-making than in any of his attempts. An artificial lake has sometimes a good effect; but neither propriety, nor beauty can arise from it, unless the heads and extremities of it are prefectly well managed, and concealed: and after all, the success is hazardous. You must always suppose it a portion of a larger piece of water; and it is not easy to carry on the imposition. If the house be magnificent, it seldom receives much benefit from an artificial production of this kind. Grandeur is rarely produced.

> Seldom art
> Can emulate that magnitude sublime,
> Which spreads the native lake; and failing there,
> Her works betray their character, and name;
> And dwindle into pools

The most natural inhabitants of parks are fallow deer; and very beautiful they are: but flocks of sheep, and herds of cattle are more useful; and, in my opinion, more beautiful. Sheep particularly are very ornamental in a park.

Their colour is just that dingy hue, which contrasts with the verdure of the ground; and the flakiness of their wool is rich, and picturesque. I should wish them however to wear their natural livery; and not to be patched with letters, and daubed over with red-ochre. To see the side of a hill spread with groups of sheep — or to see them through openings among the boles of trees, at a little distance, with a gleam of light falling upon them, is very picturesque.

As the garden, or *pleasure-ground*, as it is commonly called, approaches nearer to the house, than the park, it takes of course a higher polish. Here the lawns are shorn, instead of being grazed. The roughness of the road is changed into an elegant gravel walk; and knots of flowers, and flowering shrubs are introduced, yet blended with clumps of forest-trees, which connect it with the park. Single trees also take their station here with great propriety. The spreading oak, or elm, are no disgrace to the most ornamented scene. It is the property of these noble plants to harmonize with every species of landscape. They equally become the forest, and the lawn: only here they should be beautiful in their kind; and luxuriant in their growth. Neither the scathed, nor the unbalanced oak would suit a polished situation.

Here too, if the situation suits it, the elegant temple may find a place. But it is an expensive, a hazardous, and often a useless decoration. If more than one however be introduced in the same view, they croud the scene, unless it be very extensive. More than two should in no case be admitted. In the most polished landscape, unless nature, and simplicity lead the way, the whole will be deformed . . .

FROM scenes of art, let us hasten to the chief object of our pursuit, the wild scenes of nature — the *wood* — the *copse* — the *glen* — and *open-grove*.

Richard Payne Knight (1750–1824)

Though Gilpin could admire Brown's improvements (see p. 339), he obviously preferred the 'varied surface' and roughness of picturesque scenery. In this he was at one with Knight, whose poem, *The Landscape*, expounds extreme picturesque doctrine in 'fiction's flowery dress'. But unlike Gilpin, Knight found Brown's designs dull and vapid; they could not live up to his visual education in the schools of Claude, the Dutch landscapists and, above all, Salvator Rosa. This is vividly demonstrated (and with more point than the verses) by the engravings of two contrasted scenes (Plates 96a and 96b) published with the poem. Brown, and more especially Brown's facile imitators, lost any chance of intricacy and mystery in their landscapes; instead they relied upon such clichés as the belt of trees around an estate, tidy clumps of trees among smooth lawns and mechanically serpentine lines. Yet Knight resists Chambers' Chinese solutions to this problem of boredom, preferring to make scenery interesting by a proper manipulation of indigenous items. Knight's *Analytical Inquiry into the Principles of Taste*, eleven years later, makes clear what his verses only imply: that the picturesque is in effect a theory of association, a function of the imagination, albeit rather a mechanical one. Hence the advocates of picturesque landscapes may be seen as re-affirming the long-established principle that a garden must answer mental variety. *The Landscape* suggested this through the conventional invocation of nymphs and dryads, who could find no sanctuary among Brown's bare and tidy scenes; these spirits of the wild were a method of alluding to our thoughts and feelings among landscape, just as their presence in scenes by Claude or Poussin alerts a viewer to myth and *genius loci*. But another mode was to describe the mind's reactions, its associations, as such novelists as Sterne or such philosophers as Alison had done by the time Knight published his second work. It is this version of the picturesque, as a stimulation of minds 'richly stored', that occupies Knight in the prose extract.

from *The Landscape, A Didactic Poem* (1794)

Component parts in all the eye requires:
One formal mass for ever palls and tires.
To make the Landscape grateful to the sight,
Three points of distance always should unite;
And howsoe'er the view may be confin'd,
Three mark'd divisions we shall always find:
Not more, where Claude extends his prospect wide,
O'er Rome's Campania to the Tyrrhene tide,

96a and b Two contrasting etchings by Hearne and Pouncy from
Richard Payne Knight, *The Landscape*, 1794

(Where tow'rs and temples, mould'ring to decay,
In pearly air appear to die away.
And the soft distance, melting from the eye,
Dissolves its forms into the azure sky),
Than where, confin'd to some sequester'd rill,
Meek Hobbima presents the village mill:—
Not more, where great Salvator's mountains rise,
And hide their craggy summits in the skies;
While tow'ring clouds in whirling eddies roll,
And bursting thunders seem to shake the pole;
Than in the ivy'd cottage of Ostade,
Waterloe's copse, or Rysdael's low cascade.
 Though oft o'erlook'd, the parts which are most near
Are ever found of most importance here;
For though in nature oft the wand'ring eye
Roams to the distant fields, and skirts the sky,
Where curiosity its look invites,
And space, not beauty, spreads out its delights;
Yet in the picture all delusions fly,
And nature's genuine charms we there descry;
The composition rang'd in order true,
Brings every object fairly to the view;
And, as the field of vision is confin'd,
Shews all its parts collected to the mind.
 Hence let us learn, in real scenes, to trace
The true ingredients of the painter's grace;
To lop redundant parts, the coarse refine,
Open the crowded, and the scanty join.
But, ah! in vain:— See yon fantastic band,
With charts, pedometers, and rules in hand,
Advance triumphant, and alike lay waste
The forms of nature, and the works of taste!
T'improve, adorn, and polish, they profess;
But shave the goddess, whom they come to dress;
Level each broken bank and shaggy mound,
And fashion all to one unvaried round;
One even round, that ever gently flows,
Nor forms abrupt, nor broken colours knows;
But, wrapt all o'er in everlasting green,
Makes one dull, vapid, smooth, and tranquil scene.
 Arise, great poet [i.e. Virgil], and again deplore
The fav'rite reeds that deck'd thy Mincius' shore!
Protect the branches, that in Haemus shed
Their grateful shadows o'er thy aching head;
Shav'd to the brink, our brooks are taught to flow
Where no obtruding leaves or branches grow;
While clumps of shrubs bespot each winding vale,

Open alike to ev'ry gleam and gale;
Each secret haunt, and deep recess display'd,
And intricacy banish'd with its shade.
   Hence, hence! thou haggard fiend, however call'd,
Thin, meagre genius of the bare and bald;
Thy spade and mattock here at length lay down,
And follow to the tomb thy fav'rite Brown:
Thy fav'rite Brown, whose innovating hand
First dealt thy curses o'er this fertile land;
First taught the walk in formal spires to move,
And from their haunts the secret Dryads drove;
With clumps bespotted o'er the mountain's side,
And bade the stream 'twixt banks close shaven glide;
Banish'd the thickets of high-bow'ring wood,
Which hung, reflected, o'er the glassy flood;
Where screen'd and shelter'd from the heats of day,
Oft on the moss-grown stone repos'd I lay,
And tranquil view'd the limpid stream below,
Brown with o'erhanging shade, in circling eddies flow . . .

OFT when I've seen some lonely mansion stand,
Fresh from th' improver's desolating hand,
'Midst shaven lawns, that far around it creep
In one eternal undulating sweep;
And scatter'd clumps, that nod at one another,
Each stiffly waving to its formal brother;
Tir'd with th' extensive scene, so dull and bare,
To Heav'n devoutly I've address'd my pray'r, —
Again the moss-grown terraces to raise,
And spread the labyrinth's perplexing maze;
Replace in even lines the ductile yew,
And plant again the ancient avenue.
Some features then, at least, we should obtain,
To mark this flat, insipid, waving plain;
Some vary'd tints and forms would intervene,
To break this uniform, eternal green.
   E'en the trimm'd hedges, that inclos'd the field,
Some consolation to the eye might yield;
But even these are studiously remov'd,
And clumps and bareness only are approv'd.
Though the old system against nature stood,
At least in this, 'twas negatively good: —
Inclos'd by walls, and terraces, and mounds,
Its mischiefs were confin'd to narrow bounds;
Just round the house, in formal angles trac'd,
It mov'd responsive to the builder's taste;

Walls answer'd walls, and alleys, long and thin,
Mimick'd the endless passages within.
   But kings of yew, and goddesses of lead,
Could never far their baneful influence spread;
Coop'd in the garden's safe and narrow bounds,
They never dar'd invade the open grounds;
Where still the roving ox, or browsing deer,
From such prim despots kept the country clear;
While uncorrupted still, on every side,
The ancient forest rose in savage pride;
And in its native dignity display'd
Each hanging wood and ever verdant glade;
Where ev'ry shaggy shrub and spreading tree
Proclaim'd the seat of native liberty;
In loose and vary'd groups unheeded thrown,
And never taught the planter's care to own:
Some, tow'ring upwards, spread their arms in state;
And others, bending low, appear'd to wait:
While scatter'd thorns, brows'd by the goat and deer,
Rose all around, and let no lines appear.
   Such groups did Claude's light pencil often trace,
The foreground of some classic scene to grace;
Such, humble Waterloe, to nature true,
Beside the copse, or village pasture drew.
   But ah! how diff'rent is the formal lump
Which the improver plants, and calls a clump!
Break, break, ye nymphs, the fence that guards it round!
With browsing cattle, all its forms confound!
As chance or fate will have it, let it grow;—
Here spiring high;—there cut, or trampled low.
No apter ornament can taste provide
T' embellish beauty, or defect to hide;
If train'd with care and undiscover'd skill,
Its just department in the scene to fill;
But with reserve and caution be it seen,
Nor e'er surrounded by the shaven green;
But in the foreground boldly let it rise,
Or join'd with other features meet the eyes:
The distant mansion, seen beneath its shade,
Is often advantageously display'd:—
But here, once more, ye rural muses, weep
The ivy'd balustrades, and terrace steep;
Walls, mellow'd into harmony by time,
O'er which fantastic creepers us'd to climb;
While statues, labyrinths, and alleys, pent
Within their bounds, at least were innocent!
Our modern taste, alas! no limit knows:—

O'er hill, o'er dale, through woods and fields it flows;
Spreading o'er all its unprolific spawn,
In never-ending sheets of vapid lawn.
   True composition all extremes rejects,
And just proportions still, of all, selects;
Wood, water, lawn, in just gradation joins,
And each with artful negligence combines:
But still in level, or slow-rising ground,
The wood should always form th' exterior bound;
Not as a belt, encircling the domain,
Which the tir'd eye attempts to trace in vain;
But as a bolder outline to the scene
Than the unbroken turf's smooth even green.
But if some distant hill o'er all arise,
And mix its azure colours with the skies;
Or some near mountain its rough summits shew,
And bound with broken crags the Alpine view;
Or rise, with even slope and gradual swell,
Like the broad cone, or wide-extended bell;—
Never attempt, presumptuous, to o'erspread
With starv'd plantations its bleak, barren head:
Nature herself the rash design withstands,
And guards her wilds from innovating hands;
Which, if successful, only would disgrace
Her giant limbs with fripp'ry, fringe, and lace . . .
   The cover'd seat, that shelters from the storm,
May oft a feature in the Landscape form;
Whether compos'd of native stumps and roots,
It spreads the creeper's rich fantastic shoots;
Or, rais'd with stones, irregularly pil'd,
It seems some cavern, desolate and wild:
But still of dress and ornament beware;
And hide each formal trace of art with care:
Let clust'ring ivy o'er its sides be spread,
And moss and weeds grow scatter'd o'er its head.
   The stately arch, high-rais'd with massive stone;
The pond'rous flag, that forms a bridge alone;
The prostrate tree, or rudely propt-up beam,
That leads the path across the foaming stream;
May each the scene with diff'rent beauty grace,
If shewn with judgment in its proper place.
But false refinement vainly strives to please,
With the thin, fragile bridge of the Chinese;
Light and fantastical, yet stiff and prim,
The child of barren fancy turn'd to whim . . .
   The quarry long neglected, and o'ergrown
With thorns, that hang o'er mould'ring beds of stone,

May oft the place of nat'ral rocks supply,
And frame the verdant picture to the eye;
Or, closing round the solitary seat,
Charm with the simple scene of calm retreat.
  Large stems of trees, and branches spreading wide,
May oft adorn the scenes which they divide;
For pond'rous masses, and deep shadows near,
Will shew the distant scene more bright and clear;
And forms distinctly mark'd, at once supply
A scale of magnitude and harmony;
From which receding gradually away,
The tints grow fainter and the lines decay.
  The same effects may also be display'd
Through the high vaulted arch or colonnade:—
But harsh and cold the builder's work appears,
Till soften'd down by long revolving years;
Till time and weather have conjointly spread
Their mould'ring hues and mosses o'er its head.
  Bless'd is the man, in whose sequester'd glade,
Some ancient abbey's walls diffuse their shade;
With mould'ring windows pierc'd, and turrets crown'd,
And pinnacles with clinging ivy bound.
  Bless'd too is he, who, 'midst his tufted trees,
Some ruin'd castle's lofty towers sees;
Imbosom'd high upon the mountain's brow,
Or nodding o'er the stream that glides below.
  Nor yet unenvy'd, to whose humbler lot
Falls the retir'd and antiquated cot;—
Its roof with weeds and mosses cover'd o'er,
And honeysuckles climbing round the door;
While mantling vines along its walls are spread,
And clust'ring ivy decks the chimney's head.

from *An Analytical Inquiry into the Principles of Taste* (1805)

As all the pleasures of intellect arise from the association of ideas, the more the materials of association are multiplied, the more will the sphere of these pleasures be enlarged. To a mind richly stored, almost every object of nature or art, that presents itself to the senses, either excites fresh trains and combinations of ideas, or vivifies and strengthens those which existed before: so that recollection enhances enjoyment, and enjoyment brightens recollection. Every insect, plant, or fossil, which the peasant treads upon unheeded, is, to the n[at]uralist and philosopher, a subject of curious inquiry and speculation, — first, as to its structure, formation, or means of existence or propagation; —

and then, as to its comparative degree, or mode of connection with others of the same or different kinds; and the respective ranks and situations, which they all severally hold in the graduated system of created beings. To the eye of the uninformed observer, the sublime spectacle of the heavens presents nothing but a blue vault bespangled with twinkling fires: but, to the learned and enlightened, it displays unnumbered worlds, distributed through the boundless variety of unmeasurable space; and peopled, perhaps, with different orders of intelligent beings, ascending, in an uninterrupted scale of gradation from the lowest dregs of animated matter to the incomprehensible throne of Omnipotence itself . . .

To descend into a still lower and more confined sphere, let us apply this principle to the subjects of our present inquiry; and we shall find that much of the pleasure, which we receive from painting, sculpture, music, poetry, &c., arises from our associating other ideas with those immediately excited by them. Hence the productions of these arts are never thoroughly enjoyed but by persons, whose minds are enriched by a variety of kindred and corresponding imagery; the extent and compass of which, allowing for different degrees of sensibility, and habits of attention, will form the scale of such enjoyment. Nor are the gratifications, which such persons receive from these arts limited to their mere productions, but extended to every object in nature or circumstance in society, that is at all connected with them: for, by such connection, it will be enabled to excite similar or associated trains of ideas, in minds so enriched, and consequently to afford them similar pleasures.

Of this description are the objects and circumstances called *picturesque*: for, except in the instances, before explained, of pleasing effects of colour, light, and shadow, they afford no pleasure, but to persons conversant with the art of painting, and sufficiently skilled in it to distinguish, and be really delighted with its real excellences. To all others, how acute soever may be their discernment, or how exquisite soever their sensibility, it is utterly imperceptible: consequently there must be some properties in the fine productions of this art, which, by the association of ideas, communicate the power of pleasing to certain objects and circumstances of its imitation, which are therefore called picturesque . . .

The sensual pleasure arising from viewing objects and compositions, which we call picturesque, may be felt equally by all mankind in proportion to the correctness and sensibility of their organs of sight; for it is wholly independent of their being picturesque, or *after the manner of painters*. But this very relation to painting, expressed by the word *picturesque*, is that, which affords the whole pleasure derived from association; which can, therefore, only be felt by persons, who have correspondent ideas to associate; that is, by persons in a certain degree conversant with that art. Such persons being in the habit of viewing, and receiving pleasure from fine pictures, will naturally feel pleasure in viewing those objects in nature, which have called forth those powers of imitation and embellishment; and those combinations and circumstances of objects, which have guided those powers in their happiest exertions. The objects recall to the mind the imitations, which skill, taste, and genius have produced; and these again recall to the mind the objects themselves, and show them through an improved medium — that of the feeling and discernment of a great artist.

By thus comparing nature and art, both the eye and the intellect acquire a higher relish for the productions of each; and the ideas, excited by both, are invigorated, as well as refined, by being thus associated and contrasted. The pleasures of vision acquire a wider range, and find endless gratifications, at once exquisite and innocent, in all the variety of productions, whether animal, vegetable, or mineral, which nature has scattered over the earth. All display beauty in some combinations or others; and when that beauty has been selected, imitated, and embellished by art, those, who before overlooked or neglected it, discern at once all its charms through this discriminating medium; and when the sentiment, which it excited, was new to them, they called those appearances of things, which excited it, by a new name, *picturesque*: — a word, that is now become extremely common and familiar in our own tongue; and which, like all other foreign words, that are become so, is very frequently employed improperly.

The skilful painter, like the skilful poet, passes slightly over those parts of his subject, which neither the compass of his art, nor the nature of his materials, allow him to represent with advantage; and employs all his labour and attention upon those, which he can adorn and embellish. These are the *picturesque* parts; that is, those which nature has formed in the style and manner appropriate to painting; and the eye, that has been accustomed to see these happily displayed and embellished by art, will relish them more in nature; as a person conversant with the writings of Theocritus and Virgil will relish pastoral scenery more than one unacquainted with such poetry. The spectator, having his mind enriched with the embellishments of the painter and the poet, applies them, by the spontaneous association of ideas, to the natural objects presented to his eye, which thus acquire ideal and imaginary beauties; that is, beauties, which are not felt by the organic sense of vision; but by the intellect and imagination through that sense.

Uvedale Price (1747–1829)

It was to Price that Knight dedicated and addressed *The Landscape*, which appeared a few months before Price's *Essay on the Picturesque*. There was much in common between the two friends and they shared an enthusiasm for picturesque gardening and its inspiration from painting. What separates them may be gathered, as Humphry Repton suggested, from their respective gardens: Knight's Downton Vale (Plate 97) realized his cherished visions of Rosa in an 'awful precipice' and the 'wild but pleasant horrors' of its valley; Price's place at Foxley (Plate 98), although romantically situated, admitted 'some little sacrifice of picturesque beauty to neatness, near the house'. Price was accordingly more flexible than his friend. He was also more committed to making the picturesque aesthetic precise and definite. He chose to distinguish it from Burke's categories of the beautiful and the sublime, as the extracts here show, but this argument was not without its awkwardnesses; one reason that he encountered difficulties was because, unlike Knight's *Analytical Inquiry*, he chose to find the quality of beauty or the picturesque or sublime in the object rather than in the spectator's eye and imagination.

from *An Essay on the Picturesque* (1794)

We are therefore to profit by the experience contained in pictures, but not to content ourselves with that experience only; nor are we to consider even those of the highest class as absolute and infallible standards, but as the best and only ones we have; as compositions, which, like those of the great classical authors, have been consecrated by long uninterrupted admiration, and which therefore have a similar claim to influence our judgment, and to form our taste in all that is within their province. These are the reasons for studying *copies* of nature, though the *original* is before us, that we may not lose the benefit of what is of such great moment in all arts and sciences, the accumulated experience of past ages; and, with respect to the art of improving, we may look upon pictures as a set of experiments of the different ways in which trees, buildings, water, &c. may be disposed, grouped, and accompanied in the most beautiful and striking manner, and in every style, from the most simple and rural to the grandest and most ornamental: many of those objects, that are scarcely marked as they lie scattered over the face of nature, when brought together in the compass of a small space of canvas, are forcibly impressed upon the eye, which by that means learns how to separate, to select, and combine . . .

No one, I believe, has yet been daring enough to improve a picture of Claude, or at least to acknowledge it; but I do not think it extravagant to suppose that a man, thoroughly persuaded, from his own taste, and from the authority of such a writer as Mr. Walpole, that an art, unknown to every age and climate, that of creating landscapes, had advanced with master-steps to vigorous perfection; that enough had been done to establish such a school of landscape as cannot be found in the rest of the globe; and that Milton's description of Paradise seems to have been copied from some piece of modern gardening; — that such a man, full of enthusiasm for this new art, and with little veneration for that of painting, should chuse to shew the world what Claude might have been, had he had the advantage of seeing the works of Mr. Brown. The only difference he would make between improving a picture and a real scene, would be that of employing a painter instead of a gardener.

What would more immediately strike him would be the total want of that leading feature of all modern improvements, the clump; and of course he would order several of them to be placed in the most conspicuous spots, with, perhaps, here and there a patch of larches, as forming a strong contrast, in shape and colour, to the Scotch firs. — His eye, which had been used to see even the natural groupes of trees in improved places made as separate and clump-like as possible, would be shocked to see those of Claude, some quite surrounded, some half concealed by bushes and thickets; others standing alone, but, by means of those thickets, or of detached trees, connected with other groupes of various sizes and shapes. All this rubbish must be cleared away, the ground made every where quite smooth and level, and each groupe left upon the grass perfectly distinct and separate. — Having been accustomed to whiten all distant buildings, those of Claude, from the effect of his soft vapoury atmosphere, would appear to him too indistinct; the painter of course would be ordered to give them a smarter appearance, which might possibly be communicated to the nearer buildings also. — Few modern houses or ornamental buildings are so placed among trees, and partially hid by them, as to conceal much of the skill of the architect, or the expence of the possessor; but in Claude, not only ruins, but temples and palaces, are often so mixed with trees, that the tops over-hang their balustrades, and the luxuriant branches shoot between the openings of their magnificent columns and porticos: as he would not suffer his own buildings to be so masked, neither would he those of Claude; and these luxuriant boughs, and all that obstructed a full view of them, the painter would be told to expunge, and carefully to restore the ornaments they had hid. — The last finishing both to places and pictures is water: in Claude it partakes of the general softness and dressed appearance of his scenes, and the accompaniments have, perhaps, less of rudeness, than in any other master; yet, compared with those of a piece of made water, or of an improved river, his banks are perfectly savage; parts of them covered with trees and bushes that hang over the water; and near the edge of it tussucks of rushes, large stones, and stumps; the ground sometimes smooth, sometimes broken and abrupt, and seldom keeping, for a long space, the same level from the water: no curves that answer each other; no resemblance, in short, to what he had been used to admire; a few strokes of the

97 Thomas Hearne, 'Wooded Glen at Downton, Herefordshire', c. 1790.
Victoria and Albert Museum. Crown copyright

painter's brush would reduce the bank on each side to one level, to one green; would make curve answer curve, without bush or tree to hinder the eye from enjoying the uniform smoothness and verdure, and from pursuing, without interruption, the continued sweep of these serpentine lines; — a little cleaning and polishing of the fore-ground would give the last touches of improvement, and complete the picture.

There is not a person in the smallest degree conversant with painting, who would not, at the same time, be shocked and diverted at the black spots and the white spots, — the naked water, — the naked buildings, — the scattered unconnected groupes of trees, and all the gross and glaring violations of every principle of the art; and yet this, without any exaggeration, is the method in which many scenes, worthy of Claude's pencil, have been improved. Is it then possible to imagine that the beauties of imitation should be so distinct from those of reality, nay, so completely at variance, that what disgraces and makes a picture ridiculous, should become ornamental when applied to nature? . . .

IT seems to me, that the neglect, which prevails in the works of modern improvers, of all that is picturesque, is owing to their exclusive attention to

98 Thomas Gainsborough, 'Beech Trees at Foxley, Herefordshire', c. 1760

high polish and flowing lines, the charms of which they are so engaged in contemplating, as to make them overlook two of the most fruitful sources of human pleasure; the first, that great and universal source of pleasure, variety, whose power is independent of beauty, but without which even beauty itself soon ceases to please; the other, intricacy, a quality which, though distinct from variety, is so connected and blended with it, that the one can hardly exist without the other.

According to the idea I have formed of it, intricacy in landscape might be defined, that disposition of objects which, by a partial and uncertain concealment, excites and nourishes curiosity. Variety can hardly require a definition, though, from the practice of many layers-out of ground, one might suppose it did. Upon the whole, it appears to me, that as intricacy in the disposition, and variety in the forms, the tints, and the lights and shadows of objects, are the great characteristics of picturesque scenery; so monotony and baldness are the greatest defects of improved places . . .

PICTURESQUENESS, therefore, appears to hold a station between beauty and sublimity; and on that account, perhaps, is more frequently and more happily blended with them both than they are with each other. It is, however, perfectly distinct from either; and first, with respect to beauty, it is evident, from all that has been said, that they are founded on very opposite qualities; the one on smoothness, the other on roughness; — the one on gradual, the other on sudden variation; — the one on ideas of youth and freshness, the other on that of age, and even of decay . . .

These are the principal circumstances by which the picturesque is separated from the beautiful. It is equally distinct from the sublime; for though there are some qualities common to them both, yet they differ in many essential points, and proceed from very different causes. In the first place, greatness of dimension is a powerful cause of the sublime; the picturesque has no connection with dimension of any kind (in which it differs from the beautiful also) and is as often found in the smallest as in the largest objects. — The sublime being founded on principles of awe and terror, never descends to any thing light or playful; the picturesque, whose characteristics are intricacy and variety, is equally adapted to the grandest and to the gayest scenery. — Infinity is one of the most efficient causes of the sublime; the boundless ocean, for that reason, inspires awful sensations: to give it picturesqueness you must destroy that cause of its sublimity; for it is on the shape and disposition of its boundaries that the picturesque in great measure must depend.

Uniformity (which is so great an enemy to the picturesque) is not only compatible with the sublime, but often the cause of it. That general equal gloom which is spread over all nature before a storm, with the stillness so nobly described by Shakespear, is in the highest degree sublime. The picturesque requires greater variety, and does not shew itself till the dreadful thunder has rent the region, has tossed the clouds into a thousand towering forms, and opened (as it were) the recesses of the sky. A blaze of light unmixed with shade, on the same principles, tends to the sublime only: Milton has placed light, in its most glorious brightness, as an inaccessible barrier round the throne of the Almighty:

> For God is light,
> And never but in unapproached light
> Dwelt from eternity.

And such is the power he has given even to its diminished splendor,

> That the brightest seraphim
> Approach not, but with both wings veil their eyes.

In one place, indeed, he has introduced very picturesque circumstances in his sublime representation of the deity; but it is of the deity in wrath, — it is when from the weakness and narrowness of our conceptions we give the names and the effects of our passions to the all-perfect Creator:

> And clouds began
> To darken all the hill, and smoke to roll
> In dusky wreaths reluctant flames, the sign
> Of wrath awak'd.

In general, however, where the glory, power, or majesty of God are represented, he has avoided that variety of form and of colouring which might take off from simple and uniform grandeur, and has encompassed the divine essence with unapproached light, or with the majesty of darkness.

Again, (if we descend to earth) a perpendicular rock of vast bulk and height, though bare and unbroken, — a deep chasm under the same circumstances, are objects that produce awful sensations; but without some variety and intricacy, either in themselves or their accompaniments, they will not be picturesque. — Lastly, a most essential difference between the two characters is, that the sublime by its solemnity takes off from the loveliness of beauty, whereas the picturesque renders it more captivating.

According to Mr. Burke, the passion caused by the great and sublime in *nature*, when those causes operate most powerfully, is astonishment; and astonishment is that state of the soul in which all its motions are suspended with some degree of horror: the sublime also, being founded on ideas of pain and terror, like them operates by stretching the fibres beyond their natural tone. The passion excited by beauty is love and complacency; it acts by relaxing the fibres somewhat below their natural tone, and this is accompanied by an inward sense of melting and languor.

Whether this account of the effects of sublimity and beauty be strictly philosophical, has, I believe, been questioned, but whether the fibres, in such cases, are really stretched or relaxed, it presents a lively image of the sensations often produced by love and astonishment. To pursue the same train of ideas, I may add, that the effect of the picturesque is curiosity; an effect which, though less splendid and powerful, has a more general influence; it neither relaxes nor violently stretches the fibres, but by its active agency keeps them to their full tone, and thus, when mixed with either of the other characters, corrects the langour of beauty, or the horror of sublimity. But as the nature of every corrective must be to take off from the peculiar effect of what it is to correct, so does the picturesque when united to either of the others. It is the coquetry of nature; it makes beauty more amusing, more varied, more playful, but also,

"Less winning soft, less amiably mild."

Again, by its variety, its intricacy, its partial concealments, it excites that active curiosity which gives play to the mind, loosening those iron bonds with which astonishment chains up its faculties.

Where characters, however distinct in their nature, are perpetually mixed together in such various degrees and manners, it is not always easy to draw the exact line of separation: I think, however, we may conclude, that where an object, or a set of objects, is without smoothness or grandeur, but from its intricacy, its sudden and irregular deviations, its variety of forms, tints, and lights and shadows, is interesting to a cultivated eye, it is simply picturesque; such, for instance, are the rough banks that often inclose a bye-road or a hollow lane: Imagine the size of these banks and the space between them to be increased till the lane becomes a deep dell, — the coves large caverns, — the peeping stones hanging rocks, so that the whole may impress an idea of awe and grandeur; — the sublime will then be mixed with the picturesque, though the scale only, not the style of the scenery, would be changed. On the other hand, if parts of the banks were smooth and gently sloping, — or the middle space a soft close-bitten turf, — or if a gentle stream passed between them, whose clear unbroken surface reflected all their varieties, — the beautiful and the picturesque, by means of that softness and smoothness, would then be united.

Humphry Repton (1752–1818)

Knight's *The Landscape* and Price's *Essay* were in part directed against the landscape designs and unpublished writings of Repton, whom they took — rather mistakenly — to be a mere follower of 'Capability' Brown. Repton replied to them both in a 'Letter', which was incorporated in his *Sketches and Hints* of 1795, and the controversy flourished for some years. Misunderstandings, inevitably, obscured the debate and still tend to hamper modern assessments of it: basically, Repton did not follow Brown's schemes and styles of design, though his personal contributions to landscape history seem to emerge and express themselves more distinctly *after* the quarrel with the picturesque exponents flared. Nor was he committed to their picturesque principles, despite some affinities with them: in particular, he mistrusted Knight's landscapes which were really only 'fit . . . for the representation of the pencil'. Repton chose, in fact, an intelligent, thoughtful and independent course, which spurned effects that would appear well in a picture in favour of utility and social convenience. He was above all a professional designer: this meant not only that 'scenes of horror, well calculated for the residence of Banditti' did not suit the needs of his clients, but that they would be 'absurd, incongruous and out of character . . . in the garden of a villa near the capital, or in the more tame, yet interesting, pleasure-grounds which I am frequently called upon to decorate'. His designs catered for human society and increasingly incorporated older garden forms — terraces, raised flowerbeds, geometrical planning, trellis-covered walks, conservatories — with less appeal to an eye alert for picturesque capabilities and more respect for the convenience of those who used the garden. In this he anticipated the 'gardenesque' style of John Claudius Loudon and William Robinson, and it is significant that Loudon issued a collected edition of Repton's writings in 1840. The first extract, which is taken from the transcript made for the Bristol City Museum, shows Repton adjudicating between social needs and the extreme picturesque demands of the site of Blaise Castle (Plate 99), well known for its romantic potential (it figures in Jane Austen's mockery of the Gothic in *Northanger Abbey*). He tempers the sublime and terrible by ideas of 'agreeable surprise' and by the comfortable assurance of social values and utility. The second passage, twenty years later, suggests how Repton developed designs for small suburban villas, which increasingly involved professional designers in their improvement: suggestions for the flower garden and the conservatory arcade indicate his abilities to adapt to, and create, fresh garden tastes.

from the 'Red Book' for Blaise Castle (1795–6)

INTRODUCTION

Sir,

It has been objected to the mode in which I deliver my plans, that they do not always convey instructions, sufficiently clear, to act as guides for the detail of execution; but this ought no more to be expected in *gardening* than in *architecture*, since no work can be so well compleated as under the eye of the person who projects the improvement or designs the building. I have therefore peculiar satisfaction in marking out such lines of roads and walks as cannot be described on paper, and being very anxious to see the whole of my intentions, with respect to this place, compleated from my own directions given from time to time upon the spot, it may perhaps be asked for what purpose a plan is delivered, which rather follows than precedes the improvement? To this I must answer by observing, that upon first visiting every new subject I am obliged to conceive in my own mind such a plan as I afterwards render visible to others; and endeavour to fix on my memory the several leading features of each place by making sketches, without which from the multiplicity of various situations it would be impossible for me to pursue any regular system of improvement. Altho' much of the matter contained in this small volume has been previously hinted in conversations on the spot, I hope the repetition will not be unacceptable in this more lasting form, and if it does not serve as a minute guide in the progress of the work, it will at least record the improvements and the principles on which they are suggested. I must also beg that it may record my gratitude for the friendly attentions I have received from every part of the family at Blaise Castle.

I have the honour to be Sir   Your most obedient
and obliged humble Servant
H. REPTON

On the Spot August & October, 1795
Plan'd at Harestreet by Romford Feb. 7, 1796

SITUATION

I have been told that my predecessor, Mr. Brown, was always afraid of what is called a very fine situation, by which is generally understood, one of those lofty spots that command a boundless prospect: and as nothing can be so ill calculated for the purposes of habitation as a house on the summit of a hill, so nothing is more difficult to improve by an Art which can only perform its office by means of deception, effecting its purpose well in proportion as that deception remains undiscovered, but from a lofty eminence where the eye ranges over a vast space, and surveys the great visible horison of nature: the foreground, (or that part which falls within the improvers power) bears no comparison with the rest of the scenery and becomes little in proportion as it affects to attract the attention.

The situation of the castle from whence this place takes its name, is of the kind I have described, and however sublime in itself as an occasional spot to be visited, must be wholly inapplicable to a family residence: it was, therefore, with much pleasure that I found the comfort of the house was not to be sacrificed to extensive prospect, but that several spots had been judiciously proposed, each partaking of the quiet and sequestered scenery in which this place so remarkably abounds. It is a most singular circumstance that within a short distance of the largest City in England except London, and even in the neighbourhood of the most frequented watering place in the kingdom, the woods and lawns and deep romantic glens belonging to Blaise Castle are perfectly secluded from the "busy hum of man."

CHARACTER

Altho' I object to an exposed hill as a situation for a constant residence, yet it is not inapplicable to a Villa, which as a retreat from the bustle of the world should either be so snugly placed that nothing can intrude on its privacy, or so seated on an eminence as not to be overlooked.

The command of surrounding property, the size of the proposed mansion, and the general uses of this place as a *family residence*, seem to justify my intentions of treating the subject less under the character of a Villa than its relative situation with respect to the City of Bristol might at first suggest. It is for this reason that I think the greatest improvement in the character of the place will be the entrance from the high road, without passing thro' the village of Henbury, where a number of Villas or large country houses seem to dispute with each other by their size and cumbrous importance. Some difficulty occurs with respect to the name of Blaise Castle, and as the house neither does nor ought to partake of the castle-character, there may perhaps appear a little incongruity in making the entrance in that stile, yet I cannot propose an entrance-lodge of Grecian architecture to a house which is no where seen from the road, while the Castle, both from its giving name to the place and from its conspicuous situation, seems to demand a very different stile of entrance. I have therefore subjoined the kind of lodge which I hope will not be deemed inconsistent with its purposes or situation as the first object to attract notice in the approach to Blaise Castle.

THE APPROACH

A stranger to the shapes of the ground in this romantic Place would be at a loss to account for the crooked and distorted lines represented on the map, which can only be explained by stating, that a deep ravine crosses the wood and seemed at first to render hopeless all attempt to make any approach except that thro' the village of Henbury. I trust however that the line of road will be found perfectly easy and accessible on the ground, however violent it may appear on paper, and that when Time has thrown its ivy and creeping plants over the rawness of new walls and fresh hewn rocks, the approach will be in strict character with the wildness of the scenery, and excite admiration and surprize without any mixture of that terror which tho' it partakes of the sublime, is very apt to destroy the delights of romantic scenery. The gate being in character with the castle to which it is the prelude, introduces us to a wood with which it is in harmony, and I expect the stranger will be agreeably surprised to find that on quitting this wood, he is not going to a mouldering castle whose ruined turrets threaten destruction, and revive the horrors of feudal strife, but to a mansion of elegance, cheerfulness, and hospitality where the comfort of neatness is blended with the rude features of nature, without committing great violence on the Genius of the Place. It may perhaps be urged that I have made a road where nature never intended the foot of man to tread, much less that he should be conveyed in the vehicles of modern luxury, but where man resides, Nature must be conquered by Art, and it is only the ostentation of her triumph, and not her victory, that ought never to offend the correct Eye of Taste.

If Mr. Brown was afraid of fine situations, I am not less afraid of those beautiful scenes in nature which defy the powers of my pencil to imitate, because I cannot shew on paper the effect of improvement where no change is proposed, and this is particularly the case at Blaise Castle. I can shew the effect of a new house instead of an old one, but I cannot describe those numberless beauties which may be brought before the eye in succession by the windings of a road, or the contrast of ascending and descending thro' a deep ravine of rich hanging woods. My sketches therefore will give little idea of the grand and sublime combination of rocks and trees, which I am endeavouring to display upon the spot without fatigue; and which are at too great a distance and too inaccessible to become frequently visited from the house. This consideration makes it peculiarly desirable to have an easy road of approach thro' a part of the ground not interfering with those walks, that connect the house with the castle, and which being of course the more common objects of pleasure may therefore be deemed the home pleasure ground, in opposition to those on the other side of the glen. Yet the approach for a certain distance will serve as the line of communication betwixt the house and some objects highly interesting. Of this kind is the cottage which I shall mention hereafter, and also a view from the mouth of a cavern impossible to represent; it consists of a winding valley of wood and rock terminated by a smooth hill, and this is enlivened by frequent groups of carriages and company who visit the spot, and produce an astonishing contrast to the solemn dignity of this awful scene.

THE HOUSE

In fixing the situation for a house, the aspect or exposure should be the first object of consideration, because no landscape however delightful can compensate for the want of sunshine in this climate; it is therefore very fortunate

99 Blaise Castle, Gloucestershire. View from Repton's 'Red Book', 1795–6

that in this instance the best views are towards the south, and the two living fronts will be so placed as to command them to advantage, expecially if the house be raised a few feet above the present level, which will make it appear to stand on a small knoll with the ground gently sloping from it in every direction.

In speaking of this building I must pay a just compliment to the skill of Mr. Patty for the attention given to the internal arrangement of the whole, and for the simplicity adopted in the several fronts, especially as I cannot help mentioning a circumstance that has often occurred to me viz: that in those counties where the stone is cheap and easily worked, there is always more bad taste in external architecture, because every builder becomes an Architect. Thus houses are built without any knowledge of the first rules of that difficult Art or because those rules are stubborn to bend to the common purposes of life new proportions are adopted, new combinations attempted and all the fantastic forms of vases, urns, ballustrades, and other enrichments are added to plain houses without considering the relative propriety of such appendages. I know the difficulty of introducing columns according to the strict rules of architecture, and have hardly ever seen an house perfectly correct; it is therefore very dangerous to attempt what has so often failed, yet lest I should be thought an advocate for discarding such ornament, I will insert at the end of this volume a sketch of the portico which my ingenious friend Mr. Collison suggested, and which might at any time hereafter be added to the south-east front without making any internal alteration.

VIEWS FROM THE HOUSE

The landscape from an eating room is of less consequence than any other yet this will be very interesting, altho' from the height of some trees which ought not to be cut down till the house is built I cannot give an accurate idea of it by any sketch. But the principal view is along that rich glen of wood so feebly represented in the following sketch. This is the first instance in which I have been consulted where all improvement must depend on the axe, and tho' fully aware of the common objection to cutting down trees, yet, it is only by a bold use of that instrument that the wonders of Blaise Castle can be properly displayed.

"Nor let the axe its beak, the saw its tooth
"Refrain, when e'er some random branch has stray'd
"Beyond the bounds of beauty."

It is less necessary to explain the intention of opening a bay into the wood beneath the castle . . . because the effect has I hope already been partly produced upon the spot, by taking away the trees marked by me in the autumn. But the side of the sketch . . . will shew the improvement there suggested under the following heads viz: first, The removal of a white rail fence which catches the eye and prevents its seeing anything but itself, secondly the taking away the tops of several tall trees which hide the opposite wood, and also a corner of the lawn where, thirdly a cottage is proposed to be built. This cottage will give an air of cheerfulness and inhabitancy to the scene which would without it be too sombre, because the castle tho' perfectly in character with the solemn dignity of the surrounding woods, increases rather than relieves the apparent solitude.

THE COTTAGE

The effect of this building from the house [Plate 99] can be very little conceived from the drawing, because it is one of those objects that derives its chief beauty from the ideas of animation and movement. A temple or a pavilion in such a situation would receive the light and produce an object to contrast with the sameness of wood and lawn, but it would not appear to be inhabited; while this, by its form will mark its intention, and the occasional smoke from the chimney will not only produce that cheerful and varying motion which painting cannot express, but it will frequently happen in a summer's evening that the smoke from this cottage will spread a thin veil along the glen, and produce that kind of vapoury repose over the opposite wood which painters often attempt to describe, and which in appearance so separates the two sides of the valley that the imagination will conceive it to be much wider and more extensive than it really is. The form of this cottage must partake of the wildness of the scenery without meanness; it must look like what it is, the habitation of a labourer who has the care of the adjoining woods, but its simplicity should be the effect of Art and not of accident, it must seem to belong to the proprietor of the mansion and the castle, without affecting to imitate the character of either. I think a covered seat at the gable end of a neat thatched cottage will be the best mode of producing the object here required, and the idea to be excited is "la Simplicité soignée."

WALKS AND DRIVES

It is remarkable that no attempt should have been made to render objects of so much beauty and variety accessible in a carriage, for however interesting the walks in hilly countries may be, they can only be enjoyed by great labour and exertion; they require health of body and vigour of limbs to enjoy their romantic wonders, while the aged and the infirm have been excluded from the beauties of the place by the danger or difficulty of exploring them. I must therefore assume to myself the merit of shewing this situation in a manner before unthought of, and while I reserve some scenes for those who can walk to them, and who can climb steps or creep thro' caverns, I must endeavour to display others from the windows of a carriage with all the interest of surprize and novelty. In the drive which I have marked out from the house to the castle, I shall avail myself of that vista thro' the woods towards the river, which has always been considered as one of the striking features of the place, but instead of merely giving a glimpse of this singular effect like peeping thro' a long tube that is instantly snatched from the eye; the road ought to continue for some time in the same direction, that the most careless observer may have leisure to view the delightful scene, and before he quits the spot entirely the whole expanse of water, of shipping, and distant mountains will pass before the eye.

There is a part of the Castle wood which is seldom seen, because it lies betwixt the two walks, and properly belongs to neither; but as the carriage road is obliged to make a very long detour to ascend with tolerable facility, it must pass thro' that small lawn which surprizes by its unexpected contrast with the other wild part of this thickly wooded precipice. From this lawn the first appearance of the castle is most picturesque, because it presents the three turrets at once, and at this distance they appear of different heights. The form of this castle altho' not gothic, is well calculated for the situation, but it would give it more the character of a real castle at a distance if one of the round towers were elevated above the other two, and this I have shown both in the sketch . . . and also in the following drawing . . . which represents the first view of the castle after quitting the small lawn before mentioned, and entering the naked plain on which it is there discovered to be situated, altho' from every other point of view it appears as it ought to do —

"embosom'd high in tufted trees".

THE WATER

When we consider the vast expanse of water which the castle commands, it seems hardly possible that bad taste could for a moment suggest the idea of making an artificial river, in the bottom of a dry glen, especially as nature denies the two great requisites for such an attempt, viz., a sufficient supply of water to fill the river, and a practicable level to allow of its being retained within certain limits — but I must here record, that in defiance of all obstacles, the late possessor of these beautiful premises had prepared a number of narrow channels, about the width of a common navigation canal, secured by different heads or dams, and the sides built with stone walls, for the reception of water which it was afterwards discovered could never be expected: these dry channels became so unsightly, that various expedients were suggested to avoid the expence of filling them in, and amongst the rest an engineer proposed to raise water from the bowels of the earth by a steam engine, but instead of exposing the *Genius of the place* to all the horrors of fire and steam, and the clangour of iron chains and forcing pumps, for the sake of counter-acting the mischief already begun, I have on the contrary advised that all the yawning chasms be hid by plantations, rather than let any traces remain of works, done under the influence of such barbarous taste, as could scar those rich hanging woods by cutting furrows down their sides, and disturb the tranquil ideas suggested from this secluded spot, by planting huge wooden cannon upon every projecting rock.

While I congratulate the present possessor on having attained the command of such romantic scenes, I must rejoice that they have fallen into his hands, and am highly gratified and flattered by his having called on me, to direct how best to preserve or heighten the native beauties of such a delightful subject.

from *Fragments on the Theory and Practice of Landscape Gardening* (1816)

REPORT CONCERNING A VILLA AT STREATHAM,
Belonging to the Earl of Coventry.

MY LORD,

I CANNOT but rejoice in the honour your Lordship has done me, in requiring my opinion concerning a Villa, which, when compared with Croom or Spring Park, may be deemed inconsiderable by those who value a place by its size or extent, and not by its real importance, as regards beauty, conveni-ence, and utility. I must therefore request leave to deliver my opinion con-cerning Streatham at some length, as it will give me an opportunity of explaining my reasons for treating the subject very differently from those followers of Brown, who copied his manner, without attending to his propor-tions or motives, and adopted the same expedients for two acres, which he thought advisable for two hundred. Mr. Brown's attention had generally been called to places of great extent, in many of which he had introduced that practice distinguished by the name of a belt of plantation, and a drive within that belt. This, when the surface was varied by hill and dale, became a convenient mode of connecting the most striking spots, and the most interest-ing scenes at a distance from the mansion, and from each other. But when the same expedient is used round a small field, with no inequality of ground, and particularly with a public road bounding the premises, it is impossible to conceive a plan more objectionable in its consequences; for as the essential characteristic of a *Villa* near the metropolis consists in its *seclusion* and *privacy*, the walk which is only separated from the highway by a park paling, and a few laurels, is not more private, though far less cheerful, than the path in the highway itself. To this may be added, that such a belt, when viewed from the house, must confine the landscape by the pale to hide the road; then by the shrubs to hide the pale; and lastly, by the fence to protect the shrubs;

which all together act as a boundary more decided and offensive than the common hedge betwixt one field and another.

The Art of Landscape Gardening is in no instance more obliged to Mr. Brown, than for his occasionally judicious introduction of the Ha! Ha! or sunk fence, by which he united in appearance two surfaces necessary to be kept separate. But this has been in many places absurdly copied to an extent that gives more actual confinement than any visible fence whatever. At Streatham the view towards the south consists of a small field bounded by the narrow belt, and beyond it is the Common of Streatham, which is in parts adorned by groups of trees, and in others disfigured by a redundance of obtrusive houses. The common in itself is a cheerful object, and from its distance not offensive, even when covered with people who enjoy its verdure. Yet if the whole of the view in front were open to the common, it might render the house and ground near it too public; and for this reason, I suppose, some shrubs have been placed near the windows; but I consider that the defect might be more effectually remedied by such a mass of planting as would direct the eye to the richest part of the common only; then, by raising a bank to hide the paling in such opening, the grass of the common and of the lawn would appear united, and form one unconfined range of turf seen point blank from the principal windows; while the oblique view might be extended to the greatest depth of lawn, and to some fine trees, which are now all hid by an intervening kitchen garden not half large enough for the use of such a house.

This naturally leads me to explain the principle of improvement which I have the honour to suggest. The value of land near the capital is very great; but we are apt to treat it in the same manner as if it were a farm in the country, and estimate its produce by the ACRE, when in fact it ought to be estimated by the FOOT. An acre of land of the same quality, which may be worth £2 in Worcestershire, may be worth £5 at Streatham, for cattle; but if appropriated to the use of man, it may be worth £20 as a garden. It is therefore no waste of property to recommend such a garden establishment at Streatham as may make it amply worth the attention of the most experienced gardener to supply the daily consumption of a town-house, and save the distant conveyance or extravagant purchase of fruit and choice vegetables: especially as such an arrangement will add to the beauty and interest of the grounds, while it increases their value.

The house at Streatham, though surrounded by forty acres of grass land, is not a farm, but a Villa in a garden; for I never have admitted the word *Ferme Ornè* [sic] into my ideas of taste, any more than a butcher's shop, or a pigsty, adorned with pea-green and gilding. A garden is of different value in different seasons, and should be adapted to each. In SUMMER, when every field in the country is a garden, we seldom enjoy that within our own paling, except in its produce; but near London, where the views from public roads are all injured by the pales and belts of private property, the interior becomes more valuable, and the pleasure of gathering summer fruit should be consulted in the arrangement of the gardens. In WINTER the garden is only preferable to a field by a broad gravel-walk, from which the snow is swept, except we add to its luxury the comfort of such glass as may set the winter at defiance; and the advantage of such forcing-houses for vines and flowers will be doubly felt in the neighbourhood of the capital.

In SPRING the garden begins to excite interest with the first blossoms of the crocus and snowdrop: and though its delights are seldom enjoyed in the more magnificent country residences of the Nobility, yet the garden of a Villa should be profusely supplied with all the fragrance and the beauty of blossom belonging to "il gioventu del anno."

Lastly, the garden in AUTUMN to its flowers adds its fruits, these by judicious management may be made a source of great luxury and delight: and we may observe, that it is chiefly in spring and autumn that gravel walks are more essentially useful when the heavy dews on the lawn render grass walks almost inaccessible.

It happens at Streatham, that a long range of offices, stables, and farm buildings, fronts the south, and seems to call for the expedient by which it may be best hid, viz. a continued covered way, extending a vista from the green-house annexed to the drawing-room; houses of every kind for Grapes, Peaches, Strawberries, Vines, &c. &c. to any extent, may here be added, without darkening the windows, which may be lighted under the glass, and a low skreen of flowering shrubs in summer will sufficiently hide this long range of winter comfort, without intercepting the rays of the sun.

William Combe (1741–1823)

Combe provided the verses and Thomas Rowlandson the drawings (Plate 100) for *The Tour of Doctor Syntax in Search of the Picturesque*, a satire upon Gilpin's picturesque tours; it appeared first in *The Poetical Magazine* in 1809, from which our text is taken, and was reprinted separately in 1812. Combe manages a brisk and bathetic résumé of the foibles of the picturesque tour (though his irony lacks the incisive economy of Sydney Smith's 'The rector's horse is *beautiful*, the curate's is *picturesque*'). More accomplished and interesting are Rowlandson's contributions: he takes the basic ambiguities of regarding nature for its artistic potential and suggests that what is central to a picturesque vision — the accidents and distortions of natural scenery — is merely grotesque in human and social contexts. If Combe satirizes Gilpin's practice of providing plates that are not topographical drawings but illustrations of picturesque ideas, Rowlandson, as Ronald Paulson has suggested, mockingly examines the notions of unease and surprise by which Gilpin (and Price) distinguished the picturesque from the beautiful.

from *The Tour of Doctor Syntax in Search of the Picturesque* (1809)

Thus, as he ponder'd what to do,
A guide-post rose within his view;
And, when the pleasing shape he spied,
He prick'd his steed, and thither hied;
But some unheeding senseless wight,
Who to fair learning ow'd a spite,
Had ev'ry letter'd mark defac'd,
Which once its sev'ral pointers grac'd.
The mangled post thus long had stood,
An uninforming piece of wood;
Like other guides, as some folks say,
Who neither lead, nor point the way.
The Sun, as hot as he was bright,
Had got to his meridian height;
'Twas sultry noon — for not a breath
Of cooling zephyr fann'd the heath —
When Syntax cried, — "'Tis all in vain
"To find my way across the plain;

"So here my fortune I will try,
"And wait till some one passes by:
"Upon that bank awhile I'll sit,
"And let poor Grizzle graze a bit;
"But as my time shall not be lost,
"I'll make a drawing of the post;
"And, tho' your flimsy tastes may flout it,
"There's something picturesque about it:
"'Tis rude and rough, without a gloss,
"And is well cover'd o'er with moss;
"And I've a right (who dares deny it?)
"To place yon group of asses by it.
"Aye! that will do: and now I'm thinking,
"That self-same pond where Grizzle's drinking,
"If hither brought, 'twould better seem,
"And, faith, I'll turn it to a stream;
"I'll make this flat a shaggy ridge,
"And o'er the water throw a bridge;
"I'll do as other sketchers do —
"Put any thing into the view;
"And any object recollect,
"To add a grace, and give effect.
"Thus, tho' from truth I haply err,
"*The scene preserves its character.*
"What man of taste my right will doubt,
"To put things in, or leave them out?

100 Illustration by Thomas Rowlandson from William Combe,
The Tour of Doctor Syntax in Search of the Picturesque, 1812

"'Tis more than right, it is a duty,
"If we consider landscape beauty:
"He ne'er will as an artist shine,
"Who copies nature line by line;
"Whoe'er from nature takes a view,
"Must copy and improve it too:
"To heighten ev'ry work of art,
"Fancy should take an active part:
"Thus I (which few, I think, can boast)
"*Have made a landscape of a post* . . .

SYNTAX.

"Your sport, my Lord, I cannot take,
"For I must go and hunt a lake;
"And, while you chase the flying deer,
"I must fly off to *Windermere*.
"Instead of hallooing to a fox,
"I must catch echoes from the rocks.
"With curious eye and active scent,
"I on the *picturesque* am bent.
"That is my game; I must pursue it,
"And make it where I cannot view it.
"If in the human form you'd see
"The picturesque, — pray look at me.
"I am myself, without a flaw,
"The very picturesque I draw;
"A Rector, on whose face so sleek
"In vain you for a wrinkle seek;
"In whose fair form, so fat and round,
"No obtuse angle's to be found.
"On such a shape no man of taste
"Would his fine tints or canvass waste:
"But take a Curate, who's so thin,
"His bones seem peeping thro' his skin;
"Make him to stand, or walk, or sit,
"In any posture you think fit;
"And, with all these fine points about him,
"No well-taught painter e'er would scout him;
"For with his air, and look, and mien,
"He'd give effect to any scene.
"In my poor beast, as well as me,
"A fine example you may see;
"She's so abrupt in all her parts,
"She's quite a subject for the arts:
"Thus we travel on together,
"With gentle gale or stormy weather;

"And, tho' we trot along the plains,
"Where one dead level ever reigns;
"Or pace where rocks and mountains rise,
"Who lift their heads, and brave the skies;
"I Doctor Syntax, and my horse,
"Give to the landscape double force.
"I have no doubt I shall produce
"A volume of uncommon use,
"That will be worthy to be plac'd
"Beneath the eye of men of taste;
"And I should hope, my Lord, that you
"Will praise it and protect it too;
"Will let your all-sufficient name
"The noble patronage proclaim;
"That time may know, till time doth end,
"That Carlisle was my honour'd friend."

Jane Austen (1775–1817)

Jane Austen's novels provide fascinating glimpses of gentry's country seats. Though she invokes Repton's name as that of a typically notorious improver in *Mansfield Park*, she seems to share many of his essential notions about landscape gardens. Her satire of picturesque taste, like his, concentrates upon a 'sense of the probable' and of social exigencies (Plates 101a and 101b). In *Pride and Prejudice* Elizabeth Bennett's exclamation — 'What are men to rocks and mountains?' — might recall Knight or Price; a large part of her education in matters of human importance is conducted at the very Reptonian landscape of Pemberley Woods, the seat of Mr Darcy. The description of her arrival there forms the first extract. Emma, too, learns to appreciate her role in society at Donwell Abbey, which is presented in the second extract. Jane Austen shares Repton's confidence, as he wrote in his *Fragments*, that 'the same principles which direct taste in the polite arts, direct the judgement in morality'. What one of her heroines learns from a landscaped estate is that '*true* taste in *landscape gardening* . . . is not an accidental effect, operating on the outward senses, but an appeal to the understanding'. In making such a connection between design and social morality, Repton and Jane Austen place themselves firmly in the traditions of the English garden that Pope and Burlington and others inaugurated.

from *Pride and Prejudice* (1813)

ELIZABETH, as they drove along, watched for the first appearance of Pemberley Woods with some perturbation; and when at length they turned in at the lodge, her spirits were in a high flutter.

The park was very large, and contained great variety of ground. They entered it in one of its lowest points, and drove for some time through a beautiful wood, stretching over a wide extent.

Elizabeth's mind was too full for conversation, but she saw and admired every remarkable spot and point of view. They gradually ascended for half a mile, and then found themselves at the top of a considerable eminence, where the wood ceased, and the eye was instantly caught by Pemberley House, situated on the opposite side of a valley, into which the road with some abruptness wound. It was a large, handsome, stone building, standing well on rising ground, and backed by a ridge of high woody hills; — and in front, a stream of some natural importance was swelled into greater, but without any

101a and b Two views of 'Lord Sidmouth's' from Humphry Repton,
Fragments on the Theory and Practice of Landscape Gardening, 1816

artificial appearance. Its banks were neither formal, nor falsely adorned. Elizabeth was delighted. She had never seen a place for which nature had done more, or where natural beauty had been so little counteracted by an awkward taste. They were all of them warm in their admiration; and at that moment she felt, that to be mistress of Pemberley might be something!

They descended the hill, crossed the bridge, and drove to the door; and, while examining the nearer aspect of the house, all her apprehensions of meeting its owner returned. She dreaded lest the chambermaid had been mistaken. On applying to see the place, they were admitted into the hall; and Elizabeth, as they waited for the housekeeper, had leisure to wonder at her being where she was.

The housekeeper came; a respectable-looking, elderly woman, much less fine, and more civil, than she had any notion of finding her. They followed her into the dining-parlour. It was a large, well-proportioned room, handsomely fitted up. Elizabeth, after slightly surveying it, went to a window to enjoy its prospect. The hill, crowned with wood, from which they had descended, receiving increased abruptness from the distance, was a beautiful object. Every disposition of the ground was good; and she looked on the whole scene, the river, the trees scattered on its banks, and the winding of the valley, as far as she could trace it, with delight. As they passed into other rooms, these objects were taking different positions; but from every window there were beauties to be seen . . .

from *Emma* (1816)

It was so long since Emma had been at the Abbey, that as soon as she was satisfied of her father's comfort, she was glad to leave him, and look around her; eager to refresh and correct her memory with more particular observation, more exact understanding of a house and grounds which must ever be so interesting to her and all her family.

She felt all the honest pride and complacency which her alliance with the present and future proprietor could fairly warrant, as she viewed the respectable size and style of the building, its suitable, becoming characteristic situation, low and sheltered — its ample gardens stretching down to meadows washed by a stream, of which the Abbey, with all the old neglect of prospect, had scarcely a sight — and its abundance of timber in rows and avenues, which neither fashion nor extravagance had rooted up. — The house was larger than Hartfield, and totally unlike it, covering a good deal of ground, rambling and irregular, with many comfortable and one or two handsome rooms. — It was just what it ought to be, and it looked what it was — and Emma felt an increasing respect for it, as the residence of a family of such true gentility, untainted in blood and understanding . . .

It was hot; and after walking some time over the gardens in a scattered, dispersed way, scarcely any three together, they insensibly followed one another to the delicious shade of a broad short avenue of limes, which stretching beyond the garden at an equal distance from the river, seemed the finish of the pleasure grounds. — It led to nothing; nothing but a view at the end over a low stone wall with high pillars, which seemed intended, in their erection, to give the appearance of an approach to the house, which never had been there. Disputable, however, as might be the taste of such a termination, it was in itself a charming walk, and the view which closed it extremely pretty. — The considerable slope, at nearly the foot of which the Abbey stood, gradually acquired a steeper form beyond its grounds; and at half a mile distant was a bank of considerable abruptness and grandeur, well clothed with wood; — and at the bottom of this bank, favourably placed and sheltered, rose the Abbey-Mill Farm, with meadows in front, and the river making a close and handsome curve around it.

It was a sweet view — sweet to the eye and the mind. English verdure, English culture, English comfort, seen under a sun bright, without being oppressive.

Thomas Love Peacock (1785–1866)

Some of the misunderstandings that attended Repton's quarrel with Knight and Price inform Peacock's satire, *Headlong Hall*. Marmaduke Milestone is generally taken to be a caricature of Repton — the name being derived from an unhappy suggestion by Repton that milestones bearing the arms of the family at Tatton Park be erected in the neighbouring town of Knutsford; Milestone's provision of 'before' and 'after' sketches alludes to Repton's custom of presenting his clients with a 'Red Book' (so called because bound in red morocco) in which 'slides' or overlapping plates illustrated his proposals (see Plates 101a and 101b). But Peacock also alludes to the picturesque quarrel with Brown, whose 'corrected — trimmed — polished' landscapes with 'circular clumps' are also mocked; and there is a mention of the Chinese taste *à la* Chambers. In all, it is a sharp and intelligent satire on the general taste for improvement, a suitably sceptical note with which to close this anthology.

from *Headlong Hall* (1816)

"I PERCEIVE," said Mr. Milestone, after they had walked a few paces, "these grounds have never been touched by the finger of taste."

"The place is quite a wilderness," said Squire Headlong: "for, during the latter part of my father's life, while I was *finishing* my *education*, he troubled himself about nothing but the cellar, and suffered every thing else to go to rack and ruin. A mere wilderness, as you see, even now in December; but in summer, a complete nursery of briers, a forest of thistles, a plantation of nettles, without any live stock, but goats, that have eaten up all the bark of the trees. Here you see is a pedestal of a statue, with only half a leg and four toes remaining: there were many here once. When I was a boy, I used to sit every day on the shoulders of Hercules: what became of *him* I have never been able to ascertain. Neptune has been lying these three years in the dust-hole; Atlas had his head knocked off to make him prop up a shed; and only the day before yesterday we fished Bacchus out of the horse-pond."

"My dear Sir," said Mr. Milestone, "accord me your permission to wave the wand of enchantment over your grounds. The rocks shall be blown up, the trees shall be cut down, the wilderness and all its goats shall vanish like mist. Pagodas and Chinese bridges, gravel walks and shrubberies, bowling-greens, canals, and clumps of larch, shall rise upon its ruins. One age, Sir, has brought to light the treasures of ancient learning: a second has penetrated into the depths of metaphysics: a third has brought to perfection the science of astronomy; but it was reserved for the exclusive genius of the present times, to invent the noble art of picturesque gardening, which has given, as it were, a new tint to the complexion of nature, and a new outline to the physiognomy of the universe!"

"Give me leave," said Sir Patrick O'Prism, "to take an exception to that same. Your system of levelling, and trimming, and clipping, and docking, and clumping, and polishing, and cropping, and shaving, destroys all the beautiful intricacies of natural luxuriance, and all the graduated harmonies of light and shade, melting into one another, as you see them on that rock over yonder. I never saw one of your improved places, as you call them, and which are nothing but big bowling-greens, like sheets of green paper, with a parcel of round clumps scattered over them like so many spots of ink, flicked at random out of a pen, and a solitary animal here and there looking as if it were lost, that I did not think it was for all the world like Hounslow Heath, thinly sprinkled over with bushes and highwaymen."

"Sir," said Mr. Milestone, "you will have the goodness to make a distinction between the picturesque and the beautiful."

"Will I?" said Sir Patrick: "och! but I won't. For what is beautiful? That which pleases the eye. And what pleases the eye? Tints variously broken and blended. Now tints variously broken and blended, constitute the picturesque."

"Allow me," said Mr. Gall. "I distinguish the picturesque and the beautiful, and I add to them, in the laying out of grounds, a third and distinct character, which I call *unexpectedness*."

"Pray, Sir," said Mr. Milestone, "by what name do you distinguish this character, when a person walks round the grounds for the second time?"

Mr. Gall bit his lips, and inwardly vowed to revenge himself on Milestone, by cutting up his next publication.

A long controversy now ensued concerning the picturesque and the beautiful, highly edifying to Squire Headlong.

The three philosophers stopped, as they wound round a projecting point of rock, to contemplate a little boat which was gliding over the tranquil surface of the lake below . . .

Mr. Milestone had produced his portfolio for the edification and amusement of Miss Tenorina, Miss Graziosa, and Squire Headlong, to whom he was pointing out the various beauties of his plan for Lord Littlebrain's park.

MR. MILESTONE.

This, you perceive, is the natural state of one part of the grounds. Here is a wood, never yet touched by the finger of taste; thick, intricate, and gloomy. Here is a little stream, dashing from stone to stone, and overshadowed with these untrimmed boughs.

MISS TENORINA.

The sweet romantic spot! how beautifully the birds must sing there on a summer evening!

MISS GRAZIOSA.

Dear sister! how can you endure the horrid thicket?

MR. MILESTONE.

You are right, Miss Graziosa: your taste is correct — perfectly *en règle*. Now, here is the same place corrected — trimmed — polished — decorated — adorned. Here sweeps a plantation, in that beautiful regular curve: there winds a gravel walk: here are parts of the old wood, left in these majestic circular clumps, disposed at equal distances with wonderful symmetry: there are some single shrubs scattered in elegant profusion: here a Portugal laurel, there a juniper: here a lauristinus, there a spruce fir; here a larch, there a lilac; here a rhododendron, there an arbutus. The stream, you see, is become a canal: the banks are perfectly smooth and green, sloping to the water's edge: and there is Lord Littlebrain, rowing in an elegant boat.

SQUIRE HEADLONG.

Magical, faith!

MR. MILESTONE.

Here is another part of the grounds in its natural state. Here is a large rock, with the mountain-ash rooted in its fissures, overgrown, as you see, with ivy and moss, and from this part of it bursts a little fountain, that runs bubbling down its ragged sides.

MISS TENORINA.

O how beautiful! How I should love the melody of that miniature cascade!

MR. MILESTONE.

Beautiful, Miss Tenorina! Hideous. Base, common, and popular. Such a thing as you may see anywhere, in wild and mountainous districts. Now observe the metamorphosis. Here is the same rock, cut into the shape of a giant. In one hand he holds a horn, through which that little fountain is thrown to a prodigious elevation. In the other is a ponderous stone, so exactly balanced as to be apparently ready to fall on the head of any person who may happen to be beneath; and there is Lord Littlebrain walking under it.

SQUIRE HEADLONG.

Miraculous, by Mahomet!

MR. MILESTONE.

This is the summit of a hill, covered, as you perceive, with wood, and with those massy stones scattered at random under the trees.

MISS TENORINA.

What a delightful spot to read in on a summer's day! The air must be so pure, and the wind must sound so divinely in the tops of those old pines!

MR. MILESTONE.

Bad taste, Miss Tenorina. Bad taste, I assure you. Here is the spot improved. The trees are cut down: the stones are cleared away: this is an octagonal pavilion, exactly on the centre of the summit: and there you see Lord Little-brain, on the top of the pavilion, enjoying the prospect with a telescope.

SQUIRE HEADLONG.

Glorious, egad!

MR. MILESTONE.

Here is a rugged mountainous road, leading through impervious shades: the ass and the four goats characterize a wild uncultured scene. Here, as you perceive, it is totally changed into a beautiful gravel-road, gracefully curving through a belt of limes: and there is Lord Littlebrain driving four-in-hand.

SQUIRE HEADLONG.

Exquisite, upon my soul!

MR. MILESTONE.

Here is Littlebrain Castle, a Gothic moss-grown structure, half-bosomed in trees. Near the casement of that turret is an owl peeping from the ivy.

SQUIRE HEADLONG.

And devilish wise he looks.

MR. MILESTONE.

Here is the new house, without a tree near it, standing in the midst of an undulating lawn — a white, polished, angular building, reflected to a nicety in this waveless lake: and there you see Lord Littlebrain looking out of the window.

SQUIRE HEADLONG.

And devilish wise he looks too. You shall cut me a giant before you go.

MR. MILESTONE.

Good. I'll order down my little corps of pioneers.

Further Reading

This select bibliography is organized around the three sister arts which Walpole claimed 'dressed and adorned' nature — poetry, painting and gardening — here taken in reverse order.

GARDENING

Two surveys of garden history may be consulted for the larger perspective: Julia S. Berrall, *The Garden: An Illustrated History from Ancient Egypt to the Present Day* (London 1966), and Derek Clifford, *A History of Garden Design* (London, 2nd ed. 1966). The three best accounts of the English landscape garden are in Christopher Hussey's *English Gardens and Landscapes, 1700–1750* (London 1967), Edward Hyams' *The English Garden* (London 1964), and H. F. Clark's *The English Landscape Garden* (London 1948). Full documentation of Clark's study can be found in his pioneer article, 'Eighteenth-Century Elysiums. The Role of "Association" in the Landscape Movement', *Journal of the Warburg and Courtauld Institutes*, VI (1943), 165–89, reprinted in *England and the Mediterranean Tradition: Studies in Art, History and Literature* (London 1945). Garden design also features in B. S. Allen, *Tides in English Taste, 1619–1800: A Background for the Study of Literature*, 2 vols. (Cambridge, Mass. 1937; reprinted, New York 1958). Some of the principal gardenists have been treated separately: Switzer by William Brogden (see Introduction, note 9); Charles Bridgeman by Peter Willis (Introduction, note 6); Wise by David B. Green, *Gardener to Queen Anne: Henry Wise (1653–1738) and the Formal Garden* (London 1956); Kent by Margaret Jourdain, *The Work of William Kent: Artist, Painter, Designer and Landscape Gardener* (London 1948), and by K. Woodbridge in 'William Kent as Landscape-Gardener: A Re-Appraisal', and 'William Kent's Gardening: The Rousham Letters', in *Apollo* C (August 1974), 126–37, and C (October 1974), 282–91, respectively; Brown and Repton by Dorothy Stroud, *Capability Brown* (London, 3rd ed. 1975) and *Humphry Repton* (London 1962). Nikolaus Pevsner has written some perceptive essays on Repton, Knight and Price (Introduction, note 34). For the permeation of the English landscape garden into the continent of Europe consult Osvald Sirén, *China and Gardens of Europe of the Eighteenth Century* (New York 1950) and the essays on the picturesque garden edited by Nikolaus Pevsner (Introduction, note 16).

PAINTING

The tastes in landscape pictures before the eighteenth century are surveyed by H. V. S. and M. S. Ogden, *English Taste in Landscape in the Seventeenth Century* (Ann Arbor 1955). More detailed discussions of influential painters and schools are W. Stechow, *Dutch Landscape of the Seventeenth Century* (London 1968); Marcel Roethlisberger, *Claude Lorrain: The Paintings*, 2 vols. (New Haven 1961) and *Claude Lorrain: The Drawings*, 2 vols. (Berkeley 1968); Anthony Blunt, *Nicolas Poussin*, 2 vols. (London 1967); *Salvator Rosa*, catalogue of the exhibition held at the Hayward Gallery in 1973. Apart from some fine monographs on individual artists — Benedict Nicholson on Wright of Derby, for instance, or W. G. Constable on Richard Wilson — it is worth consulting the 'surveys' of the field in Luke Herrmann, *British Landscape Painting of the Eighteenth Century* (London 1973), and *Landscape in Britain c.1750–1850*, catalogue of the 1973 exhibition at the Tate Gallery. Two useful sources of pictures of landscape gardens themselves are Mario Praz, *Conversation Pieces* (London 1971) and J. Steegman and D. Stroud, *The Artist and the Country House* (London 1949).

POETRY

On poetry, or rather literature's relationships with landscape gardening, see Edward Malins, *English Landscaping and Literature 1660–1840* (London 1966), the first section of John Barrell, *The Idea of Landscape and the Sense of Place 1730–1840. An Approach to the Poetry of John Clare* (Cambridge 1972), and the work by John Dixon Hunt (Introduction, notes 6 and 38). Pope's gardening activities and their relationship with his political satires are explored by Maynard Mack, *The Garden and the City: Retirement and Politics in the Later Poetry of Pope 1731–1743* (Toronto, Buffalo and London 1969). Two essays of considerable relevance to landscape gardening — though the connections are not specifically made — are those on inscriptions and on the idea of *genius loci* by Geoffrey H. Hartman in *Beyond Formalism* (New Haven and London 1970). J. R. Watson, *Picturesque Landscape and English Romantic Poetry* (London 1970) has interesting things to say about the later connections between Walpole's three arts. A useful collection of relevant poetry is available in Charles Peake (ed.), *Poetry of the Landscape and the Night* (London 1967), while some aspects of literature relevant to gardenist concerns are discussed by John Chalker, *The English Georgic* (London 1969), and by R. A. Aubin, *Topographical Poetry in Eighteenth-Century England* (New York 1936; reprinted 1966).

Finally, apart from various works referred to throughout the Introduction and the notes to it, the following three books survey the aesthetic ideas of the period, which necessarily touched, and were influenced by, the landscape movement: Christopher Hussey, *The Picturesque* (London 1927; reprinted 1967); S. H. Monk, *The Sublime* (New York 1935; reprinted Ann Arbor 1960); E. W. Manwaring, *Italian Landscape in Eighteenth-Century England* (New York 1925; reprinted London 1965).

Index

Page numbers in italics refer to illustrations